Themes of Islamic Civilization

John Alden Williams
EDITOR

UNIVERSITY OF CALIFORNIA PRESS
BERKELEY LOS ANGELES LONDON 1971

University of California Press
Berkeley and Los Angeles, California
University of California Press, Ltd.
London, England

ISBN: 0–520–01685–8
Library of Congress Catalog Card Number: 78–107659
Printed in the United States of America

THEMES OF ISLAMIC CIVILIZATION

On the Day when the Hour strikes,
On that Day the doers of Vanity shall be losers.
Then shall you see every community hobbling on its knees,
Every people called unto its testament. (Qur'ān, 45:28)

Acknowledgments

The editor wishes to thank the following for permission to reprint material included in this volume:

GEORGE ALLEN & UNWIN LTD. for selections from Muhammad Mujeeb, *The Indian Muslims*; and for selections from A.J. Arberry, *Sufism*, and *Revelation and Reason in Islam*;—and A.S. BARNES AND CO. INC., for selections from A.J. Arberry, *Aspects of Islamic Civilization*;—and for selection from Seyyid Hoseyn Nasr, *Ideals and Realities of Islam*;—and THE MACMILLAN CO. (New York), for selections from Martin Lings, *A Moslem Saint of the Twentieth Century*; and for selection from A.J. Arberry, *The Koran Interpreted.*

AMERICAN COUNCIL OF LEARNED SOCIETIES—for selections from John Hardie, translator, *Social Justice in Islam.*

HAZRAT MIRZA BASHIRUD DIN MAUMUD AHMAD—for selections from *Ahmadiyyat, or the True Islam*;—and from *Tuhfat al-Muluk.*

SH. MUHAMMAD ASHRAF, PUBLISHER—for selections from J.Robson's translation of *Mishkāt al-Masabīh.*

ORIENTAL INSTITUTE BARODA—for selections from Syed Nawab Ali and C.N. Seddon (trans.) *Supplement to the Mirat-i-Ahmadi.*

CAMBRIDGE UNIVERSITY PRESS (London)—for selections from Dunlop (trans.), *Fuṣūl al-Madanī*;—and for selections from H.A.R. Gibb (trans.), *The Travels of Ibn Battuta, Vol. II*;—and for selections from A.J. Arberry, *The Doctrine of the Sufis.*

JONATHAN CAPE LTD.—for selections from R.J.C. Broadhurst (trans.), *The Travels of Ibn Jubayr.*

THE CLARENDON PRESS (Oxford)—for selections from W. Montgomery Watt, *Muhammad in Medina*;—and for selections from B.W. Andrzejewski and I.M. Lewis, *Somali Poetry, an Introduction.*

THE CRESSET PRESS, LTD.—for selections from Reuben Levy, *A Mirror for Princes.*

UNIVERSITY OF DURHAM PRESS—for selection from F.R.C. Bagley, *Al-Ghazalī's Book of Counsel for Kings.*

GIBB MEMORIAL TRUST—for selections from A.J. Arberry (trans.), *Mawāqif and Mukhātabāt of al-Niffarī*;—and for selection from R.A. Nicholson (trans.), *Kashf al-Mahjūb.*

ISLAMIC PUBLICATIONS, LTD.—for selections from the works of Syed Abul Ala Maudoodi: *Islamic Law and Constitution* and *A Short History of the Revival Movement in Islam.*

KANO STATE GOVERNMENT PRESS—for selections from F.J. Arnett, *Infāk al-Maysūr.*

KHAYAT'S LTD.—for selections from their reprint of P.K. Hitti, *Origins of the Islamic State.*

LUZAC & COMPANY LTD.—for selections from W.M. Miller (trans.), *Al-Babu-l Hadi Ashar*;—for selections from Whitting (trans.), *Al-Fakhri;* for selections from D.M. Donaldson, *The Shi'ite Religion.*

THE MACMILLAN COMPANY—for selections from Muhammad Iqbal, *Secrets of the Self*;—and THE FREE PRESS (A Division of the Macmillan Co., New York), for selection from Muhsin Mahdi, *Alfarabi's Philosophy of Plato and Aristotle.*

RICHARD J. MCCARTHY, S.J.—for selection from *Kitab al-Luma'.*

JOHN MURRAY LTD.—for selections from A.J. Arberry, *Discourses of Rumi.*

K.A. NIZAMI—for selection from *The Life and Times of Shaikh Farid ud-Din Ganj-i Shakar.*

OXFORD UNIVERSITY PRESS (India)—for selection from A.A.A. Fyzee, *The Creed of Ibn Babuya.*

OXFORD UNIVERSITY PRESS (Pakistan)—for selection from A. Guillaume, *The Life of Muhammad.*

PENGUIN BOOKS LTD.—for selection from N.J. Dawood, *Aladdin and other Tales from the 1001 Nights.* (Abridged with translator's permission.)

ROUTLEDGE AND KEGAN PAUL, LTD.—for selections from Hubert Darke, *The Book of Government*;—and CHICAGO UNIVERSITY PRESS, for selection from A.J. Arberry, *Muslim Saints and Mystics*;—and the BOLLINGEN FOUNDATION AND PRINCETON UNIVERSITY PRESS for selections from Franz Rosenthal, *The Muqaddimah: An Introduction to History,* by Ibn Khaldun (Bollingen Series XLIII).

ROYAL ASIATIC SOCIETY—for selection from D.S. Margoliouth, *Table-talk of a Mesopotamian Judge.*

Contents

Introduction

In Islam, faith in the God of revelation is prior, and it is strikingly vibrant and alive today. Like the rest of us, the Muslims are now involved in a world where continuing and radical change is a condition of life. They inhabit it as heirs of a unique past and a once integrated civilization. It was an integrated civilization, because its pattern took shape in the operating moral consensus of their faith. Its institutions reflected characteristic attitudes of faith.

This book is an attempt to illustrate, from the writings of the Muslim peoples, certain themes and archetypal ideas that have moulded Muslim minds and found expression in institutions of a civilization that, to them, was Islamic: was engaged with, was committed to, the God of revelation.

It is hoped that the book will be useful to students of Muslim institutions, but it is not a book on Muslim institutions. Rather, it is about the attitudes or the convictions that lay behind those institutions, and so helped to condition characteristic responses of the Muslims of one world civilization to history, and to the world they have encountered in history.

Deliberately, I have left aside the Muslims of Southeast Asia, for their case was significantly different. While accepting Islam as religion, they have remained—far more than other Muslims—the heirs of an older and preexisting culture, which to them appeared to be, in the main at least, satisfactorily Islamic.

Therefore, I have drawn from the writings of Muslims from Spain to Anatolia and India, who exhibited the practical consensus of a unified, although various, civilization. Basic to my method has been the conviction that faith and society are indissolubly linked. Religion is not a part of this structure; it is the structure.

It is the writings that remain of permanent value; it is in making them available in English, and intelligible to the reader, that the book's usefulness will lie. It is offered, diffidently, but without apology, to Muslims as well as to men of other faith, for it will have failed if it does not "make sense" to Muslims too, or if they feel that in selecting the texts, the editor has done violence to their spirit or their tradition.

Because this matter of selectivity is basic to the structure of the book, and the way the selections are introduced will also tinge whatever meaning emerges from them, it seems appropriate for me to state briefly the perspective from which I viewed both the texts and the themes they illustrate.

I should explain that when using the term "Islamic civilization," I do not mean a civilization which exists today. There was a great civilization which aspired to be Islamic: it grew up in less than a century under the community of those who believed they held the faith demanded of men by God through Muḥammad. By the end of the fourth century after Muḥammad's emigration from Mecca, this civilization not only controlled a mighty patrimony, but was well begun on a profound interior transformation and a vast new exterior expansion.

Islam's was thus the most spectacularly fortunate of the three great post–Hellenistic civilizations at the outset, and for centuries it appeared to be more various and more vital than either the Eastern or the Western Christian civilizations with which it was continuous and contiguous.

Yet, despite its brilliance, its success, its riches, Islamic civilization appears to have been the first of the three to lose its vital force; to "die." By the mid-eighteenth century A.D., Muslims could only respond to change by attempting to recreate the world in which their greatest success had been achieved, or by importing alien institutions. The civilization we have called Islamic, then, was dead —but Islam was certainly not. Today it is one of the most vital and expanding forms of faith.

By 1950, we might add, the specifically Western Christian civilization was as dead as that of Islam. The West had withered side by side with the growth of a new civilization, which to be sure had begun on Western soil—just as the civilization of Western Christendom had once quickened in provinces of the dying Roman Empire—but Western civilization is past. (To judge by such phenomena as the rapid self–transformation of the Roman Church, the day may soon arrive when we must also say that Western and Eastern Christianity are dead—though we may be rather confident that Christianity is here to stay.)

Today there is only one civilization—Modern Technological, as at home in Japan or China as in England or Brazil—in which men can respond creatively to change, or hope to meet the future. It is unique in not having developed within the unity of ideas offered by any religious system, and its particular weakness lies in its lack of moral consensus. There is no Islamic civilization, no Western Christian civilization, today. Yet it remains to be seen whether Modern Civilization cannot be Islamic; cannot be Christian (one suspects that it will have to be both, if it is to survive, and Confucian, Buddhist, Hindu and Jewish as well.)

But to return to the case of Islamic civilization. If we have selected correctly dominant clusters of ideas rooted in faith that we may call the themes of Islamic civilization, then they will illustrate even for non–specialists how that civilization ordered its perceptions and built its world. As elements of folk–culture today, still present in the minds of Muslims, these traditional themes will alter, deflect, or color the course of history, and affect the rate and mode of assimilation of Muslims to modernity. Ideas in Muslim minds about the nature of society, the role of government, about the omnipotence of God and the scope of human action, are today not just of importance to Muslims: in a real sense, they concern us all.

Each of the themes we have selected here produced characteristic institutions in the past, and helps produce characteristic responses to the present. Ideas about the Community produced the *millet* system (and to some extent, the Balkans) and they have helped produce the balkanisation of the Muslim World in modern times. The dream of a perfect, inspired autocrat continues to haunt Muslim politics.

Modes of thinking about the will of God brought into being the *Sharī'a* system, the *'ulamā'*, and the *madrasa,* and to some extent helped prevent any overwhelming awareness of evil or of sin. The optimism of a once–successful society, coupled with the frustration of history's recalcitrance, have made the hope for a deliverer perennial. The emphasis on struggle expanded the Community, and also at times helped to condemn it to a sterile militarism, but also has acted to prevent its ultimate submission to fate. The theme of *wilāya,* of the friends of God, helped make the transcendant Lord immanent, and gave the civilization its final justification. Today it may go far to give Muslims resilience in a civilization that seems more to happen than to be constructed.

The polyphony of themes such as these, with added grace–notes, occasional discords, and canonical variations, provided the finished composition of Islamic civilization, and a lingering accompaniment of Muslim experience.

I labor in the deliberate opinion that it is particularly useful for people unacquainted with the Muslim World to have as direct an encounter with original sources as translation will allow, and that such an encounter with the texts can be worth more than many words of exposition. That this book may fall short of its aim to bring the reader a direct apprehension of themes of Islamic civilization we may be certain, but its strong points will still lie in the texts, to which I now propose to turn.

The Community

CHAPTER 1

The Community

From the Qur'ān:

And so (O Muḥammad) We have revealed to you an Arabic Qur'ān, that you may warn Mecca, Mother of Cities, and those who dwell about her, and that you may warn of the Day of Congregating on which there is no doubt: one party in Paradise, and a party in blazing fire. If God had willed, He would have made them one community, but He admits whomsoever He wills into His mercy. (42:5)

Surely We have sent you with the Truth, to hear good tidings and a warning; no community is there but has passed away in it some warner. (35:25)

On the Day when the Hour strikes, on that Day the doers of vanity shall be losers. Then shall you see every community hobbling on its knees, every people called unto its testament. "This day what you were doing is repaid; here is Our Testament, speaking against you with truth; surely We were registering all that you were doing." (45:28)

O Mankind, surely you are the ones who have need of God; He is the All-Sufficient, the All-Praised. If He but wills, He can do away with you and bring a new creation: surely that is no great matter for God. (35:16)

To every Community there is a term: when their time comes they shall not postpone it by an hour or advance it. (7:34)

Let there be one Community among you, inviting men to good, bidding to honor, rejecting what is disapproved; such are those who prosper. And be not as those who divided and fell into disagreement after the clear signs had come to them; for them there is a mighty punishment. (3:105)

You are the best Community brought forth to men, bidding unto good, rejecting what is disapproved, believing in God (3:105)

Thus We have appointed you as a central Community, that you might be testifiers to men, and that the Messenger might testify upon you; nor did We direct how you should pray except that We might know who followed the Messenger from him who turned back on his heels. (2:134)

If God had willed, He would have made men one community, but He would test you in (the truths) that have come to you. So be foremost in good deeds; unto God you shall all return, and He will tell you of that wherein you differed. (5:48)

Among those we have created are a Community who guide by truth, and by truth act with justice. (7:180)

Surely true religion with God is Islam. (3:16)

O believers, take not as intimates other than yourselves; such people spare nothing to ruin you; they desire keenly that you may suffer. (3:112)

Men were one community, and then God sent the Prophets, bringing good tidings and warning, and He sent down with them the Book with truth, that He might judge between men in that wherein they differed. And no one differed on it save those to whom it was given, after the clear signs had come to them, rebelling amongst themselves; then God guided those who believed to the truth wherein they were in disagreement, by His leave; God guides whomsoever He wills to a straight path. (2:214)

But him who breaks with the Messenger after the guidance has become clear to him, and follows a way other than that of the believers, him We shall consign to what he had turned to, and roast in Gehenna—an evil homecoming.(4:115)

Several of man's major religious traditions have succeeded in creating in their followers a strong sense of fellow-feeling. Still it is safe to say that only in Islam has the awareness of belonging to a unique, supranational community been so strongly developed. The Arabic word the Qur'ān uses, *umma,* is often treated today as synonymous with *nation.* Yet if there is one thing the Islamic Umma is not, it is a nation, in either the Roman or the modern sense. What was most significant about the umma of Muslims in history was that it transcended national and tribal loyalties rooted in the accident of birth, and was a community of believers, bound together in a brotherhood more vital than that of blood.

The Qur'ānic texts we have cited are arranged roughly according to the order in which they were made known. Even a glance reveals that the word umma is used in more than one context. Muḥammad is first sent to warn the tribe of Quraysh, for every natural human collectivity has a "warner," to tell it of the consequences of disobeying God's will for man. But all human collectivities are mortal, and under sentence of judgement.

Later, Muḥammad is called upon to emigrate from Mecca and from his tribe, with his followers and to form a new community, of faith, based in Yathrib, or Medina. The year of the Emigration and the founding of the Community becomes the first year of the Muslim calendar.

In acting thus, he is only doing as other prophets before him have done, for a prophetic revelation divides and unites people in new and crucially important ways. The most significant groupings are religious groupings: men united by faith and acting together. The Christians and the Jews also form *ummas.* Muḥammad's own Umma, it is finally revealed, has been called into existence as a central people; an example to, and a judgement upon, all others.

Such seems to be the view of the Umma developed by the Qur'ān. And we must keep in mind that the central act of faith that bound Muḥammad's people together was the conviction that the Qur'ān was the Word of God.

In the *Ḥadīth,* or sayings ascribed to the Prophet, a new word appears often: this is the *jamā'a,* or "collectivity", used almost synonymously with umma. It is certain that many—perhaps even most—of the Ḥadīth are not genuinely Muḥammadan: they do not come from Muḥammad. Nonetheless, for centuries Muslims accepted them as authentic, and acted accordingly. They are therefore as valuable for the study of Islamic civilization as they would be if Muḥammad had actually spoken them. Some of them may even be Muḥammadan, though it would be hard to say which. But all of them reflect Islamic values; the way that Muslims thought and felt about their Community.

Ḥadīths Ascribed to the Prophet:

Ibn Mājā reports that Anas ibn Mālik, the servant of the Prophet, said: "I heard the Messenger of God—God's blessing and peace be upon him—say 'My community shall never unite upon an error, so if you should see a disagreement, you must stay with the majority.' "[1]

Tirmidhī reports that Ibn 'Umar heard the Prophet say, "In Hell there are seven doors, and one of them is reserved for those who draw the sword against my community."[2]

Bukhārī reports that Anas ibn Mālik said the Prophet said, "None of you truly has the faith, if he does not desire for his brother Muslim that which he desires for himself."[3]

Ibn Mājā, from Ibn Mas'ūd: "The Messenger of God, on whom be God's blessing and peace, said 'The blood of a Muslim is not lawful (to shed) if he testifies that there is no god but God and that Muḥammad is God's messenger, except if he be one of three: the wilful murderer, the married adulterer, and the man who has left his religion and forsaken the Collectivity.' "[4]

Bukhārī, from 'Abdallah ibn 'Umar: "The Messenger of God said: 'The Muslim is the brother of the Muslim: he shall not do him wrong or let wrong be done to him. If he comes in his brother's need, God shall come in his own need; if he delivers him from suffering, God shall deliver him from some of the sufferings of the Day of Resurrection, and if he shields a Muslim, God shall shield him at the Resurrection.' "[5]

Abū Dāwūd, from Ibn 'Umar: "The Prophet said—may God bless him and give him peace!— 'This Community of mine has been given a great mercy. It will not be punished in the next world, but in this world its punishments will be rebellions, and earthquakes, and slaying.' "[6]

Bukhārī reports that Ibn Idrīs al-Khawlānī said: "I said to the Messenger of God, 'What do you order me to do (if I should live until the time of troubles)?' He said, 'Cleave to the collectivity of the Muslims and their leader (imām).' I said, 'And what if they have neither collectivity nor leader?' He said, 'Then withdraw (*i'tazil*) from the factions altogether, even if you must gnaw the roots of trees until you die.' "[7]

Ibn Isḥāq reports that the Prophet said (on his farewell pilgrimage), "Know that every Muslim is a Muslim's brother, and that the Muslims are brethren. It is only lawful to take from a brother what he gives you willingly, so wrong not yourselves. Oh God! Have I not told you?"[8]

Bukhārī from 'Abdallah ibn 'Umar: "The Messenger of God said, 'When any man says to his brother (Muslim) "Thou infidel!" one of the two deserves the name.' "[9]

Bukhārī, from Anas: "The Messenger of God—God bless him

and give him peace—said, 'Help your brother Muslim whether he be the oppressor or the oppressed.' People said, 'Messenger of God, if he is oppressed we shall aid him, but how shall we aid him if he is the oppressor?' He replied, 'Prevent him from oppressing.' "[10]

Bukhārī reports that Aḥnaf ibn Qays said, "I was going to aid ('Ali ibn Abī Ṭālib) at the Battle of the Camel, when Abū Bakra met me and said, 'Where are you going?' 'To help this man,' I said. 'Turn back,' he told me, 'for I heard the Messenger of God say "Whenever two Muslims rush at each other with swords in hand, the slayer and the slain both go to hell," and I said to him, 'Messenger of God, one of them was a murderer, but how about the slain man?' and he said, 'He too was eager to kill his fellow.' "[11]

A Sermon of the Prophet

Praise be to God! I praise Him and implore His aid. We seek refuge in Him from the evils in ourselves and the sinfulness of our acts. He whom God guides none may cause to go astray, and him whom God leads astray none may guide. I testify that there is no god but God alone, who has no companion. Surely the finest speech is the Book of God—blessed be He, and exalted! The man in whose heart God has made his Word seem beautiful, whom God has caused to enter Islam after unbelief, the man who has chosen it above the words of men, that man shall prosper. Truly it is the finest speech, and the most penetrating. Love what God loves. Love God with all your hearts—never weary of the Word of God and its mention, and harden not your hearts to it.

Of all that God creates, He selects and chooses; the acts He chooses He has called Good, the people He chooses He has called Chosen; the speech He chooses He has called Virtuous. In all that comes to man, there is the lawful and the forbidden. Serve God and associate nothing with Him; fear Him with proper fear, affirm for God in righteousness what you profess with your lips.

Love one another in the spirit of God. Verily God is wrathful when His covenant is broken. Peace be upon you.[12]

THE CONSTITUTION OF MEDINA

A highly important document from the Medinan period of the Prophet's career has been preserved as the "Constitution" of Medina. The date is uncertain, and the archaic and often ambiguous language presents many difficulties of understanding. Yet the main lines are fairly clear. One striking feature of this constitution is that the Jews of Medina are considered as a part of the Community, and there are detailed clauses regulating their relations with the Muslims. One might suppose that this is because they were too powerful to ignore, but since there is no mention of the main groups of the Medinan Jews, there is good reason to assume that in the form in which it survives, it comes from the time *after* Muḥammad expelled and executed the main body of the Jews, when those who remained were only the weaker groups. If so, there was nothing to constrain him to consider them a part of his Community, as this unquestionably genuine text shows that he did. However, the date is not given.

Apart from the fact that non-Muslims are included, the most remarkable aspect of the document is the way in which it transcends the sovereign concept of blood-relationship—the whole basis of all pagan Arabian values—by the concept of a theocratic, super–tribal grouping *in a physical locality*. The tribes, like families, still exist, but the new bonds of mutual faith can make the participants consider even blood brothers as enemies, if they oppose the Umma, and there is a new emphasis on individual responsibility. It is a profoundly significant transformation. At the same time, the intensity of the old tribal tie is carried over into the new grouping. In a barbaric social context, a new "moral communalism" has emerged, which will be as absolute for its members as the old Arabian tribe.

From "The Constitution of Medina"

The Messenger of God wrote a document, concerning the emigrants from Mecca and the helpers of Medina, in which he reconciled the Jews and convenanted with them, letting them act freely in the religion and possessions which they had, and stated reciprocal obligations.

In the name of God, the Merciful, the Compassionate!

This document is from Muḥammad the Prophet, governing relations among the Believers and the Muslims of Quraysh and Yathrib (Medina) and those who followed them and joined with them and struggled with them.

1. They are one Community (umma) to the exclusion of all other men.

2. The emigrants of Quraysh shall pay the price of blood among themselves according to their present custom, and shall redeem their captives with the justice proper to true believers.

3. The Banu 'Awf shall pay the blood–price they paid before:

every group shall redeem its prisoners with the justice proper to true believers.

4. Similarly with those of Banu al-Khazraj: with the Banu Sa'ida; 5) the Banu al-Ḥārith 6) the Banu Jusham; and 7) the Banu al-Najjār.

8. Similarly with those of al-Aws; with the Banu 'Amr ibn 'Awf; 9) the Banu al-Nabīt; and 10) Banu al-Aws.

11. The Believers shall not desert any poor person among them, but shall pay his redemption or blood-money, as is proper.

12. No Believer shall seek to turn the auxiliary of another Believer against him.

13. God-fearing Believers will be against whoever among them is rebellious or whoever seeks to sow injustice or sin or enmity among the Believers; every man's hand shall be against him, though he were the son of one of them.

14. No Believer shall kill a Believer for the sake of an unbeliever, or aid an unbeliever against a Believer.

15. The protection of God is one: even the least of them may extend it to a stranger. The Believers are friends to each other, to the exclusion of all other men.

16. The Jews who follow us shall have aid and equality, except those who do wrong or aid the enemies of the Muslims.

17. The peace of the Believers is one: no Believer shall make peace separately where there is fighting for God's sake. Conditions (of peace) must be just and equitable to all.

18. In every raid, the riders shall ride close together.

19. And the Believers shall avenge one another's blood, if shed for God's sake, for the God-fearing have the best and strongest guidance.

20. No idolator (of Medina) shall take Qurayshī property or persons under his protection, nor shall he turn anyone against a Believer.

21. Whoever kills a Believer shall also be killed, unless the next of kin of the slain man is otherwise satisfied, and the Believers shall be against him altogether; no one is permitted to act otherwise.

22. No Believer who accepts this document and believes in God and Judgement is permitted to aid a criminal or give him shelter. The curse of God and His wrath on the Day of Judgement shall fall upon whoever aids or shelters him, and no repentance or compensation shall be accepted from him if he does.

23. Whenever you differ about a case, it shall be referred to God and to Muḥammad.

24. The Jews shall bear expenses with the Muslims as long as they fight along with them.

25. The Jews of the Banu ʿAwf are one community with the Believers; the Jews have their religion and the Muslims have theirs. This is so for them and their clients, except for one who does wrong or treachery; he hurts only himself and his family.

26–35. The same is true for Jews (who are members and confederates) of the other clans of Yathrib: honorable behaviour is without treachery.

36. None of them may go out (to war) without Muḥammad's permission, but they shall not be prevented from taking vengeance for a wound. Whoever murders a man murders himself and his family, unless he has been wronged. God is (the guarantor).

37. The Jews shall bear their expenses and the Muslims shall bear theirs, and they shall render mutual aid to whoever wars against the people of this document. There shall be mutual advice and consultation, and honorable behavior, without treachery. A man is not guilty of treachery by the act of his confederate, and help shall be due to one who is wronged.

38. The Jews shall bear expenses with the Muslims as long as they fight along with them.

39. The Valley of Yathrib shall be a sacred enclosure for the people of this document.

40. A stranger under protection shall be as his host, without doing harm or treachery.

41. A woman shall only be given protection with the permission of her family.

42. Whatever incident or dispute arises from which trouble is feared shall be referred to God and to Muḥammad, God's messenger; God is the most scrupulous and truest (guarantor) of what is in this document.

43. No protection is to be given to Quraysh and to those who help them.

44. The (contracting groups) are bound to render aid against whoever attacks Yathrib.

45. When they are called upon to conclude or to maintain peace, they must do so, and when they call for concluding a similar peace,

this shall be observed by the Muslims, except one who fights for the sake of religion.

46. Everyone shall have his portion from the side to which he belongs; the Jews of al-Aws, their clients and themselves, are in the same position as the people of this document. Honorable dealing is without treachery.

47. Whoever acquires any (guilt) does not acquire it for any but himself. God is the most just and loyal fulfiller of what is in this document. This writing will not protect a wrongdoer or a traitor. Whoever goes out is safe, and he who stays at home is safe in the town, unless he has done wrong or treachery. God is the protecting neighbour (*jār*) of whoever does good and fears Him, and Muḥammad is the Messenger of God. Verily God is wrathful when His covenant is broken. Peace be upon you.[13]

Letters of the Prophet

The Messenger of God (God bless and preserve him) wrote to al-Hilāl, the master of al-Baḥrayn:

Peace to you; I praise to you God, beside whom there is no god, and who has no partner; and I summon you to God alone, that you believe in God, and obey, and enter into the community (*jamā'a*). That is better for you. Peace be upon whoever follows the guidance.[14]

While pagans were invited, in no uncertain terms, to join the community, Christians and Jews were tolerated. Muḥammad's treaty with the Arab Christians of Najrān, to the South, served as the model of the Umma in many later treaties of toleration with "People of the Book."

This is a letter of Muḥammad the Prophet, the Messenger of God, to the people of Najrān. To him belonged the decision in respect of every fruit, and every slave; but he was gracious to them and left (them) all that for the payment of 2,000 suits of clothes (yearly), each suit worth one ounce (of silver). Where these tribute-suits exceed or fall short of the ounce, that is taken into account. Whatever was taken from them of the coats of mail and horses and riding camels and equipment they possessed is taken into account. Najrān is to give lodging to my messengers for twenty days or less (and) to lend thirty coats of mail, thirty horses, and thirty camels if there is war (*kayd*) in the Yemen. Whatever is destroyed of the coats of mail or horses or camels they lend my messengers is guaranteed by my messengers until they repay it. Najrān and their followers have protection (*jiwār*) of God and the *dhimma* of Muḥammad the prophet the Messenger of God, for themselves, their community, their land, and their goods, both those who are absent and those who are present, and for their churches and services (no bishop will be moved from his episcopate, and no monk from his monastic position, and no church–warden from his church–wardenship) and for all, great or little, that is under their hands. There is no usury, and no blood–revenge from pre–Islamic times. If any of them asks for a right, justice is (in their own hands, to see that they are) not doing wrong and not suffering wrong; it belongs to Najrān. If any one takes usury after this, my dhimma is free from (responsibility for) him. No one of them is punished for the wrongdoing of another. On the terms stated in this document (they have) protection of God and dhimma of the Prophet forever, until God comes with His command, if they are loyal and perform their obligations well, not being burdened with wrong.[15]

A writer who can always be read with instruction, and one of the most interesting minds of the Middle Ages of Islam, is Abū Ḥāmid al-Ghazālī. He so well sums up the religious attitudes, interests, and statements of his time that it is frequently difficult to say whether he is the leader and creative innovator, or simply a very lucid spokesman for the spirit of an age. In any case, one finds set forth in his works—particularly the great "Revivification of the Sciences of Religion"—an almost unparalleled presentation of all that was typical of the best Sunnī theology until the Eighteenth century. Characteristically, he is deeply concerned with ethics—with the right things for Muslims to do—and much that he says here on what Muslims have the right to expect from their fellowmembers in the Umma still holds today. It lives in the specific forms and coloring of communal solidarity and the traditional ethics honored in many parts of the Muslim world.

The Duties of a Muslim to a Muslim
from Revification of the Sciences of Religion
Abū Ḥāmid al–Ghazālī (d. A.H. *505*/A.D. *1111)*

The duties of a Muslim to a fellow–Muslim are that you say "Peace be upon you" if you encounter him, and respond if he gives you an invitation, that you bless him if he sneezes, visit him if he is ill, and attend his funeral if he dies. They are to honor his oath, if he swears something to you, to advise him when he seeks advice, and take care of his interests when he is absent; to want for him what you want for yourself, and to dislike for him what you would dislike for yourself. All of this has come to us from the sayings of the Prophet and his companions. Anas, with whom may God be well pleased, tells how the Messenger of God—God's benediction and peace be upon him—once said, "The Muslims have four claims upon you: that you assist those who do good, ask forgiveness for those who do ill, pray for those who turn their backs, and love those who repent." Ibn 'Abbās—God be well pleased with him and with his father—in discussing God's words "(The Muslims are) merciful one to another" (Qur. 48:28), said: "He has called the righteous Muslim to the bad Muslim and the bad Muslim to the righteous Muslim: whenever the bad regards the righteous in Muḥammad's Umma, he says, 'O God, bless him for the goodness you have given him and strengthened him in, and cause us to benefit by him.' And when the righteous Muslim sees the bad Muslim, he says, 'O God, guide him and forgive him, and pardon his stumbling.' " And Nu'mān ibn Bashīr said, "I heard the Messenger of God—God bless him and give him peace—say 'The Muslims in their mutual affection and mercy should be as a single body: if one member is affected, the other members suffer fever and sleeplessness.' "

Abū Mūsa says that he (God bless him and give him peace) also said, "One believer is to another like the parts of one structure, each strengthening the others."

One should never cause any injury to another Muslim by word or deed. The Messenger of God once said in a longer *ḥadīth* ordering good deeds, "And if you cannot do that, then turn people from evil, and it will be as an alms you have given to yourselves." He once asked, "Do you know what a Muslim is?" They said, "God and His Messenger know best." He said, "A Muslim is one from whose tongue and hand the Muslims are at peace." They asked him, "Then what is a Believer?" and he said, "A man to whom believers can entrust themselves and their possessions." They said, "And what is one who makes the Emigration (Muhājir)?" "One who leaves wickedness and avoids it." A man asked, "What is Islam, Messenger of God?" and he said, "To deliver your heart to God and deliver Muslims with tongue and hand." [Each of these responses involves a pun.—Ed.]

Abū Hurayra, God be pleased with him, once said "Messenger

of God, teach me something that will do me good," and he said, "Remove something harmful from the way of the Muslims." He also said "A Muslim may not cast at a brother Muslim so much as a glance that might hurt him," and, "It is not permissible for a Muslim to frighten a Muslim."

One of (the rights of Muslims) is that one be humble with all of them and not act haughtily, for God loves no conceited braggart. Ibn Abī 'Awf says that even the Messenger of God used to act humbly with every Muslim, and not scorn anyone. He was not too proud to walk with the widowed and the poor, to look after their needs.

Another is that one not listen to people's exaggerations about each other, or pass them on to other people. The Prophet has said —God bless him and give him peace—"Slanderers do not enter paradise."

Another is that one should not stay apart from one whom he knows for longer than three days, when he is angry with him. The Prophet has said, "A Muslim may not avoid his brother (Muslim) more than three: if they meet, he who gives the first greeting is the better of the two," and "Whoever forgives a Muslim a fault will be forgiven by God on the Day of Resurrection."

And another is that one should treat all of the Muslims well so far as he is able, without regard to whether they are worthy of it. 'Alī ibn Ḥusayn reports, from his father and his grandfather, that the Messenger of God, on whom be God's blessing and peace, said "Do good to those who are worthy of it and to those who are not; if he is a good man, then because he is good, and if he is not, then because you are." He reports also that the Messenger said "The most intelligent thing after service to God is affection for people, and doing good to every man, pious or dissolute."

Another is that one should not enter (the quarters of) one of them without permission: in fact, one should seek permission three times [as, by knocking or clapping the hands.—Ed.] and if it is not given, go away.Abū Hurayra—God be pleased with him—said that the Messenger of God, God bless him and give him peace, said "Seeking entrance is threefold. The first alerts, the second greets, and the third receives permission or brings."

Another is to behave well with a good temper to everyone, and act with them according to their state of life, for if one meets the ignorant with knowledge, the illiterate with erudition, and the unpractised with fine exposition, he suffers harm and does harm.

Another (duty) is to honor old men and be mild with children. Jabīr—God be pleased with him—says that the Messenger said "No one is one of ours who does not honor our old men and treat our children mildly."

And one of them is that one should with all people be cheerful, joyful of countenance and companionable. The Prophet—God's blessing and peace be upon him—once asked "Do you know whom hellfire has been forbidden to hurt?" They said "God and His Messenger know best." He said "The supple and clear, the easy and near." Abū Hurayra reports him as saying "Truly God loves people with easy ways and cheerful faces."

And another is that one should never promise a Muslim anything without performing it. The Prophet—God bless him and give him peace—said "A promise is like a gift." He also said "A promise is a religious duty." He also said "There are three things about a hypocrite: when he tells you something, he lies; when he promises something, he breaks it, and when he is entrusted with something, he betrays." And he said "If he does those three things, then he is a hypocrite, though he fasts and prays (like a Muslim)."

Another is to share with people willingly, and give them nothing that one would not like to be given. . . . The Prophet, on whom be peace and God's benediction, said "If it pleases anyone to be snatched from hellfire and allowed to enter paradise, he shall gain his desire if he testifies that there is no god but God and that Muḥammad is God's messenger, and then gives to people what he would like to be given."

Another is to show more honor to those whose aspect and clothing indicate their higher station, and to come down to the level of other people. It is told that 'A'isha, the Prophet's favored wife—God be well pleased with her—was once on a journey, and made a halt and spread out her food. A beggar came, and she said, "Give this poor man a loaf of bread." Then a man passed on a fine mount, and she said "Invite him to eat." Someone said, "You send bread to the poor, and invite the rich to dinner?" She replied, "God the Exalted has assigned people their stations, and we must treat them accordingly. That poor man is pleased with a loaf of bread, but it would be abominable for us to give this rich man, with such an appearance, a loaf of bread."

Another of their rights is for one to reconcile any enmity between Muslims insofar as he finds any means to do so. The Prophet, on him be God's benediction and peace, said "Shall I tell you what is better than prayers, fasting, and almsgiving?" The Companions said "Of course!" and he said "Reconciling enmity. The evil of enmity is death."

Another duty is to cover the shame of the Muslims, all of them. The Prophet, God bless him and give him peace, said "Whoever draws the veil over a Muslim, God will draw the veil over him on the Day of Judgement." It is related that the Caliph 'Umar, with whom God be well pleased, was walking one night in Medina, and saw a man and a woman engaged in an immoral act. When morning came, he said to the people "How do you view it? If the Imām sees a man and woman in an immoral act, should he give them the prescribed Qur'ānic punishment (*ḥadd*) for what they were doing?" They said "But you are the Imām!" Then 'Alī, with whom God be well please, said "It is not for you to impose the prescribed punishment, for God does not accept (as condition) fewer than four witnesses, and so He has left them what He wills to leave them." Then 'Umar asked the people again, and they replied as before, while 'Alī gave his previous opinion. Now this shows that 'Umar was perplexed as to whether the ruler should give judgement according to his own knowledge, where God's prescribed punishments are concerned, and so limited them to a discussion of his powers, rather than of (the truth of) his information, fearing lest he be guilty of defamation, while the opinion of 'Alī was that he had no right to punish them. This is one of the strongest indications of how the Shar', the law of God, seeks to veil immorality, of which adultery is the worst sort, since it makes (the prosecution) conditional on four just and credible witnesses testifying that they saw this of his in that of hers, like a kohl-stick in its bottle, which is hardly likely to happen. And even if the judge knows certainly, it is not for him to pursue the question. Now see the wisdom of closing the door on an immorality which involves death by stoning, the greatest punishment of the Law—and see how thick God has made the veil he casts over sinners among His creatures, by narrowing the way to pursue them. Let us hope that we too shall not be deprived of His generosity on the Day when hearts shall be tried, and secrets made manifest. . . . [Ghazālī is arguing here for a relaxation of the censorious, prying application of the Law favored by many legalists, and embodied in such institutions as the *ḥisba*; cf. Chapter 3.—Ed.]

'Abd al-Raḥman ibn 'Awf said, "I went out with 'Umar, God be pleased with him, one night in Medina, and while we were walking there appeared a lamp, and we followed its flickering until we came near to it, and found a door bolted upon people with (loud) voices and (thick) language, and 'Umar took my hand and said 'Do you know whose house that is?' I told him. 'No', and he said, 'It is the house of Rabī'a ibn Umayya ibn Khalaf, and they have been drinking. What do you suggest?' I told him, 'I suggest that we have come to where God has told us to stop, when He said, "Do not spy upon each other." ' (49:12) Then 'Umar turned back and left them." And this too indicates the necessity of covering over faults and giving over pursuing people's weaknesses.

Another is to guard against occasions of suspicion, and keep the hearts of people from bad thoughts, and their tongues from the absent, for if they disobey God in what they say of him, and one is the occasion of it, then one becomes their accomplice. God Most High has said, "Do not abuse those (gods) on whom they call apart from God, or they will abuse God in ignorant hostility." (6:108) The Prophet, on whom be God's blessing and peace, said "How do you view those who curse their parents?" They said, "And does anyone curse his parents?" He replies "Yes indeed; if he curses the parents of another (Muslim) then he has cursed his own parents." Anas ibn Mālik relates that the Messenger of God was speaking once to one of his women, and a man passed by. He called the man to him, and said "Such-a-one, this is my wife, Ṣafīya." The man said, "O Messenger of God, who would think anything of it? I would never think anything (wrong) about you!" And he said, "Verily, Satan runs in the sons of Adam like the blood in the veins."

And another is to intercede for whoever has need among the Muslims, with those of rank, and to strive to fulfil his need so far as one is able. . . . The Messenger of God, God's blessing and peace be upon him, said "There's no alms finer than an alms of the tongue." Someone said "How is that?" He said "Intercession. With it, you may prevent bloodshed, and pour benefits upon one, and divert hateful things from another."

Another is to greet every Muslim with "Peace be upon you," before speaking, and shake hands while greeting. The Prophet, on whom be God's benediction and peace, has said "When anyone begins with talk before salutations, do not answer him until he has begun with "*al-salāmu alaykum!*" One of the companions related that he once entered the Prophet's presence, and did not salute him or ask his leave. The Prophet said "Go back, and say '*salāmu alaykum,*' and come in." Anas said "I served the Prophet on eight pilgrimages, and he told me, 'Anas, be copious in the ablutions: it lengthens your life. And greet those you meet of my community with "Peace be upon you:" it increases your good qualities. And when you enter your quarters, say "Peace be upon you" to the people of your family: it increases the good things of your household.' " Anas also said that the Messenger of God—God bless him and give him peace—said "When two Muslims meet and clasp hands, seventy pardons are distributed between them—and sixty-nine of them go to the best man of the two." And God, be He exalted, says "And when you are greeted with a greeting, greet with another better than that, or return it." (Qur. 4:86) And the Prophet, on whom be peace, said "By Him in whose hand is my soul, you will not enter paradise until you believe, and you do not believe until you love one another, so shall I not tell you of a work which if performed will make you love each other?" They said "Of course, Messenger of God!" He said "Spread 'Peace' among yourselves." He also said "If a Muslim says 'Peace' to another and he answers, the angels bless it seventy times," and "The angels are astonished by a Muslim who passes another and does not wish him 'Peace!' " And he said "Let the rider salute the walker, and the walker salute the walker, and the walker salute the sitter, and if one person in a party wishes 'Peace,' it suffices for all of them." Clasping hands is also *sunna* (approved practise) along with the *salām*. A man once came to the Messenger of God—may God bless him and give him peace—and said "Peace be unto you!" And he said "Ten merits! (*ḥasanāt*)." Another came and said "Peace be upon you, and the mercy of God!" And he said "Twenty merits!" And a third man came and said "Peace be upon you, and the mercy of God, and His blessings!" And the Prophet said "Thirty." Anas, with whom God be well pleased, when he passed by little boys would say "*al-salāmu 'alaykum,*" and he related of the Messenger of God that he used to do that too. The Prophet, on whom be peace, said "Do not begin talk with a Jew or a Christian by 'Peace,' and if you encounter them on the street, then crowd them over to the narrow-

he went out, I said to him 'When he came, you said what you said, and then you made your speech gracious to him!' And he said 'O 'A'isha, the worst place at the resurrection will be that of those whom people avoided fearing their mischief!' "

Another duty is to avoid mixing with the rich and to seek the company of the poor and do good to orphans. Fuḍayl ibn 'Iyāḍ said, "I have heard that one of the prophets once said, 'O Lord, how shall I know if you are pleased with me?' And God said 'Look to see how pleased with you are the poor.' " The Prophet too, said "Beware of sitting with the dead!" Someone asked "And who are the dead?" He answered "Those who do not need (*al-aghniyā'*)." He also said, may God's blessing and peace be on him, "Whoever places his hand on an orphan's head in compassion, God shall give him merit for every hair his hand goes over." And he said, God bless him and give him peace, "The best Muslim home is one where an orphan is well-treated, and the worst is where an orphan is ill-treated."

Another is to give good advice to every Muslim and strive to cause joy to enter his heart . . . for the Prophet, on whom be blessing and peace, said "None of you really believes, until he wants for his brother (Muslim) what he wants for himself." And he said "The dearest act in the eyes of God is to cause joy to enter the heart of a Muslim, or to relieve it from some distress, or pay a debt for him, or feed him when he is hungry."

(The ascetic) Ma'rūf al-Karkhī said, "Whoever prays every day 'O Lord, have mercy on Muḥammad's Community,' will be registered by God among the Guardian Saints (*al-abdāl*)." And 'Alī ibn Fuḍayl one day wept, and people said "What makes you weep?" He said "I weep for him who did me wrong, for he may someday stand before God and be questioned on his wrongdoing, and have no defense."

Another (duty) is to visit their sick. Spiritual knowledge and Islam (*al-ma'rifa wa al-Islām*) both fully establish this duty, and (the desirability of) obtaining its graces. Good behavior for the visitor is a short, pleasant stay, asking few questions, showing delicacy, praying for the quick recovery of the sick man, and not noticing any of the defects of the place. When one seeks permission to enter, he should not go to the door and tap gently, or answer "I" when asked who is there, or speak patronisingly (*lā yaqūl yā ghulām*), but rather praise and magnify. The Prophet, God bless him and give him peace, said "It completes a sick visit to put one's hand on his forehead or his hand and ask how he is. A handclasp completes the salutations." He also said "Abū Hurayra, shall I tell you something having the property that if one says it when he first takes to his bed in sickness, God will deliver him from hell-fire?" Abū Hurayra said "Certainly, Messenger of God!" (The Prophet replied), "Let him say 'There is no god but God, who causes to live and causes to die; the Living, the Immortal. Glory be to God, the Lord of lands and men; praise be to Him, praise great and good, and blessed be He in every estate. God is most great! And His grandeur and glory and power are everyplace. O God, it is You who have made me sick, so take my soul in this illness and place it with the souls on whom You have poured out Your grace, and exile me from the Fire, as You have exiled your friends, on whom You have poured out Your grace.' "

Another duty is to take part in their funerals. The Prophet, God bless him and give him peace, said "Whoever attends a funeral shall have one *carat* of reward, and if he waits until they have buried him, he shall have two *carats*." In a ḥadīth it states that such a carat is equal to one mountain. . . . The object in attending funerals is to perform the duty of the Muslims, and show consideration. . . .

Another is to visit their tombs, and the object in this is to pray for them, show consideration, and soften the heart. The Prophet, God's blessing and peace be upon him, once said "I have seen no sight so terrifying as the tomb." 'Umar, God be well satisfied with him, related "We walked out with the Messenger of God—God bless him and give him peace—one day, and he came to the cemetery and sat by a tomb. I was nearer to him than anyone—and he began to weep, so we wept too. Then he said 'What makes you weep?' and we said, 'We wept to see your tears.' He said, 'This is the tomb of Āmina bint Wahb (his mother). I asked leave of my Lord to visit it, and He permitted me to do it. Then I asked permission to beg forgiveness for her, and He refused [because she had died in paganism. —Ed.] and so there overtook me the pity that overtakes a son.' " 'Umar, when he stopped by a tomb, used to weep until his beard was wet. . . . And Ḥātim al-Aṣamm said, "Whoever passes by graves and does not bethink himself or pray for them, has betrayed himself and betrayed them." The Messenger of God—blessing and peace be upon him—said "Not a night passes but a Caller calls 'O people of the graves, whom do you count happy?' And they say 'Happy are the people of the mosques, for they fast, and we may not fast, and they pray, and we may not pray, and they mention God's name, and we may not.' " And Rabī'a ibn Khuthaym dug a grave in his house, and when he found any hardness in his heart, he would enter it and lay himself down there a while, and then say "Lord, let me return: perhaps I may yet do a good work in what I forsook" (23:99). Then he would say "Rabī'a, you have returned, so act now, before you go back."

Good manners in a visit of condolence is humble behavior, a show of sorrow, little talk, and avoiding smiling.

Good manners in attending a funeral is behaving with humility, avoiding conversation, showing esteem for the dead, reflection on death and preparing oneself for it, and walking before the bier, near it. Hastening the funeral procession is approved practice (sunna).

That is the sum of good social behavior with the generality of people, and the general summation of it all is that you should not treat anyone as insignificant, whether he be alive or dead, and that because you do not know if perhaps he is not a better man than you. Even if he were a transgressor, he might yet affect you by the example he affords, while you, by righteousness, may affect him.

Regard no one with an eye that sees his worldly estate as great, for this lower world is insignificant in the eye of God, and all that it holds is little. No matter how much the people of this world may exalt you, they have exalted worldly matters, while you dwindled in the eye of God. Therefore, do not exchange godliness to participate in their worldliness, for you will only be less in their eyes, and may yet be deprived of their worldly state, and even if you are not deprived of it, you will have exchanged what is better for what is lower. . . . And do not be submissive to them because of their affection for you and their praise of you to your face and their fine appearance, for if you sought for the truth of that, you would not find that it was more than one part in a hundred—and perhaps you would not find that it was even that much. Or (on the other hand) if you receive evil from them, and something from them strikes you that may hurt you, then (remember that) their affairs are all under God, so seek refuge with Him from their evil and do not worry about requital, for that adds to the distress and wastes one's life. Never say to them "You have not known my place," for I believe that if you are worthy of it, God will prepare a place for you in their hearts, since it is God who inclines hearts to love and to aversion. Be very attentive to the right and deaf to the wrong in what they say.[16]

SUNNĪ VIEWS

The communal solidarity, or "catholic tendency" of the Umma was preserved among the Sunnīs, or majority group, whose name for themselves is "People of the Tradition and the Collectivity."

The following creedal statement is from Aḥmad ibn Ḥanbal, who gave his name to the fundamentalist school of the Sunnīs, the Ḥanbalīs. He was a formidable opponent of the rationalist school (*mu'tazila*) and the Partisans of 'Alī, or Shī'a, and this is not a tolerant document or a conciliatory one. He takes a very harsh view of differing opinions. At the same time, he insists that "all who pray in the direction of Mecca" are his brothers, and must be left to God to judge. Here where one might expect to find it least is still the sense of the unity and fraternalism of the Umma of Muḥammad.

Some Essential Ḥanbalī Doctrines from a Creedal Statement
Aḥmad ibn Ḥanbal (d. A.H. *241/*A.D. *855)*

Aḥmad ibn Ḥanbal said: The principles of the tradition (sunna) for us are holding fast to the practise of the companions of the Messenger of God, and seeking guidance from that; and abandoning innovation, for every innovation is an error. Also, abandoning quarrels, and not consorting with people who do as they please (*ahl al-hawa*), and leaving off strife and contentiousness in religion. The Sunna to us means the footsteps of the Messenger of God, may God bless him and give him peace, and the Sunna explains the meaning of the Qur'ān, and is the indication of the Qur'ān. There is no use of logical analogies in the Sunna, or coining of similitudes, or perception by use of reason or inclination. It is only following, and giving up one's own inclinations.

A part of the essential Sunna, such that if one leaves any part of it, not accepting it and believing in it, he cannot be considered as being of the people of the Sunna, is belief in the predestination (*qadar*) of good and bad, and affirmation of the ḥadiths about it and belief in them, not saying "Why?" or "How?", but simply affirming them and believing them. If anyone does not know the explanation of these ḥadīths or his intelligence does not comprehend them, it is still sufficient, and his sentence is, that he shall believe in them and submit to their authority, such as the ḥadīths (affirming predestination), and the ḥadīths that the beatific vision is possible, in their entirety. And even if he turns away from hearing about this, or feels dislike at hearing about it, still he must *believe* in it, and must not contradict a single letter of it, or any other ḥadīth transmitted by dependable narrators. [Aḥmad himself decided who was dependable.—Ed.] No one should dispute this, or speculate about it, or recognize any contention about it, for speaking about predestination and the beatific vision and the (nature of) the Qur'ān and other matters established by the traditions is disapproved of and to be avoided. Whoever speaks about them, if he criticises the Sunna, is not one of the people of the Sunna, until he abandons contention and submits, and believes in the tradition.

The Qur'ān is the Word of God, and it is not created. It is not wrong to say "It is not created," for God's Word is not separated from Him, and there is nothing of Him that is created. Beware of discussing this with those who speak about this and talk of "the creation of sounds" and such matters, and those who go midway and say "I don't know whether it is created or uncreated, but it is God's Word." Such a one is guilty of a religious innovation, and is as one who says "It is created," for it is God's Word, and that is not created.

Similarly with the vision of God on the Day of Resurrection, as it is related from the Prophet—God bless him and give him peace—in sound ḥadīths. The Ḥadīth is to be taken by us without interpretation (*al-ḥadīth 'indanā 'ala ẓāhirihi*) as it came from the Prophet, God's blessing and peace be on him. To discuss it is an innovation, but we believe it as it came, without interpretation, and not one of us speculates about it.

Similarly belief in the Scales on the Day of Resurrection, as it came: "A man will be weighed on the Day of Resurrection, and crimes will not be weighed with a compensation." And a man's acts will be weighed, as one finds in the tradition (*al-athar*), and belief and affirmation of this (is necessary), and opposition to those who reject it, and leaving contentiousness. And that God will speak to His servants on the Day of Resurrection, without any spokesman between Him and them, and belief in this, and affirmation of it. Also belief in the Tank, and that the Messenger of God will have a tank on the Day of Resurrection where he will quench the thirst of his Community, and it will be as broad as it is long, a journey of one month. Its ewers are as the stars of heaven for number, just as the traditions assert, without embellishment. Also belief in the Torments of the Grave, and that this Community will be tried in its graves. Also that one will be asked about his faith, and if he is a Muslim, and who is his Lord? and that Munkar and Nakīr will come to him, as God wills and desires, and faith in this and affirmation of it. Also belief in the Prophet's intercession, God bless him and give him peace, and in the people who will be brought out of the Fire after they have been burned and become as coal, and that they shall be brought to a river at the Gate of Paradise, as the traditions state, as God wills, and how He wills, only with faith in it, and affirmation.

And belief that the False Messiah will rise up, with the word "Unbeliever" written between his eyes, and in the ḥadīths that have come about this. And faith that this shall really be so, and that Jesus will descend from Heaven and slay him at the Lydda Gate.

Faith is word and act, and increases and decreases, as it is stated in the ḥadīths. "The most perfect of believers in faith is the best of them in morality." Also, "He who leaves off the ritual prayers has rejected God," and there is no act which when neglected occasions infidelity except the ritual prayers. Whoever quits them is an infidel, and God makes killing him lawful.

The best of this Umma—after its Prophet—is Abū Bakr al-Ṣiddīq, then 'Umar ibn al-Khaṭṭāb, then 'Uthman ibn 'Affān. We give the preference to those three (over 'Alī) as the Companions of God's Messenger gave preference: they did not differ about it. Then after those three come the Five Electors chosen by 'Umar as he lay dying (*aṣḥāb al-shūra*): 'Alī ibn Abī Ṭālib, Zubayr, Ṭalḥa, 'Abd al-Raḥman ibn 'Awf, and Sa'd ibn Abī Waqqāṣ. All of them were suited for the Caliphate, and each of them was an Imām. On this we go according to the ḥadīth of 'Umar's son: "When the Messenger of God was living—God bless him and give him peace—and his Companions were still spared, we used to number first Abū Bakr, then 'Umar, then 'Uthmān, and then keep silent." After the Electors come those who fought at the battle of Badr from among the Emigrants from Mecca, and then those at Badr from among the Helpers of Medina, because the Emigrants had left their homes, and been first (in Islam), so they come first.

The best of mankind after these are the Companions of God's Messenger from the period in which he was sent among them. Anyone who knew him for a year, or a month, or a day, or an hour, or even saw him, is of the Companions, to the extent that he was with him, took precedence with him, heeded his words and regarded him. The least of these in companionhood is better than the generation which did not see him. If they should come before God with all their works like those who were Companions of the Prophet—God bless him and give him peace—and beheld him and listened to him, the one who saw him with his eye and believed in him even for a single hour is better for his companionship than those who followed after, even if they should have performed all good works.

And hearing and obeying the Imāms and the Commanders of the Believers (is necessary)—whoever receives the Caliphate, whether he is pious or profligate, whether the people agreed on him and were pleased with him, or whether he attacked them with the sword until he became Caliph and was called "Commander of the Believers." Going on a holy war (*jihād*) is efficacious with a pious or with a dissolute commander until the Day of Resurrection: one does not abandon him. Division of the spoils of war and applying the punishments prescribed by the Law is for the Imāms: it is not for anyone to criticise them or contend with them. Handing over the alms-money to them (for distribution) is permissible and efficacious: whoever pays them has fulfilled his obligation whether (the Imām) was pious or dissolute. The collective prayer behind the Imām and those he delegates is valid and complete; both prostrations. Whoever repeats them later is an innovator, abandoning the tradition and opposed to the Sunna. There is no virtue in his Friday prayer at all, if he does not believe in praying with the Imāms, whoever they are, good or bad: the Sunna is to pray two prostrations with them and consider the matter finished. On that let there be no doubt in your bosom.

Whoever secedes from the Imām of the Muslims—when the people have agreed on him and acknowledged his caliphate for any reason, either satisfaction with him or conquest—that rebel has broken the unity of the Muslims and opposed the tradition coming from God's messenger, God's blessing and peace be upon him.

If the seceder dies, he dies as ignorant carrion. It is not lawful for anyone to fight against the authority or to secede from it, and whoever does is an innovator, outside the tradition and the way.

It is permitted to fight against robbers and attackers. If they threaten the life or property of a man, then he has the right to fight for his life and property and to repel them by whatever means he can. If they turn away from him and leave him, it is not for him to seek them or follow their footsteps: that is only for the Imām or the governors of the Muslims. It is only for him to protect his life in the place where he finds himself. Also, he should not intend, so far as he is able, to kill one of them. If he should (unintentionally) kill one of them while defending himself in the battle, God curses the slain man. And if one is killed while defending his life and property, he may be considered a martyr, as it says in the Ḥadīth and all the traditions of the Companions. It is only ordered to fight the attacker, not to kill him or pursue him, or to despatch him if he is downed or wounded. If he is taken prisoner, it is not permissible to kill him, or to inflict (on one's own initiative) the penalty of the Law upon him, but only to submit the matter to the higher authorities whom God has put in power, and let them sentence him.

We do not testify that anyone who prays in the direction of Mecca is in heaven or hell because of some deed he has committed: we hope for his welfare, and we fear for him. Likewise we fear for the evildoer and the sinner, and hope for God's mercy for him.

When anyone meets God with a sin deserving of hellfire, repenting truly of it, God pardons him, for God accepts the repentance of His servants and pardons their offenses. When one meets Him after having been given the penalty of the Law for that sin in the world, he has expiated it, according to information from the Messenger of God. Whoever is constrained to meet God unrepentant for the sins which could bring punishment upon him, is at God's mercy: He will afflict him if He wills, or pardon him, but whoever meets him rejecting Him (*kāfirān*) He punishes and does not pardon.

It is right to stone to death one who has committed adultery after marriage, if he confesses it or it is proved. The Messenger of God used to stone (such) and so did the rightly guided Imāms.

Whoever speaks ill of one of the Companions of the Messenger of God, or hates one for something he did, or mentions his bad actions, is an innovator, until he asks God's mercy for them all, and his heart is reconciled to them.

Hypocrisy (in religion) is infidelity: it is to reject God and worship another, while making a public display of Islam, like the hypocrites at the time of the Messenger of God (may God bless him and give him peace). He said, "Three things in one make him a hypocrite." (*sic*) That is a hard saying (*'ala al-taghliẓ*), but we relate it as it came, and do not interpret it. He also said, "Do not turn back, after me, as infidels, cutting one another's throats," and "If two Muslims come at each other with their swords, both the slayer and slain man go to hellfire," and "Abuse of a Muslim is disobedience (of God), and fighting one is disbelief," and "Whoever says to his (Muslim) brother 'Thou infidel!' one of the two is worthy of that name," and "Whoever denies his origins (*nasab*), rejects God, even if they were base," and similar ḥadīths from those which have been found sound and were kept, so we are obedient to him, even if we do not know the interpretation, and we do not discuss them or contend about them. We do not interpret the traditions, except by a similar one which has come down, or disregard one except for another which is better than the first.

Paradise and Hell are two created places which God has created, as has come down from the Messenger of God, on him be peace and God's blessing: "I entered Paradise, and saw a palace," and "I saw (the fountain of) al-Kawthar," and "I considered hellfire, and saw that most of the people there were women," and "I looked into hellfire, and I saw this or that," so whoever asserts that they are not created things has made a liar of the Qur'ān and the traditions of God's messenger, on whom be peace and God's blessing, and cannot be considered as believing in Paradise and Hell.

Whoever among those who pray in the direction of Mecca dies believing in One God should be prayed over, and forgiveness asked for his sins. He may not be deprived of the prayer for forgiveness, and we do not neglect to pray for him for any sin he committed, whether it was great or small. It is for God, the Mighty and Glorious, to judge him.[17]

THE DOCTRINE OF IJMĀ'

With a few important exceptions, the Sunnī theorists agree that since the Umma cannot come together on an error, it is infallible. If there is a difference of opinion within the collectivity, right is with the majority. In practise, this has not meant *vox populi vox dei*, since by a further refinement of the principle, the only voices heard were those of the *'ulamā'*, the professional religious learned class, and the rulers. When 'ulamā' and rulers joined together on a question, they provided an authority which was unchallengeable in practise and infallible in theory. (In the case of a disagreement between 'ulamā' and rulers, it was usually the rulers who lost.)

The founder of the Shāfi'ī Sunnī law school, who died before Ibn Ḥanbal, develops the doctrine of *ijmā'* ("joining together") as an authority next only to Qur'ān and Ḥadīth.

On Ijmā', *or General Consensus*
from the Legal Treatise
Abū 'Abdallah Muḥammad al-Shāfi'ī (d. A.H. *204/*A.D. *820)*

Al-Shāfi'ī said: Someone has told me, "I understand your doctrine about God's commands and then about the commands of His messenger, and that whoever receives from the Messenger has received from God, since God has ordered obedience of His messenger, and (I understand) that the proof of what you hold lies in the fact that a Muslim who knew Scripture but not tradition could not lawfully contradict the one by the other. I recognize that this (obedience) is commanded by God. But what is your proof for following what people have agreed upon, where there is no command in a text from God, or related from the Prophet? Would you assert what others have held, that 'joining together' can never occur except on a firm tradition (sunna), even though it may not have been related?!"

I told him, "As to what they agree upon, and say that it has been related from the Prophet, let us hope (*inshā'allāh*) that that is as they say. However, as for what is not related, it may be that it was actually said by the Messenger of God, and it may be otherwise. It is not permissible to attribute sayings to him, for one is only permitted to relate what one has heard, and is not permitted to relate anything one fancies, in which there may be things (the Prophet) did not say.

"Therefore, we hold to what they held to, following them. We know that if these were practises of the Messenger, they would not be remote to the generality of Muslims, though they are remote to the few, and we know that the generality of Muslims will not agree on what is contradictory to the Sunna of the Messenger of God, or on an error, please God."

If it is asked, "Is there anything to indicate that or prove it?" we reply "Sufyān informs us on the authority of 'Abd al-Malik ibn 'Umayr from 'Abd al-Raḥman the son of 'Abdallah ibn Mas'ūd, from his father, that the Messenger of God said, 'God prospers a servant who listens to what I say, remembers it, pays attention to it, and passes it on. Often one may transmit insight (*fiqh*) who is not himself perspicacious, and often he transmits it to one with more insight than he. There are three things which cannot be resented by the heart of a Muslim: sincerity of action for God, good advice to the Muslims, and cleaving to the collectivity, for the claims of these protect them in advance (*min warā'ihim*)' ".

Sufyān also informs us, from 'Abdallah ibn Abī Labīb from Ibn Sulaymān son of Yasār, from his father, that 'Umar ibn al-Khaṭṭāb addressed the people of al-Jābiya (the Syrian garrison town) saying: "The Messenger of God stood among us as I am standing among you, and said, 'Show regard for my Companions, and then for those who follow them, and then for those who follow those. Then falsehood will become manifest, so that a man will make oaths without being asked to swear, and testify without being asked to testify. Then let him who is pleased by the joys of paradise cleave to the Collectivity, for Satan is with the one who stands alone, but he is further from two. But let no man be alone with a woman, for Satan will be the third of them. Whoever is pleased with his good actions and grieved by his bad actions is a Believer.' "

(The questioner) asked "What is the meaning of the Prophet's command to cleave to the Collectivity?"

I (Shāfi'ī) said "There is but one meaning to it."

He said "How may it have only one meaning?"

I replied "When the Collectivity of Muslims was dispersed in (various) countries, one could not cleave to a Collectivity whose members were scattered, and besides, they were found together with Muslims and unbelievers, with pious men and profligates. Thus it could not mean a physical 'cleaving,' because that was not possible, and because physical nearness would (in itself) effect nothing, so that there is no meaning in cleaving to the Collectivity except in agreeing with them in what they make lawful and forbidden, and obedience in both these matters.

"Whoever holds to what the Collectivity of Muslims holds has 'cleaved to their collectivity,' and he who contradicts what the Collectivity holds has separated from the Collectivity he was ordered to cleave to. Error comes only with separation, but as for the Collectivity, there can be no error in it, and no heedlessness of the Book, or the Tradition, or Analogy, if God wills."[18]

A sharp protest against the doctrine of the infallible community was registered by the Ḥanbalī doctor Ibn Taymīya (d. A.H. 728/A.D. 1328), the figure in Islam whom one may best liken to Martin Luther in Western Christianity.

For al-Shāfi'ī, the Muslim majority could not agree on an error. For Ibn Taymīya, they had already done so, repeatedly, and the point was that Islamic "joining together" should not depart from Scripture and the Ḥadīth. Much of what was accepted in his own day he found unacceptable. As a reformer, desiring a return to what he considered the fundamentals of Islam, he necessarily rejected much of the cumulative tradition of the Community.

It was natural that such a figure would tend to rise only in the right wing of the Ḥanbalī school, though Ibn Taymīya's intolerance is rather different from that of Ibn Ḥanbal.

It is instructive to compare Ibn Taymīya's career with that of Luther. While political, economic and social circumstances combined to make Luther's doctrines the justification of a great revolution, the social situation of fourteenth century Syria was quite different from that of sixteenth century Northern Europe. It was relatively stable and content at home, and threatened militarily by the Mongols from without. Social forces were more centripetal than centrifugal. Thus Ibn Taymīya was easily suppressed, and virtually ignored. It was not until more than four centuries had passed that Muslim society, in the disintegrating state of the Ottoman Empire, was favorable for the social and military propagation of his doctrines. This was first done in Arabia by Muḥammad b. 'Abd al-Waḥḥāb (d. A.H. 1201/A.D. 1787). Today, most Muslim fundamentalist reform movements derive their characteristic doctrines from Ibn Taymīya.

On Ijmā', *or General Concensus*
from The Ladders of Attainment
Taqī al-Dīn Aḥmad ibn Taymīya (d. A.H. *728/*A.D. *1328)*

Many doctors (*mujtahids*) of the early Community and those who followed them have held or practised what was innovation, not knowing that it was so, either because of weak ḥadīths they thought sound, or because of understanding from a Qur'ānic verse what does not follow, or for some personal view held in ignorance of definitive texts on the matter. If (such) a man fears God as much as possible (he may still hope for mercy).

The point here is that the Messenger has clearly shown all of religion in the Scripture and in his Sunna. Ijmā'—the joining together of the Community—is right, and it shall not join together on an error. . . .

The verse cited as a proof-text for "joining together" is (Qur'ān 4–115): "But him who breaks with the Messenger after guidance has become clear to him, and follows other than the way of the believers, him We shall consign to what he had turned to, and roast in Gehennā—an evil home—coming."

(We may sum up the possible exegeses of this) thus: The blame attaches to those who break with the Messenger only, or those who follow other than the way of Believers only, or else blame does not attach to one of these but to both of them, because they both are the same, or to both of them although they are separate from one another, or to both of them because they are closely connected with each other. The first two positions are false, because if only one of the two (categories) is affected, there would be no point in mentioning the other. That the blame should not attach to one of these two (categories) is absolutely untenable.

Breaking with the Messenger clearly entails the divine threat, apart from anything else. Attaching blame to both categories but treating them as separate is not indicated by the verse; it concerns both together.

There remains the last position, which is that all those described thus incur the threat, because they are closely connected, just as the like is said of those who rebel against God and the Messenger, and as it is said (in the ḥadīth) that one who opposes the Qur'ān and Islam or leaves the Qur'ān and Islam is of the people of hell, and God's saying (4–136) "He who disbelieves in God and His Angels, His Books, and His Messengers has strayed into extreme error," so that disbelief in each of these fundamentals involves disbelief in the others, and whoever disbelieves in God has disbelieved in all of them.

It is similar with breaking with the Messenger and following other than the way of the Believers: whoever breaks with him has followed other than the way of the Believers—that is obvious. And whoever follows other than the way of Believers has broken with him, and exposed himself to the Divine threat. . . . Any one departing from their "joining together" has followed another way absolutely, and accordingly exposed himself to the Divine threat. If anyone says that they are only blamed because at the same time they broke with the Messenger, we say, "yes"—because the two acts are intimately connected, for the reason that *whatever the Muslims join together on must be based on texts from the Messenger of God* [italics supplied.—Ed.], so that whoever opposes them has opposed also the Messenger, and whoever opposes him opposes God. It necessarily follows that everything on which they join together should have been demonstrated by the Messenger, and that is our point.

Thus there is absolutely no question on which they are joined together that has not been clearly demonstrated by the Messenger, but this has escaped some people, and they know about "joining together" and try to use it as a proof, as one would use a text, if they do not know any proof-texts. However, "joining together" is a second proof, to be added to the text, like an example given in the Qur'ān. . . . Whatever joining together indicates has also been indicated by Scripture and by the (Prophet's) Sunna. All that the Qur'ān indicates has come by the way of the Messenger, since both Qur'ān and Sunna came through him, so there cannot be any question on which "joining together" has occurred, unless it has been based on a text. . . .

Many 'ulamā' have not known the texts, and still have concurred with the Collectivity, just as they have used logic on a matter where "joining together" had occurred without their knowing it, and still agreed with the consensus. . . .

Whatever modern says that "joining together" is the basis of the greater part of the Law has given himself away, for it is lack of knowledge of the Scripture and the Sunna that drives him to say it. Similarly when they say that most new events require use of logical analogy, because there is no indication in the texts—that is only the statement of one who has no knowledge of the Book and the Sunna with their clear rules for making judgements. . . .

The Sunna cannot abrogate the Book . . . if there be anything abrogated in the Qur'ān, the abrogation is written there, since nothing can take precedence over it. If one does not find something in it, he may look for it in the Sunna, and nothing can abrogate a ḥadīth except another ḥadīth: the Sunna is not abrogated by "joining together" or anything else . . . for joining together cannot contradict Scripture or the Sunna.[19]

SHĪʿĪ VIEWS ON THE COMMUNITY

It may be said that every revealed religion must have an infallible link between the believer and the revelation. Without an infallible authentication of the original revelation, the God of Revelation becomes only a dubious hypothesis, and indeed "dies" to faith. Thus for Protestantism, the Scripture which told of the revelation has been infallible, while for Catholics, the Church which wrote the Scriptures and bears witness to their truth is the infallible link between the Worshipped and the worshipper.

Islam has an infallible Book and an infallible Prophet, but its emphasis on Divine Law has necessitated an infallible connecting link for the living Muslims. In traditional Sunnī Islam, as we have seen, this infallibility reposes in the Community—although strict Ḥanbalīs tended rather to stress the infallibility of the Ḥadīth material which transmitted the Prophet's Sunna.

For Shīʿī Islam, the case was quite different. There could be no question of the infallibility of the majority of Muslims joined together. For Shīʿīs, it is axiomatic that the community had gone deeply and tragically wrong almost as soon as the Prophet was dead. Instead of recognizing the rights of his family, many of the Prophet's Companions then living combined against it. Eventually, the majority of Muslims accepted rulers who had no right to rule, and then—a Shīʿī would feel—they despicably acquiesced or assisted while the Prophet's descendants were defrauded of their rights, persecuted and murdered. The Muslims could be infallible only so long as they followed their rightful leaders, from the House of the Prophet.

Thus, we find two nuances in the Shīʿī attitude toward the Umma. The first is here outlined by the early Twelver doctor Ibn Babūya al-Sadūq. For him, the Umma is simply his own sect.

On the Umma
from a Twelver Shīʿī Creedal Statement
Ibn Babūya al-Sadūq (d. A.H. *381/*A.H. *991)*

Every verse in the Qur'ān which begins with the expression "Oh you who believe" refers necessarily to ʿAlī ibn Abī Ṭālib as their leader (*qāʾid*) and prince (*amīr*) and the most noble among them.

And every verse which directs the way to Paradise applies to the Prophet or the Imāms, the blessing of God upon them all and their partisans and followers. . . . Among the Prophets none is better than the Prophet Muḥammad, the blessings of Allah upon him, and among the plenipotentiaries (*awṣiyā'*) none is better than Muḥammad's plenipotentiaries (i.e. the twelve Imāms) and among the communities none in reality is more excellent than this Community—the partisans (Shī'a) of the Prophet's family, and none else. And among the wicked, none is more wicked than those who are their enemies and opponents.

The (twelve Imāms) are immune from sin and error . . . they may be likened in this Community to the Ark of Noah; he who boards it attains salvation or reaches the Gate of Repentance.[20]

A Shī'ī may thus concede the infallibility of the Community, and restrict the Community to the Partisans of 'Alī. Another possible view is to deny it outright. Here is an Ismā'īlī statement of doctrine written between 1209 and 1215 in the Yemen by the head of the Musta'lī sect of Ismā'īlīs. It is based no doubt upon the creeds used by the Ismā'īlī Imāms of the Fāṭimī Empire (909–1171), who had many Sunnī subjects.

On the Umma
From an Ismā'īlī Creedal Statement of the 7th/13th Century

The Imām cannot be elected by the Community. He is the absolute ruler, who imposes his final judgement upon his followers. The principle of *ijmā'*, or consensus of the community in accepting certain religious laws and practises, is completely false. If one were to accept this principle, he should regard Muḥammad as not a real Prophet, because all the people to whom he at first addressed himself, or at least the majority of them, did not at first recognise him as such. . . . Only the Imām, appointed by God, is *ma'ṣūm*, or infallible, but the community, obviously, cannot be considered as infallible.

Everyone who makes an attempt on the rights of an Imām [hence, the Sunnī leaders.—Ed.] is Taghūt the demon. This means that every action intended to oppose the Imām to prevent him from occupying his office, etc. is to be considered as a great sin.

The Umma became split and fell into disagreements after the death of the Prophet, thus taking the way of error. This was chiefly due to their reluctance to follow the *ahl al–bayt,* i.e. the Imāms. Only a small group amongst the Muslims remained faithful to the commandments and the will of the Prophet, suffering for this reason at the hand of different oppressors. Only the Ismā'īlīs preserved the correct belief and followed the true path.[21]

One who blindly follows the religion of his ancestors, by tradition, without having ascertained for himself whether it is correct or wrong, is not right. He should know and act in accordance with the Qur'ān and Sunna as taught by the Imāms of the family of the Apostle. . . .

Association with *munāfiqīn* [hypocrites: often used for non–Shī'ī Muslims.—Ed.] is undesirable. Such are those who ridicule religion or its representatives.

True religion *(al–Ḥaqq)* is always the lot of only a small minority of mankind, as can be proved from the Qur'ān. The great majority usually take up various false and mistaken beliefs.

(Religion) and faith are to be found only in Shī'ism (along with true) following the Sunna of the Prophet. . . . The Prophet predicted the splitting up of the Islamic Community into seventy-three sects after his death; of these only one is that which brings salvation. It is the one which follows the Prophet and his descendants, who are the Ark of Noah, giving religious salvation. . . . Walāya, or support for 'Alī and love for him and his cause, is the greatest religious virtue in Islam.[22]

EXCLUSIVISM

Although the Prophet had included Jews in his Umma, and the Muslims made use of the cultural contributions of the conquered peoples, the Muslim sense of exclusiveness grew. How orthodox Muslims tended to regard their own relation to the Peoples of the Book is suggested by this selection from the *Book of Politics* of Niẓām al–Mulk, the great Persian minister and adviser of the Saljūqs. The Saljūq Turks had recently come to power, and were notable for their tolerance toward all their subjects. The intent of the argument seems to be that the Saljūq Sulṭāns should rely only on men of the Muslim administrative class. While the stories from early Islam on which it draws are too full of anachronisms to be authentic, they had the persuasiveness of truth for the Niẓām and his contemporaries, and helped to justify the medieval social system by which power and most of its fruits were with few exceptions restricted to Muslims.

On Giving State Employment to Non-Muslims
from the Book of Politics
Abū' Alī Ḥasan ibn Isḥāq, the Niẓām al-Mulk (d. A.H. *458*/A.D. *1092)*

The Commander of the Faithful 'Umar was sitting in the mosque at Medina; Abū Mūsā Ash'arī was sitting in front of him, and was presenting the accounts for Isfahan—written in a fair hand and exactly reckoned, so that all who saw them admired them. Abū Mūsā was asked, "Whose writing is this?" He said. "My secretary's." They said, "Send someone to bring him here." He said, "He cannot come into the mosque." 'Umar said, "Is he unclean then?" He said, "No, he is a Christian." 'Umar gave Abū Mūsā a slap on the thigh—so hard that he said he thought his thigh was broken—and said, "Have you not read the command of The Lord of Majesty: 'O ye who believe, take not Jews and Christians as friends; they are friends to one another.' " Abū Mūsā said, "This very hour will I dismiss him and give him his leave.' "[23]

It so happened that in the days of Sa'd (ibn Abī) Waqqāṣ in the neighbourhood of (southern Iraq) there was a Jewish tax-collector. Now the people of these districts wrote a letter to The Commander of the Faithful 'Umar (may Allah be pleased with him) and complained against that Jewish collector, saying, "This man is humiliating us; we cannot endure it further. Appoint a Muslim collector over us; being of the same religion as ourselves perhaps he will not oppress us; (but) at least we would prefer to suffer such indignity from a Muslim than from a Jew." When 'Umar read the petition, he said "Is it not enough for a Jew that he should be alive in the world? Does he also expect preference over the Muslims?" He immediately ordered a letter to be written to Sa'd Waqqāṣ telling him to dismiss the Jew and give the appointment to a Muslim. . . .

Sa'd Waqqāṣ was at a loss to know what to do. Of necessity he kept the Jew in the appointment and wrote, saying: "There was no one at all who understood the duties of tax collection and administration as well as the Jew. I was obliged to keep him."

When the letter reached 'Umar, he took up his pen and wrote at the top of the letter, "The Jew is dead!" and sent it back to Sa'd Waqqāṣ. What he meant was, "Every man has to die; and death may dismiss the tax-collector. Suppose the Jew is dead." When

Sa'd received the letter and 'Umar's post–script, he immediately recalled the Jew and gave the post to a Muslim. After a year had passed it was observed that the Muslim discharged his duties even more efficiently than the Jew; the same revenues came in, the peasants were contented, yet public works were increased. Sa'd Waqqāṣ then said to the Arab nobles, "What a great man is The Commander of the Faithful! He gave the answer in two words, and it turned out as he said, not as we thought." (A saying which will be) applauded and will be cited as (a proverb) by Muslims until the resurrection was that saying of 'Umar, may Allah be pleased with him: "The Jew is dead." (Whenever it is argued that an unsuitable person should be retained because he is efficient) then the ruler must say at once "The Jew is dead!" When the Prophet—upon him be peace—went out from the world, not one of his Companions dared to say that the Prophet was dead: (then) Abū Bakr said, "Whoever used to worship Muḥammad, verily Muḥammad is dead; whoever used to worship Muḥammad's Lord, verily He is living and immortal." The Muslims approved this speech, and it became a proverb among the Arabs; and whenever any great affliction befalls the Arabs or a dear one passes away, and they want to ease the burden of suffering for the unfortunate relative, people cry out "Muḥammad is dead!" for of all mankind had it been possible for one man not to die, then that person should have been Muḥammad the Elect.[24]

How important it seemed to a devout medieval Muslim to live within the territory of the Umma, under Muslim rule, can be seen from the remarks of the Spanish Muslim traveller Ibn Jubayr, who journeyed from A.D. 1183 to 1185 through the eastern Muslim domains, and set down what he saw for his western Muslim readers.

It was the period of the Crusades, when Muslims and Western Christians were often in contact, not always hostile. Ibn Jubayr also passed through the Crusader Kingdom in Syria, and was in Sicily, where the Norman kings were such tolerant patrons of Muslim culture that they aroused the anger of Popes. The pious Andalusian writer is frank to admit that he saw there much that was attractive—and he rejects it.

What he has to say must be seen in the context of his times. Ibn Jubayr was a civil servant in Muslim Spain under the North African Muwaḥḥids ("Almohades"), who had taken over the remaining Muslim provinces of Andalusia. It was the period of the *Reconquista* —Spanish Crusader armies were threatening to retake all of Spain, and many Muslims were already living under the (then tolerant) protection of Spanish Kings. By the orthodox Mālikī standards of the Spanish Muslims, the Berber Muwaḥḥids were, strictly speaking, heretics and not popular. Ibn Jubayr, orthoprax Muslim that he was, felt strongly that any foreign Muslim rule was preferable to government by Christians, whether Spanish or no.

On Residing in Non-Muslim Territories
from the Travels
Ibn Jubayr of Valencia (d. A.H. *614/*A.D. *1217)*

We moved from Tibnin (in Syria)—may God destroy it—through continuous farms and ordered settlements whose inhabitants were all Muslims, living comfortably with the Franks. God protect us from such temptation. They surrender half their crops to the Franks at harvest time, and pay as well a poll-tax of one dinār and five *qirāt* for each person. Other than that, they are not interfered with, save for a light tax on the fruits of trees. Their houses and all their effects are left to their full possession. All the coastal cities occupied by the Franks are managed in this fashion, their rural districts, the villages and farms, belonging to the Muslims. But their hearts have been seduced, for they observe how unlike them in ease and comfort are their brethren in the Muslim regions under their (Muslim) governors. This is one of the misfortunes afflicting the Muslims. The Muslim community bewails the injustice of a landlord of its own faith, and applauds the conduct of its opponent and enemy and is accustomed to justice from him. He who laments this state must turn to God.[25]

During our stay in Tyre, we rested in one of the Mosques that remained in Muslim hands. One of the Muslim elders of Tyre told us that it had been wrested from them in the year 518 (June 27, 1124). They thereupon decided to abandon the town, and to make good their escape. So it happened, and they dispersed among the Muslim lands. But there were some whose love of native land impelled them to return and, under the conditions of a safeguard which was written for them, to live amongst the infidels. "God is the master of His affair" (12:21). Glorious is God, and great is His power. His will overcomes all impediments.

There can be no excuse in the eyes of God for a Muslim to stay in any infidel country, save when passing through it, while the way lies clear in Muslim lands. They will face pains and terrors such as the abasement and destitution of the capitation (tax) and more especially, amongst the base and lower orders, the hearing of what will distress the heart in the reviling of him (Muḥammad) whose memory God has sanctified, and whose rank He has exalted; there is also the absence of cleanliness, the mixing with the pigs, and all the other prohibited matters too numerous to be related or enumerated. Beware, beware of entering their lands. May God Most High grant His beneficent indulgence for this sin into which our feet have slipped (of setting foot there), but His forgiveness is not given save after accepting our penitence. Glory be unto God, the Master. There is no Lord but He.[26]

The (Muslim) people of the island of Sicily suffer, amongst other tribulations, one that is very sore. Should a man show anger to his son or his wife, or a woman to her daughter, the one who is the object of displeasure may perversely throw himself into a church, and there be baptised and turn Christian. Then there will be for the father no way of approaching his son, or the mother her daughter. Conceive now the state of one so afflicted in his family, or even in his son. The dread of their falling to this temptation would alone shorten his life. The Muslims of Sicily therefore are most watchful. The most clear-sighted of them fear that it shall chance to them all as it did in earlier times to the Muslim inhabitants of Crete. There a Christian despotism so long visited them with one (painful) circumstance after another that they were all constrained to turn Christian, only those escaping whom God decreed. But the word of chastisement shall fall upon these infidels. God's will shall prevail: there is indeed no God but He. . . .

We came upon another striking example of their state, such as breaks the spirit in pity and melts the heart in compassion. One of the notables of this town of Trapani sent his son to one of our pilgrim companions, desiring of him that he would accept of him his daughter, a young virgin who was nearing the age of puberty. Should he be pleased with her, he could marry her; if not, he could marry her to any one of his countrymen who liked her. She would go with them, content to leave her father and her brothers, desiring only to escape from the temptation (of apostasy), and to live in the lands of the Muslims. The man sought after, in order to win a heavenly reward, accepted the offer, and we helped him to seize an opportunity which would lead him to the felicities both of this world and the next.

We ourselves were filled with wonder at a situation which would lead a man to give up so readily a trust tied to his heart, and to surrender her to one strange to her, to bear in patience the want of her, and to suffer longings for her and loneliness without her. We were likewise amazed at the girl—may God protect her—and at her willingness to leave her kin for her love of Islam.[27]

MODERNIST REFORMERS

In recent times, the Syrian educator-reformer Shaykh from al-Azhar, Rashīd Riḍā, who died only in 1935, lived in a time when the Caliphal powers of the Ottoman Sultans had been abolished by the Turkish Republic. Suddenly, the Islamic Community found itself without any visible head or political expression, even in theory.

Although Riḍā was a modernist reformer, deeply influenced by the doctrines of Ibn Taymīya and exercising in turn a great influence on modern Muslim thought, he still belongs more to the medieval than to the modern world. His world of concern was naturally still the universal Umma, and he devoted much energy to the problems of what Muslims should now do. The unity of the Community was real for him, and it demanded political structures. A Caliph was necessary. He argues that sovereignty is really delegated to the Community, and it in turn delegates it to a leader. The Community should now choose and obey a new leader, whose authority must be more than merely symbolic, since he is the executive of the infallible Collectivity: in a sense, he is the will of a most absolute democracy.

The Power of the Community and the Meaning of "Collectivity"
from Caliphate, or the Great Imamate
Rashīd Riḍā (d. A.H. *1354*/A.D. *1935)*

God has said of the believers, "Their affairs are by mutual counsel." (Qur. 42:36) As we have pointed out in our commentary on the Qur'ān, the Qur'ān prescribes law for the collectivity of Believers, even on waging war and other matters of the general interest, and apart from that, it orders obedience to those in authority —that is to say, the Collectivity—and those representing them. This is because the one who wields the power is one of the Believers, and he is obeyed because he has the support of the Community who took allegiance to him and gave him their trust. This is shown by sound ḥadīths, which stress that one must cleave to the Collectivity, and that obedience is due the ruler because of the obedience due the Collectivity, and "joining together" is only possible when there is power. There is the sound ḥadīth of Ibn 'Abbās from the

Prophet: "Let him who sees something (bad) in his commander resign himself, for whoever willfully quits the Collectivity dies the death of the Jāhilīya (when there was no Islam)," and what the Prophet told Hudhayfa ibn al-Yamān in the well-known ḥadīth about the trials (to come) in the Community: "Cleave to the Collectivity of the Muslims and their leader." "What when there is no Collectivity and no leader?" "Then withdraw from all the factions." In other ḥadīths it is shown that the "Collectivity" is the majority, going back to the dawn of Islam.

One of the proofs of the sovereignty of the Community, used also to justify "joining together" is the ḥadīth, "My Community shall not join together in error." Al-Ṭabarī, in discussing differences about the meaning of "Collectivity," since some [mostly Ḥanbalīs.—Ed.] reduce it to majority only of the Prophet's companions, says "The exact meaning of "cleaving to the Collectivity" is to obey him they have set in authority: whoever breaks his allegiance to him has seceded from the Community." He also says "It is in the Ḥadīth that when there is no leader for the people, and they have split into parties (*aḥzāb*), then one ought not to follow any faction, but withdraw from all of them so far as one is able, lest he fall into evil." This is also accepted by al-Ḥāfiz in his commentary on Bukhārī.

It is the Collectivity which is "those in authority," and "those who loose and bind," "who must be obeyed when joined together." From among them come the "higher authorities" and "those who give counsel" before the leader (*imām*). Now, when the Muslims are instructed about a matter of general interest in the Qur'ān, the Sunna, and the example of the Companions, they are obliged to see that it is put into effect.

As an example of the Companions, we have the words of Abū Bakr at his election to the caliphate. "You have put me in power, though I am not the best among you. If I do well, help me, and if I do wrong, then set me right," and the like was said of 'Uthman: "They were given the rank of the caliphate as neither the highest nor lowest of the Emigrants (from Mecca.)"

In the text of the *Mawāqif* of 'Aḍud we read, "The Community may depose its leader in case of necessity, but if that will lead to a schism (*fitna*), one should choose the lesser of two evils." In defining the Caliphate, we have already cited the authority of al-Rāzī: "The supreme authority belongs to the Community, which may depose the Imām (the Caliph) if it sees the necessity for doing so." Al-Sa'd says "By 'Community' is meant 'those with power to loose and bind,'" that is: those who represent the Community by possession of authority and prestige; their authority extends to the others, that is, the individuals in the Community. In his commentary on the verse "Obey God, His Messenger, and those in authority among you" (Qur. 4:58), he makes it clear that "Those in authority" means those who may loose and bind, who represent the power of the Community. He is followed here by Nīsabūrī, and by our teacher and shaykh (Muḥammad 'Abdūh). It is necessarily known that "those in authority" at the Prophet's time were consulted in the general welfare; they were not 'Ulamā' of the Law, or judges, but men of counsel among the leading Muslims.[28]

The Muslim Brotherhood (*al-Ikhwān al-Muslimūn*) was founded in Egypt, by Shaykh Ḥasan al-Bannā' (d. 1949), of the following of Rashīd Riḍā. A man of charismatic magnetism, he transformed the reformist program into a mass movement, a Brotherhood intent on purifying Egyptian and other Muslim society.

Although the movement (almost inevitably) ran afoul of the Egyptian Revolution under Gamāl 'Abd al-Nāṣir, its ideas have gained very wide currency in the modern Muslim world, even among the Nāṣirists.

Like Riḍā and the Revolution, the Ikhwān rejects parties. The prime concern of Brotherhood spokesmen is: how may society be made Islamic again? Necessarily, it can be achieved at first only within one of the existing Muslim states: the development of consensus demands power. The Brotherhood's lack of squeamishness about means, including subversion and assassination, has done more than anything else to turn people against it as an organization. Sayyid Quṭb, one of the leading Egyptian writers of the movement (executed in 1965), develops some characteristic ideas about the individual and the Community in his book *Social Justice in Islam*, from which this selection is taken. Very striking is the tendency to talk of "Islam" as if it were some abstract ideology, like Marxism, or National Socialism. A faith to be lived is transformed into a penal code.

Mutual Responsibilities of the Individual and the Umma
from Social Justice in Islam
Sayyid Quṭb (d. A.H *1385/*A.D. *1965)*

We must think also of the responsibility which the individual has to society, and that of society to the individual. Islam tries as far as possible to harmonize their interests. Every individual is charged in the first place conscientiously to perform his own work; (this is) in the long run advantageous and beneficial to the community. . . .

Again every individual is charged with the care of society, as if he were the watchman over it, responsible for its safety. Life is like a ship at sea, whose crew are all concerned for her safety; none of them may make a hole even in his own part of her, in the name of his individual freedom. No individual, then, can be exempt from this care for the general interest. Similarly the welfare of the community must be promoted by mutual help between individuals —always within the limits of honesty and uprightness. "Help one another in innocence and piety, but do not help one another in crime and hostility" (5:3). Each individual will be held personally responsible for having urged to virtue; and if he has not done so, then he is a criminal and will be punished for his crime. "Take him and chain him; then roast him in Hell; then thrust him into a chain of seventy cubits' length. Verily he would not believe in Allah the Great; he would not urge the feeding of the poor. So he has no friend here today, nor any food save foul corruption which only sinners eat" (69:30–36).

Every individual, again, is charged with the duty of putting an end to any evil-doing which he sees. Thus every individual will be held responsible for every evil-doing in the community, for society is a unity which is harmed by evil-doing. . . . The whole community is to blame and merits injury and punishment in this world and in the world to come if it passively accepts evil-doing in its midst. . . . "When We wish to destroy a town We command its luxury-loving citizens and they deal corruptly in it; thus the sentence upon it is justified, and We destroy it utterly" (17:17). There is no injustice in this, for the community in which evil-doing flourishes unchecked is a community which is exhausted and decayed, on the way to its end. . . . "Those of the Children of Israel who became unbelievers were cursed by the tongue of David and of Jesus son of Mary. That was because they rebelled and transgressed; they did not restrain one another from evil-doing, but practised it. Bad indeed is what they were doing" (5:82).

Now concerning the verse: "O you who believe, look after yourselves, he who goes astray will not harm you, so long as you let yourselves be guided" (5:104). What this verse actually contains is a statement of individual responsibility. Wickedness which is negative, which has no compulsive force on others, is a matter which concerns only him who indulges in it; the duty of others is to seek guidance; if the sinner does not, the responsibility is on himself and his own possessions.

The Community is also responsible for the care of its weak members . . . it has also the duty of fighting in defense of those whom it guards. It must also guard the property of the young until they attain to years of discretion.

The Community has the care of the money from the poor–tax and of its expenditure on various objects. If this is not enough, the rich are obliged to contribute as much as will meet the wants of the needy; there is no restriction and no condition, except that there shall be sufficient. If any individual pass the night hungry, the blame attaches to the Community because it did not bestir itself to feed him. . . . Where neighborliness is concerned, prosperity obliges a man even to give away one garment out of two. . . .

The whole Islamic Community is one body, and it feels all things in common. On this foundation the laws against social crimes are built up; they are very severe, because mutual help cannot exist except on the basis of the safety of a man's life, property, and rights. Thus the penalty for killing or wounding is laid down as an exact equivalent: "Free–man for free–man, slave for slave, female for female." (2:173) "We have prescribed a law for them in this matter; a life for a life, an eye for an eye, a nose for a nose, an ear for an ear, a tooth for a tooth, and for wounds the equivalent" (17:35). "In this retaliation there is life for you, O ye who have understanding; perhaps you may be pious" (2:175) and in fact it does mean life; for it safeguards life by discouraging murder, and because it preserves the vitality and the power of the life of society.

The punishment for immorality, again, is severe, because it involves an attack on honor and a contempt for sanctity and an encouragement of profligacy in society. From it by a gradual process there comes license, the obscuring of family ties, and the loss of those essential features of fatherhood and son-ship. The penalty for this must be severe; for married men and women it is stoning to death; for unmarried men and women it is flogging, a hundred lashes, which in most cases is fatal. "The man or woman guilty of fornication shall be flogged with a hundred lashes; and let no pity for them affect you in the faith of Allah" (24:2).

A punishment of eighty lashes is fixed for those who (impugn) chaste women Believers who have been innocently careless: in this case, the crime is closely akin to that of immorality; an attack on reputation and honor, an incitement to hatred and bitterness, and an evidence of corruption of thought.

The punishment of theft is likewise severe, because it is an offense against property; it is fixed at the cutting off of a hand; for a second offense the other hand is cut off, for a third offense a foot, and then the other foot. There are some today who profess to find this a shocking punishment, but Islam looks at the matter only from the point of view of safety, the security, and the stability of society. . . . Such secret crimes have need of stern punishments to recompense the criminal and to make him an example. . . . (It) is not exacted in full if the theft was committed under compulsion, such as hunger. . . .

As for those who threaten the general security of society . . . "The punishment of those who war on Allah and His Messenger and who strive to cause revolt in the land is to be put to death, to be crucified, to have their hands and feet cut off on opposite sides, or to be banished from the land" (5:37). Consensus holds that revolt and civil war are a greater crime than individual crimes. . . .

Thus Islam legislates for mutual responsibility in society in all shapes and forms; these forms take their rise from the basic principle that there is an all-embracing identity of purpose between the individual and society, and that life in its fullness is all interrelated. . . .

On these three foundations, then—an absolute freedom of conscience, a complete equality of all mankind, and a permanent mutual responsibility in society—social justice is built up and human justice is assured.[29]

THE NATIONALIST TRANSFORMATION

The Muslim world today is divided into separate "nation states." In most cases, nationalism began in Muslim areas as an effort to reject the control of aliens. In each case, it was closely involved with specifically Muslim sentiments, and for the masses, it is safe to say that it was identical with Islam. As W. Cantwell Smith has put it, "No Muslim people has evolved a national feeling that has meant a loyalty to or even concern for a community transcending the bounds of Islam."[30] Nowhere has this identification of the nation with the Umma gone further than with the Arabs. The very word for "nation" in modern literary Arabic is "umma"; thus "United Nations" becomes "United Ummas." Appeals to voters are made in the name of the name of the Iraqi umma, the Tunisian umma, the Arab umma.

The use of this hallowed word, addressed to an Arab audience, is profoundly significant: it appropriates to a geographic or ethnic entity the same transcending loyalties that Muslims traditionally gave to the universal community of Muḥammad. Here is a representative view of the umma and history, from a political statement by a prominent Pan-Arabist, Munīf al-Razzāz, secretary general of the Ba'th political party. The Nāṣirist Pan-Arabists, although they differ vehemently with the Ba'th, do not differ on this basic secularization of the Community. The specific quality of Muslim nationalism has also been inevitably colored by Muslim religious ideas. The corporate responsibility of the Community for its members, so dear to the Muslim revivalists, is translated by the Ba'th and the Nāṣirists into socialism, and that aspect of Marxist thought has an undeniable appeal to Muslims everywhere. The corollary of the equation of Arabism with Islam—that the sizable minority of Arab Christians are equals, more worthy than the Indian or African Muslims—remains a bone discarded unswallowed, for most Arab Muslims.

On the Umma of the Arabs
from Development of the Idea of Nationalism
Munīf al-Razzāz

In these times, the Arabic Umma is going through a period of development such as it has not passed through since the beginning of the Islamic era. After these long centuries of decadence, disintegration, and Turkish and Persian usurpation, the Arabs have begun to know their own identity, and realize themselves. With the middle of the 19th century, life has begun to stir in them as it has not stirred for centuries.

It was quite natural that an awakening be at first sluggish and uncertain and occur in a few scattered centers, and that this consciousness be dubious and vague, like that of a new-born child who has no clear sense of direction or definite goal. But then the awareness grew, assumed an instinctive primitive form, striving to express its attitudes and its objectives. For each small gain it suffered many setbacks.

But as it grew, it gained momentum until it was transformed into a massive movement encompassing the entire Umma. The confused and feeble cries and wails grew into a powerful, articulate act which announced that the Umma as a whole was entering the phase of maturity, and the battle of living responsibly.

Since the growth of the new Arab consciousness stretched over a century, we are fortunate indeed to assist the entry to the stage of maturity and responsibility. Before this, we passed through a time when we thought that we had reached this stage, and were taking on the forms of mature ummas, without realizing how much this maturity required of us in basic changes of belief, objectives, relationships, responsibilities and rights, like an adolescent who fancies that he has attained manhood, and so takes on the outward mannerisms of an adult, not understanding that maturity is something more profound and more important than outward behavior.

For us, there was no escaping of catastrophe—a great disaster, to overwhelm us and threaten our very existence, and open our eyes to realities, to teach us the profound difference between surfaces and depths, and that the rotten foundations that characterised our life in the past were still there. Instead of altering them, we had only tried to cover them from view, to gloss them over with a delicate veneer which pleased the passing eye, but did not change the actuality.

There was no escape from a catastrophe, to strip off the glittering veneer and lay bare our desperate need—not for more illusions, but for truths, for changes in the very fundamentals, and for change in the methods and techniques—in short for a total revolution in all those things that had led to our weakness and impotence and stultification in past centuries; in one word, for a total revival.

The catastrophe came, in the form of the Palestine tragedy; the ice melted, the truth became clear; the revolt began. The imperialist powers sensed the vigor of this revolt, and gathered like a pack of hounds to worry and destroy it. But the reply of the revolt was joined together, and the real awakening began: the awakening based on realities. The Arab people stood together for the first time in modern history: a united Umma confronting a united usurper, and the manhood of the Arab Umma was born.

We are not, therefore, at the end of a period, but at the beginning of one: that of building solidly on sound foundations.[31]

Islam first appeared in the Arabian Peninsula brought by the hands of Muḥammad, the Messenger of God. The Arabs carried that message to most of the neighboring countries as Arabs, and they conquered the lands of the Persians, the Byzantines, the

Copts, Indians, Afghans and Turks, founding a purely Arab empire. . . . They felt that they could be both Arabs and the bearers of Islam. However, the ummas of the conquered countries, who had newly entered Islam—especially those with strong ethnic feelings (*qawmīya*)—felt a contradiction. They could not free themselves from their ethnic feelings for the sake of the new message. . . . Thus the rule passed from Arabs to Persians to Turks. . . . Then the Ottoman state rose as a Turkish Islamic state, and the Arabs were subjected to it, entirely without power. Were the Arabs pleased to be ruled by the Persians or Turks, simply because they were Muslims? Not at all. Although at times these people all united when followers of another religion attacked them, as in the Crusades, these temporary coalitions did not endure, and they were succeeded by lasting and powerful antagonisms.[32]

NOTES

1. Ibn Mājā. Book 36, Bāb 8. (Editor's translation.)

2. Tirmidhī. Book 44, commenting on Qur'ān Sūra 15, tradition 2. (Editor's translation.)

3. Bukhārī. Book 2, Bāb 9, no. 14. (Editor's translation.)

4. Ibn Mājā. Book 20, Bāb 2; also Book 36, Bab 2. (Editor's translation.)

5. Bukhārī. Book 46, Bāb 3. (Editor's translation.)

6. Abū Da'ūd. Book 34, Bāb 7. (Editor's translation.)

7. Bukhārī. Book 92, Bab 11; cf. Book 61, Bāb 25. (Editor's translation.)

8. A. Guillaume. *The Life of Muḥammad.* Oxford, 1955. p. 651.

9. Bukhārī. Book 78, Bāb 73. (Editor's translation.)

10. Bukhārī. Book 46, Bāb 14. (Editor's translation.)

11. Bukhārī. Book 2, Bāb 22. (Editor's translation.)

12. Ibn Hishām. *Sīrat al-Nabī.* Cairo, 1937. Vol. II, pp. 118, 119. (Editor's translation.)

13. Ibid. pp. 119–24. For a discussion of this document see also Montgomery Watt's *Muḥammad in Medina* (Oxford, 1956), p. 227ff.

14. Montgomery Watt. *op.cit.*, p. 360.

15. Ibid. pp. 350–60.

16. Al-Ghazālī. *Iḥyā' 'Ulūm al-Dīn,* Book 15, Chapter 3. (Editor's translation and abridgement.)

17. In Ibn Abī Ya'la's *Ṭabaqāt al-Ḥanābila.* Cairo, 1952. pp. 241–46. (Editor's translation.)

18. Al-Shāfi'ī. *al-Risāla.* Shākir edition, Cairo, 1940. pp. 471–76. (Editor's translation.)

19. Ibn Taymīya. *Ma'ārij al-Wuṣūl,* in *Majmū'at al-Rasā'il al-Kubra.* Vol. I, Cairo, 1323/1905. pp. 208–17. (Editor's translation.) Also in French translation by Henri Laoust.

20. A. A. A. Fyzee. *A Shi'ite Creed.* London, 1942. p. 89.

21. W. Iwanow. *A Creed of the Fāṭimids.* Bombay, 1936. pp. 41–42.

22. Ibid. pp. 50–53. (Here abridged.)

23. *The Book of Government, or Rules for Kings.* Translated by Hubert Darke. London, 1960. p. 169. (Here abridged.)

24. Ibid. pp. 176–78. (Here abridged.)

25. *The Travels of Ibn Jubayr.* Translated by R. J. C. Broadhurst. London 1952. pp. 316–17.

26. Ibid. pp. 321–22.

27. Ibid. pp. 359–60.

28. Rashīd Riḍā. *al-Khilāfa aw al-Imāma al-ʻUẓma.* Cairo, 1923. pp. 13–15. (Editor's translation.) Also in French translation by Laoust.

29. Sayyid Quṭb. *Social Justice in Islam.* Translated by John Hardie. Washington, D. C., 1953. pp. 61–68. (Here abridged.)

30. Wilfred Cantwell Smith. *Islam in Modern History.* Princeton, 1957. p. 77.

31. Munīf al-Razzāz. *Taṭawwur Maʻna al-Qawmīya.* Beirut, 1960. pp. 9–12. (Editor's translation.) Also in paraphrastic translation by Ibrahīm Abū Lughod.

32. Ibid. pp. 21–22.

The Perfect Ruler

CHAPTER 2

The Perfect Ruler

From the Qur'ān:

O you who believe, obey God, and obey the Messenger, and those in authority among you. (4:62)

And when his Lord tried Abraham with certain words, and he fulfilled them, He said "I have made you an Imām unto men." He replied "And of my seed?" Said He, "My covenant shall not extend to evildoers." (2:124)

And what of him who is upon a clear proof from his Lord, and a witness from Him recites it, and before him there was the Book of Moses as an Imām and a mercy? Those believe in it; and whoever disbelieves in it from among the factious, his appointed place is the Fire. Be therefore not in doubt of it: it is the truth from your Lord. Yet most of the people do not believe. (11:17)

And those who say, "Our Lord, give coolness to our eyes in our wives and children, and make us as an Imām to the god–fearing." (25:74)

God has promised those of you who believe and do wholesome deeds that He will surely make you successors in the land, as he made successors of those before you, and He will surely establish for them as their service (*dīn*) what He approves for them, and exchange for them, after their fear, security: "They shall serve Me, not associating with Me anything." (24:55)

He it is who has made you successors in the earth, and raised some of you above others in rank, that He may try you in what He has given you. Surely your Lord is very swift in retribution, and surely He is One forgiving, compassionate. (6:165)

O David, we have made you a successor in the earth, so judge between the people with truth, and do not follow your own desire, lest it cause you to stray from the way of God. Surely for those who stray from the way of God there is a severe punishment, in that they forgot the Day of Reckoning. (38:26)

When your Lord said to the angels, "Verily I am placing on the earth a successor," they said, "Will you place there one to do mischief therein and shed blood, while we give glory with your praise, and call you Holy?" He said, "Assuredly I know what you know not." (2:30)

THE ORIGINS OF THE IMAMATE

The titles of the supreme Muslim ruler have been—almost interchangeably—Imām: "him before you," hence both "example" and "leader," and *Khalīfa,* or Caliph: "successor." Both words are found in the Qur'ān more than once, but in such contexts that it is difficult to connect them with the office as it later developed. In the first three Qur'ānic verses cited here, "Imām" can be understood easily as meaning "example." In the following verses, we have translated *Khalīfa* as "successor." The first two of them appear to refer to the Muslims who are to become the successors of earlier communities. But in the next, reference is made to David as a successor to supreme authority, while in the last, Adam, the first man, is indicated as a successor to authority over the earth.

Sir Thomas Arnold has pointed out that

"these two verses have produced volumes of commentary. It would seem that the word 'Khalīfah' here means something more than mere 'successor,' though some commentators say that when God declared his intention of creating Adam, He called him a Khalīfah, a successor, because Adam was to be the successor of the angels who used to live upon the earth before the creation of man. But other Muslim authorities interpret 'Khalīfah' as meaning a viceregent, a deputy, a substitute—a successor in the sense of one who succeeds to some high function, and they accordingly explain that Adam and David are given the designation because each was on earth a viceregent of God, in their guidance of men and in the warnings they gave as to the commands of God. It is obvious that such an interpretation could be used to enhance the dignity and authority of the Caliph."[1]

The Qur'ān is a revelation, and the interpretation of these two words is a good example of how later generations read back into it meanings that it probably did not have for those to whom it was first revealed.

The origins of the caliphate–imamate have been the most troubled question in Islamic history. The majority party, the Sunnīs, have left documents that seem to indicate the caliphate came into being suddenly, and as a response to the death of the Prophet, in 632. So long as the Prophet lived, he had been the perfect ruler—accessible, humane, fatherly, a warrior and a judge, and "always right" for his people. Although he often complained of their turbulence, he was almost always successful in leading them. Now he was unexpectedly dead. Confronted by this loss, and with no successor to him, the Community began to split into its component tribes. By quick action, Abū Bakr and 'Umar, two of his fathers–in–law and closest associates, succeeded in having one man accepted by all as ruler. A detailed version of the events by 'Umar, when he in turn was ruler, is as follows:

'Umar I, on the Election of a Successor to the Prophet
from The Way of the Prophet
by Ibn Isḥāq (d. ca. A.H. *151*/A.D. *768)*

I am about to say to you something which God has willed that I should say. He who understands and heeds it, let him take it with him whithersoever he goes. I have heard that someone said, "If 'Umar were dead, I would hail So–and–so" [i.e., 'Ali.—Ed.]. Let no man deceive himself by saying that the acceptance of Abū Bakr was an unpremeditated affair which was (then) ratified. Admittedly it was that, but God averted the evil of it. There is none among you to whom people would devote themselves as they did to Abū Bakr. He who accepts a man as ruler without consulting the Muslims, such acceptance has no validity for either of them . . . (both) are in danger of being killed. What happened was that when God took away His apostle the Anṣār (Medinans) opposed us and gathered with their chiefs in the hall (*saqīfa*) of the Banu Sā'ida; and 'Alī and Zubayr and their companions withdrew from us [to prepare the Prophet's body for burial.—Ed.] while the Muhājirīn (emigrants from Mecca) gathered to Abū Bakr.

I told Abū Bakr that we should go to our brothers the Anṣār in the hall of Banu Sā'ida. In the middle of them was (their leader) Sa'd ibn 'Ubāda (who) was ill. Their speaker then continued: "We are God's helpers and the squadron of Islam. You, O Muhājirīn, are a family of ours and a company of your people come to settle." And lo, they were trying to cut us off from our origin [in the Prophet's tribe—Ed.] and wrest authority from us. I wanted to speak, but Abū Bakr said "Gently, 'Umar!" I did not like to anger him and so he spoke in his inimitable way better than I could have done. He said, "All the good that you have said about yourselves is deserved. But the Arabs will recognize authority only in this clan of Quraysh, they being the best of the Arabs in blood and country. I offer you one of these two men: accept which you please." Thus saying he took hold of my hand and that of Abū 'Ubayda ibn al-Jarrāḥ who (had come with us). Nothing he said displeased me more than that. By God, I would rather have come forward and have had my head struck off—if that were no sin—than rule a people of whom Abū Bakr was one.

One of the Anṣār said "Let us have one ruler and you another, O Quraysh." Altercation waxed hotter and voices were raised until when a complete breach was to be feared I said, "Stretch out your hand, Abū Bakr." He did so and I paid him homage; the Muhājirīn followed and then the Anṣār.

Al-Zuhrī told me (Ibn Isḥāq) on the authority of Anas ibn Mālik: On the morrow of Abū Bakr's acceptance in the hall he sat in the pulpit and 'Umar got up and spoke before him. "O men, yesterday I said something based on my own opinion [he had denied that the Prophet could be dead.—Ed.] but I thought that the apostle would order our affairs until he was the last of us alive. (But) God has left His Book with you, by which He guided His apostle, and if you hold fast to that, God will guide you as He guided him. God has placed your affairs in the hands of the best one among you, the companion of the apostle, 'the second of the two when they were in the cave,' (9:40) so arise and swear fealty to him." Thereupon the people swore fealty to Abū Bakr as a body after the pledge in the hall.[2]

The Shī'īs retain an altogether different memory of the events. Both they and the Sunnīs agree that during his return from his Farewell Pilgrimage, the Prophet told the people that whoever was his friend must be 'Alī's also. Sunnīs have explained this as the Prophet's defense of a none too popular son-in-law. The Shī'īs maintain that at this time the Prophet designated 'Alī as his successor and the future Imām, and made his choice common knowledge. However, the actions of Abū

Bakr and 'Umar on the night of the Prophet's death precluded 'Alī's coming to power, and to maintain the unity of the Community he did not press his claim. He was again deprived of his right when Abū Bakr made 'Umar his own successor. When 'Umar died, the electors 'Umar had designated passed over 'Alī to select the Prophet's other son-in-law, the wealthy, aristocratic, ineffectual 'Uthmān. Not until 'Uthmān was slain during an army revolt did 'Alī have an opportunity to come to power, but the strife and factionalism generated in the weak reign of 'Uthmān, and fanned by the violence of his death, cast a shadow over 'Ali's caliphate. Dissension continued, and at last 'Alī too was murdered by a rebel. The histories of new states in modern times are rich in analogies.

The designation of 'Alī is celebrated by the Shī'īs as the 'Īd (feast) of the Ghadīr. This account of what occurred at the marshy pool of Khumm is by a famous Shī'ī scholar of Ṣāfavī Persia, Muḥammad Bāqir Majlisī.

The Designation of 'Alī as Muḥammad's Successor.
from The Life of Hearts
Muḥammad Baqīr Majlisī (d. A.H. *1111*/A.D. *1700)*

When the ceremonies of the pilgrimage were completed, the Prophet, attended by 'Alī and the Muslims, left Mecca for Medina. On reaching Ghadīr Khumm he halted, although that place had never before been a *manzil,* or stopping place for caravans, because it had neither (drinkable) water nor pasturage. The reason for encampment in such a place was that illustrious verses of the Qur'ān came powerfully upon him, enjoining him to establish 'Alī as his successor. He had previously received communications to the same effect, but not expressly appointing the time for 'Alī's inauguration, which, therefore, he had deferred lest opposition should be excited and some forsake the faith. This was the message from the Most High in Sūra 5:66.

> *O Messenger, publish that which has been sent down to you from your Lord, for if you do not, then you have not delivered His message. God will protect you from men; surely God guides not unbelieving people.*

Being thus peremptorily commanded to appoint 'Alī his successor, and threatened with penalty if he delayed when God had become his surety, therefore the Prophet halted in this unusual place, and the Muslims dismounted around him.

As the day was very hot, he ordered them to take shelter under some thorn trees. Having ordered all the camel–saddles to be piled up for a *minbar* or rostrum, he commanded his herald to summon the people around him. When all the people were assembled, the Prophet ascended the minbar of saddles, and calling unto him the Commander of the Believers ('Alī), he placed him on his right side. Muḥammad now rendered thanksgiving to God, and then made an eloquent address to the people, in which he foretold his own death, and said "I have been called to the gate of God, and the time is near when I shall depart to God, be concealed from you, and bid farewell to this vain world. I leave among you the Book of God, to which if you adhere, you shall never go astray. And I leave with you the members of my family who cannot be separated from the Book of God until both join me at the Fountain of al–Kawthar." He then with a loud voice demanded, "Am I not dearer to you than your own lives?" and was answered by the people in the affirmative. He then took the hands of 'Alī and raised them so high that the white of (his shirt) appeared (at the open armpits of his cloak) and said, "Whoever receives me as his [*mawla*: master, ally, or friend.—Ed.], then to him 'Alī is the same. O Lord, befriend every friend of 'Alī, and be the enemy of all his enemies; help those that aid him, and abandon all that desert him."

It was now nearly noon, and the hottest part of the day. The Prophet and Muslims made the noon prayers, after which he went to his tent, beside which he ordered a tent to be pitched for the Commander of the Believers. When 'Alī was rested Muḥammad commanded the Muslims to wait upon 'Alī, congratulate him on his accession to the Imamate, and salute him as the *amīr*, or commander. All this was done by both men and women, none appearing more joyful at the inauguration of 'Alī than did 'Umar.[3]

(Other traditions state that in his sermon, the Prophet said) "Nothing is lawful or unlawful but God has made it so, of all of which he has given me knowledge, and I have communicated the same to 'Alī, son of Abū Ṭālib, and I have conferred it all upon 'Alī, who is the Imām mentioned in (Sūra 36:12):

> *Surely We restore the dead to life and write down what they have forwarded and what they have left behind: everything we have reckoned in a manifest* Imām.

Stray not from him. He is the first person of the religion who believed in God and the Prophet, for whom he exposed his own life. God will not accept the repentance of anyone that rejects the authority of 'Alī."[4]

The bitter dispute over the leadership of the Community dragged on, and men "remembered" all manner of things they thought the Prophet had told them or their grandfathers. A great profusion of these traditions were collected in the early 'Abbāsī period, and approved as "sound." None of them can escape the suspicion of being forged, or being at least uttered by the Prophet in some other context, and they no doubt tell us more about the opinions of Muslims in the first and second centuries of Islam than they do about the prophetic milieu, but that is not the point. They were accepted as authoritative, and have colored the political thinking of Muslims ever since.

Ḥadīths on the Ruler
taken from Niches of Lamps *(an anthology of Ḥadīth) of al-Khaṭīb al-Tibrīzī (written* A.H. *737*/A.D *1336)*

Bukhārī and Muslim, from Abū Hurayra: The Messenger of God, may God's blessing and peace be on him, said "Whoever obeys me obeys God, and whoever disobeys me disobeys God. Whoever obeys the Commander obeys me, and he who disobeys him disobeys me. The Imām is simply the shield behind whom the fighting takes place, from which one seeks protection. So when he orders fear of God and is just, he shall receive his reward, but if he holds otherwise, it will bring guilt upon him."

Muslim, from Umm al-Ḥuṣayn: The Messenger, may God bless him and give him peace, said "Even if a mutilated slave is made your commander, and he leads you in accord with the Book of God, hear him and obey."

Bukhārī, from Anas: The Messenger of God, the blessing of God and peace be upon him, said "Hear and obey, though an Abyssinian slave with a head like a raisin be placed over you."

Bukhārī and Muslim, from 'Umar's son: The Messenger of God —God's benediction and peace upon him—said "Hearing and obeying are incumbent on a Muslim man, so long as he is not ordered to disobey God. When he is ordered to do that, there is no hearing it and no obeying." 'Alī reported a similar tradition.

Bukhārī and Muslim, from Ibn 'Abbās: The Messenger of God, may God's blessing and peace be on him, said "If anyone sees something hateful in his commander, let him be patient, for no one separates from the collectivity by a handspan without dying the death of the Jāhilīya (before there was Islam)."

Muslim, from 'Awf ibn Mālik al-Ashja'ī, from the Messenger of God, on whom be the benediction of God, and peace: "Your best Imāms are those you love, who love you, whom you bless, and who bless you. The worst are those you hate, who hate you, whom you curse and who curse you." He says, we said "Messenger of God, should we not depose them when that happens?" but he said "No, not so long as they keep the ritual prayers with you; not so long as they keep the prayers. When anyone has a ruler placed over him who is seen doing something which is rebellion against God, he must disapprove of that rebellion, but never withdraw his hand from obedience."

Bukhārī and Muslim, from Abū Hurayra from the Prophet, God bless him and grant him peace: "The children of Israel were governed by the prophets; whenever a prophet died, another prophet became his successor. There will be no prophet after me, but there will be successors, and they will be many." They asked "So what do you order us to do about that?" and he answered "Keep the allegiance to each of them, and give them what is due them, for God will hold them responsible for what He entrusted to them."

Bukhārī and Muslim, from 'Umar's son: The Messenger said—may God give him peace and blessing—"Is not each of you a shepherd, who must answer for his flock? The Imām of the people is a shepherd, and is answerable for his flock. A man is the shepherd of the people in his house, and he is answerable for his flock. A woman is shepherdess of her husband's house and children, and is answerable for them, and a slave is the shepherd of his master's wealth and is answerable for that. Thus each of you is a shepherd, and each of you is responsible for his flock."

Muslim, from Abū Sa'īd: The Messenger of God, on whom be God's blessing and peace, said "If two successors are given the oath of allegiance, kill the second of them."

Bukhārī from Abū Hurayra from the Prophet, God bless him and give him peace: "You will be eager for commandership, but it will be a matter for regret on the Resurrection Day, for it is a good suckler, but a bad weaner" [i.e., becomes a burden—Ed.].

Muslim, from 'Arfaja: I heard the Messenger of God, peace and God's blessing be upon him, say "If anyone comes to you when you are united under one man, and tries to split you or divide your Umma, then kill him."

Muslim, from 'Amr ibn al-'Aṣ: The Messenger of God—may God bless him and give him peace—said "The Just shall be at the right hand of the All-merciful on thrones (*manābir*) of light, and both His hands are right. These are they who are just in ruling their people, and what is in their charge."

Bukhārī from Abū Bakra: When it came to the Messenger of God—peace be upon him and the blessing of God—that the people of Persia had made Chosroe's daughter queen over them, he said "A people who gives a woman charge of their affairs shall never prosper."

Bayhaqī from Mu'āwiya: The Messenger of God—may God bless him and give him peace—told me, "Mu'āwiya, if you are ever put in a position of authority, then fear God and do justly." And I never stopped thinking that I would be tried with authority, according to the Prophet's word, until I *was* tried.

Bayhaqī, from 'Umar's son: The Prophet, God bless him and give him peace, said "The Government (*al-Sulṭān*) is the shadow of God on the earth; all of His servants who are oppressed shall turn to it. When it is just, it shall be rewarded, and the flock must be grateful. When it is tyrannical, the burden is upon it, and the flock must be patient."

Abū Nu'aym al-Isfahānī, from Abū al-Dardā': The Messenger of God, may God's benediction be on him and peace, said "God says 'I am the God than whom there is no other; the Lord of kings and King of kings, in whose hands are the hearts of kings. When My servants obey Me, I turn the hearts of kings to them in mercy and kindness, and when My servants disobey me, I turn the kings' hearts against them in anger and harshness, and they afflict them with dire punishments.' "[5]

Bukhārī, from Jābir ibn Sumura: I heard the Prophet, may God bless him and give him peace, say "There will be twelve commanders," and then he said something I did not hear, but my father said he said "All of them will be of Quraysh."[6]

THE IDEAL OF THE IMAMATE

For the Sunnīs, the ideal of the successors of the Prophet can be found perfectly in the reigns and sayings of Abū Bakr and 'Umar, although much later they added the controversial 'Uthmān and 'Alī both to the list, to conciliate disputants, and called all four 'the Rightly-Guided Caliphs.'

Anecdotes Concerning the First Caliphs from the Book of Land-tax *of Abū Yūsuf (d.* A.H *182/*A.D. *798)*

"I have heard," says Abū Yūsuf, "from Ismā'īl ibn Abī Khālid, on the authority of Zubayd ibn al-Ḥārith, that when death was drawing near to Abū Bakr, he sent for 'Umar to make him the Caliph, his successor, and people said 'Will you appoint as Caliph over us this hard, harsh man to be hard and harsh to us? What will you say to your Lord when you meet Him having appointed 'Umar over us?' He said 'Would you frighten me with my Lord? I shall tell Him "God, I have appointed over them the best of Thy people!" ' Then he sent for 'Umar and said 'I shall give you a piece of advice such that if you follow it, nothing will be dearer to you than your death when it comes, and if you do not follow it, nothing will be more hateful to you than the death you shall not escape. You have obligations to God at night that He will not accept from you by day, and obligations by day that He will not accept at night, and a work of supererogation is not accepted until after the performance of the obligatory works. The scales on Judgement Day will not weigh lighter for anyone than for those who sought light things, and they will not weigh heavier for anyone than for the man who sought justice in the world. . . . I have only appointed you my successor thinking of those whom I leave behind me. For I was a Companion of the Prophet, and saw one who preferred us to himself, and our people to his own family, so that we should give to them from the abundance of what is given to us. You have been my companion, and you have seen that I have only followed the path of him who was before me, and the first thing I counsel you against, 'Umar, is your self, for every self has selfish desires, and if one gives in to one of them, it demands another. Beware also of those persons among the Companions of the Messenger of God who have filled their bellies and raised their eyes. Every man of them loves himself, and all of them will be in perplexity if one of them stumbles. Take care that that one is not you. They will never cease to fear you so long as you fear God, or cease to go straight with you so long as your way is straight. That is my counsel to you, and now I wish you farewell.' "

When 'Umar was dying, he left this advice: "I advise my successor to fear God, and to respect the rights and the merits of the first emigrants to Medina; and as to the Anṣār, who lived in Medina, and in the Faith, to accept their good deeds and to be indulgent to the bad among them. As to the people of the garrison towns, (*amṣār*), they are the help of Islam, the fury of the enemy, and the bringers of wealth, so he should take only their superfluity, and by their agreement. I advise him as to the beduins that they are the source of the Arabs, and the raw stuff of Islam, and he should take only a little of their possessions, to return to the poorest among them. As to the protected peoples, let him fulfill his agreement with them and fight their enemies and not burden them beyond their endurance."

And 'Umar wrote to Abū Mūsā al-Ash'arī (whom he had made governor of Baṣra). "The happiest shepherd with God will be the one whose flock was happy. Take care not to stray, or your subordinates will stray too, and in God's eyes you will be like a brute, who looks only at the green stuff of the earth, grazing upon it to fatten itself, and dying with its fat."

Ismā'īl al-Bajalī told me from 'Abd al-Mālik ibn 'Umayr that a man of the Thaqīf tribe said, "(The Caliph) 'Ali made me tax-collector for 'Ukbarā', and said to me while the people of that place were with me listening, 'See that you take what they owe in taxes; beware of lessening it for them in any way, and beware of showing any weakness.' Then he sent for me that noon, and I went to him and he said, 'I only advised you thus before the people because they are a deceitful lot. But see when you are over them that you do not sell (to raise tax money) a single garment of theirs, summer or winter, or the provisions they eat, or a work animal, and that you do not strike anyone even a blow, for tax money, or hang him up by one leg to extort money, or sell any of their land to raise taxes, for we have only been ordered to take the abundance. If you act contrary to my orders, it is God who will punish you in my stead, and if I hear that you do, I shall remove you.' I told him, 'Then I shall leave here as I came.' He said, 'And what if you do?' Then he went, and I did as he ordered, yet the tax collection did not suffer in any respect."[7]

After the first caliphs, the Sunnī model Imām is to be seen in 'Umar ibn 'Abd al-'Azīz, the Umawī (d. aged 39, in A.H. 101/A.D. 720). While his family, the first Islamic dynasty, are accused by Sunnīs and Shī'īs alike of subverting the perfect government of the early period, all agree that 'Umar was a just and pious Muslim ruler. He reduced the hostilities which divided the Umma, encouraged mass conversion by the conquered peoples, and was regarded as the "renewer" of Islam. His correspondence with al-Ḥasan, the great and saintly ascetic of Baṣra, whether genuine or not, is famous for the standard it upholds, one held up to Muslim monarchs from that time forward. Its demands are simple: total responsibility and human perfection.

'Umar ibn 'Abd al-'Azīz
from The Necklace *(an encyclopedic anthology),*
by Ibn 'Abd Rabbihi (d. A.H. *328/*A.D. *940)*

When 'Umar ibn 'Abd al-'Azīz became Caliph, he wrote to Ḥasan al-Baṣrī to write him the description of a just Imām, and Ḥasan wrote him—"Know, Commander of Believers, that God has made the just Imām the prop of every leaner, the straightener of every deviator, the reform of all corrupt, the strength of all weak, the justice of all oppressed, the refuge of all who are pitied. The just Imām, O Commander of Believers, is like a herdsman, solicitous for the camels he tends, desiring the sweetest pasture for them, driving them away from any dangerous grazing place, protecting them from beasts of prey, and shielding them from the harms of heat and cold.

"And the just Imām, Commander of Believers, is the guardian of the orphan, and the treasury of the poor, fostering the little ones, and providing for the old ones. The just Imām, Commander of Believers, is as the heart is to the members of the body: all are sound when it is sound, and all corrupt when it is corrupted. The just Imām, Commander of Believers, stands intermediary between God and His servants; hearkening to God's Word, and making them to hearken; looking to God, and making them to look; obedient to God, and making them obedient.

"Therefore, O Commander of Believers, act not in what God the Mighty and Glorious has given you like a slave whose master has trusted him and given into his care his wealth and his children, who then squanders his master's wealth and drives his children away, and reduces the family to poverty and scatters their fortune.

"And know, Commander of Believers, that God has sent down (His prescriptions for) the legal punishments to chide (people) away from wickedness and immorality. How shall it be, if he who administers them, deserves them? And He sent down (the law of) retaliation to give life to His servants. How will it be if the man who gives them retaliation puts them to death?

"Remember, O Commander of Believers, death and what comes after it, and how few partisans you have there, or aids against it. Therefore make provision for death, and against the greater terror which follows it.

"And know, Commander of the Believers, that there is a place for you other than the place where you now are. Your stay there will be long, and your friends will be separated from you. You will be committed to its depths as a completely solitary individual. Therefore, make provision of what you may take with you—"On the Day when a man shall flee from his brother, his mother, his father, his consort, his sons" (80:36), and remember, Commander of the Believers, "When that which is within the tombs shall be cast out, and that which is in the breasts be exposed" (100:9), when secrets are made manifest, and "The Record leaves nothing, great or small, without numbering it." (18:49)

"And now, Commander of Believers, you are in leisure, before the dissolution of death and the severing of hope. Therefore Commander of Believers, do not give judgement among the servants of God according to the usages of the pre-Islamic period (*bi-ḥukm al-jāhilīn*), and do not travel the way of transgressors with them, and do not put the arrogant in power over the humble, for such will not watch over any believer or the protected religious groups (*dhimma*), so that you will have to acknowledge your own faults and the faults of others, and bear your own burdens and other burdens too. Do not be deceived by those who would lead a pleasant life by causing damage to you, and eat the good things of this world by causing the good things of your afterlife to disappear. And do not regard your power in this world, but look toward what will be your power when you are a captive in the bonds of death, and forced to stand before God Most High in the company of the angels and prophets and apostles, and faces are turned to the Living and Self-subsisting One.

"And I, O Commander of the Believers, though I have not attained by my rigors what prudent men attained before me, yet have I not desisted from offering you solicitude and advice, sending you my letter as a doctor causes a beloved friend to drink disagreeable medicine, because he hopes thus to offer him health and soundness. And peace be upon thee, O Commander of the Believers, and the mercy of God, and His blessing."[8]

'Umar ibn 'Abd al-'Azīz
from the Book of Land-tax,
by Abū Yūsuf (d. A.H. *182*/A.D. *798)*

When 'Umar ibn 'Abd al-'Azīz died, the learned men came to his wife to express their sympathy and say how great a calamity had struck the people of Islam by his death. And they said to her, "Tell us about him—for the one who knows best about a man is his wife." And she said, "Indeed, he never used to pray or fast more than the rest of you, but I never saw any servant of God who feared Him more than 'Umar. He devoted his body and his soul to the people. All day he would sit tending to their affairs, and when night came, he would sit up while business remained. One evening when he had finished everything, he called for his lamp—for which he used to buy the oil from his own money—and prayed two prostrations. Then he sat back on his folded legs, with his chin in his hands, and the tears ran down his cheeks, and this didn't stop until dawn, when he rose for a day of fasting. I said to him, 'Commander of the Believers, was there some matter that troubled you this night?' And he said 'Yes, I saw how I was occupied with governing the affairs of our Community, all its black sheep and its white sheep, and I remembered the stranger, beggared and straying, and the poor and needy, and the prisoners in captivity, and all like them in the far places of the earth, and I realized that God Most High would ask me about all of them, and Muḥammad would testify about them, and I feared that I should find no excuse when I was with God, and no defense with Muḥammad.' And even when 'Umar was with me in bed, where a man usually finds some pleasure with his wife, if he remembered some affair of God's (people), he would be upset as a bird that has fallen into the water. Then his weeping would rise until I would throw off the blankets, in kindness to him. 'By God,' he would say, 'How I wish that there was between me and this office the distance of the East from the West!'[9]

For the Shī'īs, the ideal of the Imām may be found in the lives of their Imāms, and particularly in the sufferings of 'Alī and his descendants. And in a very special sense, it is found for popular piety in the death of 'Alī's son, Ḥusayn. While he was for Shī'īs the legitimate Imām, he reigned without ruling, because the caliphate had been usurped by the Umawī family. Invited by the people of Kūfa, 'Alī's old capital, to lead them, he set out across the desert to Iraq with his family and retainers, but the Umawī governor of Kūfa in the meantime had put down the revolt there, and sent a force which surrounded Ḥusayn's small caravan at Karbalā, near Kūfa. Although cut off from water, he refused to surrender, and at last the party was slain to the last man. Mourning for him and meditation on the significance of his death have characterised the Shī'a ever since. The following text is from a Persian "passion-play" for the anniversary of the martyrs of Karbalā, the *'Ashūra* (tenth) of Muḥarram, and is from the nineteenth century. However, it stands in a long tradition of mourning pieces, of which one very prominent text is the *Rawḍat al-Shuhadā'* by Mullā Ḥusayn Kāshifī of Sabzawar, who died in A.H. 910/A.D. 1504–5. The Imamate is the necessary fulfillment of the Prophethood of Muḥammad. The suffering and rejection of the Imāms has a cosmic meaning. Ḥusayn dies for the sins of the Umma, and becomes their special intercessor on the Day of Judgement.

In this scene the Imām, having seen his sons and brothers die one by one and alone at the last, is visited by a darwīsh, who represents the mystical tradition.

The Death of Ḥusayn
from a Shī'ī Passion Play
(Traditional)

DARWĪSH FROM KĀBUL: O Lord God, wherefore is the outward appearance of a man of God usually without decoration, and the lap of the man of this world usually full of gold and jewels? Either Islam, the religion of peace and charity, has no true foundation in this world, or this young man, who is so wounded and suffers from thirst, is still an infidel.

ḤUSAYN: Why are thy eyes pouring down tears, young darwīsh? Whither is thy face set?

DARWĪSH: It happened, young man, that last night I arrived in this valley. When one half of the night had passed, I heard a child bemoaning and complaining of thirst. I have therefore brought some water in this cup for that poor child. I humbly beg thee, dear sir, to direct me to the place where the young child may be found, and tell me what is its name.

ḤUSAYN: O God, let no man be ever in my pitiful condition!—

young man, the child mentioned by thee is the peace of my troubled mind; it is my poor little girl. If I will, I can make the moon, or any other celestial orb, fall down on the earth; how much more can I get water for my children! I voluntarily die of thirst to obtain a crown of glory from God, and offer myself a sacrifice for the sins of my people, that they should be saved from the wrath to come.

DARWĪSH: What is thy name, sir? I perceive that thou art one of the chief saints, and the brightness of the Lord's image, but I cannot tell to which sacred garden thy holy rose belongs.

ḤUSAYN: O darwīsh, thou wilt soon be informed. What is the end thou hast in view in thy hazardous enterprise?

DARWĪSH: I intend to set out, if God wills, from Karbalā to Najaf, where 'Alī, the supreme master of all the darwīshes, is buried.

ḤUSAYN: Be it known unto thee that I am Ḥusayn (ibn 'Alī), the intercessor on the Day of Resurrection, the rose of the garden of glory.

DARWĪSH: May I be offered a sacrifice for thy blessed arrival! Pardon me my fault, and give me permission to fight the battle of faith, for martyrdom is one of the glories of my faith.

ḤUSAYN: Go forth, O atom which aspirest to the glories of the sun; go forth, thou hast become at last worthy to know the hidden mysteries of faith. He who is slain for the sake of Ḥusayn shall have an abundant reward from God; yea, he shall be raised to life with 'Alī Akbar the sweet son of Ḥusayn.

(*The Darwīsh is slain.*)

JA'FAR (*the king of the jinns, coming to Ḥusayn's assistance*): O king of men and jinns; O Ḥusayn, peace be on thee! O judge of corporal and spiritual beings, peace be on thee!

ḤUSAYN: Peace be on thee, thou handsome youth! Though thine affairs are not hidden from me at all, still it is advisable to ask thy name.

JA'FAR: O lord of men and jinns, I am the least of thy servants, Ja'far, the chief ruler of all the tribes of the jinns. Today while on the throne of my majesty, I heard thy voice, and behold I am come with troops of jinns to lend thee assistance.

ḤUSAYN: In this perishable kingdom, O Ja'far, none can attain to immortality. What can I do with the empire or its tempting glories, after my dear ones have died and gone? Is it proper that I should live, and Akbar, a blooming youth, die? Return thou, Ja'far, to thy home, and weep for me as much as thou canst.

JA'FAR (*returning*): Alas for Ḥusayn's helplessness! Alas for his groans and sighs!

(*Ibn Sa'd orders the army to stone Ḥusayn.*)

ḤUSAYN: Ah, woe to me! My forehead is broken; blood runs down my face.

THE PROPHET (*appearing*): Dear child, thou hast at length suffered martyrdom by the cruel hand of my own people! This was the reward I expected from them; thanks be to God! Open thine eyes, dear son, and behold thy grandfather with dishevelled hair. . . . Be not grieved that 'Alī Akbar thy son was killed, since it tends to the good of my sinful people on the day of universal gathering.

ḤUSAYN: Seeing his martyrdom contributes to the happiness of thy people, seeing my sufferings give validity to thy office of mediation, I would offer my soul a thousand times for the salvation of thy people!

THE PROPHET: Thou shalt be a mediator too, in that day. At present thou art thirsty, but tomorrow thou shalt be the distributor of the water of al-Kawthar.

ḤUSAYN: My mother is not alive, that she might close my eyes when I die.

FĀṬIMA (*appearing*): I am come to see thee, my child, my child! May I die another time, my child, my child! How shall I see thee slain, my son, my son!

ḤUSAYN: I am now, dear mother, at the point of death. Come, close my eyes with your kind hand.

FĀṬIMA: O Lord, how difficult for a mother! I am Zahrā' who make this moan, because I must close the eyes of my son Ḥusayn. O tell me, if thou hadst any desire long cherished, for I am much distressed in mind.

ḤUSAYN: Go, mother, my soul has come to my throat; go, I had no desire except one, with which I must rise on the Day of Resurrection, namely, to see 'Alī Akbar's wedding.

(*Shimr prepares to cut Ḥusayn's throat.*)

ḤUSAYN: O Lord, for the merit of me, the dear child of Thy Prophet, O Lord; for the sad groaning of my miserable sister, O Lord; for the sake of young 'Abbās in his blood, even that young brother of mine who was equal to my soul; I pray Thee, in the Day of Judgement, forgive, O merciful Lord, the sins of my grandfather's people, and grant me, bountifully, the keys of the treasure of intercession. (*Dies.*)[10]

SUNNĪ LEGAL THEORY ON THE CALIPHATE

The following excerpt is from a work on taxation by the great Ḥanafī doctor Abū Yūsuf (d. A.H. 182/A.D. 798) for his 'Abbāsī master, the caliph Hārūn al-Rashīd. In his admonitions to his sovereign, he shows what the Sunnī legalists of his time expected of the Imām; he repeatedly plays on the ancient Near Eastern motif of the ruler as the shepherd of the people. On his wisdom and piety depend the health and soundness of the all-important Umma, and for so weighty a matter he is to be held strictly accountable.

An Orthodox Legalist's Admonitions to the Caliph
from the Book of Land-tax
Abū Yūsuf (d. A.H. *182/*A.D. *198)*

Commander of the Believers, God has invested you with a great matter, whose reward is the greatest reward, and whose punishment is the greatest punishment: He has entrusted you with the affair of the Community of Believers. Day and night you build for many people, of whom God has made you the shepherd, whom He has confided to your care and tried you with, and of whose affairs He has made you the administrator. A structure not founded on piety shall not abide, for God will attack its foundations and cause it to fall on him who built it and trusted in it against Him. Therefore do not waste what God has entrusted you with: the matter of this Community and these subjects, for power to act is by God's leave.

Do not put off the work of today until tomorrow, for if you do, you waste. Death is without hope, so go to death with deeds, for there are no deeds after death. Shepherds of men must settle with their Master, as a shepherd must settle with his; therefore establish the right in what God has set you over and entrusted you with for an hour. The happiest shepherd on the Day of Resurrection will be he whose flocks were happy with him. Do not deviate, and thus cause your subjects to deviate, and beware of giving orders in passion or punishing in anger! When confronted by the matter of this world and the matter of the next, choose the next world, for it will abide and this world will pass away. Act cautiously, in fear of God, and where God's command is concerned, let people be equal in your sight, whether they are near or far from you. When you are on God's side, fear no one's blame. Be wary—and wariness is a matter of the heart, not of the tongue. Fear God, for piety is only fear of God, and God keeps him who fears Him.

Act for a term delayed, and a road travelled, and a way taken, and an act preserved, and a goal attained, for that is the true stopping place; the grand station, where hearts shall fly and arguments be cut off, by the might of a King whose power is overwhelming, for this is (so certain that it is) as if it had already been. There will be requited with sorrow and regret those who knew but did not act, on the Day when feet shall drag and colors change, the Day of long standing and severe accounting. God—blessed be He and exalted—has said in His Book, "A day with thy Lord is as a thousand years of your counting." (22:49) and "This is the Day of Decision, We have joined you with the ancients." and "It shall be on that Day that they see what they are promised, and if they had not lingered but for one hour of a single day" (61:34). Alack for mistakes that are not found small, alas for useless regrets! Only the difference of a night and a day will wear out every new thing, and make imminent every remote matter, and bring the fulfillment of every thing promised, and God will pay every soul what it has earned—and surely God is swift at the accounting and He judges His servants by their acts, not by their rank. The Prophet, God bless him and give him peace, has said "No one shall retire on the Day of Judgement until he has been asked about four matters: on his knowledge and what he did with it, on his life and how he passed it, on his money and where he got it and how he spent it, and on his body, and how he used it." Therefore, Prince of the Believers, prepare the response for these questions, and what you have done establish securely, for tomorrow you must recite the answers.

I advise you, O Commander of the Believers, to keep what God has entrusted to you, and to guard the flock He has given you, and to regard it all as His for His sake, for if you do not, the easy path of guidance will become hard, and your eye will be blind to it; its landmarks will be effaced, and its width will be narrow for you, so that you reject what you see and see what you should reject. Contend with your self (*nafs*) so as to obtain victory for it, and not against it. . . . Beware of causing loss to the flock which its Master will require you to make good, causing you loss. A house can only be buttressed before it falls. . . . Do not neglect to take charge of that which God has entrusted to you, and you will not be neglected. . . . Your time in the world will not be wasted, and God in His grace and mercy and goodness has made those in charge of affairs His viceregents on His earth, and given light to His subjects; the light which He causes to shine on those in charge of affairs is in applying the legal punishments and rendering justice to His people. The violence of the shepherd causes loss to the flock, and the aid he seeks from those who are unworthy of confidence causes general ruin. Nothing is dearer to God than doing good, and nothing more hateful to Him than corruption, while to act sinfully is to reject His grace.

I have written for you what you ordered, and explained it and made exposition of it, so ponder it and apply yourself to it and reread it until it is yours, for I have exerted myself for you, and neglected no advice for you and the Muslims, seeking God's favor and reward and fearing His chastisements. May God assist you to that which will be pleasing to Him, and best for you![11]

Abū Yūsuf's advice to his caliph still upholds the patriarchal ideal of early Islam: the Imām should live simply, a shepherd and steward who will answer for his stewardship. But Abū Yūsuf was expressing a view already out of tune with the times. Since the late Umawī period, caliphal theory had been more and more affected by the Persian concept of kingship as a divine institution. With the transfer of the capital to Iraq under the 'Abbāsīs in 750 A.D. the way had been opened for wholesale Persianisation of the Caliphate. The Caliph now was an all-powerful emperor, and Persian institutions were hurriedly being adapted to Islamic government—chiefly by the Persian *debherān* or bureaucrats, who converted easily to Islam and served the Caliphate. Beginning with the famous Ibn Muqaffa', they translated Persian books of ethics and courtly literature into Arabic. The final triumph of the Persian view of kingship came with the transfer of the capital to Samarra on the Tigris in 836 A.D., where the Caliphs lived as absolute monarchs in magnificent isolation, surrounded by elaborate ceremonial and upheld by their Turkish slave guards, as the "Shadow of God on Earth."

A manual of court etiquette, the "Book of the Crown," written in this period by a now unknown Persian courtier has survived, composed between 847 and 861 A.D. in the reign of al–Mutawakkil and dedicated to his Turkish favorite, Fatḥ ibn Khaqān. In 861 the Caliph and Ibn Khaqān were both murdered by Turkish guards, in the first of a series of military slave-intrigues that greatly weakened the caliphate, and brought the Samarran period to a gloomy close.

The author sees the caliphs simply as the successors of the Sasanian Great Kings. He takes it for granted that there is a civilized, Persian, way of doing things, and now that God has exalted the Arabs and

Turks to positions of importance, the least that they can do is to learn it. His book contains so many references to Sasanian court practise that it is used as a source for Iranian history. The culture and usages of the 'Abbāsī court of the ninth and early tenth centuries were eagerly imitated even in those parts of the Muslim world which, like Spain, were outside the 'Abbāsī empire.

Life at the Caliphal Court

from the Book of the Crown

(Anonymous: between 847–861 A.D.*)*

The etiquette of the Great King has no limit which can be imagined, or comprehended by reflection. For you see, it continues from the first king who ruled the earth until this period, and one who thinks that he can attain the far reaches of that stretch of time is to me like someone who believes in anthropomorphism, for example, or in the corporeal body (of God).[12]

On entering the presence of the king: If the visitor is one of the nobles (*ashrāf*) or the upper class, it is his duty to the king to stand in a place not too far and not too near, and to salute the king while standing. If the king gestures to him to approach, he should draw near, prostrate himself over the fringe of the king's garment, and kiss it, and then retire standing, to the place of his rank. If he is given a sign to sit, he sits, and if he is spoken to, he answers in a low voice, with few movements of the body. If the king is silent, he rises immediately, before he has taken his seat, and retires without further salutation or waiting for commands.

If the visitor is of the middle class, his duty to the king, if he sees him, is to stop where he is, even if it is far. If he is beckoned, he advances three steps, or thereabouts, and stops again, and if he is beckoned, he draws near by about the same distance, without regard for the trouble it is for the king to make signs or gestures. Although this may be embarassing for the king, it is still due to him in veneration for him.

If one enters by the front door facing the king, opposite him, if he can go to the right or the left he should take a way which does not put him in front of the king's visage, then move toward where the king is sitting, and salute him standing, with his eyes fixed on the king. If the king is silent, he retires, retreating without further greeting or any word. If the sign is given, he advances a few steps with downcast eyes, and then raises his head, until the king ceases to make any sign or gesture, and stops in that place. If he is signalled to sit, he sits crouching or kneeling. He answers if he is addressed, in a low voice with few gestures, and paying close attention. When the king ceases to speak to him, he rises and retires walking backwards. When it is possible for him to veil himself from sight by a wall or corridor so that he is not before the king if he turns, he may walk as suits him.

If a prince is visited by one who is his equal in power, following, majesty, birth, and family, he should rise, move toward him a few paces, embrace him, take him by the hand, seat him, and seat himself lower, for that is the sort of treatment the prince would himself want if he visited his visitor, and whenever either of them goes outside the law and commandments, bad blood is born of it.

Such were the manners of the Sasanian dynasty of kings and princes, and it was the policy adopted by Ardashīr I (the founder of that dynasty).[13]

On eating with kings: It is due to the king, if he is so generous and familiar as to share a meal with one, not to serve oneself before him in eating, for there are very blameworthy defects in such behavior. (Serving oneself) indicates one's gluttony, shows bad education and lack of distinction, and is bold. . . .

Similarly it is a duty to the king for one not to behave greedily during the meal, or have as aim to fill one's stomach and leave [this contradicts the table behavior recommended by the early Muslims: to eat quickly and silently, with full attention to one's food, and rise—Ed.], unless one is a near relative of the king. The kings of Persia, when they saw such a person, considered that he was not a serious person, but a jester, and not worthy of respect, but of contempt and mockery.

If the king places a dish before one, one should realize that he did not place it there so one might finish it. Perhaps he even wished to know if one could restrain oneself. A man may be content, if the king offers him some rare dish, simply to toy with it. That is sufficient, and it indicates one's good breeding.

It is royal etiquette that before every guest is placed a dish served with the same foods that the king has. The king does not eat special foods not served to his companions, for that would be below him, and indicate that he was arrogant.

It is due the king that no one should wash his hands in the king's presence after eating (unless he were his complete equal). The manners of kings are not like those of common people; in fact, they do not resemble them at all since they are raised far above (them)....

It is also due the king that when he stops eating, all who are with him should rise from the table and retire.[14]

Amusements: It is a trait of kings to rank their courtiers in a hierarchy. We have observed that a king may have need of a base fellow for his diversion, just as he has need of a brave man for his strength, and may need an amusing raconteur for his stories, just as he needs an ascetic to preach to him, and may need buffoons just as he needs serious people, and may need a skilled flautist just as he needs wise scholars.

And such is the character of kings that each class is found about them, for they pass quickly from a serious mien to joking, and from laughter to reflection, and from diversion to pious exhortation. Thus each of these classes of people is raised up at one time and put down at another, and given to at one time and deprived at another, except nobles and learned men, for to these is due a high position so long as they keep to their obedience and fulfil its duties.

All of the Persian kings, from Ardashī son of Pāpāk to Yazdagird, separated themselves from their courtiers by a curtain....

I once asked the (great court musician) Isḥāq ibn Ibrahīm al-Mawṣilī, "Did the Umawī caliphs show themselves to their familiars and singers?" He replied, "'Mu'āwiya and Marwān I, 'Abd al-Malik, Walīd I, Sulaymān, Hishām and Marwān II were separated from their familiars by a curtain, so that none of the courtiers saw what the caliph was doing, if he was transported by the music, or shook his shoulders, or danced, or threw off his clothing, so none but his special slaves saw him. As for the rest of the Umawī caliphs, they were not ashamed to dance or throw off their garments and expose their nakedness in the presence of their familiars and singers. But for that, none of them was like Yazīd ibn 'Abd al-Malik and Walīd ibn Yazīd for shamelessness and obscene speech in the presence of their familiars, and taking off their clothes, not caring what they did."

I said, "What about 'Umar ibn 'Abd al-'Azīz?" He said, "Not a note of music came to his ears from the time the Caliphate came to him until he took leave of this world."

I said, "And our ('Abbāsī) caliphs?" He said, "At the beginning of his reign, Abū al-'Abbās showed himself to the courtiers; then after a year he curtained himself off from them. As for Abū Ja'far Manṣūr, he never showed himself to his familiars at all, and no one saw him drink anything but water . . . sometimes he wanted to clap his hands, but he would rise from where he was sitting and enter the chamber of one of his women, and do it there.

"Al-Mahdī veiled himself from his familiars for a year, like al-Manṣūr. Then he showed himself to them. When (General) Abū 'Awn counselled him to screen himself, he said 'Clear out, you clod! My pleasure is only in observing happiness and in contact with people who amuse me. What good or pleasure is there in hiding behind a curtain?'

"Hārūn al-Rashīd had the same habits as al-Manṣūr, except in giving gifts and pensions and robes of honor: here his acts were those of Abū al-'Abbās and al-Mahdī (very generous) . . . and if anyone ever tells you that he saw him drink anything but water, then tell him he's a liar, for no one ever was present when he drank, except his favorite slaves."

"And the deposed caliph (al-Amīn)?" I asked Isḥāq; "Where was he, in what you are saying?"

"How curious all his ways were!" he said. "He was so familiar that he never cared where he was or with whom he sat. If there had been a hundred curtains between him and his familiars, he would have torn them all down, so he might sit where they were sitting. And he was the most generous of creation with gold and silver if he liked a song or was amused. One day I saw him when one of his slave boys was near by. He looked at him, and cried, 'You wretch! Your robe needs washing. Here, take thirty thousand dirhams, and have it washed!'

" 'Allawayh told me about him: 'When he was besieged (by Ma'mūn's generals), a stone from a mangonel struck the carpet where we were sitting with him while one of his slave girls was singing a song to him, and she left something out in confusion. He shouted "Adulteress! You're singing it wrong! Take her away!" They carried her off, and that was the last time we saw her.' "

"And Ma'mūn?" I asked. He replied, "He stayed twenty months after he came (to Baghdad) without listening to a single note. Then he listened from behind the curtain, like al-Rashīd, their father. It was like that for seven years; then he appeared before the courtiers and singers. But when he wanted to see a concert before his eyes, his family and his brothers made a big thing of it."[15]

The king's sleeping-place: It is a peculiarity of kings that the place they sleep, by day or night, should not be known (and the king should not be careless about this matter.)

It is said that the Sasanian kings' sleeping places were never known to anyone (but) they used to have forty beds prepared in forty different places, and at times not sleep in any of them. . . .

And it is due the king that his son should behave to him as a slave would behave, and not enter his presence except by his bidding, and that the veil between them be thicker for him than for those who are less than he among the king's entourage and servitors, so that lack of restraint will not lead him to exceed his rights. We have been told that one day in the reign of al-Mu'tasim (General) Itākh saw (the heir) al-Wāthiq standing in a place he should not have been, and said to him, "Get out of there! By God, if I had not failed to tell you earlier, you'd get a hundred blows of the stick!"

There may occur in the temper of kings some weariness (toward a person) due to a simple desire for change. But it is not for the king's familiar, if the king's temper changes, to display the like of that to him, for if he does that, his intentions are bad, and one who is bad-intentioned will see his obedience become disobedience and his friendship turn to hostility—and one who is hostile to the king is hostile to himself, and hurts only himself.[16]

The garments of kings: Ardashīr ibn Pāpāk, Yazdagird, Bahram, Khusraw Parvīz and Khusraw Anūshirvān and Kavādh all used to wear a gown and then have it washed. After three washings, it was not washed again, but put among the robes of honor given to princes of the royal family and to no one else.

Among the Arab kings, those who wore a gown more than once and had it washed were Mu'āwiya, 'Abd al-Malik, Sulaymān, 'Umar ibn 'Abd al-'Azīz, Hishām and Marwān II, as well as Abū al-'Abbās and Abū Ja'far Manṣūr and al-Ma'mūn.

But as for Yazīd I, Walīd II, and Yazīd III, as well as al-Mahdī, al-Hādī, al-Rashīd, al-Mu'tasim and al-Wāthiq, they never used to put a gown on more than once, unless it was some rare, remarkable, unusual garment.

As for the outer garments, kings have always worn them during one year, or thereabouts, and some of them have even kept outer gowns and robes for several years.[17]

Of classical Sunnī legalist views of the Imamate, one of the most typical and lucid is that of the Shāfi'ī judge al-Māwardī (d. A.H. 450/A.D. 1058). The caliph is the divinely instituted executive of the Community; hence all power, to be legitimate, must emanate from him and be sanctioned by him.

Al-Māwardī was describing a system which no longer functioned except in legal theory. The absolute monarchy of the early 'Abbāsī period had broken down, and while caliphs of the family were allowed to reign, actual power was wielded by warlords and local rulers. Persian Shī'is of the Buwayhī family, with the significant title "Commander of Commanders," dictated to the caliph in Baghdad, and in Spain and Egypt two other rulers had adopted the caliphal title and pomps. Against this state of affairs, Māwardī's careful detailing of the laws of rule takes on a poignant quality of "it *should* be so."

Sunnī Legal Theory on the Imamate
from the Governing Statutes
al-Māwardī (d. A.H. *450/*A.D. *1058)*

The Imamate: God, whose power be glorified, has instituted a chief of the Community as a successor to Prophethood and to protect the Community and assume the guidance of its affairs. Thus the Imamate is a principle on which stand the bases of the religious Community and by which its general welfare is regulated, so that the common good is assured by it. Hence rules pertaining to the Imamate take precedence over any other rules of government. . . .

The Imamate is placed on earth to succeed the Prophet in the duties of defending the Religion and governing the World, and it is a religious obligation to give allegiance to that person who performs those duties. . . .

Abū Hurayra related that the Prophet, on whom be God's blessing and peace, said "Other rulers will govern you after me. The pious will govern you with his piety, and the libertine with his immorality. Hear them both, and obey them in all that conforms with the truth. If they do well, it is to their credit and yours, but if they do evil, it will be to your credit and their discredit."

Thus the obligatory nature of the Imamate is established, and it is an obligation performed for all by a few, like fighting in a holy war, or the study of the religious sciences, and if no one is exercising it, then there emerge two groups from the people; the first being those who should choose an Imām for the Community, and the second those who are fitted to be Imām, of whom one will be invested with the Imamate. As for those of the Community who do not belong to either of these two categories, there is no crime or sin if they do not choose an Imām. As to these two categories of people, each of them must possess the necessary qualifications. Those relating to the electors are three:

1. Justice, in all its characteristics.
2. Knowledge, sufficient to recognize who is worthy to be the Imām by virtue of the necessary qualifications.
3. Judgement and wisdom to conclude by choosing the best person, who will best and most knowledgeably direct the general welfare.

As for those persons fitted for the Imamate, the conditions related to them are seven:

1. Justice, in all its characteristics.
2. Knowledge requisite for independent judgement (*ijtihād*) about revealed and legal matters.
3. Soundness of the senses in hearing, sight, and speech, in a degree to accord with their normal functioning.
4. Soundness of the members from any defect that would prevent freedom of movement and agility.
5. Judgement conducive to the governing of subjects and administering matters of general welfare.
6. Courage and bravery to protect Muslim territory and wage the *jihād* against the enemy.
7. Pedigree: he must be of the tribe of Quraysh, since there has come down an explicit statement on this, and the consensus has agreed. There is no need to take account of Dirār ibn 'Amr, who stood alone when he declared that anyone could be eligible. The Prophet said "The Quraysh have precedence, so do not go before them," and there is no pretext for any disagreement, when we have this clear statement delivered to us, and no word that one can raise against it.

Some have held that the election is valid only with participation of all those who may "bind and loose," from every region, so that consent may be general, but this school is refuted by the fact that Abū Bakr was recognized as Caliph by those who were present without waiting for the recognition of those who were absent.

Others (basing themselves on 'Umar's selection of six electors to choose his successor) say there must be at least five electors uniting in their choice in order to confer the Imamate, or that one may choose with the approval of the other four. This is the opinion of most of the legalists and theologians of Baṣra. Others, among the learned men of Kūfa, say that three may confer the Imamate, while others say it may be conferred by one, as when 'Abbās said to 'Alī, "Stretch out your hand, that I may acclaim you, and the people will say, 'The Prophet's uncle acclaims the Prophet's cousin,' and then two of them will not contest you."

There is a difference of opinion among legalists as to what to do when there is competition between two equally qualified candidates. Some say it should be settled by casting lots; others that the electors have a free choice of the one they prefer. If they select the best person and acclaim him, and later there comes one who is better than he, they may not turn aside from the Imām to the one who is better (since he was validly elected).

If the Imamate has been conferred on two imāms in two different regions, they are not both legally imāms, for there cannot be two imāms of the Community at the same time, even though a few isolated authorities would permit it. The correct opinion among the best legalists is that only the Imamate of the first acclaimed is legal.

If the Imamate has been conferred through the designation by the previous Imām of his successor, the consensus is that this is lawful because Abū Bakr designated 'Umar and 'Umar designated the electors of his successor. . . .

When the Imām has designated his successor, he cannot afterwards remove him from the succession, so long as the conditions of the heir have not altered, even though he may legally remove all the rest of his own appointees. . . .

There are ten things incumbent on the Imām as matters of the common interest:

1. He must maintain the Religion according to the principles established and agreed upon by the earliest Muslims (*salaf al-umma*), and if an innovator appears, or someone with dubious opinions who deviates from those principles, then he must clarify matters by logical proofs, and show him the correct way, and finally apply the rules and punishments to which he is

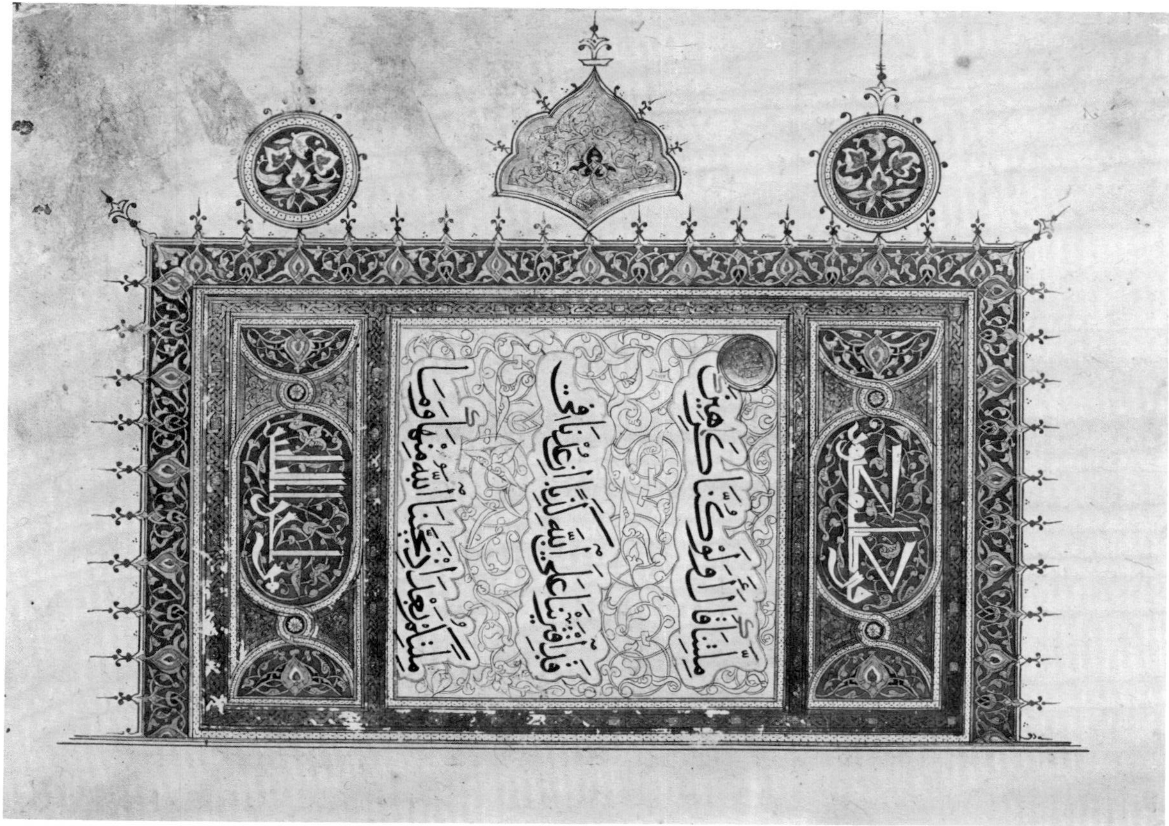

An illuminated Qur'ān page. Fourteenth century; period of Mamlūk rule in Egypt and Syria. *Courtesy, Trustees of the British Museum.*

A North African Qur'ān. 1568 A.D. Pages from a Qur'ān in the Maghribī (Western) script, made for the Moroccan Sharīfī Sulṭān Mawlay 'Abdallah. *Courtesy, Trustees of the British Museum.*

Mosque of Sulaymān the Regulator ("Qanūnī") at Istanbul. Built from 1550–1557 A.D. by Sinān, the greatest Ottoman architect. This imperial mosque is a fine example of the domed and inclosed style developed under Turkish hegemony in a country long exposed to Byzantine influence. *Courtesy of the Turkish Tourist Bureau.*

bound, that religion may be preserved from disorder, and the Community from stumbling.

2. He must apply legal judgements for litigants, and stop contention among plaintiffs, so that equity reigns, without aiding the oppressor or weakening the oppressed.
3. He must guard Islamic territory and protect what is sacrosanct, so that people may gain their bread and move from place to place secure from any threat to life and property.
4. He must apply the punishments of the Law, so as to secure God's prohibitions from violation, and preserve the rights of God's servants from attack or destruction.
5. He must fortify the marches with adequate garrisons and deterrent power, so that the enemy may not appear due to neglect, committing misdeeds or shedding the blood of any Muslim or confederate.
6. He must struggle with holy war against those who have been invited to join Islam and rejected it, until they either convert or enter into the status of tribute–paying non–Muslim subjects, to make victorious the truth of God over every (other) religion.
7. He must collect the taxes on conquered territories and the poor–tax in conformity with the Law as written and interpreted, without fear or oppression.
8. He must administer the outlays and proper expenditures of the public treasury, without lavishness or niggardliness, and with punctuality.
9. He must see to it that trustworthy and loyal men are delegated to look after the offices and the monies under his control.
10. He must himself oversee matters and examine the circumstances, in order to direct the affairs of the Community and safeguard the Religion, and not delegate his authority seeking to occupy himself with pleasures or devotion, for a loyal person can yet turn traitor, and a faithful commander can yet deceive. God, be He exalted, has said, "O David, We have made you a caliph on earth, so judge between the people with the truth, and follow not your own desire, lest it lead you astray from God's way" (38–26).[18]

The Caliph's position in the Buwayhī period can be seen in the following ironic account. The 'Abbāsī Caliph was maintained by the Shī'ī Buwayhīs both to give the aura of legitimacy to their usurpation of power, and to justify their reluctance to acknowledge the sovereignty of the Ismā'īlī Shī'ī caliphs of Cairo, but he was little more than a piece of the state apparatus.

Weakness in the Caliphate
from a History of Mecca
by Quṭb al-Dīn al-Nahrawalī (d. A.H. *990/*A.D. *1582)*

This was in the days of the weakness of the caliphate and the usurpation of the power by the family of Buwayh. Matters went on like this until the Caliph abdicated, God have mercy on him, and the oath of allegiance was taken to his son Abū Bakr 'Abd al-Karīm in the year A.H. 363/A.D. 974, who took the title of al-Ṭā'i'Lillāh. His greatness was only outward, and not otherwise, so that in the year A.H. 369/A.D. 979–80 when the envoy of al-'Azīz Billāh the Master of Egypt (i.e. the Fāṭimī Caliph) came to Baghdad, 'Aḍud al-Dawla ibn Buwayh, who had been given the titles of authority by al-Ṭā'i' and in whose hands were the affairs of the state, asked him to give him more titles, so that he should have the title of Tāj al-Milla (Crown of the Community), and to give him new robes of honor and crown him, and he complied. Al-Ṭā'i' sat on a high throne, while around him stood a hundred men with drawn swords. Before him was the Qur'ān of the Caliph 'Uthman, and on his shoulders the mantle of the Prophet, in his hands the Prophet's staff, and he was girded with the sword of the Prophet, God's benediction and peace be upon him, all of which the caliphs have inherited and make part of their general regalia. He was hidden by a long curtain, so that the army's sight should not fall on him until it was raised; the Turkish and Daylamī officers were in attendance, and all those who received state allowances were drawn up in ranks. 'Aḍud al-Dawla was summoned and entered, and the curtain was raised, so he kissed the ground before him. Then the envoy of al-'Azīz, Master of Egypt, was admitted, and he was awed and astonished by what he saw, so that he asked 'Aḍud al-Dawla, "Is this God the Exalted?" but he answered, "No, this is God's Successor on the earth." He then began to advance, kissing the ground seven times. Al-Ṭā'ī' turned to his chamberlain, who was called Khāliṣ, and said "Let him draw near." He brought him to the foot of the throne, and he kissed the Caliph's foot. Then al-Ṭā'i' placed his right hand on the head of 'Aḍud al-Dawla and ordered him to sit on a stool which was placed for him near the throne. At this, 'Aḍud al-Dawla begged to be excused, but he swore that he must sit, so he kissed the stool, and then sat upon it. When he was seated, al-Ṭā'i' said, "I have delegated to you what God has entrusted to me, the affairs of my subjects in the East of the earth and in the West." He replied, "May God assist me to obey the Commander of the Believers!" and he kissed the ground. Thereupon the Caliph bestowed seven robes of honor upon him, and as they were presented to him, he kissed the ground before each one. Then he departed, and the people left after him, awed by what they had beheld and making much of what they had seen. Yet all this grandeur was only a contrived image and artificial pomp, weak in reality and frail of strength. The authority passed to Naṣr ibn Buwayh, and al-Ṭā'i' mounted the throne and bestowed seven robes of honor on him, and placed a jewelled collar around his neck, and bracelets on his wrists, and gave him the title Bahā' al-Dawla (Splendor of the State), and Ḍiyā' al-Milla (Light of the Community), in the year 379. Then in 381 "Splendor of the State" came to al-Ṭā'i' and kissed the ground before him, and sat upon the stool, and gave orders to his Daylamīs, and they pulled al-Ṭā'ī' off his throne and muffled him with garments, and "Splendor of the State" ordered him to abdicate, so he did. Then he brought in Abū al-'Abbās Aḥmad, grandson of the Caliph Muqtadir, and entitled him the Caliph al-Qādir Billāh (The Potent in God).[19]

By the 8th/14th century, Baghdad had been sacked by the Mongols, and descendants of the 'Abbāsīs lived in Cairo with the caliphal titles, as the pensioners of the Mamlūk sultans. They had no power, but they were acknowledged by many sultans, who did hold supreme power in their own areas, and often fought wars against each other.

A representative statement of how Muslim legalists of the later medieval period viewed the problems of power and Islamic leadership is well shown by a Syrian contemporary of Ibn Taymīya (and with whom the Ḥanbalī naturally disagreed), Ibn Jamā'a (d. 1333 A.D.) who was one of the highest officials of the Mamlūk religious establishment, and twice Chief Qāḍī of Cairo. Although he was a Shāfi'ī, like al-Māwardī, it is Ibn Jamā'a's view which conforms to that of Aḥmad ibn Ḥanbal in the creedal statement found in Chapter One: the Imām in power is to be obeyed regardless of how he came there. In a conflict between unity and justice, the unity of the Umma must have precedence. By extension, whoever wields effective power in any area must be recognized by the Imām, if he has no means of removing him. In short, rulers must be treated as if they were perfect whether they are or not: the needs of the Community guarded from error require it. It is a logical view, but Ibn Taymīya may be excused if he felt that it was morally bankrupt.

Yet one cannot understand Ibn Jamā'a by treating him simply as a cynic or opportunist. The plain facts of his day were that Muslim life went on, even in political chaos, and that sultans still had to take account of Muslim sentiment. Some minimal demands could still be made of any local king: he must provide for defense and a certain degree of security, and he must not interfere with the fulfilment of his subjects' religious obligations. The continuing concern of the medieval 'ulamā' was to try to ensure that if evil or injustice occurred, it would still occur in a context of Islamic morality.

The Imām and Legality
from Emancipated Judgement in the Governance of Muslims.
by Ibn Jamā'a (d. A.H. *733*/A.D. *1333)*

The Imamate is of two sorts: that by election, and that by usurpation. For that of election, ten conditions are required. These are that the Imām be 1) male, 2) free, 3) adult, 4) rational, 5) Muslim, 6) upright, 7) brave 8) of Qurayshī descent, 9) learned, and 10) equal to the duty of guiding the Community and taking care of its interests. When a man of this description has been acclaimed and there is no other Imām at that time, then his acclamation and his Imamate are valid, and obedience to him is a duty insofar as it does not constitute rebellion against God, be He exalted.

The elected Imamate is confirmed by two methods, and the usurped Imamate by a third method. The first method in the elected Imamate is by an oath of acclamation of "those with power to loose and bind:" those of the amīrs and 'ulamā' and chiefs and leaders of the people whose presence at the Imām's city is practicable, as happened at the acclamation of Abū Bakr, with whom may God be well pleased, in the Hall of the Banu Sā'ida. Everyone agrees on the necessity of acclamation, and no conditions are posed about any particular number of those making it, but it should be those whose participation is practicable at the acclamation. Its validity does not depend on the agreement of the people of the provincial capitals (al-amṣār) but rather when the news reaches them they are bound to agree, if the one acclaimed is worthy of the office.

The second method is for the Imām to be chosen as successor by the one before him, as Abū Bakr designated 'Umar–may God be well pleased with him. All agree that this is valid. If the Imām chooses a body of electors from the Community and they then agree upon one of themselves, it is also valid, as 'Umar did in appointing the six who then chose 'Uthman. If the Imamate is contracted to one, and after him to another, that is also valid, and succession goes after him to the one next in line, as the Prophet—God's blessing and peace be on him—did in appointing the Commanders for the raid on Mu'ta. If the heir designate refuses the succession, then the acclamation has no validity.

As for the third method, by which the acclamation of a usurper is made valid, it is effected by overcoming the wielder of effective power (*ṣāḥib al-shawka*), and if there is no Imām at the time, and one sets himself up who is otherwise not qualified for the office, and overcomes people by his power and his troops without any election or appointment to the succession, then his acclamation is valid and one is bound to obey him, so that the unity of the Muslims be assured and they speak with one voice. It makes no difference if he is ignorant or unjust, according to the most correct opinion, and if the Imamate has been secured by force and conquest by one, and then another rises and overcomes the first by his power and troops, and the first is deposed, then the second becomes the Imām, for the sake, as we have said, of the welfare of the Muslims and their unity of expression. For this reason, 'Umar's son said at the Battle of the Ḥarra, "We are with the one who wins."

It is not permissible for the Imamate to go to two persons whether in one land together or in two different lands. . . .

The Imām of the Muslims has the right to delegate authority over any region, country, area or province to whoever is able to hold general authority there, because necessity demands it—not least in a far country. Thus the Messenger of God—on whom be blessing and peace—set 'Attāb ibn Asīd over Mecca. . . . If it is a general delegation of power, such as is customary for sultans and kings in our own time, it is lawful for the delegate then to appoint the qāḍīs and governors and rule the armies, with full disposition of the wealth from all quarters, but not to have anything to do with a region over which he is not delegated, because his is a particular government. The same qualifications apply to the delegate ruler when the Imām selects him that would apply to his own office, except that of Qurayshī descent, because he is standing in the Imām's place.

If a king attains power by usurpation and force in a (Muslim) country, then the caliph should delegate the affairs of that place to him, in order to call him to obedience and avoid a split with him, lest there be disunity and the staff of the Community be broken. In this way usurpation becomes legitimate government, issuing effective orders. . . .

The rights and duties of the Ruler. To the Sultan and the Caliph are due ten duties from the Community, and they owe ten duties to it. . . .

The first duty to the ruler is to render him outward and inward obedience in all he commands or forbids, unless it means committing rebellion against God. "Obey God and the Messenger and those in authority among you" (4:62). These are the Imām and his representatives, according to most, and some also say, the 'ulamā'.

The second duty is to give him good counsel, secretly or openly. . . .

The third is to exert oneself to render them help outwardly and inwardly, because it is a help to all the Muslims, and gives protection to religion and stops the activities of adversaries.

The fourth is to recognize how great is his rank, and how necessary it is that his power be magnified, and to treat him (accordingly). . . .

The fifth is to remind him when he is forgetful and to guide him when he strays, with compassion for him. . . .

The sixth is to protect him from any enemy or anything which can be feared, and this is one of the most important duties to him, and the most necessary. . . .

The seventh is to inform him of the ways of his officials, for whom he is responsible, and those charged with the protected communities (al-dhimma) so that he may attend to carrying out the protection, and see to the Community in the interests of his government and his flock.

The eighth is to help him to carry the burdens imposed by the interests of the Community as far as possible.

The ninth is to turn disaffected hearts to him for the benefit of the Community and the good order of the affairs of the Muslims (*al-milla*).

The tenth is to defend him in word and deed, and possessions and person and family, outwardly and inwardly, secretly and openly. . . . If the subjects do all (this) hearts will be pure and sincere, unity will prevail, and victory will ensue.

As for the ten duties of the ruler to the subjects, the first is to protect the Muslim heritage (*bayḍa*) and defend it, whether in every region, if he is caliph, or in his own country if he is delegated over it, and to struggle against idolators and put down rebels. . . .

The second is to guard the religion in its principles and beliefs, and put down innovation and heretics and encourage the religious sciences and study of the Law, venerate learning and the 'ulamā', and raise places from which the light (of Islam) may shine. . . .

The third is to uphold the rites of Islam, such as the obligation of prayer and the congregational prayers and the call to prayer and performance of it, and the sermons and leadership of the prayers, and looking after the matter of the fast and the feasts, and keeping the calendar, and the pilgrimage; and part of the last is facilitating the pilgrimage from all the districts, and keeping the roads clear and giving people security on the way and appointing people to look after them.

The fourth is to make the final decisions on court cases and sentences, by appointing the governors and judges, so as to reduce contentiousness and keep oppressors from the oppressed, and not to appoint any but those who may be depended on: virtuous 'ulamā'.

The fifth is to wage the jihād himself and with his armies at least once a year, if the Muslims have strength enough, and oftener than that if necessity demands it.

The sixth is to apply the punishments imposed by the Law, and make no distinctions when doing so between the powerful and the weak. The Messenger of God—God bless him and give him peace—said, "(The communities) before you only perished because they used to apply God's punishments to the lowly and let the high ranking alone, but by Allāh! if Fāṭima were to commit theft, I would cut off her hand!"

The seventh is to collect the poor–tax (*zakāt*) and the protection money (*jizya*) from those who are to pay it, and the booty (*fay'*) and the land–tax, and to use it as the Law stipulates. . . .

The eighth is to supervise pious and family foundations, keep bridges and roads in good repair, and make smooth the ways of welfare.

The ninth is to supervise the division and distribution of booty. . . .

The tenth duty is justice in the ruler in all his affairs.

The Laws of the prophets and the opinions of sages and prudent men all agree that justice is the cause of blessings and the growth of good things, and that oppression and tyranny are the cause of ruin to kindgoms. . . It is said that king (Bahram Gūr) travelling incognito once stopped at the house of a man who had a cow that gave the milk of thirty ordinary cows. He was astonished, and made up his mind to take her for himself. The next day she gave only half as much milk and the king asked the reason for this. The man replied, "I imagine our ruler has decided to take her, for oppression in a king drives away blessings." The king decided to leave her alone, and took an oath to God. The next day she gave her customary quantity, and the ruler swore to his Lord that he would be just all his life.[20]

In effect, the Umma entrusted its affairs to a Caliph, and asked him to be a perfect absolute ruler. Apart from the question of whether this is not usually a contradiction in terms, there was no sure apparatus for choosing him or ensuring a peaceful transmission of his power, and often or even usually men came to power by violent means. Once they were there, there was no mechanism for removing them except more violence, which was forbidden by the Law. It was a melancholy fact that in most states, except those few like the Ottoman and Mughal empires who succeeded in establishing the principle of hereditary succession, nothing so well suited a man for power as criminal instincts.

The great North African scholar Ibn Khaldūn, who also was a qāḍī in Cairo, and died in A.H. 808/A.D. 1406, had his own solution for the problem. The Mālikī school, to which he belonged, had long since accepted the principle in North Africa and Spain that there might validly be more than one caliph at a time, in different parts of the Umma. The caliphate, for him—and here he was influenced by the Muslim philosophers—was not just a title, but a function: that of ruling as a Muslim ruler should. Thus any king who ruled according to the tenets and ideals of Islam might be a successor to the Prophet in his own area. To put it in dynamic terms, the caliphate is not an office, but a challenge. This view was attractive later on, when the visible caliphate had disappeared, and some such understanding of it led to the general acceptance of the Ottoman sultans as caliphs. It is still attractive, for a divided Muslim world.

Royal and Caliphal Authority
from the Prolegomena
Ibn Khaldūn, (d. A.H. *808*/A.D. *1406)*

The real meaning of royal authority is that it is a form of organization necessary to mankind. (It) requires superiority and force, which express the wrathfulness and animality of human nature. The decisions of the ruler will therefore, as a rule deviate from what is right. . . . Therefore, it is necessary to have reference to ordained political norms, which are accepted by the mass and to whose laws it submits. . . . If these norms are ordained by the intelligent, the result will be a political institution on an intellectual basis. If they are ordained by God through a lawgiver who establishes them as religious laws, the result will be a political institution on a religious basis, which will be useful for life in both this and the other world.

This is because the purpose of human beings is not only their worldly welfare. . . . This makes it clear what the caliphate means. Natural royal authority means to cause the masses to act as required by purpose and desire. (But) the Caliphate means to cause the masses to act as required by religious insight into their interests in the other world as well as in this world. . . . In reality (it) substitutes for the Lawgiver (Muḥammad) in as much as it serves, like him, to protect the religion and exercise leadership in the world.[21]

It is not possible to appoint two men (as Imām) at the same time (in the same place). . . . Others hold that where there are great distances, it is possible to set up another Imām there to take care of public interests.

Among the famous authorities who are reported to have held this opinion are Abū Isḥāq al–Isfarāyinī (and) the Imām al–Ḥaramayn. . . . The opinions of the Spaniards and Maghribīs often make it evident that they, too, inclined to it. . . . Some scholars have rejected (it) with reference to 'the general consensus.' This is not evident proof, for if there existed a general consensus on the point, neither Abū Isḥāq or the Imām al–Ḥaramayn would have opposed it. They knew better than anyone else what the consensus ment.[22]

Royal authority, if it be Muslim, falls under the Caliphate and is one of its concomitants. (That) of a non–Muslim nation stands alone. . . .

Even though (caliphate) includes royal authority in the sense mentioned, its religious character brings with it special functions and ranks peculiar to the Muslim caliphs . . . all the religious functions of the religious law fall under the Caliphate.[23]

SHĪʿĪ LEGAL THEORY ON THE IMAMATE

As we would expect, the Shīʿī legal views of the Imamate differ quite significantly from the Sunnī theories. First of all, the Imām can only be a descendant of ʿAlī and Fāṭima, and for the Twelvers and Ismāʿīlīs, the perfect ruler cannot be chosen by fallible men, but only by a merciful God. It may happen that he is prevented from ruling, by Sunnīs, but he reigns and is the Imām of the true Community. In fact, for the Twelvers, human perversity so increased that the last true Imām, the twelfth, has been veiled from human sight, but still he lives and reigns and shall come again in glory. The Ismāʿīlīs on the other hand, who split with the Twelvers on the question of which of two sons of the sixth Imām should be considered the seventh and then followed the continuing line of Ismāʿīl, succeeded in founding the Fāṭimī caliphate. One branch of the Ismāʿīlīs reveres the Agā Khān as the true Imām today.

The following brief statement of the chief points of difference is taken from an 8th/14th century commentary on the doctrinal statement of a Twelver doctor who lived in the Mongol Sultanate in Iran and Iraq, ʿAllāma Muḥaqqiq al-Ḥillī (d. A.H. 726/A.D. 1326). He is said to have converted one of the Mongol Sultans to Twelverism.

Necessary Qualities of the Shīʿī Imām
from The Eleventh Chapter *(a Twelver doctrinal statement.)*
by ʿAllāma al-Ḥillī (d. A.H. *726/*A.D. *1326)*

1. The Imamate is a universal authority in the things of religion and of the world, belonging to some person and derived from the Prophet. And it is necessary according to reason. 'Belonging to a person' (means that) he who is worthy of the Imamate is a person appointed and specified by Allāh and His Prophet, not any chance person, and that it is not possible that there be more than one individual at any one period who is worthy of it. Men have disagreed as to whether the Imamate is *wājib* [necessary or incumbent.—Ed.] or not. The Khārijites say it is not. The Ashʿarites and Muʿtazilites say it is incumbent on man. The Imamites say it is incumbent on Allāh the Most High by reason, and this is the reality, (for) the Imamate is *luṭf* [kindness or goodness.—Ed.], and every sort of kindness is incumbent upon Allāh. [Here the point is that for the

Shī'a, God is *essentially* good. Sunnī theologians stress rather that He is free to act as He wills, since He is absolute and sovereign, and above good and evil.—Ed.] Those who hold that it is incumbent upon man say that it is incumbent to guard against harm. We have no quarrel with them as to the Imamate's being a protection against harm and incumbent. Our quarrel is about its being bestowed upon men (to appoint him), for in this case there would be an actual conflict (between Allāh and men) regarding the appointment of Imāms and it would result in harm, whereas what is sought is a decrease of harm. . . .

2. It is necessary that the Imām be *ma'ṣūm* [free from error. If he were not, then he would need an Imām himself.—Ed.] and because if he commited sin (*ma'ṣīya*) he would lose his place in men's hearts. And because he is the guardian of the Law, (and) must be immune from sin in order that it be safe from addition or loss and because of the Word of the Most High, "My covenant embraceth not the evildoers" (2–118).

3. It is necessary that the Imām be specified (*manṣūṣ*) for the Imamate, because immunity from sin is a matter which no one perceives except Allāh. Hence the specification must be made by one who knows that the Imām has the immunity to sin (necessary) for it. Sunnites say that whenever the Umma acknowledges any person convinced of his ability for it, and his power increases, he becomes the Imām. The (Zaydī Shī'īs) say that any rational Fāṭimite who comes forth with the sword and claims the Imamate is the Imām. Reality is contrary to all this, for the Imamate is a succession from God and His Messenger, and acknowledging anyone or any rational Fāṭimite would result in fightings and struggle. . . .

4. It is necessary that the Imām be the best of the people of his age, because if there were one better than he then the worse would take precedence over the better. . . .

5. The Imām after the Messenger of Allāh is 'Alī ibn Abī Ṭālib . . . (here follow proofs.) And the proofs of this cannot be numbered for multitude. Then after him his son al–Ḥasan, then al–Ḥusayn, then 'Alī ibn Ḥusayn, then Muḥammad ibn 'Alī al–Bāqir, then Ja'far ibn Muḥammad al–Ṣādiq, then Mūsā ibn Ja'far al–Kāẓim, then 'Alī ibn Muḥammad al–Hādī, then al–Ḥasan ibn 'Alī al–'Askarī, then Muḥammad ibn al–Ḥāsan the Lord of the Age (*ṣāḥib al–zamān*)—the blessing of Allāh upon them—Because each one of them who preceded appointed his successor. . . .

The Twelfth Imām is alive and existent, for in every age there must be an Imām immune to sin. . . . The thought that it is unlikely that anyone should remain alive (so long) is false, since it has occurred in previous times to (some) to live longer than he has lived. Their cause of his being hidden is either some advantage which Allāh has kept to Himself, or else the number of enemies and the paucity of helpers.

O Allāh, hasten his joy, and cause us to behold his victory, and make us his helpers and followers, and sustain us with his obedience and his good pleasure, and protect us from his opposition and anger![24]

In A.H. 447/A.D. 1055, the family of Saljūq, leaders of semi-nomadic tribal Turks who operated as warlords in Eastern Persia, drove the Buwayhīs out of power and took over the protection of the 'Abbāsī empire. The chief was given the new official title of Sulṭān, or "authority." As Sunnīs, they sincerely honored the Caliph, though they left him little more than the role of supreme Muslim religious leader, while they themselves held virtually all temporal power. The classical age of Islamic civilization had ended, and its medieval period had begun. There was a new wave of Islamic expansion, and new economic, social, and religious institutions were developed. In all this one of the most prominent figures was the great Persian wazīr of the Saljūqs, Niẓām al-Mulk, patron of 'Umar Khayyām and al-Ghazālī. Niẓām al-Mulk wrote a book on politics for the third Sulṭān, young Malikshāh, that served as a model for sultans long after. The new concept of Muslim kingship that was the sultanate is nowhere better illustrated. Typically, it was a military dictatorship, often hereditary, based on 'feudal' armies who received estates and the right to collect taxes in return for military service. There was an elite corps of household troops—usually military slaves—called *ghulāms* or *mamlūks*: the "pages" of this selection. These elite troops were used to control the feudal levies, and their officers often filled the highest state posts. Court etiquette attempted to imitate Persian and 'Abbāsī practise.

The Art of Muslim Kingship: The Sultanate from the Book of Politics *Niẓām al-Mulk (d.* A.H. *485/*A.D. *1092)*

Now in the days of some of the caliphs, if ever their empire became extended, it was never free from unrest and the insurrections of rebels, but in this blessed age there is no one in the world who in his heart meditates opposition to our lord and master. . . . Such is the happy state of this great empire; and in proportion to its greatness, it is blessed with an abundance of wise and good institutions. (The Sulṭān) has no need of any counsellor or guide; nevertheless he is not without cares, and perhaps he wishes to test his servants and assess their intelligence and wisdom. So when he commanded (me) his humble servant to write down some of those qualities that are indispensable to a king, whatever came to the mind of his humble servant that he had seen, learnt, read or heard, was written down, and The Sublime Command was fulfilled.[25]

Of a certainty the Master of the World (i.e. the Sulṭān) should know that on that great day he will be asked to answer for all of God's creatures who are under his command, and if he tries to transfer (his responsibility) to someone else he will not be listened to. Since this is so, it behooves the king not to leave this important matter to anyone else [e.g. the caliph.—Ed.] and not to disregard the state of God's creatures. To the best of his ability, let him ever acquaint himself, secretly and openly, with their conditions; let him protect them from cruel tyrants, so that the blessings resulting from those actions may come about in the time of his rule, if Allah wills.

It is absolutely necessary that on two days of the week the king should sit for the redress of wrongs, to extract recompense from the oppressor, to give justice, and to listen to the words of his subjects with his own ears, without any intermediary. . . . For when the report spreads, all oppressors will be afraid and curb their activities.[26]

Tax collectors, when they are given a fiscal district, must be instructed to deal honorably and take only the due amount, with civility and courtesy, and not to demand any taxes from [the peasants] before the time comes to pay. . . . If any peasant is in distress, let him be given a loan, lest he be cast out of his home.[27]

It is well known how Alexander defeated Darius. The reason for this was that Darius' wazīr had secret dealings with Alexander . . . at no time must the king be ill-informed about his officers (and) should any impropriety or treachery be found, let (the officer) be removed and chastised so that others will take warning.

Officers who hold lands in fief (*iqṭaʿ*) must know that they have no authority over the peasants except to take from them the due amount of revenue which has been assigned to them to collect;

the assignees are to have no further claim upon them. If peasants want to come to the court to state their cases, they are not to be prevented. . . . In this way the peasants will be contented and the king will be secure from punishment and torment in the world to come.[28]

It is necessary for full information to be available about every judge in the country. . . . Let each be paid salary and allowances so that he will have no excuse for dishonesty. . . . All other officers must strengthen the hand of the judge and uphold the dignity of the court. If anyone fails to appear in court, however exalted he may be, he must be forcibly compelled to be present. For in the time of The Companions of The Prophet, upon him be peace and blessings, justice was dispensed by them in person and not delegated to anyone else, so that there could be no scope for injustice or evading the law.[29]

Let observation be kept in every city to see who there is in it who shows interest in religious matters, fears God—be He exalted—and is not self-seeking. Let such a person be addressed thus: "We desire that you make constant enquiries and be always well-informed in matters small and great concerning the conduct of the tax-collector, the judge, the prefect of the police, and the inspector (of weights and measures) towards the people. Make us acquainted with the truth, whether your findings are kept secret or made public. . . ." If persons who are of the right quality refuse this trust, they must be coerced and however reluctantly commanded to do it.[30]

Spies must constantly go out to the limits of the kingdom in the guise of merchants, travellers, ṣūfīs, peddlers, and mendicants, and bring back reports of everything they hear. In the past it has often happened that (people) plotted mischief against the king; but spies forestalled them and informed the king, who was thus enabled to strike them down and frustrate their plans. Likewise they brought news about the condition of the peasants.[31]

A king cannot do without suitable boon companions with whom he can enjoy complete freedom and intimacy. The constant society of nobles tends to diminish the king's majesty and dignity because they become too arrogant. As a general rule people who are employed in any official capacity should not be admitted as boon companions nor should (boon companions) be appointed to any public office. . . . They should have a fixed time for their appearance; after the king has given audience and the nobles have retired, then comes the time of the boon companions. . . . They are company to the king, secondly they are in the position of bodyguards, thirdly the king can say things, frivolous and serious, to (them) which would not be suitable to (say to) his wazīr or other nobles, and fourthly all sorts of sundry tidings can be heard from boon companions, for through their freedom they can report on matters, good or bad, whether drunk or sober, and in this there is advantage and benefit.[32]

Twenty special sets of arms, studded with gold, jewels, and other ornaments, must always be kept ready and stored at the treasury so that whenever ambassadors arrive from distant parts of the world, twenty pages finely attired can take these weapons and stand round the throne. The pomp and circumstance of the kingdom and kingship must accord with the highmindedness of the king so it is fitting that wherever other kings possess one of a thing, our sovereign should have ten.

Whatever treatment is given to an ambassador, whether good or bad, it is as if it were done to the very king who sent him; and kings have always treated envoys well, for by this their own dignity has been enhanced. And if at any time there has been disagreement and enmity between kings, never have (ambassadors) been molested or treated with less than usual courtesy.[33]

The troops must receive their pay regularly. Those who are assignees of course have their salaries to hand independently as assigned, but in the case of pages who are not fit for holding fiefs, money for their pay must be made available and always be paid to them at the proper time. . . . The king should with his own hands put it into their hands, for this increases their feelings of affection and attachment.

The rulers of the Arabs, Kurds, Dailamites, Rūmīs and others who have only recently come to terms of submission must be told that each of them should keep a son or a brother resident at the court; there should be, if not a thousand, never less than five hundred of them. In this way no one will be able to rebel against the king, because of the hostages.

Although there has arisen a certain amount of aversion to the Turkmans, and they are very numerous, still they have a long-standing claim upon this dynasty, because at its inception they served well and are attached by ties of kinship. So it is fitting that about a thousand of their sons should be enrolled as pages of the palace. When they are in continuous employment they will learn the use of arms and settle down with other people and serve as pages, and the dislike felt for them will disappear. . . . In this way the empire will not leave them patronless, the king will acquire glory, and they will be contented.[34]

Raising of the curtain is the sign that an audience is in progress; when the curtain is lowered it indicates that there is no audience, except for persons who are summoned. There is nothing more annoying for nobles and officers than to come to the court and have to return without seeing the king. If they come several times and fail to gain audience, they form a bad impression of the king and begin to plot mischief. There is no better rule for the king than to hold frequent audiences. When (a set) system has been in force for some time, it will become habitual and remain established. Then all crowding will be avoided. . . . Any arrangements other than these should not be permitted.[35]

Men who are promoted and elevated to high rank have to spend time and trouble in the performance of their duties, and when, as sometimes happens, they make a mistake, if they are publicly reprimanded they suffer loss of honor, and no amount of goodwill or favour will restore them to their positions. . . .

Kings have always paid attention to having well supplied tables in the mornings so that those who come to the royal presence may find something to eat there. If the nobles have no desire for it at the time, there is no objection to their eating their own provisions in due course, but it is essential to have the table well spread in the morning.[36]

If reports come in from any district showing that the peasants are being ruined and scattered abroad, and if it seems likely that the bearers of the report are actuated by self–interest, one of the private staff should be appointed and bring back verified reports, because officials (when they are questioned) always (make excuses and counter–accusations). This is even now a cause of decline in population; the peasants are becoming impoverished and uprooted, and taxes are being unfairly levied.[37]

In all ages the office of commander of the guard was one of the most important posts, because his office is concerned with punishment. When the king is angry with anyone, it is the commander of the guard whom the king orders to cut off his head, to chop off his hands and feet, to hang him on a gibbet, to give him the bastinado, to put him in prison or to throw him into a pit; and to save their skins and lives people do not hesitate to sacrifice their goods and wealth. The people proverbially feared (the commander of the guard) more than the king. But in our epoch this post has fallen into disuse and has been robbed of its prestige. There should be at least fifty mace-bearers constantly at the court, the equivalent and outfit of the commander of the guard must be of the finest, and he must be surrounded with the utmost possible pomp.[38]

That part of the Siyāsat-nāma was apparently written in 1086. About 1091 the aged minister began to write again, and now his words had an urgent note. Times had changed. Much of his earlier advice had not been heeded, and Malikshāh's favorite wife was his enemy. The Sulṭān was engaged in a quarrel with the Caliph, and had also come under the influence of adventurers and heretics. The elder statesman outlined the dangers that particularly threatened the Saljūq empire, and states like it. Before the addition to his book could be presented to Malikshāh, however, Niẓām al-Mulk was dismissed from office. In A.H. 485/A.D. 1092 he was murdered by Ismā'īlī assassins in circumstances suggesting that they may have been sent with the knowledge of the Sulṭān or his queen. Malikshāh himself died a month later, and wars over the succession began soon after.

At any time the state may be overtaken by some celestial accident, or influenced by the evil eye. Then the government will change and pass from one house to another, or the country will be thrown into disorder through seditions and tumults; opposing swords (will be drawn and there will be) killing, burning and violence. In such troubled days men of noble birth will be crushed; evil-doers will gain control and whoever has strength will do as he likes, and any wretch will not hesitate to take upon himself titles reserved for the king and the wazīr; he might give himself ten titles with impunity and nobody would ask if he were worthy or not. Turks will adopt titles proper to civil dignitaries, and the latter will take those belonging to Turks [who are military.—Ed.], while Turks and Tazīks (Persians) alike will decorate themselves with titles of learned men and issue orders on behalf of the king. The religious law will be held in contempt, the peasants will become unruly and the soldiers oppressive; all discretion and decency will vanish away and no one will be able to remedy matters. . . .

Later, God will bring forth a just and wise king from princely stock, and will give him the power to vanquish his enemies, and the wisdom and intelligence to judge matters right. He will test the merit and estimate the rank of everyone; those who are worthy he will reinstate and the unworthy he will dismiss. He will be the friend of religion and the enemy of oppression; he will assist the faith and remove vanity and heresy.[39]

Amīrs and Turks have always been given the titles Ḥusām al-Dawla (Sword of the Empire), Saif al-Dawla (Sabre of the Empire), Shams al-Dawla (Sun of the Empire) and such like, while civil dignitaries have received titles like 'Amīd al-Mulk (Pillar of the Kingdom) Ẓāhir al-Mulk (Protector of the Kingdom) Qiwām al-Mulk (Support of the Kingdom) Niẓām al-Mulk (Harmony of the Kingdom). Nowadays all discretion has vanished, and Turks give themselves the title of civil officials, and Tazīks take those of Turks, and think it no wrong. Yet titles always used to be held dear. . . . After the time of the Fortunate Sulṭān Alp Arslan (may Allah have mercy on him) customs changed, discretion disappeared and titles became mixed up: the smallest person demanded the biggest title and was given it.[40]

When two appointments are given to one man, one of the tasks is always inefficiently and faultily performed; and when two men are given a single post each transfers (his responsibility) to the other, and the work remains forever undone.[41]

Nowadays all distinction has vanished; and if a Jew administers the affairs of Turks it is permitted, and it is the same for Christians, Zoroastrians, and Qarmaṭīs. Everywhere indifference is predominant; there is no zeal for religion, no concern for the revenue, no pity for the peasants. Your humble servant knows not where this state of affairs will lead.

(In the days of the Ghaznavīs and the early Saljūqs) those who administered the affairs of the Turks were all professional civil servants and secretaries from Khurasān, who belonged to the orthodox Ḥanafī or Shāfi'ī (law schools). The (Shī'ī) heretics of Iraq were never employed as secretaries and tax collectors. Now things have reached such a state that the court and the divan are full of them. One day the Turks will realize the iniquity of these people and recall my words when the divan becomes empty of Khurasānī secretaries and officials.

One day it was reported to the martyr Sulṭān Alp Arslan (may God sanctify his soul) that Ardam was going to appoint a certain village headman (known to be a Bāṭinī or Ismā'īlī) as his secretary.

He said, "Go and bring this man here." He was brought in immediately. The Sulṭān said, "Thou wretch, thou sayest that the Caliph of Baghdad is not the lawful caliph; thou art a Rāfiḍī." The wretched man said, "O Master, your slave is not a Rāfiḍī; I am a Shī'ite." The sulṭān said, "O cuckold, what is so good about the Shī'a that you give it precedence over the Bāṭinī sect? The one is bad, the other is worse." He commanded the mace bearers to beat the man, and they threw him half dead out of the palace.[42]

The king's underlings must not be allowed to assume power. This particularly applies to women, for they are wearers of the veil and have not complete intelligence. Their purpose is the continuation of the lineage, and the more chaste (and veiled) their bearing the more admirable they are. But when the king's wives begin to assume the part of rulers they are not able to see things with their own eyes. . . . They give orders following what they are told by such as chamberlains and servants. In all ages, nothing but disgrace, infamy, discord and corruption have followed when kings have been dominated by their wives. The first man who suffered loss and underwent pain and trouble for obeying a woman was Adam, who did the bidding of Eve.[43]

Seceders have existed in all ages. Never has there been a more vile, more perverted or more irreligious crowd than these people. The greatest reinforcement of their strength comes from the Rāfiḍīs and Khurramdīns. The kingdom of the Master of the World has no worse opponent. They try to persuade the Master of the World to overthrow the house of the ('Abbāsī caliphs). Worse than that, as a result of their representations the Master of the World has become weary of his humble servant, and is not prepared to take any action in the matter. One day the Master will realize their iniquity and treachery when I have disappeared.[44]

In the advice of Kay Kā'ūs ibn Iskandar, the Ziyārī ruler of a little kingdom in the Caspian provinces of Persia, to his son Gīlānshāh, we have a valuable insight into Islamic kingship as it appeared to a Muslim king in the fifth/eleventh century. Kay Kā'ūs is a professional member of a ruling class, and an affectionate father who wishes to pass his knowledge to his son. He is very conscious that even if a king cannot have lordly morals, he must appear to have them. He knows that a king must sometimes tell lies and kill, but it is not expedient to get a name for it. Virtue, or its appearance, is *useful;* it is one of the means by which a king in his civilization must try to secure his power. The Ziyārīs were experts at retaining their throne in turbulent times, by skilful marriages, changing from Shīʿī to Sunnī, and fearlessly serving whatever great power had the upper hand. The son for whom this was written reigned for seven years, and in 1090 was overthrown by Ḥasan-i Sabbāh, leader of the Ismāʿīlīs of ʿAlamūt.

Practical Advice from a King
from the Book of Qābus *(a "Mirror for Princes")*
by Kay Kāʾūs ibn Iskandar, written A.H. *475*/A.D. *1082*

You must realize, my son, that the day of my departure approaches and the day when you will succeed me is near. Know that this world is ploughland; as you sow, be it good or ill, you reap. Yet no man enjoys on his own ground what he has reaped there. It is in the place of Delight that he enjoys it, and that is the Everlasting Abode. Now in this present world virtuous men are imbued with the spirit of lions, whereas wicked men have the spirit of dogs, for while the dog consumes his prey where he seizes it, the lion takes it elsewhere. Your quarry is knowledge and virtuous conduct. Carry through your pursuit to the end here, so that when the time comes for enjoyment in the Everlasting Abode it may be with the greatest degree of pleasure. The one way to achieve it is by submission to God Almighty.[45]

Be of ready speech, my son; yet never tell lies and do not gain the reputation of being a liar. Rather become known for veracity, so that if ever in an emergency you utter a lie it will be believed. Never utter a truth which has the appearance of a lie; for a lie which has the air of truth is preferable to an accurate statement which seems to be false, and this kind of lie will be believed where that kind of true statement will not.[46]

Do not be over hasty in shedding innocent blood, and regard no killing of Muslims to be lawful, unless they are brigands, thieves, and grave–robbers or such whose execution is demanded by the law. Torment in both worlds is inflicted for the shedding of innocent blood; you will find retribution for it on the Day of Resurrection, but also in this world your name will be besmirched. . . .

Yet do not neglect your duty where blood must rightfully be shed, for the general welfare demands it and out of remissness evil is born.[47]

As for your companions of the cup, regard them only as drinking associates and not as true friends; they are well–disposed to your cups, not to you. But make friends with persons both good and bad and be affable with both classes of men, having sincere friendship with the good and making a show of friendship towards the bad. One's need is not always for good people, occasionally help in need comes from the bad ones, because what one can do cannot always be done by the other. Yet do not attach yourself so closely to either group that the other becomes hostile to you; tread the path of wisdom and understanding, thereby securing your safety.[48]

If you become king some day, my son, be Godfearing, keep eye and hand away from other Muslims' women–folk and let your robe be unspotted. In every task you propose, first consult with wisdom. As long as you see any possibility of leisurely action avoid haste; and whenever you propose to enter upon an undertaking, first ascertain the way by which you will emerge from it.

Be ever one that speaks the truth, but speak rarely and laugh rarely, so that those subject to your kingship may not become emboldened against you. Expose yourself to the public gaze only rarely, and so prevent yourself from becoming a spectacle commonplace in the eyes of your troops and your people. Maintain stern discipline, more especially with your wazīr (and) never be completely dependent upon his counsel. Hearken to what he has to say, but make inquiry into the circumstances of the case to ascertain if it is your welfare he is seeking, or his own benefit. Thus he will be unable to regard you as being governed by his views.

Whether you are young or elderly, have an old man as your wazīr. It is inexpedient for an old man to take a young one as administrator and controller of affairs. If you are young and your wazīr is likewise young, the fire of your youth will be added to his, and between the two fires the kingdom will be destroyed.

Next, it is essential that the wazīr be of imposing appearance. He should be well formed, strongly built, and of corpulent person. . . . (He) must have a beard, and a large one.

Grant him full powers in his office to ensure that the affairs of your kingdom shall not be hindered. Be generous to his kinsmen and adherents, but never appoint them to office (the whole of the sheep's fat tail may not be given to the cat at once), for he will not in any circumstances render a true account of his adherents' dealings nor condemn his kinsmen to penalties for the benefit of your revenues. . . .

Have no compassion upon robbers and never allow a pardon for them, nor grant any forgiveness to the shedder of blood. For if he deserves (Qur'ānic) retaliatory punishment and you pardon him, you will be associated with him on the Day of Resurrection.

Assign to every man a task, and grudge no man employment. Adherents are maintained for the purpose of working, yet when you make an appointment be careful to allot it to the man adapted to it. As the poet says:

This gift on thy behalf of God I ask
That you appoint men fitted for their task.

In the course of your kingship, never permit your commands to be treated with indifference. The king's solace and pleasure lie in giving commands; in other respects the king is like his subjects, and the difference between them is that the king issues commands while the subjects obey. . . .

When your maternal uncle, the martyred Sulṭān Mas'ūd (of Ghazna) sat upon the throne he preferred dalliance with his slave girls to ruling as a king. His troops and viceroys began to tread the path of disobedience and both bodyguard and peasantry were stirred to insubordination. At last one day an old woman arrived lodging a complaint against the governors of (her distant) province. Sulṭān Mas'ūd commanded that she be given a letter. However, the governor concerned paid no attention to it, thinking (that she) would never again be able to go to Ghazna. Nevertheless, she did return to Ghazna and demanded justice. The Sulṭān once more ordered that she should be given a letter, but to this (she) objected that she had once before taken a letter, without effect.

"What am I to do?" asked Mas'ūd. To which she replied "Your course of action here is simple. Maintain your authority (so) that your instructions will be acted upon, or else resign your authority and let another possess it, leaving you to occupy yourself with your pleasures. Thus mankind will cease to be held fettered in the miseries of tyranny." Mas'ūd was shamed into procuring justice for the old woman and the governor was hanged at the gate of Farawa. Thereafter Mas'ūd awoke from the sleep of indifference and no man dared to fall short in the fulfillment of his commands. . . .

It is inexpedient for the king to place soldiery in authority over the people, else the realm will fail to retain its population, and it is through the people that the country is made prosperous (if they are) given what is rightfully theirs. Therefore let there be no place in your heart for extortion; the dynasty of kings who recognize rights endures long and becomes old, but the dynasty of extortioners swiftly perishes, because fair treatment means prosperity, and extortion means a depopulated land. The sages say that the wellspring of gladness in the world is a just king. . . .

As for your bodyguard, do not let it consist entirely of a single race, for the reason that the members of one race will be in alliance together. If they are of all races, one is held in check by another.

Then also, you should frequently invite the chiefs of your soldiery to food and wine; treat them generously in respect of robes of honor and gifts of various kinds, yet if you wish to make (a small gift) do not announce it in public. Declare it secretly.

For eight years I was at Ghazna as intimate companion of the Sulṭān Mawdūd, whom in all that time I never saw commit three particular acts. One was that he never announced any gift of less than two hundred dīnārs in public, another was that he never laughed in such fashion as to display his teeth, and the third was that when in anger he refrained from insulting language. This was most excellent behaviour.

I can tell you nothing further on the subject of open–handedness except that you should be lavish with money. In brief, never be petty–spirited; if you cannot resist your own disposition, at least follow my advice in not displaying your meanness of spirit in public.

Strive against becoming intoxicated with the wine of kingship and permit no shortcoming in your fostering of these six qualities: awesomeness, justice, generosity, respect for the law, gravity, and truthfulness. If any of these is lacking in a king, he is near to intoxication with kingship, and no king who becomes intoxicated with kingship regains sobriety except with its disappearance.

During your reign as king do not neglect to inform yourself of the position of other kings in the world. The ideal at which you must aim is that no king shall be able to draw a breath without your being aware of it.

Then in the same measure that you are informed of affairs in the world generally and of the doings of its princes, it is your duty to be acquainted with your own country and people and bodyguard. Most particularly you must be vigilant concerning the doings of your wazīr. He should not be able to swallow a drink of water without your knowing it, for you have entrusted your life and possessions to him. If you are neglectful of him, you are neglectful of your own life and possessions.

As for the rulers of the various parts of the world who are your fellow sovereigns, if you are on terms of friendship with them do not let it be half-friendship; but if you are at enmity with them let it be overtly. Do not be at secret enmity with your equal.

Let your actions be habitually on a noble scale. Do not affix (your sign) to anything trivial. Once you have affixed (it) do not contradict yourself except with obvious justification; self-contradiction is always unworthy, and especially so in a prince.

These are the requirements for kingship. It is a rarely acquired position, and not everyone attains it, but I speak of it because it is demanded by this work. If some other career falls to your lot, such as agriculture or one of the crafts practised in the bazaar, whatever it be, you must keep its laws to ensure that your work shall prosper.[49]

The following aphorisms are from a manual of politics presented to the Mongol prince of Mosul in Iraq in 1302 A.D. by the Shī'ī civil servant Ibn al-Ṭiqṭiqā'. The barbarian Mongols who had occupied Iraq and Persia had only recently converted to Islam, and had fairly cordial relations with their Shī'ī subjects, who least regretted the vanished 'Abbāsī empire. Ibn Ṭiqṭiqā's treatise on the art of rule and the brief political history of Islam he appended to it were a part of the process by which the Il-Khān Mongols were transformed from destroyers to patrons of Muslim civilization.

Advice on Muslim Kingship for a Barbarian Prince
from the Fakhrī *(written* A.H. *702/*A.D. *1302)*
by Ibn al-Ṭiqṭiqā'

Knowledge adorns kings more than it adorns their subjects, and when the king is learned, the learned rule. The best thing for a king to look into is books dealing with the manners of rulers, and historical biographies comprising interesting stories and wonderful things of the past, although ministers of old used to dislike kings to study biography and history, fearing that kings might come to understand matters which ministers do not like kings to understand.

The best prince is one in whom are combined certain qualities, while others are not found in him. Of these is intelligence—it is the basic one and the noblest. On it are built dynasties, even communities, and to say that is sufficient. Another is justice, through which wealth becomes abundant and provinces are developed and men are made better. Another is knowledge by which the ruler is adorned in the eyes of the common and the elite, and numbered among the greatest rulers. Desirable knowledge is only for him to have enough familiarity with the sciences to be able to converse with experts so that a present situation may be dealt with. For that, there is no need to go into minutiae. Studies of princes vary according to their views. The Persian rulers studied maxims and moral counsel, polite letters, history, geometry, and the like. The kings of Islam studied philosophy, grammar, poetry, and history to the point that an error of speech was reckoned among the worst defects a prince might have, and a man's rank might be raised by a single anecdote or verse; nay, by a single word. In the Mongol state all these sciences have been rejected, and other sciences taken up, such as economics and accounts for control of the realm and balancing income and expenditure, and medicine, and astrology for choosing auspicious occasions. More than that of science and literature was unpopular with them, except the Prince of Mosul—may God lengthen his shadow and cause his excellence to spread. Another quality is fear of God, exalted be He, and this is the root of every good and key to every blessing, for when a king fears God he is trusted by God's servants.

Some have claimed that rancour is a praiseworthy quality in a king. I disagree with this, for men are composed of error, and swift to act according to their nature. How often they furnish occasions for rancour! A ruler would never cease from it all his life long, and it would embitter his pleasure and distract his attention from affairs of state. How often we have seen subjects or the army rise up against their rulers and divest them of the kingdom or of life itself (even) in the early Islamic period, when men were men and religion was religion! Of all creatures, a prince needs most to conciliate hearts and improve intentions. One of the qualities to be desired in a ruler is generosity, for it is the basis of inclining hearts, obtaining good advice from the world, and enlisting the service of notable men. The poet says

> If the ruler has no gold,
> Leave him, for his state is departed.

Another is (to inspire) awe by which order is preserved from the ambition of subjects. Kings used to go to extremes in this, even tying up lions and elephants and leopards, sounding great trumpets, and kettle-drums and cymbals, all to inspire awe in the subjects and create reverence for his rule.

Another is policy (*siyāsat*), which is the ruler's capital, trusted upon to spare bloodshed, protect property, strengthen gaps, prevent evils, restrain evil–doers and mischief makers and check the oppression that comes from rebellion and upheaval. Another is fidelity to promises, for calming hearts and contenting minds and giving the subjects confidence in the ruler. Another is to look into the minutiae of the affairs of state and subjects, and recompense the doer of good and the doer of evil according to their deeds. Whoever has these ten qualities deserves the highest power. If only men of theories and religious sects would truly consider, these would be the conditions for the Imamate. All else is useless.

Know too that a king has properties which are peculiar to himself and distinguish him from common people. When he likes a thing, or dislikes it, or delights in a thing, the people do likewise, either naturally or in imitation to gain his favor. Thus it is said, "People have the religion of their princes." Consider the manners of people in the time of the 'Abbāsīs. When this (Mongol) dynasty—God expand its good–doing and elevate its estate—took power, people changed their manners in all affairs and imitated those of the rulers, in speech, costume, furnishings and custom, without the rulers obliging them or ordering them to do so, or forbidding them. It was only that people knew that their former manners were scorned by the rulers and contrary to their choice, so they sought their favor through their manners. This is one of the peculiarities of royal power and a secret of kingship. Another peculiarity of kingship is that association with it brings haughtiness and pride and courage and arrogance. Association with other than a ruler does not do this.

Another peculiarity of the ruler is that when he turns from a man, the man becomes faint–hearted even though the ruler does nothing to him. And when he approaches a man, the man is encouraged, though he has not benefitted him. Mere turning away or approaching does that, and none of mankind but the ruler has this quality.

Among qualities preferably not found in a ruler are impetuosity (as well as) disgust, weariness and ennui, which are among the most hurtful and damaging things to his position.

Subjects owe duties to a ruler, and he owes duties to them.[50]

He should ever make mention of and be grateful for (God's favor to him), in conformity with the Word of the Most High, "As for the favor of your Lord, speak thereof," and "If you are grateful I will surely give you more." I see no harm in here recording a royal prayer of my own composition. "God, I relinquish to Thee my strength and power, and I take refuge in Thy strength and power. I magnify Thee, for that Thou gavest me being from naught; exalted me over many peoples; placed in my hands the reins by which to control Thy creatures, and made me (a successor) over Thy earth. God, take me by the hand in straits; reveal to me the aspects of truth, help me to do Thy will and protect me from error; snatch not from me the cover of Thy beneficence, and save me from the blows of evil; shield me from the craftiness of the envious and the exultation of foes; treat me kindly in all my vicissitudes; shelter me with Thy wing on every side, Most (Merciful of those who have mercy)."

One of the things disliked in a ruler is excessive inclination to women. To consult them in affairs is to induce inefficiency, and an indication of weakness of judgement. As the Prophet,—peace be upon him—said, "Consult them and do the opposite."

To each type of subjects corresponds a type of administration. The upper classes are administered by nobility of character and gently guiding aright. The middle classes are administered by a combination of interest and fear, while the common people are administered by fear and by being constrained to the straight path and forced to the obviously right. Understand that a ruler stands to his subjects as a doctor to an invalid. If the latter's constitution is delicate, the former's regimen is delicate too, and he insinuates nasty medicines into pleasant tasting things, and by every possible means tricks the latter, to attain his objective of curing him. It is not fitting for a ruler to threaten one for whose instruction the cold shoulder or a frown is enough, nor to execute (where) chastisement is enough. A ruler should be circumspect in ordering an execution and taking life. He should realize that if all the people in the world (struggled to restore the dead to life) they could not do so. This is one of the most dangerous things for a ruler, and it is proper that he should always himself dislike executions. Perpetual imprisonment in hidden dungeons replaces execution with (the added benefit of) security from the remorse to be feared in the case of the latter. The perfect ruler should also pay close attention to the various kinds of punishments. How many a punishment has resulted in spilling the lifeblood of the punished man though the taking of his life was not intended! Of them the severest is surely punishment by fire, and it is an unhallowed punishment, because punishment by fire is especially reserved for the Deity, and it is not for His servant to share it with Him.

It is said that the determined ruler is he who reviews and scrutinizes himself until none of his people know his faults better than he knows them (and) who schools his subjects to adopt his own good habits and manners by kindliness, winning methods and affability.

Men have differed as to the strong unjust ruler and the weak just ruler. They (mostly) prefer the strong unjust, arguing that his pride preserves (his people) from being damaged by others than himself. So his subjects are spared damage by all men but suffer damage by one. The weak just ruler neglects the interests of his subjects and every hoof tramples them, so that they are spared damage by one and suffer damage by all. A wise man said "A ruler whom his subjects fear is better than a ruler who fears them." (Another) said, "There are two important matters, one of which can only be achieved singly and in isolation, the other only in being shared. The former is rule. If shared, it is spoiled. The latter is opinion. If shared, it can be trusted to be right."[51]

KING OF THE VIRTUOUS CITY

Muslim concern with virtuous society and the perfect ruler was naturally reflected in the writings of a series of illustrious medieval Islamic philosophers. One of the chief figures in this series was the Turk al-Fārābī, educated at Baghdad, in close contact with the Syriac Christian Aristotelians who flourished in Iraq and Syria. Later he moved to the brilliant court of the Shī'ī Arab prince of Aleppo, Sayf al-Dawla the Ḥamdānī, where he died in A. H. 339/A.D. 950. While a devout Muslim, of mystical bent, al-Fārābī believed that reason was superior to faith, that Greek philosophy provided satisfactory answers to all important Islamic questions, and that religion was a symbolic presentation of the truths of philosophy for the masses. While in logic, science and metaphysics an Aristotelian, in political philosophy he based himself on Plato's *Republic* and *Laws*. He envisages not only a perfect city–state, but also a perfect *umma* and perfect world–state, in which the perfect ruler is the philosopher–king.

Islamic Political Philosophy
from The Virtuous City
by Abū Naṣr al-Fārābī (d. A.H. *339/*A.D. *950)*

He who treats bodies is the doctor, and he who treats souls is the statesman, who is also called the king. Just as the doctor who treats bodies needs to know the body as a whole, diseases and method of removal, so the statesman and king who treats souls needs knowledge of the soul as a whole, the parts of the soul, the defects and vices which are liable to affect it and every part of it, whence they occur and from what amounts of a thing, what are the states of a soul by which a man does good deeds, and how many they are, how the vices are to be removed from the people of the cities, the devices for establishing (the virtues) in the souls of the citizens and the method of proceeding for their preservation among them, so that they do not cease. But it is requisite for him to know about the souls only so much as he needs in his art.

The virtues are of two kinds, ethical and rational. The rational virtues are the virtues of the rational part, such as wisdom, intellect, cleverness, readiness of wit (and) excellence of understanding. The ethical virtues are the virtues of the appetitive part, such as temperance, bravery, generosity, justice. The vices are similarly divided into two classes.

The ethical virtues and vices are established in the soul simply by repeating the actions and becoming accustomed thereto, just as in the case of the arts, e.g. writing. If the actions of writing which we repeat and accustom ourselves to are bad actions, bad writing is established in us.

A man cannot be created from the beginning naturally endowed with a virtue or defect. But it is possible that he should be naturally disposed to the conditions of a virtue or vice. . . .

Between the man who restrains himself and the virtuous man is a difference, viz., that the man who restrains himself does the opposite of what his state and desire prompt him to do. . . . The virtuous man does good deeds liking and desiring them, not feeling pain but pleasure in them. . . .

Actions which are good deeds are the moderate, or mean actions between two extremes, both of which are bad. . . .

He who brings out and produces the mean and moderate in foods and medicines is the doctor. The art by which he brings it out is medicine. He who produces the mean and moderate in morals and actions is the ruler of the city and the king. The art by which he brings it out is the political art and the kingly craft.

Just as the body is composed of different parts, each doing a different work, so the city and the household are each composed of different parts, some less, some more excellent, each doing a certain work independently . . . and there is combined in their actions mutual help towards the perfection of the aim in the city or the household. It is not disallowed that there is a man who has the power to produce the mean in actions and morals as far as he himself is concerned (just as a man may doctor himself, but) if in what he produces he does not seek the advantage of the city or the rest of its parts (he) operates with a part of a corrupt political art.

The indispensable (or 'minimum') city is that in which the mutual help of its members is restricted to attaining merely what is indispensable for continuance, livelihood, and preservation of life. The ideal city is that in which the inhabitants help each other towards the attainment of the most excellent of things, by which are meant the true existence of man, his continuance, his livelihood and the preservation of his life. . . . Socrates, Plato and Aristotle thought that man has two lives (and) man, according to them, has a first and a last perfection. The last results to us not in this life but in the afterlife, when there has preceded it the first perfection in this life of ours.

The first perfection is that a man does the actions of all the virtues, not that he is merely endowed with a virtue without performing its actions. This perfection affords us the last perfection, which is ultimate happiness, i.e. the absolute good. It is that which is chosen and desired for itself, and not for the sake of anything else. The ideal city (thus) according to them is that whose inhabitants help one another towards the attainment of the last perfection, i.e. ultimate happiness.

The true king is he whose aim and purpose in the art by which he rules are that he should afford himself and the rest of the people true happiness, which is the aim and end of the kingly craft. It is quite necessary that the king of the ideal city should be the most perfect of them in happiness, since he is the cause of the happiness of the city. The king is king by the kingly craft, whether he is known for his art or not, whether he has found implements to use or not, whether he has found people to receive from him or not, just as the doctor is doctor by the medical craft, whether he is known for it or not. . . . Some people think that they should not apply the name of king to him without his being obeyed and honored in a city. Others add to that riches, while others (add) force, subjection, terrorizing and fear. None of these things belong to the essential conditions of kingship, but are things which may be useful to the kingly craft.

The parts of the ideal city are five: the most virtuous or excellent, the interpreters, the assessors or measurers, the fighting men, and the rich. The most excellent are the wise; next come the bearers of religion and the interpreters, who are the orators, the eloquent, the poets, the musicians, the secretaries and the like. The measurers are the accountants, geometers, doctors, astrologers and the like. The fighting men are the army, watchmen, and the like. The rich are the gainers of wealth, such as the farmers, herdsmen, merchants, and the like. . . .

The chiefs and rulers of this city are of four descriptions:

A. The king in reality. He is the first chief, and it is he in whom are combined six conditions: a) wisdom; b) perfect practical wisdom; c) excellence of persuasion d) excellence in producing an imaginative impression; e) power to fight the holy war (jihād) in person; f) that there be nothing in his body to prevent him attending to the holy war. . . . It is for this man to rule according as he thinks right and wishes.

B. The second case is when no man is found in whom all these are united, but they are found separately in a group of men. This group then together takes the place of the king. Their system of rule is called the rule of the most virtuous.

C. The third case is when these are not available either. The chief of the city is then the man in whom are united a) knowledge of the ancient laws and traditions which the first generations of imāms acknowledged . . . b) excellent discrimination of the conditions in which those traditions may be employed; c) power to produce what is not found explicit in the old traditions, oral and written, imitating therein the model of the ancient traditions; d) excellence of idea and practical wisdom in the events not such as to be in the ancient traditions, in order to preserve the prosperity of the city; and e) excellence of rhetoric and persuasion and in producing an imaginative impression. At the same time, f) he should be able to go on the jihād. Such a one is called the king according to the law, and his rule is called lawful kingship (*malik al-sunna*).

D. The fourth case is when no man is found in whom all these are found united, but they exist separately among a group, and they together take the place of the king according to the law. This group is called the chiefs according to the law.[52]

It follows, then, that the idea of Imām, Philosopher and Legislator is a single idea. However, the name "philosopher" signifies primarily theoretical virtue. . . . "Legislator" signifies excellence of knowledge concerning the conditions of practical intelligibles, the faculty for finding them, and the faculty for bringing them about in nations and cities. . . . It will follow that the theoretical virtue must precede the others. The name "prince" signifies sovereignty and ability. His ability to do a thing must not result only from external things; he himself must possess great ability as a result of his art, skill, and virtue being of exceedingly great power. This is not possible except by great power of knowledge, great power of deliberation, and great power of (moral) virtue and art. Otherwise he is not truly able or sovereign. For if his ability stops short of this, it is still imperfect. Similarly, if his ability is restricted to goods inferior to supreme happiness, his ability is incomplete and he is not perfect. Therefore the true prince is the same as the philosopher-legislator. As to the idea of the Imām in the Arabic language, it signifies merely the one whose example is followed and who is well received. . . . Only when all other arts, virtues, and activities seek to realize his purpose and no other, will his art, his (moral) virtue, his deliberation (and) his science be the most powerful. . . . For with all these he will be exploiting the power of others so as to accomplish his own purpose. This is not possible without the theoretical sciences, without the greatest of all deliberative virtues, and without the rest of those things that are in the philosopher. . . . So let it be clear to you that the idea of the Philosopher, Supreme Ruler, Prince, Legislator, and Imām is but a single idea.[53]

A Sulṭān of India who for his contemporaries and for later generations came near to incarnating the ideal of a medieval Muslim monarch was Fīrūz Shāh of the Tughluq dynasty, who ruled from A.H. 752/A.D. 1351 to his death in A.H. 790/A.D. 1388. He was a great builder and a champion of Sunnī orthopraxy, he came to power after a tyrant spendthrift and restored justice and prosperity, he was charitable and a patron of learning and piety; he had all the admired virtues but one—for he was an incompetent general. Probably conscious of this, he compiled a list of the blessings of his reign, had it inscribed in the dome of the mosque of his capital at Delhi, and entitled it his "victories" (Futūḥāt). It is an appealing testimony by a pious ruler. Although the Muslims of India remembered him as an almost perfect king, his case illustrates the maxim that the ruler who appears perfect to one age may not appear so to another. His mildness led to feudalistic tendencies among the ruling class, and serious loss of revenues. Corruption flourished in the state by the end of his reign, and the vigor of the military class on which the Sulṭānate depended for its existence in Hindustān was undermined by peace and ease, so that it fell easy prey to Tīmūr's invasion only ten years later.

The Record of an Ideal Sulṭān
from the Victories of Fīrūz Shāh
Fīrūz Shāh Tughluq (d. A.H. *790/*A.D. *1388)*

Praises without end, and infinite thanks to that merciful Creator who gave to me, His poor abject creature Fīrūz son of Rajab, his impulse for the maintenance of the laws of His religion, for the repression of heresy, and the prevention of things forbidden. My desire is that, to the best of my human power, I should recount and pay my thanks for the many blessings He has bestowed on me, so that I may be found among the number of His grateful servants.

1. In the reigns of former kings the blood of many Muslims had been shed, and many varieties of torture practised. Amputation of hands and feet, ears and noses; tearing out of the eyes, pouring molten lead into the throat, crushing the bones of the hands and feet with mallets, burning the body with fire, driving iron nails into the hands, feet, and bosom, cutting the sinews, sawing men asunder; these and many similar tortures were practised. The great and merciful God made me, His servant, hope and seek for His mercy by devoting myself to prevent the unlawful killing of Muslims, and the infliction of torture (so that) whoever transgressed the Law should receive the punishment prescribed by the Book and the decrees of judges.

2. The repetition of the names and titles of former sovereigns had been omitted from the prayers on (Fridays) and Feasts. The names of those sovereigns of Islam had fallen into neglect and oblivion.

So I decreed that their names and titles should be rehearsed in the *khuṭba,* and aspirations offered for the remission of their sins.

3. In former times they used to collect frivolous, unlawful, and unjust cesses at the public treasury. I had these abolished. . . . The money received in the public treasury should be derived from sources recognised by the Sacred Law: first the *kharāj* or tenth from cultivated lands, then the zakāt or alms, then the jizya or poll tax on Hindus and other separatists, then the *khums* or fifth of the spoil (of war) and of (the produce of) mines. No tax unauthorized by the declarations of the Book should be received in the public treasury.

4. Before my time, in repressing infidelity four-fifths of the spoil was appropriated to the public treasury and one-fifth was given to the captors, but the rule of the Law is (exactly the contrary). To prevent these irregularities I decreed that one-fifth should be taken by the State, and four-fifths given to the captors.

5. The sect of the Shīʿā, also called Rāfiḍīs, had endeavoured to make proselytes, and traduced and denied the first (caliphs). I seized them all and I convicted them of their errors and perversions. On the most zealous I inflicted punishment, and the rest I visited with censure and threats. Their books I burnt in public, and so by the grace of God the influence of this sect was entirely suppressed.

6. There was a sect of heretics (*mulḥid*) who labored to seduce the people into heresy and schism. They met by night. Wine was served and they said that this was their religious worship. They brought their (womenfolk) to these meetings (and had promiscuous intercourse with them). I cut off the heads of the elders of this sect, and imprisoned and banished the rest, so that their abominable practices were put an end to.

7. (Punishment of a sect of Muslims who worshipped their leader.)

8. (Killing of a man who claimed to be the Mahdī.)[This and Article 7 will be found in Chapter 4.]

9. A person had set himself up as a *shaykh* in the province of Gujarat, and used to say "*Ana al-Ḥaqq*" ("I am the Truth"). He commanded his disciples to say "Thou art, thou art!" He further said "I am the king who dies not." The charges being proved, I condemned him to punishment, and his book I ordered to be burnt, so that his (corruption) might be prevented from spreading among the faithful people of Islam.

10. A custom unauthorized by the Law of Islam had sprung up in

Muslim cities. On holy days women went out of the city to the tombs. Rakes took the opportunity for improper and riotous actions. Under pain of exemplary punishment now, thanks to the great God, no lady or respectable Muslim woman can go out on pilgrimage to the tombs. The practice has been entirely stopped.

11. The Hindus and idol–worshippers had agreed to pay the money for toleration (dhimma) and had consented to pay the poll–tax (jizya) in return for which they and their families enjoyed security. These people now erected new idol–temples in the city and environs in opposition to the Law of the Prophet. Under Divine guidance I destroyed these edifices and I killed those leaders of infidelity who seduced others into error. I forbade any chastisement of the Hindus in general, but I destroyed their idol–temples, and in place thereof raised mosques. Where infidels and idolators once worshipped idols, Muslims now, by God's mercy, perform their devotions to the true God. Others were restrained by threats and punishments as a warning to all men that no *dhimmī* could follow such wicked practises in a Muslim country.

12. It had been the practise in former times to use vessels of gold and silver at the royal table, and sword–belts ornamented with gold and jewels. I forbade these things, and commanded that only such should be used as are recognised by the Law.

13. In former times it had been the custom to use ornamented garments, and figures were painted and displayed upon all articles and utensils. I ordered all pictures and portraits to be removed from these things, and that such articles only should be made as are approved by the Law. Those pictures on the doors and walls of palaces I ordered to be effaced.[54]

14. Before this, most of the garments of the great were of silk and gold thread, contrary to the Law. By the grace of the All–Praised, the All–High, my order was given that such should be worn as are approved by the Law of Muḥammad, on whom be peace and God's blessing, and all that was unprescribed, unpermitted, forbidden or opposed to the Law was discarded. Praise be to God for Islam.

15. One of the gifts of God to me, His humble servant was His assistance to raise charitable buildings. Thus I built many mosques and madrasas and dervish—convents, that 'ulamā', shaykhs, ascetics and devotees might truly worship the Adored One, and aid the pious builder by their prayers. And I dug canals and planted trees and gave endowments of land, for it is in accordance with the Law,

and in the Community of Islam the 'ulamā' of the Law are in complete agreement, so there is no doubt or hesitation about it, that allotments should be made to them in proportion to their expenditures, so that income may always come to God's servants. The details are mentioned in our registers of *waqfs*.

16. Another of God's gifts was that I was led to repair edifices and structures of those past, the ancient kings and former princes, which from the passage of days and the march of years had fallen into decay, and I gave the repair and restoration of these preference over my own buildings.

As the Friday mosque of Old Delhi, which was built by Sulṭān Mu'izz al-Dīn Sām of Ghūr, had come to need repair and rebuilding, I repaired it so that it stood like new.

The tomb of this Sulṭān I restored.

The Quṭb Minaret, built under him, which had been struck by lightning, I made better than before, by raising it higher than it had been.

The tank of Sulṭān Iletmish had been deprived of water by irreligious men who cut the supply. I punished these presumptuous and unpreserving fellows severely, and opened the channels again.

The tank of Sulṭān 'Alā' al-Din had filled up and gone dry, so that some people of the town carried on cultivation in it, and dug wells in it and sold the water of the wells. After a generation, I cleared it out, so that this great reservoir might again be filled from year to year.

The buildings of the madrasa of Sulṭān Shams al-Din Iletmish, God be pleased with him, which had fallen into decay, I rebuilt, and gave it doors of sandalwood, and the columns in his tomb which had fallen down I replaced with even better ones. In the dome, a staircase of hewn stone was added, and in the four towers, supports of masonry.

The tomb of Sulṭān Mu'izz al-Dīn son of Iletmish at Malikpūr had become so overgrown that one could say it was no longer to be seen; and I built up anew the dome, terrace and enclosure walls with masonry. At the tomb of Sulṭān Rukn al-Dīn son of Iletmish at Malikpūr I repaired the enclosure wall, added a new dome, and built a *khānqāh* for ṣūfīs.

The tomb of Sulṭān Jalāl al-Dīn I repaired and built a new monumental gate for it.

The tomb of Sulṭān 'Alā al-Dīn was repaired, and given doors of sandalwood. I repaired the walls of the foundation for drinking water, and repaired the *qibla* wall of the madrasa mosque, and the flagstone pavement.

I repaired and renovated the tombs of (all the family of) Sulṭān 'Alā' al-Dīn.

At the tomb of the Sulṭān of Shaykhs, Saint Niẓām al-Dīn the Chishtī, the beloved of God—God sanctify his mighty secret—I constructed doors and lattice work of sandalwood, and hung gold candelabra on gold chains in the four corners of the dome-chamber, and built a new *jamā'at-khāna* (congregational house), for before this there was none in that place.

At the tomb of Mālik Nā'ib Tāj al-Mulk Kāfūr, who had been the great wazīr of Sulṭān 'Alā' al-Dīn, wise and intelligent, who had taken many kingdoms where the horses of former Muslim kings had never set hoof, where he had caused the Friday sermon to be made in the name of Sulṭān 'Alā' al-Dīn, and who had had fifty-two thousand horsemen, his grave had been razed level with the earth, and his tomb laid low [by his successors.—Ed.] The tomb was completely reconstructed, for he was zealous for the state, and an honest man.

In the Dār al-Amān, the last couch and resting place of great men, I placed doors of sandalwood and on the tombs of these distinguished persons I put curtains and hangings. These repairs of tombs and colleges were paid for from their original waqfs, and in cases where no provision had already been made for purchase of carpets, lights and furnishings I assigned villages whose revenues would be used for this in perpetuity.

And I caused the city of Jahān Panāh, built by the divinely pardoned and forgiven late Sulṭān Muḥammad ibn Tughluq, my gracious patron, who had me educated and brought me up, to be restored.

All the fortifications which past Sulṭāns had built in the district of Delhi I had repaired.

17. (Endowing of madrasas, tombs and shrines.)

18. Also I was enabled by God's help to build the Dār al-Shifā, the House of Healing, where high or low, all who were suddenly taken ill or overcome with suffering might come. Physicians are in attendance to diagnose the illness, prescribe the cure and diet, and provide the medicines. The cost of the food and medicines is paid for by endowments, and all patients, whether residents or

travellers, humble or highborn, free or slave, resort there for treatment, and with God's blessing and mercy, they are cured.

19. Another gift given by the Majesty of the Lord of Might and Power to this His rebellious slave was that I arranged that the heirs of all those who in the time of the late Sulṭān Muḥammad, my lord and patron who nurtured me, had been fated to be killed, and those who had been deprived of their members, an eye, the nose, or a hand or a foot, should be reconciled to the late Sulṭān and appeased with gifts, so that they wrote deeds declaring their satisfaction, which were attested by witnesses, and sealed in a box and placed in the tomb of the divinely pardoned and forgiven Sulṭān beside his head, that God might be generous to him who was my master and nurtured me, and show him His mercy.

21. In former times, villages and estates and ancient patrimonies had been seized for the exchequer. I ordered that all who had claims to property should come forward in the court of the Law, and after one established his claim it was restored to him.

22. Another of the divine gifts to me has been that the lands and wealth of God's servants in my reign have been safe and secure, protected and guarded (from confiscation.) Men often whispered to me, "This merchant has so many hundred thousand, and that tax–official this many," but by reproof and punishment I made informers hold their tongues.

23. God disposed me to turn the hearts of *faqīrs* and ascetics to myself. Whenever I heard of a devotee or a religious recluse, I would go and visit him and ask for the help of his prayers, that I might gain the reward promised to the prince who visits the poor.

24. Whenever a person had finished his natural span of life, after providing for his necessities, I would advise him to busy himself in preparation for the world to come, and repent of any faults against the Law and religion in his youth.

25. When by God's decree one who had prestige and rank was taken from the house of this world to the Palace of Delights, I gave his employment and rank to his son, so that he might have the same place and rank and comfort as his father, and suffer no diminishing.

26. The greatest and best of the honors given this slave by the Sovereign Lord (glorified be His Majesty!) was that by obedience, sincerity, zeal for the State, and submission to the Caliph, the Prophet's cousin and successor, my Sulṭānate was confirmed with legitimacy, for no kingship is legal until it has submitted itself to

that lofty presence and received investiture from that sacred court. From the holy majesty of the Abode of the Caliphate [i.e. Mamlūk Cairo.—Ed.] diplomas were issued conveying upon me absolute powers as deputy of the Caliphate, and the Commander of Believers was graciously pleased to honor me with the title 'Lord of Sulṭāns' (*Sayyid al-Salāṭīn*). He also conferred upon me court robes of honor, a *taylasān*, a banner, a sword, a signet ring and stirrups as badges of honor and distinction.

My object in writing this was that I might mention at least one part in a thousand of the great blessings that have been given me, and express my gratitude for God's grace. And that those who desire to be good and happy may read this and know that this way has been approved, for there is a short maxim by observing which men may obtain guidance: "Men shall be judged according to their works, and rewarded for the good they have done."

The growing tradition of thirteen centuries is obviously not to be dispelled by a few years of modern statehood. The next selection, written in 1963 as an editorial in the *Journal* of al-Azhar, the great Muslim University in Egypt, by its editor Aḥmad Ḥasan Zayyāt, was first delivered as a speech before President 'Abd al-Nāṣir. It shows with great clarity how the longing for the archetypal perfect ruler is intensified by the bewilderments of modernity and the sense of departed but renascent glory. The image of the ruler desired by vast numbers of Muslims is still the traditional one; a man endowed with near-prophetic charisma, an enlightened military autocrat free of sin, perfectly just and wise, on whose power and term of office there can be no human limitation, because he is the executive of the Umma.

The endurance of this image is of course much more significant than the fact that it is identified here with this, there with that, frail mortal figure.

The Survival of the Traditional Ideal

from the Journal of al-Azhar, *January 1963*
by Aḥmad Ḥasan Zayyāt

Mr. President: There were three golden Arab periods in which science developed, literature flourished, civilization was refined, and life progressed: the age of al-Rashīd and his son al-Ma'mūn in Baghdad, the age of al-'Azīz and his son al-Ḥākim in Cairo, and the age of al-Nāṣir and his son al-Ḥakam in Cordoba. These three periods were landmarks in human progress. Yet they were branded with the mark of aristocracy, and their good scarcely went beyond the elite, the throne halls, the corridors of palaces and the offices of chancelleries, which abounded with men of learning, literature, art, and wisdom. As for the common people, they were herds to be sheared and milked; resources to be exploited, and only a limited amount of the excellence of those times reached them. At last God saw fit to send the Arabs a fourth golden age which should make up for the deficiencies of these earlier periods, and that was your age, Mr. President, in which were applied the principles of Islam, which had been understood but not believed in, or believed in but not applied. Now government is by mutual consultation, and the rule is just; sustenance is shared, men are equal, and the people rule.

Your age has been singled out as the age of the dignified man, the free citizen, the eager worker, the working scholar and the independent writer, and each of them feels today that he has rights he receives, duties he performs, sustenance to suffice, and a country to take pride in.

It is an age of peace, harmony, and unity, for you strive persistently for peace among nations, harmony among peoples, and unity among Arabs. In this you seek for yourself only what was sought by those who were sent before you with prophetic missions.

The light of your National Charter will expand in every soul and every country as does the Word of God, for it is the truth He has placed in His Holy Law, and the course He has prescribed for His creatures.

Mr. President, the same literature you honor this evening gave good news of your coming, prepared the way for you, and called for you. In August 1945 (my) magazine *al-Risāla* said, "Our infirmity is that our statesmen and leaders are all men of words, not men of deeds, and men of the pen rather than of the sword; of the forces of law, rather than of the forces of action; cultivated in the research of books, and trained at the desks of government offices; deprived of military training, which alone can provide planning, order, command, efficiency, sacrifice and honor." In April 1940, it said "There are signs which prepare the way and point to the man who is awaited by the Arab Umma. Some of the signs preparing for his appearance are the dissolution of morality, and the lack of cohesion between words and deeds; hearts sundered from each other, attached neither to homeland nor to religion; selfishness of spirits, such that they are pure neither in friendship nor in family ties; wildness of passions such as may be controlled neither by gentleness nor severity. Of the signs indicating his presence will be that he will be for others, not for himself; his Umma will be before his family, and his humanity will be after his nationalism. What will confirm these signs will be that the 'I' will die on his tongue and live in his conscience; his own existence will be united in his mind with that of his people. He will feel their pains because in them unite all his feelings. He will perceive their shortcomings because his mind is fully conscious of them. He will possess the leadership because he is the manifestation of their will. In the loftiness of his soul and the purity of his desire, he will be above the sins of mankind and the filth of the earth. He will not be greedy, because his goals are far from this world; he will not hate, because his concerns are above enmity. He will not play favorites because his merit is above clannishness. He will say and do nothing that does not accord with the religion he holds, the principles he supports, the people he heads. In the sagacity of his mind, the serenity of his heart, the steadfastness of his character, the width of his concern, he will triumph over circumstances and rise above obstructions. He will not bring an idea to maturity without enacting it, he will not aim without hitting the mark, or meditate a desire without achieving it. . . .

"O God, our wandering has carried us through the unknown parts of the earth for generations, and the belief in life has degenerated in us to opinion. When shall we end this wandering as did Moses, so that we may attain the forefront of active life as did Muḥammad? Lord, send us the shepherd who will drive away the wolf, the thread that will bind love, the guide who will carry the lamp, the leader to raise high the banner, the teacher who will instruct us how to manufacture the needle and the cannon, to dig the mine and the field, to reconcile religion and the world, to unite the private interest and the public good; all this, O God, united in one man, most similar to the awaited Mahdī and the promised Christ."

All this, Mr. President, the *Risāla* foretold twelve years before your blessed revolution. The prophecy has come true, and the prayer has been answered.[55]

NOTES

1. Sir Thomas Arnold. *The Caliphate.* Oxford, 1924. p. 45.

2. Alfred Guillaume. *The Life of Muḥammad.* Oxford, 1955. pp. 684–87.

3. Majlisī, *Hayyāt al-Qulūb.* Translated by James Merrick. Boston, 1850. p. 334. (Here abridged by editor.)

4. Ibid. p. 339.

5. Tabrīzī. *Mishkāt al-Maṣābiḥ.* Karachi, 1367/1948. pp. 318–23. (Editor's translation.)

6. Bukhārī. Book 93, Chap. 51, no. 6. (Editor's translation.)

7. Abū Yūsuf. *Kitāb al-Kharāj.* Cairo, 1352/1933. pp. 11–16. (Editor's translation, here abridged.) Also available in a French translation by E. Fagnan.

8. Ibn 'Abd Rabbihi. *Al-'Iqd al-Farīd.* Cairo, 1953. Bk. I, pp. 25–26. (Editor's translation.)

9. Abū Yūsuf. *op. cit.* pp. 16–17.

10. Sir Lewis Pelly (translator). *The Miracle Play of Hasan and Husayn.* London, 1879. Book II, pp. 100–103. (Here abridged.)

11. Abū Yūsuf. *op. cit.* pp. 3–6, (Editor's translation, here abridged.)

12. *Kitāb al-Tāj.* Cairo, 1914. p. 5. (Editor's translation, here abridged.) Also in French translation by Ch. Pellat.

13. Ibid. pp.7–9.

14. Ibid. pp. 11–20.

15. Ibid. pp. 21–43.

16. Ibid. pp. 123–29.

17. Ibid. pp. 153–54.

18. Māwardī. *al-Aḥkām al-Sulṭānīya.*

19. Quṭb al-Dīn al-Nahrawālī. *Kitāb al-I'lam bi A'lām Bayt Allāh al-Harām.* Leipzig, 1857. Edited by Wüstenfeld. pp. 168–69. (Editor's translation.)

20. Ibn Jamā'a Taḥrīr. *al-Aḥkām fi Tadbīr Ahl al-Islām.* In *Islamica,* vol. VI, pp. 349–414. Edited by Kofler, with a German translation in vol. VII, pp. 1–64.

21. Ibn Khaldūn. *Muqaddimah.* Translated by Franz Rosenthal. London, 1958. vol. I, pp. 385–88.

22. Ibid. pp. 392–93.

23. Ibid. p. 449.

24. 'Allāma al-Hillī. *al-Bābu-l Hādī 'Ashar.* Translated by Wm. McElwee Miller. London, 1928. pp. 62–81. (Here abridged.)

25. Niẓām al-Mulk. *The Book of Government,* or *Rules for Kings.* Translated from the Persian by Hubert Darke. London, 1960. pp. 9–11. (Abridged here and following.)

26. Ibid. pp. 13–14.

27. Ibid. p. 23.

28. Ibid. pp. 32–33.

29. Ibid. p. 44.

30. Ibid. p. 49.

31. Ibid. p. 78.

32. Ibid. pp. 92–93.

33. Ibid. pp. 97–98.
34. Ibid. pp. 102–105.
35. Ibid. pp. 121–22.
36. Ibid. pp. 125–27.
37. Ibid. p. 132.
38. Ibid. p. 135.
39. Ibid. pp. 143–44.
40. Ibid. pp. 152–61.
41. Ibid. p. 163.
42. Ibid. pp. 165–66.
43. Ibid. pp. 185.
44. Ibid. pp. 193–94.
45. Kay Kā'ūs ibn Iskandar. *A Mirror for Princes*. Translation of the *Qābūs–Nāma* by Reuben Levy. London, 1951. p. 3.
46. Ibid. p. 35.
47. Ibid. p. 88.
48. Ibid. p. 129.
49. Ibid. pp. 222–36. (Here abridged.)
50. Ibn al–Ṭiqṭiqā'. *al–Fakhrī*. Cairo, 1927. pp. 3–18. (Editor's translation and abridgement.)
51. *al–Fakhrī*. Translated by Whitting. London, 1947. pp. 31–68. (Here abridged.)
52. al–Farābī. *Fuṣūl al–Madanī*. Translated by D. M. Dunlop as *Aphorisms of the Statesman*. Cambridge, 1961, pp 27–51. (Here abridged.)
53. From *The Attainment of Happiness*. Translated by Muḥsin Mahdī in *Alfarābī's Philosophy of Plato and Aristotle*. New York, 1962. pp. 46–47.
54. The text through No. 13 is abridged from the translation found (pp. 378–89) in Vol. II of Elliot and Dowson's *The History of India, as told by its own Historians: The Muḥammadan Period* (London, 1867–77). As the text Elliot used was corrupt in the latter half, I have used the Persian edition of *Futūhāt–i Fīrūz Shāhī* (Aligarh 1954) to emend the sections following.
55. Aḥmad Ḥasan al–Zayyāt. In *Majallat al–Azhar*. Vol. 34 (January, 1963). pp. 573–75.

The Will of God

CHAPTER 3

The Will of God

From the Qur'ān:

O ye who have believed, eat of the good things wherewith We have provided you, and give thanks to God, if it is Him you serve. He has only forbidden carrion, blood, and the flesh of swine, and what has been dedicated to other than God. Yet if anyone is forced, without craving or transgressing, then no sin is on him; surely God is most forgiving, most compassionate. (2:172–173)

O believers, ordained for you is retaliation for the slain: freeman for freeman, slave for slave, female for female. Yet if somewhat is forgiven a man by his brother, then prosecution according to good usage, and payment to him in kindliness. That is a lightening and a mercy from your Lord, and for him who transgresses after that, there is a painful torment. (2:177–178)

O believers, devour not usury, doubled and re–doubling, but fear God; haply you may prosper. And fear the Fire that is prepared for the unbelievers. Obey God and the Messenger; so you may find mercy. Run the race for the forgiveness of your Lord, and a paradise wide as the heavens and the earth, prepared for those who fear God, who give alms in prosperity and in hardship, who restrain their rage and pardon the offences of others; for God loves those who do good; who, when they commit an indecency or wrong themselves remember God, and ask pardon for their sins—and who shall pardon sin but God?—persevering not in what they did wittingly. Those—their recompense is forgiveness from their Lord, and gardens beneath which rivers flow, wherein they shall abide forever; excellent the wage of the laborers! (3:130—136)

This is a declaration for mankind, and guidance, and admonition for those who fear God. Be not faint, neither sorrow; you shall be the upper ones, if you are believers. (3:138–139)

He has prescribed for you of religion what He charged Noah with, and what We have revealed to you, and what We charged Abraham with, and Moses, and Jesus: to perform the religion and scatter not in it. (42:13)

He is the All–creating, the All–knowing; His order when He wills a thing is to say to it "Be," and it is. So glory be to Him, in whose hand is the dominion of every thing, unto whom you shall be returned. (36:82)

God's is the kingdom of the heavens and the earth; He forgives whom He will, and He torments whom He will, and God is most forgiving, most compassionate. (48:14)

He who is guided is guided only for himself, and he who is led astray is only led against himself; none shall bear the burden of another. We use not to cause torment until We have sent a Messenger. When We desire to cause a city to perish, We give commands to those who dwell at ease therein, and they commit wickedness. Then the Word against it is justified, and We utterly destroy it. How many of the generations after Noah We have caused to perish! Your Lord is a match for the sins of his servants: He is perfectly aware, all–seeing. He who desires this hasty world, We hasten therein for him what We desire, and We appoint for him Hell; he shall roast therein condemned, rejected. And he who desires the life to come, and strives after it as he should, being a believer—each have had their striving thanked. (17:15–19)

He whom God desires to guide, He makes wide his breast for Islam, and he whom God desires to lead astray. He makes his breast tight, narrow, as if he were climbing to the sky. (6:125)

They say, those who commit idolatry, "If God had willed, we should have served naught but Him; we and our forefathers, and we would have forbidden naught without Him." Thus did those who were before them: yet is there anything for the Messengers except to deliver the clear message? Surely We have sent to every community a Messenger saying "Serve God and eschew idols." And some of them God guided, and to some of them error was charged. Journey therefore in the land, and see how was the requital of those who cried that it was lies. Though you be ever so eager for their guiding, God guides not those whom He leads astray; for them there are no helpers. (16:35–37)

FULFILLING THE WILL OF GOD

The Qur'ān is replete with references to God's commanding and forbidding certain actions. The Community is called into being to do the will of God, and so the study of the Law is the characteristic activity of Islamic scholarship. God commands: Islam is commitment to His will. By the fourth century of the Hijra, the scholars had produced well defined systems of Law, based on the Qur'ān and the Ḥadīth.

The implementation of the Sharī'a, the Law, is of course first of all the affair of the ruler, to whom the Community gave extraordinary powers. Yet, though he might be treated as if he were perfect, few rulers—as we have seen—were so in fact. Extraordinary powers all too often led to extraordinarily arbitrary behaviour. In this case, the implementation of the Law became the task of the scholars of the Sharī'a. A scholar of Seville, Ibn 'Abdūn, put it clearly, and somewhat plaintively, in the late eleventh century A.D.

On the Prince

from a Treatise on Implementation of the Law
by Muḥammad ibn Aḥmad ibn 'Abdūn of Seville,
(fl. ca. A.H. *473–505/*A.D. *1080–1110)*

It is necessary first of all to look into the conditions of the prince, who is the pole, like the center of a circumference which cannot be harmonious, perfect in its periphery, and sound, unless the center is well fixed and sound. He is also like the faculty of the intelligence in man: if that in him is sound, then his views and opinions will be fair and weighty. By the righteousness of the prince, mankind becomes righteous, and by his corruption all order is corrupted.

It is incumbent on the men of learning and religion first of all to look into his character and examine carefully his words and deeds; whether he inclines to the world and ease and vanity and pays little attention to the necessary conduct of affairs in his country or to looking after his subjects and all the Muslims, or whether he is harsh-tempered, easily angered, quick to quarrel, a man of force and violence; in such a case, one must behave kindly with him, and handle him adroitly, and cause him gradually to love the good and strive for it and take it for his own, and mention in his presence that the lower world does not endure for any man, and has destroyed past generations and previous communities, and in the course of stories and historical anecdotes, to weave in admonitions which will burn the soul. It is for the men of learning to transmit from books of the prophets this and that about fatal catastrophes which occurred to long-past peoples—all this in a gentle and politic way. This is a part of one's obligation to give him good counsel, for if the men of learning and religion do not treat with him thus, he will perish and the Muslims will perish with him.

It is not necessary to follow him in his ways and his wilful inclination to worldly things not pleasing to God, for every prince or jurist who does not live by the Law (*nāmūs*) dies by the Law. This is what the prophets—God's benediction be upon them—used to do: to terrify people with threats of God's punishment and the Balance, until they despaired and their livers burned from what they heard, and then to comfort them with talk of God's generosity and mercy and forgiveness, and what God has promised in Paradise.

It is necessary always to so mention the good as to make it seem fair to the prince, and to make evil deeds appear ugly, while he should exert himself to look into the affairs of his people personally, and watch over the marches and fortify the frontiers against his enemies, and curb tyranny and assaults upon the people, as well as excess and excuses for it, and not entrust that to his chamberlain or ministers, lest one of them conceal or disguise the facts to him, for that would ruin his affairs, destroy love for him, and dissolve the order of his realm.

And if the prince by his character, his acts, and his aspirations shows that he loves the good and those who love it, and is attached to the Law, he shall find rest and give rest. That will be a great blessing for him. But where shall one find such a prince? Where indeed?[1]

Here Ibn 'Abdūn touches on a notable feature of much Islamic historiography: the use of history for didactic purposes. And if history did not seem to reflect the will of God, it could be made to seem to reflect it. History in the service of morality rather than of truth produced many edifying distortions of fact, particularly in books of belles lettres and counsel. Behind this, of course, lay a conviction that the actions of individuals are deeply interesting, and that God is the Lord of events, even when these were forced to conform to rigid patterns. An example from al-Ghazālī's *Counsel for Kings*, written for a Saljūq Sulṭān around 1105 A.D., will suffice.

The Example of the Ruler
from Counsel for Kings
by Abū Ḥāmid al-Ghazālī (d. A.H. *505/*A.D. *1111)*

Muḥammad ibn al-Faḍl said, "I did not know that the activities of the people depend on the activities of the Sulṭān of the epoch. However," he continued, "in the reign of Walīd ibn 'Abd al-Malik, the people concerned themselves with planting gardens and orchards and building houses, and in the reign of Sulaymān ibn 'Abd al-Malik with eating well—they used to ask one another, 'What have you cooked?' and 'What have you eaten?' Whereas in the reign of 'Umar ibn 'Abd al-'Azīz the people concerned themselves wholly with serving God, reciting the Qur'ān, giving charity and doing good works." In view of this, you will understand that the people in every epoch choose to do as their Sulṭān does. Now every individual's nature contains envy, ambition, spite, cupidity, and love of pleasure; and when people get a (free) hand from kings they indulge their desires, but when a king is right-minded they likewise repress these things and cease indulging their desires—as I heard in the following story. In the days of Anūshīrvān the Just, a certain man bought a house from another man and found a (hoard) of treasure in it. He immediately went to the seller and told him, "You sold me such and such a place, and the things which are in it are yours." There was a long dispute between them, and they went to Anūshīrvān. "Do you have children?" he asked. One of them replied, "I have a son," and the other, "I have a daughter." Then the king said, "Become kinsmen forthwith, so that it may belong to you both and to your children also." This they did, and they were well satisfied with each other.

Now what would you say if those two men had lived in the days of an unjust Sulṭān? Each would have asserted that the treasure was his own property. But because they knew that their king was just, they strove to be honest.[2]

Modern Muslim writers often make the point that in Islam there is no theoretical distinction between church and state, and the observation is certainly true. Nonetheless, because of the inevitable tendency of rulers to abuse their enormous powers, there did develop a marked practical distinction between the religious scholars, or 'ulamā', and the court and military class. Rulers to some extent bridged the gap by their control of teaching and legal posts, and by endowments. While the 'ulamā' were not priests, they formed a clerical class, and many of them were implacably suspicious of the state. While the early history of the Community and its factional divisions had meant that some religious men sometimes opposed some ruler, development of the 'ulamā' class seems to have been concurrent with the development of the ruling institutions, and began in the heyday of 'Abbāsī autocracy. The same Ghazālī who counselled kings shows well in his counsels to Muslims the ambivalent attitude of the medieval 'ulamā' toward the ruler. He uses very doubtful ḥadīths here, and his anecdotes are tendentious and distorted, but they no doubt reflect what he and other pious 'ulamā' thought.

On Visiting Princes
from Revivification of the Sciences of Religion
by Abū Hāmid al-Ghazālī (d. A.H. *505/*A.D. *1111)*

Know that you can have three sorts of relations with princes, governors, and oppressors. The first and worst is that you visit them, the second and better is that they visit you, and the third and surest that you stay far from them, so that neither you see them nor they see you.

As for visiting them, it is severely reproved in the Law and there are reproofs and threats for it in both the Ḥadīth and the examples of the pious forefathers. Abū Hurayra relates that the Messenger of God, may God bless him and give him peace, said: "The best princes are those whom the 'ulamā' visit, and the worst 'ulamā' are those who visit the princes." There is also the ḥadīth "The 'ulamā' are God's trustees for the servants of God, so long as they do not mix with the rulers, and if they do that, they have betrayed the prophets; beware of them and stay far from them." It was related by Anas.

As to the examples of the forefathers, Hudhayfa said "Beware the occasions of temptation!" They asked him "What are they?" and he replied "The doors of princes, where you may enter to agree with them on lies and say what you do not mean." Sufyān al-Thawrī said "In Hell there is a valley entirely inhabited by Qur'ān readers who used to visit kings."

Muḥammad ibn Salāma said "A fly on a pile of excrement is finer than a Qur'ān reader at the door of those people."

These ḥadīths and anecdotes show what temptations and sorts of corruption there are in frequenting kings. However, we shall analyze this and look into it from a legal point of view, to distinguish the forbidden from the disapproved and the permitted. We may say that one who enters the ruler's presence is exposed, because he will offend God either by act or silence or speaking or credulity: he cannot avoid one of these matters.

If anyone says "The early Muslim 'ulamā' used to visit the rulers," I reply: "Yes. First learn how they did it, and then do it." It is told that Hishām ibn 'Abd al-Malik (the Umawī caliph) went on pilgrimage to Mecca and asked there for one of the Companions of the Prophet. "But Commander of the Believers!" they replied, "they have all passed away." "Then bring one who knew them," he said, so they brought him Ta'ūs the Yamanī. When he came in, he took off his sandals at the edge of the carpet, and did not call him "Commander of Believers," but said "Peace to you, Hishām," without even using his name of respect (*kunya*), and sat down in front of him, saying "How are you, Hishām?" Hishām was greatly enraged, and wanted to kill him, but they told him "You are in God's sanctuary, the sanctuary of His messenger. Such a thing is not possible!" Then he said "Ta'ūs, what possessed you, to do what you have done?" He replied "And what have I done?" Hishām's anger and irritation increased, and he said "You have taken off your sandals at the edge of my carpet, and not kissed my hand nor saluted me with my title or my name of respect, and then sat down in front of me without permission, and said, "How are you, Hishām?" Ta'ūs replied "I take off my sandals before the Lord of Majesty every day five times, and He does not punish me or grow angry with me. As to your hand, I heard 'Alī the Commander of Believers say—God be well pleased in him—'No man should kiss anyone's hand, unless it be that of his wife, in sensuality, or that of his child, in tenderness.' As for not calling you Commander of the Believers, not all the Believers accept your commands, and I hated to lie. As to the name of respect, God, exalted be He, addresses His prophets and friends simply as 'David,' 'John,' and 'Jesus,' and uses the name of respect for His enemies, saying 'Accursed is the hand of Abū Lahab' (111:1). As for sitting in front of you, I heard the Commander of Believers 'Alī, God be well pleased in him, say, 'If you want to see one of those who are for hellfire, find a man who sits and lets people stand around him.' " Hishām told him "Well, preach to me," and he said "I heard 'Alī, the Commander of Believers, God be pleased in him, say 'In Gehenna there are snakes like ranges of hills and scorpions like mules, to torment every prince who does not lead his flock aright.' "

And Sufyān al-Thawrī, God be pleased in him, said "Abū Ja'far Manṣūr (the second 'Abbāsī caliph) came to me on the pilgrimage at Minā and said 'Tell me what you need.' 'For you to fear God,' I told him. 'You have filled the earth with oppression and tyranny.' He hung his head, then raised it and said 'Tell me what you want.' I said 'You only came to this rank because of the Muḥājirīn and Anṣār (Meccans and Medinans) and now their descendants are starving. Fear God, and give them their due.' He hung his head, then raised it and said 'Tell me what *you* need.' I told him, 'When 'Umar ibn al-Khaṭṭāb made the pilgrimage, he asked his treasurer "What were our expenses?" and he said "Almost ten pieces of silver." But here I see wealth that many camels could not carry.' Then he went away."

That was how they kept company with rulers, when they had to—at the risk of their lives, for they stood for God against oppression.[3]

The great poet-saint of Anatolia, Jalāl al-Dīn Rūmī (d. A.H 623/A.D. 1273) had a less paradoxical view of relations with the ruler, but with a characteristically Ṣūfī proviso: the motives of the religious scholar who assisted a prince must be pure.

On Visiting Princes
from What is in It is in It
by Jalāl al-Dīn Rūmī (d. A.H. *623/*A.D. *1273)*

When the scholar has not become qualified with learning on account of princes but rather his learning from first to last has been for the sake of God; when his way and wont have been upon the path of rectitude because it is in his nature so to comport himself and he cannot do otherwise—just as a fish can only live and thrive in water—such a scholar is subject to the control and direction of reason. All men living in his time are held in check by the awe of him and derive succour from the reflection of his countenance, whether they are aware of the fact or no. If such a scholar goes formally to visit the prince, it is himself who is visited, and the prince is the visitor, because in every case the prince takes from him and receives help from him. That scholar is independent of the prince. . . . His trade is giving: he dispenses and does not receive.[4]

The religious scholars who maintained closest association with the ruler were the qāḍīs, the judges. In point of fact, they were the sovereign's appointees and representatives, for the first qāḍīs seem to have been simply administrative assistants to the governors of the provinces. With the development of accepted legal procedures, however, judging became a special profession. The 'Abbāsīs made a point of conciliating religious men by appointing them as qāḍīs, and the development of the class of 'ulamā' meant that qāḍīs were virtually always members of that class, while the process of the sacralization of legal procedures was greatly assisted.

Among the purist 'ulamā' the qāḍīship, with its opportunities for bribes and its dependence on the rulers, was a suspect office. And when better men avoided the responsibility, the way was open for incompetent opportunists to pursue the post for very worldly reasons. Nonetheless, since the qāḍī applied the Law in the Community, his office helped to bridge the divine and the temporal orders.

One of the most frequently cited texts detailing the duties of the qāḍī was the supposed letter of 'Umar to Abū Mūsa al-Ash'arī, a Companion whom, according to story, 'Umar made a qāḍī. While the document is certainly a forgery of 'Abbāsī times, it was as much the expression of an ideal for later generations as a genuine letter.

On the Duties of the Qāḍī
from the supposed letter of 'Umar I to Abū Mūsā al-Ash'arī
early third/ninth century (?)

'Umar ibn al-Khaṭṭāb—God be pleased in him—wrote a letter to Abū Mūsā al-Ash'arī in which was the following:

"In the name of God, the Merciful, the Compassionate, from the servant of God 'Umar, Commander of the Believers, to 'Abdallāh ibn Qays (Abū Mūsā): Peace be upon you. As to the rest, qāḍīship consists of applying either a clear injunction (of the Qur'ān) or a practise which is followed. Understand this when cases are put before you, for it is useless to discuss rights which are not valid.

"Make all Muslims equal in your sessions and in your sight, so that the highborn will not expect your favor, and the weak will not despair of your justice.

"The plaintiff must adduce evidence, and if the defendant denies, he must take an oath. Compromise between the parties is permissible, unless it makes the forbidden lawful, or the lawful forbidden. If you have given a decision, and then reconsidered and come to a better decision, the first decision must not impede you from returning to what is right, for nothing may invalidate what is right. Know that this is better than persistence in error.

"Use your understanding for the matters which perplex your heart for which there is neither a Qur'ānic text nor any precedent (sunna). Know the similarities and like cases, and then make an analogy after that and base yourself on what is most pleasing to God and appears to you to be what is right.

"Appoint a fixed term for a man who has a claim brought against him while he is absent; after that, if proofs are given against him, allow the claim; otherwise it is permissible to give judgement against the plaintiff.

"All Muslims may be legal witnesses except those who have been flogged for an offense which carries a Qur'ānic punishment, or have had false witness proved against them, or are suspect on grounds of their friendship or kinship to the parties. God must judge the secrets of the heart; He leaves you to judge the evidence.

"Beware of displaying fatigue and weariness and annoyance in the place of justice, wherein God allows you to win a reward and earn good pay at the same time. For when a man has a clear conscience as to what is between him and God, God makes good what is between him and others, but whoever adorns himself in the eyes of the world with false pretences, God will mar him. Peace be to you."[5]

Ibn 'Abdūn, the qāḍī of eleventh century Seville, goes into detail on the duties of a qāḍī, and how he can best conduct himself with the ruler and be effective in his position.

On the Duties of the Qāḍī
from a Treatise on Implementation of the Law
by Muḥammad ibn 'Abdūn of Seville
(fl. ca. A.H. *473–505/*A.D. *1080–1110)*

The qāḍī—may God stay him!—should be prudent in speech, decisive of manner, sure in his judgements, respected by commoners, prince and public alike. He must be knowledgeable in God's Law, for judgement is the scale of God's justice on the earth to divide the oppressor from the oppressed, to take the part of the weak against the strong, and to institute God's prescribed punishments according to right practices.

He should not be swayed by personal desires, nor should he be familiar with the jurists or the bailiffs, for embarrassments may come of it. As the poet says,

> Beware your enemy, and thousandfold when 'ware your friend;
> Full many a friend has changed to one most skilled in harms.

Thus he should see to it that none of them is familiar with him in word or deed, so that he loses in consideration and his orders are slighted and his position alters so that his sentences are changed by addition of some word or act and people come to despise him. In that case, the religion will be undermined, and the conduct of both worlds will be corrupted.

His orders too must be firmly established, and he should never act hastily in word or deed, but only after having formed an opinion, reached a decision, and then looked at the matter from the point of view of his own afterlife. He should not take frequent vacations or incline to ease, for it will be held against him. Rather, he should be resolute and apply himself, and consider that he belongs totally to God's service, exactly as if he were on a holy war, or in a military convent (*ribāṭ*) or on a pilgrimage. God—be He exalted—has said, "Truly the believers are brothers: therefore set things right between your brethren and fear God, and so you may find mercy." (49:10).

The qāḍī should be of a merciful disposition, clement and gentle, and compassionate to the Muslims, a man of urbanity, learning, and good repute, and he should not delegate his authority to others, for that opens the way to its corruption, and people may prefer his delegate and he himself may be esteemed lightly and not respected, while his appointee may create a great opposition to him, particularly if he is susceptible to bribery, is careless, or lacks experience. This will not be so, if he appoints an arbitrator (*ḥākim*) who is also learned, beneficent and well-to-do, to judge petty cases of the common people, but with no competence over the disposition of property, or the affairs of orphans, or affairs of the ruler and the governors.

Every day two jurists should sit with him in turn for consultation.

This will be serviceable to the people and more efficient and just for judgement. He may then examine their opinions, and accept or reject them. These jurisconsults should never be more than four: two in the qāḍī's office and two in the cathedral mosque [often used for hearing cases.—Ed.] each day in their turn. Any who do not accept this disposition should be deposed. None of them should be consulted in his own house, for at one time he may easily be absent, at another time be napping, or relaxing, or diverting himself, and not care for visitors, while the work to be done increases and the time for it grows shorter: does a healthy man feel the pain of the sick person? It also becomes an occasion for devouring the public treasury with (costs of) the cases, and the page will say, "I was walking with him all day, and he only gave me so much! Let the jurists also be responsible for my fees!" So then the page will become both a seeker and a plaintiff! Thus consultation in the houses of the jurists and going to see them (there) is a great abuse.

Neither the qāḍī, the judge or the muḥtasib should employ bailiffs who are easily irritated, drinkers, or violent, or babblers, talkative persons, or quibblers. That must be amended; such people are rascals. None of them should be allowed to speak to a woman, except one who is virtuous, continent, and advanced in age, for it is an occasion for bribes, suspicion, and rascality. And if he is young, the first thing he will do is try to entice her, to awake desire in her and seduce her. Matters go much better when the judge attends carefully to this matter, and puts an end to it altogether. The qāḍī should look carefully into the affair of female plaintiffs, and take charge of it, for when they have need of his offices, they are exposed. Thus he should not continue his work and leave them to sit so that men stare at them.

As for advocates who plead cases for others, they should be suppressed, for they find many pretexts to devour the wealth of the people with deceit. Whoever makes use of one of them only does it to change a wrong to a benefit, making all of his sweet speeches to flatter and lie and disguise matters to the judge. If they are used at all, let it be the minimum possible, and only such as are known for continence, virtue, piety, and learning, who do not drink or take bribes, and these are qualities not to be found in them! None shall plead the case of a woman, for thus he has access to her to speak with her, and the first thing he will do for her is seduce her and then lengthen her case so as to have access to her. I have seen with my own eyes those who boasted openly of such affairs, and I have heard them.

The arbitrator should not give judgement in his house, but in the chief mosque or some other suitable place. He should present himself each day at the qāḍī's sitting, and consult him on the more important matters, so that the qāḍī may have some control over him and look into his matter, and review his judgements and his procedures.

The qāḍī should be able at any time to summon a minister of the government and ask him to visit him at morning and evening. In this way he will have a certain control of him and receive respect from him, so that he does not say something in the ruler's presence which has harm in it for the Muslims. Thus (the qāḍī) can settle matters with (the minister) before he takes them up with the ruler, and if the ruler takes up something with the minister the qāḍī can know about it to arrange his affair. By frequent visits of the minister to the qāḍī some of the ruler's roughness can be mitigated.

If the qāḍī knows that the minister is two–faced, he should observe him closely and counsel the ruler to replace him, for he damages himself and him whom he serves by bad intentions.

As a matter of policy, the qāḍī should arrange to be ill from time to time and make excuses, and see to it that the minister counsels the ruler to visit him, so that the public may see this and respect for the qāḍī be increased among the people and among the officials. If the qāḍī sees that one of the ministers seeks to harm him or is jealous of him, he should visit him in his house and consult him for his opinion in some matter he has arranged beforehand, to soften him and quiet him and his envy, so that his enmity may become friendship. When the minister sees this, he will surely visit the qāḍī in return. This is an action that it hurts no intelligent, prudent, or sagacious man to perform; I mean, that if he sees the face of evil, he repels it by a stratagem and courtesy, and if he sees the face of good, he attracts it to himself by such procedures.[6]

The distrust of advocates and lawyers shown by Ibn 'Abdun was not confined only to his time. The medieval attitude survives as a factor in modern Muslim states, and has been recently restated with characteristic force by the influential Pakistani neo–orthodox reformer Abū al–'Alā' Mawdūdī.

Reforming the Modern Legal System,
from Islamic Law and Constitution
by Abū al-'Alā' al-Mawdūdī

In order to prepare the ground for the enforcement of Islamic law, we will have to introduce many reforms in our judicial system also. The first problem which deserves attention is the legal profession which is one of the worst and probably the greatest banes of the present judicial system. From a moral point of view not a single argument can be put forward in its favour and, in the practical field, there is not a single requirement of court procedure for which a better alternative cannot be provided. This profession stands in such contrast with the principles of Islam that as long as it exists, it would be extremely difficult to enforce the Islamic law in its real spirit. Moreover, if the same jugglery is practised with the Law of God as is being practised day in and day out with the man-made law, that may not only deprive us of justice but may also rob us of our faith. It is, therefore, imperative that this profession in its present form is gradually abolished. . . .

It is the supposed duty of a lawyer to put forward only such interpretations of the law as serve his client's purpose, and to strengthen it by referring to legal precedents. Thus, he tries, in a way, to mislead the judge and circumvent the process of justice. All this is done only to extract from the judge a judgement which is in favour of his client, and not the one which is desirable from the point of view of justice. . . .

It is, therefore, apparent that incalculable disservice has been done to the cause of law and justice by making law a profession. . . . Then, this malady does not end here. When these people, with this moth-eaten character, enter the arena of public life and politics, they poison the academic, cultural and political life of the whole nation.[7]

The ruler did not relinquish his duty to act as a magistrate, despite the presence of the qāḍīs. As a sort of court of appeals and complaints, he (or at times a relative or royal appointee) personally looked into cases brought to him by the public. These royal courts, or courts of *maẓālim* (wrongs) at times conflicted with the qāḍī's jurisdiction, but it was a recognized part of the ruler's duty to "right the wrongs of the people" at regular sessions open to all. Al-Māwardī describes the jurisdiction of these courts, and how they differed from the qāḍī's court.

On Looking into Wrongs
from the Governing Statutes
by al-Māwardī (d. A.H *450/*A.D. *1058)*

None of the first four caliphs was called upon to hold courts for maẓālim because they lived at the first period, when the religion was in the ascendancy, among people who turned to the right with alacrity, or whom a mere admonition would deter from wrongdoing. The disputes which arose among them were only about perplexing matters which the qāḍī's decisions could set straight, and if one of their wild bedouins did behave tyranically or try to, a warning would set him right or a little roughness would lead him to improve. The first caliph to set aside a day to look into the complaints of those who had been wronged—though he did not make personal investigations—was 'Abd al-Malik ibn Marwān the Umawī. When he was stopped by some problem or needed an effective pronouncement, he would refer the difficulty to his qāḍī Abū Idrīs al-Awdī, and he would take care of it. After that, acts of tyranny by governors and wrongdoing by high people increased to such an extent that they could be restrained only by two strong hands and effective authority. 'Umar ibn 'Abd al-'Azīz, God have mercy on him, was the first to take over in person the investigation of wrongs.

The one conducting the court should be of easy access, and have well chosen companions of five categories indispensable for proper order: 1) The guards and sergeants-at-arms to tame the strong and make the bold tractable; 2) the qāḍīs and judges, so that he may ask what took place in their courts and know how matters between the disputants proceeded; 3) the legalists, to ask about difficult questions and consult on embarrassing or obscure matters; 4) the scribes, to take down what happens and what decisions are taken; 5) the witnesses.

The person in charge should confine himself to ten categories of acts.

1. Acts of injustice committed by governors. . . .
2. Tyranny by tax collectors in levying the collecting taxes. . . .

3. Acts by secretaries of state offices, for they are trustees for the Muslims in taking care of their wealth and interests. . . .
4. Complaints of the army of shortages or arrears in their pay and rations.
5. Restitution of things seized wrongfully, of two sorts:
   a. Things seized by those in authority: here restitution must be made as soon as it is known (as, from records) even without any complaint having been made. . . .
   b. Things seized by powerful individuals: here a complaint must be made and witnesses appear.
6. Surveillance of pious bequests and foundations (*waqf*) of two sorts, general and particular. General foundations must be investigated even if no–one has alleged any wrongdoing, to see if they fulfill their purpose according to the condition established by the donors, after these have been established by one of three sources:
   a. Registers of the officials in charge of caring for waqfs.
   b. State archives, to the extent that they mention the operations (of foundations) or name them and thus establish their existence.
   c. Old writings which are obviously genuine, if there are no litigants (who might have reason to falsify them).

   Jurisdiction in these matters is broader than in the case of particular foundations. In their case, investigation takes place at an allegation of injustice, by those concerned, and evidence is taken from the registers of the waqf officials. It is not permitted to refer to the state archives or to what is stated in old writings, unless there is right evidence that they are genuine.
7. Enforcing decisions of qāḍīs not carried out due to weak enforcement. . . .
8. Investigation of matters which those in charge of the injunction to do good and reject the reprehensible (*al–ḥisba*) were powerless to enforce in the general interest, and making people respect the rights of God, exalted be He, and ordering that these be carried out as they should.
9. Surveillance of the public acts of service to God, such as Friday prayers, feasts, pilgrimage; and holy war, if they are curtailed or wrongly performed, for the rights of God are those most worthy to be upheld, and His orders those most deserving of performance.

10. Looking into disputes and judging between those making allegations, without however departing from the rules and procedures of the qāḍīs (but hearing appeals from the decisions).

The differences between maẓālim jurisdiction and that of the qāḍīs are ten (here summarized):

1. The investigator of maẓālim has greater dignity and power.
2. His jurisdiction is wider and less fettered.
3. He employs greater powers of intimidation and investigation.
4. He can check wrongs and set matters right at once.
5. He may postpone his decision in order to make an investigation, while the qāḍī has to give an immediate decision.
6. He can require quarreling parties to submit to arbitration by a third, while a qāḍī can only do this by consent of both sides.
7. He has full power to put both parties under surveillance if their depositions seem dubious, and may require them to put up security that their contentions will cease.
8. He can hear the depositions of people of veiled circumstances whom it would be irregular for the qāḍī to hear.
9. He can put to the oath witnesses of whom it is doubtful that they would give evidence spontaneously, and hear as large a number as he requires to remove doubt, which is not permitted to a judge.
10. He can summon and interrogate witnesses at his pleasure, while the qāḍī must wait until litigants have produced their own witnesses and interrogated them in his presence.

These are the ten aspects of difference between the two jurisdictions, even when they deal with the same matters.[8]

VIOLATING THE WILL OF GOD: THE *ḤADD*

All of the Law was considered the command of God for His Community, but there was one aspect of it which is particularly mentioned: the prescribed penalties. These were in most cases penalties specified in the Qur'ān, though in the case of that for drinking wine it was based on early tradition. For certain sins, according to the legalists, no discretion was left to the judge: he was obliged to apply a given punishment, the *ḥadd*: it was a claim of God upon His servants.

The question of ḥadd is a particularly controversial one today. Modern minds tend to recoil at the harshness of these penalties, while willing to concede that they may have been necessary in an earlier day, but the fundamentalists call for reviving them as a necessary part of religion. In Saudi Arabia and a few other areas, they are still applied, while in other countries they are in abeyance. The section on *ḥudūd* following has been taken from one of the definitive books of the Shāfi'ī school of Sunnī law, the *Minhaj al-Ṭālibīn,* written by the Syrian al-Nawawī.

The Legal Punishments
from The Goal of Seekers
by Muḥyī al-Dīn al-Nawawī (d. A.H. *676/*A.D. *1277)*

Apostacy: This consists of abjuring Islam by intention or words or acts of rejection, whether the words were said in jest, or contradiction, or belief. They consist of a declaration:

1. That the Creator or the Messengers do not exist, or
2. That one of the prophets was a liar, or
3. That one considers lawful what the "joining together" has considered unlawful—as for instance, fornication, or
4. That one considers unlawful what the joining together makes lawful, or
5. That one does not have to follow what has been decided by joining together, or
6. That one intends to reject Islam, or doubts it.

An *act* making one an apostate is one based on an obvious mockery or denial, such as throwing a copy of the Qur'ān on a muck heap, or prostration to an idol or the sun. An effort should be made to convince an apostate to return from error, though one authority says that it is only desirable, either at once or for three days. Then he is put to death. Where the guilty one repents, his submission is accepted and he is let alone, unless (according to some), he has turned to an esoteric infidelity such as Zandaqa [i.e. Manicheeism or Mazdakism.—Ed.], in which one can profess Islam outwardly but deny it inwardly.

The infant of two apostates (not one only) should be considered an apostate, according to the best opinion.

As to his property, the best opinion is that if he dies an apostate, he has lost it, but if he submits, he regains it. Debts contracted beforehand are however charged to his estate.

Fornication: This consists of introducing the male organ into the vagina of a forbidden woman, without any ambiguity or doubt,

A Cairo royal madrasa. Facade of the madrasa, hospital, and tomb (marked by dome) of Sulṭān Qalāwūn (d. 1290 A.D.). The panels of the recessed pointed arches and form of the windows were probably inspired by Gothic architecture built there by the Crusaders. *U.A.R. Antiquities Service.*

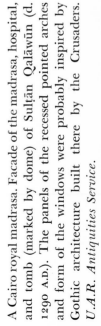

A madrasa and Ṣūfī retreat. 1303–1304 A.D. An unusual combined establishment built in Cairo by two Mamlūk comrades-in-arms of high rank, the amīrs Salar and Sanjar. The small tomb-dome at the left is that of a holy man they venerated. *U.A.R. Antiquities Service.*

Wood door panel. Eleventh century A.D. From the Fāṭimī Western Palace, Cairo. Animal elements are found only rarely among predominantly floral arabesques. *Islamic Museum, Cairo.*

Wooden cenotaph. From the shrine (constructed in 1211 A.D.) of the Sunnī doctor al-Shāfiʿī (d. A.H. 204/A.D. 820). Cairo. The shrine was constructed during the post-Saljūq Sunnī revival of the Ayyūbīs. Cenotaph shows rich arabesques and geometric design, a frequently occurring combination. *Islamic Museum, Cairo.*

Decoration in a Qur'ān of Uljaytu Khudabanda the Mongol sultan (from Mosul, 1310 A.D.). The Qur'ān does not forbid figural representations. Pictures are commonly found on objects for secular use, but only abstract design was fully approved by the 'ulamā', whose strictures are applied most severely in the ornamentation of objects for religious use. *Courtesy, Trustees of the British Museum.*

or into the anus of a man or woman as well, according to our school, and it receives a prescribed penalty (ḥadd), regardless of whether it was done for payment or by consent, and is applied as well for (relations with) a woman within the forbidden degrees of kinship or marriage [e.g., sister of a living wife.—Ed.] even if a marriage was performed. The guilty person must be adult, sane, and aware that it was wrong. Drunkenness is no excuse.

1. The ḥadd of an adult free Muslim or member of a protected community, who has consummated a legal marriage before this, is stoning to death. If one of the two partners has not, it does not lessen the guilt of the other.
2. The ḥadd of a fornicator who is not adult and free or was never married is one hundred lashes and banishment for a year, and if the Imām designates a place of banishment, that must be accepted.
3. For a slave the ḥadd is fifty lashes and banishment of half a year.

Defamation (qadhf): For a false accuser to receive the ḥadd, he must be a sane adult Muslim, drunk or sober, who acted freely. A child of reasonable age is punished at the discretion of the court. The penalty for a free person is eighty lashes, and for a slave forty. If two people accuse each other, the two punishments do not cancel each other.

Crimes punishable by amputation: For theft the amount necessitating punishment by amputation is of a value equal to the quarter of a (gold) dīnār. Two persons stealing together must have stolen twice the minimum amount. There is no amputation if what was stolen was impurity (which cannot constitute property) such as wine, or a pig or dog, or the skin of an animal not ritually slaughtered. But if the container of the wine was worth the minimum amount, amputation follows.

Theft by a minor, insane person, or one forced against his will is not punished by cutting off the hand, but cutting may be performed on members of a protected community, subject to our laws.

The right hand is cut off for the first offense (even if more than one theft was involved), the left foot for the second, the left hand for the third, and the right foot for the fourth.

Brigands (highwaymen and bandits): Those who do not rob or murder travellers may be given a lesser punishment. One guilty of theft of the legal amount has his right hand and left foot cut off. Murder by a brigand makes his death mandatory. He is then hung on a cross for three days and taken down. Some say the body should hang until ichor runs from it, and others that he should be crucified for a time and then taken down and killed.

Forbidden beverages: Every drink that inebriates in a large quantity is forbidden in a small quantity. The *ḥadd* for drinking it is not given to a child, an insane person or a non–Muslim subject. One may take wine in immediate necessity, according to our school, *e.g.* to dislodge food in the throat which is choking one, if nothing else is available, but one is liable to punishment if he uses wine for medicine or for thirst. The ḥadd of a free person is forty blows, and that of a slave twenty; by whip, hand, sandal, or a rolled–up garment. It is said that it should be with a whip. The Imām may double the number if he sees fit.

Sins not punishable by a prescribed penalty or expiation may be punished by imprisonment, beating, slapping, or threatening. The nature of this is at the discretion of the Imām or his deputy.[9]

INTERPRETING THE WILL OF GOD: A GNOSTIC VIEW

"Islam" may be translated, and has been understood, as commitment to the will of God. Hence for most Muslims, the Law has been a thing to be joyfully fulfilled.

It was often alleged that the Islamic philosophers and the esoteric Shī'a set no store by the Law, but the truth of the matter was simply that they had their own ways of understanding it. The following selection is taken from the *Treatises* of the Brothers of Purity (or, the Sincere Brethren), a circle of syncretising philosophers imbued with gnostic, Hellenistic, and esoteric Shī'ī ideas, who flourished in Baṣra in the tenth century A.D. Their praise of the Law would have pleased a fundamentalist, but their rationalization of what it was about was felt to detract from the immediacy of the divine command.

On Fulfilling the Law

from the "Treatise on (Divine) Judging and Enabling"
in Treatises *of the Brothers of Purity (fourth/tenth century)*

Know, my brother, that the prime support of faith and its most powerful pillar is subservience to the bearers of the divine Laws (*nawāmīs*) in that which they command of obedience and that which they forbid of rebellion; it consists of hearkening to them and obedience to them. This is so because the noblest works of mankind, the most delightful deeds of humanity and the highest rank to which the wise may attain next to the rank of angels is the establishment of the divine Laws. Know, my brother, that the lawgivers and their followers possess many good qualities and characteristics, a part of which we have mentioned in the Treatise on the Laws, part in the Treatise on the Doctrine of the Brethren of Purity, and part in the Treatise on the Mutual Fellowship of the Brethren.

Know then that the relation between the lawgivers and their followers, and that which the latter hear from them with regard to knowledge, and that to which they are commanded in the prescriptions of the Laws, resemble the heavens with its rain and the earth with its vegetation. That is because the speech and utterances of the lawgivers are like the rain, and the hearkening of their followers is like the earth; and what is produced through both of them of the benefits of the sciences, by way of both ideas and deeds, is like the plants, animals, and minerals. To these He points in His Word:

> He sends down out of heaven water
> and the wadīs flow each in its measure,
> and the torrent carries a swelling scum;
> and out of that over which they kindle
> fire, being desirous of ornament or ware,
> out of that rises a scum like of it.
> So God strikes both the true and the false.
> As for the scum, it vanishes as jetsam,
> and what profits men abides in the earth.
> Even so God strikes His similitudes.
> For those who answer their Lord, the reward
> most fair: and those who answer Him not—
> if they possessed all that is in the earth,
> and the like of it with it, they would
> offer it for their ransom. (13:17)[10]

Know, my brother, that the Law is fulfilled only by means of commands and prohibitions. Command and prohibition are carried out only by means of promise and threatening. Promise and threatening are made effective only through providing incentive and deterrent. Incentive and deterrent are efficacious only for those who fear and hope. Fear and hope become apparent or known only through subservience to command and prohibition, for whoever does not fear anything nor hope for anything has no desire or apprehension. Whoever has no desire or apprehension, for him promise and threatening are not efficacious, nor are command and prohibition (and hence) he has no share at all in the Divine Law.

The attainments to be hoped for are of two kinds: the one pertaining to this life and the other to the next. The earthly is such things as rule, honour, power, wealth, and earthly possessions while the soul is joined to the body, and that which remains of it after death, such as offspring and descendants. That pertaining to the next life is the escape of the soul from the sea of material existence and captivity to nature, the departure from the abyss of bodily existence, (namely) the world of being and corruption which exists in the sub-lunary world, and the realization of one's ascension to the Kingdom of Heaven, entry amongst the company of the angels, floating through celestial space and the vast expanse of the heavens, and the enjoyment of that rest and bliss mentioned in the Qur'ān, which fails of description except in summary fashion, as God, exalted be He, has said, "No soul knows what comfort is laid up for them secretly." (32:17)[11]

THE *ḤISBA*: THE WILL OF GOD AND THE PUBLIC WEAL

You are the best community brought forth to men, bidding unto good, rejecting what is disapproved, believing in God.—Qur'ān 32:17

To bid to good and reject the disapproved is not obligatory on every single individual, but is to be carried out as far as is possible, and since the Holy War is its completion, it is exactly like the Holy War. Any man who performs his (other) duties and does not fight the Holy War sins; thus every one must act according to his ability, as the Prophet said: "Whoever sees something disapproved, let him change it with his own hand, and if he is unable, with his tongue, and if he is unable to do that, in his heart."

So if it is thus, then it is known that bidding to good and rejecting the disapproved, together with their completion, the Holy War, are among the most important things we are ordered to perform.[12]—Ibn Taymīya (d. A.H 728/A.D. 1328)

The Community existed to bid to good and reject what is disapproved. The Imām existed to assist men to be virtuous. The state was a moral institution, for the fulfillment of God's will on earth.

Morality was a Community affair—and thus delegated to the Community's executive, but still a matter of public concern. This distinctive moral framework was referred to as the *ḥisba,* and its institutionalization went by the same name.

An official of singular importance was the *muḥtasib,* who was charged with carrying out the ḥisba under the ruler. He was a censor *cum* market inspector, under whose purview came such apparently separate matters as sanitation, morality, and public order. Historically, his office had developed out of that of the Byzantine market prefect, but as it did develop, no office could have been more revealing of the spirit of Islamic civilization than that of the muḥtasib, with its peculiar jurisdiction.

Here, Ibn 'Abdūn of Seville, with his characteristic pessimism and asperity, describes the duties of the office in eleventh century Spain.

On the Muḥtasib
from Treatise on Implementation of the Law
by Muḥammad Ibn 'Abdūn (written ca. A.H. *439/*A.D. *1100)*

The qāḍī must not appoint a muḥtasib without informing the prince of it, so that the qāḍī will have a proof, if he later wishes to remove him or keep him. The muḥtasib must be continent, honest, pious, learned, well–to–do, accomplished, experienced, seasoned and sagacious. He should not be partial or accept bribes, so that he loses his dignity and is taken lightly, and so that those who are brought before him do not blame him and upbraid him to his face. The office must not be entrusted to people of low condition, or those who would eat up the wealth of others by false practises and reprehensible methods, for it is suited only for those who have property and prestige.

The office of the muḥtasib is closely akin to that of the qāḍī, and thus the occupant should only be a model person. He is the spokesman of the qāḍī, his chamberlain, assistant and successor, and if the qāḍī is prevented, he may give judgement in his place in what pertains to him and is within his competence.

He receives a salary from the public treasury, for he takes care of many matters for the qāḍī which in principle belong to the qāḍī's office, thus sparing him fatigue and tiring scenes, and being tried by vulgar and low people, and insolent and ignorant persons from among the artisans and laborers. He is the qāḍī's tongue, and recourse to him is necessary, for the common people are crooked and deceiving and wicked, and if one puts up with them and averts his eye, the conduct of the state will be corrupted and many doors will be opened for abuses.

It is better to mend a thing than to endure it; like a garment; if it is mended it will yet give service, but if worn it will quickly go to rags.

Thus this office, if one sees to it properly, brings health to the world, the prince, and the people altogether, because in its observance lies the performance of many affairs of religion, the Law, and traditions, as well as physical labours and trades and the livelihood of the people and all the matters which concern them, for the competence and administration of this office is not concerned so much with matters of litigation and protecting property, as with what is incumbent upon the individual in the Law of Islam. Look into this: thou shalt find that it is so, O man![13]

Duties of the Muḥtasib: mosques: One must not allow any beggar to beg inside the mosque on Friday; whoever does shall be given corporal chastisement. The mosque servants and muezzins shall be told to prevent it. Also no beggar is allowed to beg at the entrance of the mosque in a loud voice once the imām of Friday prayers has gone into the pulpit to preach.

The muḥtasib must not allow any beast of burden to stand near the entrance, for it may make droppings or urine which destroy the ritual purity of people coming in.

The mosques are the houses of God, places of recollection and worship, and known for purity. They are not for payments, or arguments, or any of the acts of this world, since they are for the acts of the next world. Thus boys should not be taught in them, because they are careless about impurities on their feet and clothing. If it is absolutely necessary, they can be taught in the galleries (of the court). Boys should not be disciplined with more than five blows of the cane to the big ones, and three blows to the small ones, with severity proportionate to their ability to bear.

Schoolmasters: They must be prevented from attending dinners and funerals and acting as witnesses, except on days when they are free, for they are salaried people, and cause ignorant people to lose their money (thus). Schoolmasters should not increase the number of their students: they are forbidden to do it, yet I may say that they will never observe it, for one does not voluntarily rise to serve the Collectivity; especially in the matter of schoolteaching. Also they never teach anything as they should. Most schoolteachers are ignorant of the art of teaching: to know the Qur'ān is one thing, and to teach it is another.[14]

Cemeteries: The worst thing about the cemeteries, and one much blamed by the people of our city, is that people go there among the tombs to drink wine and even commit debauchery. One must not allow any tradesmen there, because they see the women who come to mourn (with bare faces), and also not allow any young men to sit in the ways so as to encounter the women. The muḥtasib must be careful to forbid that. It is necessary to forbid the storytellers and reciters of romances to be alone with women in the tents (they pitch nearby) to tell stories in, for they do it to seduce or rob them, and only loose women go to them anyway. If the storytellers stay at home and the women go there to hear them, that must be forbidden too, for it is worse than the first case. One must always maintain close control of these people, for they are profligates.

Market regulations: milk: No one but honest people should sell milk, for water is sometimes added to it to dilute it, which is deceit of the Muslims. It is also necessary to keep it clean. Milk must be kept in wood or pottery, and not in copper, for that produces a poisonous substance (verdigris) harmful to the Muslims.

Vegetables: Lettuce, chicory, carrots and the like shall not be washed in ponds or garden pools, which may be unclean; but only in the river itself, for it is cleaner and purer.

Oil: Oil must not be sold near the chief mosque, nor any dirty thing, nor anything which will leave a stain that cannot be brushed off.

Rabbits and poultry: These may not be sold near the chief mosque, and there must be a special place for them. Partridges and slaughtered poultry shall have the tails plucked, so that spoiled birds can be told from fresh ones. Rabbits may only be sold skinned, to show their state of freshness, and if they are left in their skins they soon spoil.

Eggs: The sellers must have vessels of water before them, for testing whether the eggs (float, and so) are spoiled.

Truffles: These may not be sold near the mosque, for they are sought after by debauchees.

Slaughter: Animals shall not be slaughtered in the market except within enclosures, and the blood and contents of the tripes must be taken outside the market. Beasts must be slain with long knives, and animals still fit for farmwork must not be slaughtered, unless they have a defect or are females unfit for breeding. Animals already slaughtered cannot be sold until the owner gives evidence that they were not stolen. The tripes may not be sold with the meat at one price.

Marketwomen: They shall be forbidden to wash things in the gardens (around the town), for these become brothels for fornication.

Grapes: These may not be sold in large quantity to one of whom it is known that he will press them for wine: this is a matter for caution.

Fruits: Not to be sold except when ripe, for that is deceit, except only for grapes, which are good for pregnant women and sick people.

The Riverbanks: Women shall not sit there in the summer, if men appear there.

Barbers: They may not be alone in their shops with a woman, but only in the marketplace, or where they may be observed.

Professions: No one may be allowed to pretend to mastery in something he cannot do well, especially the profession of medicine, which involves the loss of life, for the mistake of the physician is covered by the earth. The same is true of the housebuilder. Each should be fitted for his profession, and not lay claim to it unless he knows it, especially when it has anything to do with women, for ignorance and error are most frequent with them![15]

Baths: The reservoirs of public baths must be covered, for if they are open, they are not secure from impurities, and baths are for purification. The bathman, the masseur, and the barber may not go about in the bath except in a shirt and drawers.

Masseurs: A Muslim may not massage a Jew or a Christian, or empty their garbage or clean their latrines, for Jews and Christians are fitter for such work. Also, a Muslim may not look after the riding animal of a Jew or a Christian.

Churches: Muslim women must be forbidden to enter the infamous churches, for the priests are profligates, adulterers and sodomites. The Frankish women too should be forbidden to go in the church except on days of offices or feasts, because they go to eat and drink and fornicate with the priests, and there is not one of the priests who does not have two of them or more to sleep with him. This is well known among them, since they forbid what is lawful and find lawful what is forbidden. The priests should be ordered to marry, as done in the eastern lands; if they wanted to, they could do it.

No woman should be let in a priest's house, whether he is old or otherwise, if he refuses marriage. The (priests) should also be forced to be circumcised, as al-Mu'tadid 'Abbād did with them. For they persist in alleging that they follow the example of Jesus—the blessing of God be upon him, and peace!—and Jesus was circumcised, and they celebrate the day of that circumcision as a feast, and yet do not practice it! . . .

Jews: They must not butcher an animal for Muslims, and the Jews should be ordered to set aside butcher shops for themselves.[16]

Prostitutes: The women of the tax-paying houses shall be forbidden to uncover their faces outside the public houses, to confuse honest women with their adornments, and shall be forbidden to reveal their secrets to married women or come to wedding parties, even if husbands permit it. Dancing girls also shall be ordered not to uncover their heads (in public).

Costumes: No tax-farmer or police agent or Jew or Christian shall be allowed to dress like an important person, or as a jurist, or virtuous person: rather they should be known and avoided. They must not be greeted with "Peace be on you!" for "Satan has taken the mastery over them, and caused them to forget the recollection of God. They are Satan's party: shall not Satan's party be the losers?" (58:20). A distinctive badge should be given to them by which they may be known, as a way to disgrace them.

Catamites: Pleasure–boys (*hiwā*) should be expelled from the city, and chastised whenever one of them is found (in it). They should not be allowed to circulate among the Muslims or participate in festivities, for they are fornicators cursed by God and all men! . . .

Games: Youths and boys must be forbidden to play at boxing and with clubs, because it leads to misunderstandings and disorders. It is necessary to forbid the playing of chess, backgammon, the pebble–game, and darts, as they are forms of gambling, which is forbidden and distracts one from his religious obligations.[17]

Villagers: When a villager or someone else is caught with long hair, he should have it cut off or be shaved. He may be given corporal punishment and forced to cut it, for it is a mark of bad people and good–for–nothings. Arms must not be sold to the unmarried men of the countryside, and if one appears with a spear in his hand it should be taken from him, for long hair and carrying arms works on their spirits.

Riding animals: These must not be left standing in the streets, for they get in the way and cut off the passage of the people, and sometimes trample them.

Bells: In the territory of Islam, the sound of (church) bells must be prohibited. They should only sound in infidel territory.[18]

Books: No book of learning should be sold to a Jew or a Christian, unless it treats of their own law, for they translate the books and then attribute them to their own people and their bishops, although they are of Muslim authorship. It would be best to allow no Jewish or Christian doctor to treat any Muslim, for they do not have true friendship with Muslims and should treat only the people of their own community. Since they do not have sincere friendship for Muslims, how shall one trust them with his life?

Stolen fruit: Ripe olives and all sorts of fruit must not be bought from one of whom it is known that he has no property, for that is participation in the theft of people's goods. It should be confiscated from one who shows up with it, particularly if he is a youth, a country person, or suchlike.[19]

Moneychangers: These must be prevented from usury. No currency shall be circulated except that of the land, for differing currencies lead to inflation, higher prices, and unstable conditions.

Public scales: The weighers must be honest men advanced in age, for that work calls for dependability, religion, and piety.

Daggers: It is necessary to prohibit the manufacture of poignards, for no one buys them except ruffians, good-for-nothings, and evil men.[20]

Conclusion: In general, people have corrupted their religions, and this is only because the world is perishable and the times are near their end. To do other than this (that we have described) is to initiate disorder and herald corruption and the ruin of the world. No one could better the (present state of affairs) except a prophet with the help of God, and this is no time for a prophet. It is the qāḍī who is responsible for all of that. But whoever assists the Muslims shall have God for his own assistance. Therefore it is for the qāḍī to declare for justice, and give himself to virtue, equity and sincerity, and look to himself. Thus he may be saved, and God in His might may support him and assist him unto good, for it is He who is the Dispenser of good, and who is powerful over all things.[21]

ACCEPTING THE WILL OF GOD

The will of God was perceived by Muslims as a command, and this found expression in distinctive institutions. In the earliest period, while an empire was being built, this perception was a predominantly ethical one, and Muslims joyfully set out to build the Kingdom of God on earth. Toward the end of the first century, when contradictions and frustrations were beginning to be felt, men began to discuss what the sovereignty of God implied for human action. There were verses enough in the Qur'ān to suggest that all that happened was God's will: if one failed to perform God's command, was this not also by God's decree? The following exchange on the subject, between an Umawī Caliph and al-Ḥasan of Basra, is probably genuine, and reflects early thinking on this matter.

On God's Enabling Man to Disobey Him
from a letter to an Umawī caliph
by al-Ḥasan of Baṣra (d. A.H. *110*/A.D. *728)*

From 'Abd al-Malik ibn Marwān to al-Ḥasan ibn Abī al-Ḥasan al-Baṣri: Peace be to you, and I extol to you God, beside whom there is no god. As for what follows, there has come to the Commander of Believers about you that concerning the description of *al-qadr* [literally: "the power" (of God).—Ed.] the likes of which have never come to him from any of the past. The Commander of Believers cannot remember any of the Companions of the Prophet whom he knew saying what it has come to him that you have said. He has always known good things of you in your ways; your excellence in religion and knowledge of religious insight (fiqh) and your search and your eagerness for that. And then the Commander of Believers found repugnant this doctrine ascribed to you; therefore write to him about your doctrine and the position you take; whether it is a tradition from a Companion of God's messenger, on whom be peace and God's blessing, or only an opinion of yours, or something you know how to prove from the Qur'ān. For truly, we have heard no one discuss this matter before you. Present your opinion to the Commander of Believers and clarify it. Peace be to you, and the mercy of God and His blessings.

From al-Ḥasan al-Baṣri to God's servant 'Abd al-Malik: Peace be to you, O Commander of Believers, and the mercy of God. I extol to you God, beside whom there is no god. As for what follows, may God bless the Commander of Believers; may He place him among His friends who do works of obedience and desire His good pleasure and hasten to follow what He has commanded.

Those among the Companions who accomplished God's command and related His wisdom and followed the tradition of His messenger, on whom be peace and God's blessing, never denied a truth or justified a wrong or attached to the Lord anything He did not attach to Himself. God has said "I have not created the Jinn and mankind except to serve Me: I desire no sustenance from them, neither do I desire to be fed." (51:56–57). Now God would not create them for something and then come between them and it—He is no oppressor of his servants. None of those who went before denied that, or even discussed it, because they were in agreement about it. We ourselves only began to talk about it when people began to deny it following their misleading desires and committing grave sin: distorting the Book of God. What God forbade is not from Him, because He is not pleased with what He is angry about, and not angry with what He is pleased about, and if infidelity (*kufr*) were by God's decree and ordaining, then it would please Him from whomever it came. It is inconceivable that He would decree something and then be displeased with His own decree. God would not openly forbid His servants something, and then covertly decree it for them, as stupid and ignorant men say. Were that the case, He would not have said "Let him who wills believe and him who wills disbelieve" (74:40). That is because God has placed in them the power (*qudra*) by which they go forward or lag behind, so that the doer of good may merit Paradise and the doer of bad may merit hellfire. If the matter were as falsifiers have interpreted it, it would not be in them to go ahead or remain behind, and there would be no praise for him who went forward or blame for him who lagged. According to what they say, power does not come from them and should not be attributed to them; rather, it is a thing that works by means of them. They follow what is ambiguous in the Qur'ān, seeking dissension.

They argue that God, be He exalted, has said "God leads astray whomsoever He will, and guides to Him all those who repent" (13:27), and they do not look at what comes before it and after it. (If they did) they would not go astray.

Know, Commander of Believers, that those who differ from God's commands and Book and justice are those who transgress in the matter of their religion, and who in their ignorance transfer (responsibility) to predestination (al–qadr). If you order any of them concerning the matter of his religion, he says "The Pen has run dry, and it is written on our foreheads whether we shall be happy or miserable (in this world and the next.)" But if you said to one of them "Do not weary yourself seeking the world, or go out in the morning in the heat and cold, and endanger your life on a journey, for your sustenance is decided about that," then he would find fault with you.

Their idea is that God has charged His servants to take what they have no power to take, and to leave what they have no power to leave, but God, be He exalted, gives them the lie with His Word: "God imposes on no soul beyond its capacity" (2:286). No, surely God has known that infidelity will come from them just as it happens, by their own choice.

Know, Commander of Believers, that God did not foreordain matters for His servants, but He said "If you do such and such, I will do with you such and such, and if you do thus and so, I will do with you thus and so."

Speak to yourself, Commander of Believers. Do not say "God has foreordained for His servants what He forbade them, and come between them and what He ordered them to do, and sent the prophets to call them to the opposite of what He has decreed for them, so as to torment them everlastingly if they did not do what He did not let them do." God is exalted far above what wrongdoers claim! This is the answer to what you asked me about; I have explained it and clarified it. Reflect on it and ponder it, for it is a cure for what is in the heart. Here ends the letter.[22]

In essence, this was the position of the *Qadarīs*, who believed that God gave men power to do good and evil, without willing that they do evil. For many of the early legalists, however, the matter was a question of God's sovereignty. If, as they believed, all power was from God, then the power to do evil was from Him. If He was the cause of all things, then He was the cause of men's acts as well, and all that occurred, good and evil, was from Him, as were damnation and salvation.

GOD'S WILL AND HUMAN FREEDOM

We enjoin what is just and prohibit what is evil. What reaches you could not possibly have missed you, and what misses you could not possibly have reached you.—The *Fiqh Akbar* of Abū Ḥanīfa (d. A.H. 150/A.D. 767)

A part of the essential Sunna, such that if one leaves any part of it not accepting it and believing it, he cannot be considered as being of the people of the Sunna, is belief in the predestination (qadar) of good and bad, and affirmation of the ḥadīths about it and belief in them, not saying, "Why?" or "How?" but simply affirming them and believing them.—A creed of Aḥmad ibn Ḥanbal (d. A.H. 241/A.D. 855)

A party that developed from among the followers of al-Ḥasan, who took up the doctrine that God does not will evil, were the Mu'tazila, or "withdrawers," apparently so called originally because they withdrew from the Sunnī–Shī'ī disputes over the Imamate. They called themselves "People of the (Divine) Justice and Unity," because they maintained that God's unity meant that His attributes, such as His speaking (and hence His words in the Qur'ān) must be created, if they were not to be considered coeternal partners of God, while His justice meant that He could not will man to do evil, since He punishes evil.

The traditionalists however held that the Qur'ān was God's uncreated Word, and that being all–powerful meant being able to do anything at all. If this seemed paradoxical, then man must be content with a paradox: he could not force God to conform to the dictates of his limited reason.

It is clear that the Mu'tazila were attempting to preserve the immediacy of the divine command undiluted by fatalism, but the times were against them, and after a few initial successes they fought a long, losing battle. Their books were burned by their opponents, and their teachings were known chiefly by hearsay. Only recently, the work of a Mu'tazilī writer has come to light, and it casts much light on their method of reasoning. This was the Qāḍī 'Abd al-Jabbār (d. A.H. 415/A.D. 1024), who served as the chief justice of the Shī'ī Buwayhī ruler Fakhr al-Dawla at Rayy, near modern Tehran. The Shī'ā were more tolerant of the Mu'tazila than the Sunnīs, and 'Abd al-Jabbār's books were preserved among the Shī'ī Zaydīs of Yaman. As he was a later authority of the school, his writings are a compendium of Mu'tazilī thought.

What God Wills and Does not Will in the Deeds of His Servants *from* Commentary on the Five Principles *of Qāḍī 'Abd al-Jabbār al-Mu'tazilī (d.* A.H. *145/*A.D. *1024)*

As for the acts of God's servants, they are of two sorts: one sort has an attribute additional to what it was created with, as well as the attribute of its kind. The other sort has no other attributes, and since this is so, God neither desires them nor hates them.

The sort which has an attribute additional to what it was created with is of two kinds, one bad, the other good. What is bad, God absolutely does not desire, but detests and is angered by.

What is good is also of two kinds: one has an attribute additional to its goodness, and the other does not. This second one is the permissible act: God—be He exalted—cannot possibly will it, as we hope to show later.

As for the first sort, those with an attribute additional to their goodness, these are the obligatory and recommended acts, all of which are a part of what God desires. We may say that the utmost way to know what another wills is when he gives a command. Now a command has issued from God, and more too, for when God commanded it He also expressed His desire for it and promised a great reward for it, while He forbade its contrary, deterred from it, and threatened it with a great punishment. Thus God must will it, according to our doctrine.

Now if the servant is obedient to God, be He exalted, in performing mandatory and supererogatory deeds, then God must will that, for a heedful person is one who does the will of one he obeys, as in God's word, be He exalted: "And for the wrongdoers there is no loyal friend, and no intercessor to be heeded." (41:18).
That is to say, no one who will do what they will to be done. Another citation that gives the sense of the word is the verse of Suwayd ibn Kāhil:

> "Perhaps he whose bosom I made swell with rage
> Wished me death, but it heeded him not."

That is, it did not do what he willed.

Similarly, it is related that the Prophet, God's benediction be on him, and peace, once struck the earth with his heel before his uncle 'Abbās, and water gushed forth. Then 'Abbās said to him "Truly your Lord is heedful of you, son of my brother," and the Prophet—God bless him—said "And of you, my uncle: be heedful of God, and He will be heedful of you."

Now if anyone says "Did you not say that a heedful person is one who does what another commands him to do?" We reply: When a command is stripped of willing to do, then it is not distinguishable from a prohibition, or something carrying the sense of a threat, so that the disobedient would all be heedful of God, because they did as they would, according to His word, be He exalted: "Do what you will; surely He sees what you do." (41:40), and even the devil would be heedful of God, since he startles whom he can, and rallies against them, according to God's word, be He exalted: "Depart! Those of them who follow thee, surely Gehenna shall be your reward; an ample reward! And startle those of them thou canst with thy voice, and rally against them thy horses and thy footsoldiers, and promise them!" (17:62–63), when of course the opposite is known.

What we mean here is that God does not will bad things, but hates them and is angry with them, and what shows this is that the utmost by which another can show his dislike of something is that he prohibits it, and prohibitions have issued from God which are the greatest prohibitions, for when He, be He exalted, prohibited the bad, He also deterred us from it, and promised painful punishments for it, commanding the opposite, expressing His desire for it, and promising a great reward for it—all of which shows that He, be He exalted, did not desire bad things, but hates them.

And God's mercy has also indicated verses in the Qur'ān giving notice that the definitive Book of God agrees with what we have already said about His Unity and Justice. One of these is the verse "And God does not will wrong to His worshippers." (40:31) The indication is in the fact that "wrong" here is indefinite, and the indefinite in a prohibition has a universal scope. The plain meaning is that He, be He exalted, does not want anything at all which bears the name of wrong, so that it is just as one would say "I did not see man," where the plain meaning is that one did not see anything that is called man.

If anyone says "All that this means is that God does not will to wrong any man, but where does it say that He does not will that they should wrong one another?", we reply: Due to the fact that the verse applies generally to anything that bears the name of wrong, one must conclude that He does not will any of it.

What also indicates that God wills obedience and the mandatory and recommended acts is His word "I have not created the Jinn and mankind except to serve Me" (51:56). This "except" here is the except of express intention, and will, as if He should say "We did not create them or will of them anything except that they should serve."

Another thing that shows that God does not will what is bad is that He, be He exalted, if He willed what is bad would have to make a bad intention, and a bad intention is bad, and God does not intend the bad because He knows what it is and has no need of it.

If anyone says "Why is the will to do bad bad?" We reply: This is known perforce, and we also do not doubt that a command to do bad would be bad, because it causes bad.

If anyone says "Then the power to do bad must also be bad, because it causes bad," we say: There is a difference. The power makes free from impotence, and its influence is by way of completion, quite the contrary of willing.[23]

The most influential opponent of the Mu'tazila was their onetime pupil, al–Ash'arī (d. A.H 324/A.D. 935), because the school of theology he founded came later with the patronage of Niẓām al-Mulk and the Saljūqs to dominate Sunnī teaching, and finally drove the Mu'tazilīs completely into the arms of the Shī'īs. His exposition follows in question and answer form.

God's Creation of Man's Disobedience
from the Book of Brightness
by Abū al–Ḥasan al–Ash'arī (d. A.H. *324/*A.D. *936)*

QUESTION: Tell us about the case of a king of this world who passes by a blind and paralyzed cripple and is cursed by him, though the king does not will that the man should curse him: do you hold that in this case the king is overtaken by weakness, feebleness, and failure to attain his desire, since he wills that the man not curse him, and yet he does curse him?

ANSWER: Certainly . . . if the king did not desire to be cursed by the blind cripple, and yet the man cursed the king without regard for the king's desire or disapproval—why this is the very description of weakness and feebleness. Moreover, when someone wills something from us and it is, and when he does not will it, and it is not, he deserves to be described as "having power" much more than one who wills the being of what will not be, and the not being of what will be. And the Lord of the Worlds is not to be described save in the way which best accords with the attribute of "having power."

QUESTION: Has not God, then, created the injustice of creatures?

ANSWER: He created it as their injustice, not as His.

QUESTION: Then why do you deny that He is unjust?

ANSWER: God is not necessarily unjust because He creates injustice as another's injustice and not as His. Moreover, if what they say were compelling, then, if God were to make a volition and a desire and a motion for another and not for Himself, He Himself would have to be willing, desiring, and moving. Since this is not necessary, neither is what they have said.

QUESTION: Has God decreed and determined acts of disobedience?

ANSWER: Yes, in the sense that He has created them, and has written them down, and has announced that they will be. But we do not say that God has decreed and determined acts of disobedience in the sense that He has commanded them.

QUESTION: Is God free to inflict pain on infants in the next life?

ANSWER: God is free to do that, and in doing it He would be just. Nor would it be evil on His part to punish the believers and to introduce the unbelievers into the Gardens. Our only reason for saying that He will not do that is that He has informed us that He will punish the unbelievers—and He cannot lie when He gives information.

QUESTION: Then lying is evil only because God has declared it to be evil.

ANSWER: Certainly. And if He declared it to be good, it would be good; and if He commanded it, no one could gainsay Him.

OBJECTION: Then allow that God can lie, just as you allow that He can command lying-

ANSWER: Not everything that God can command can be predicated of Him. He cannot lie, not because it is evil, but because it is impossible for Him to lie. So He cannot be qualified by the power to lie, just as He cannot be qualified by the power to move or be ignorant.[24]

The brutality of al-Ash'arī's reasoning would not have been a match even for the naiveté of the Mu'tazila without state support. The historical context, and the legal and political theory and structure of medieval Muslim government considerably influenced the outcome.

A more subtle Sunnī school, but one which never obtained much currency, developed among the Ḥanafīs. It owes its name to al-Māturīdī of Samarqand (d. A.H 333/A.D. 944). The Māturīdīya were much more successful in threading the narrow way between ascribing creation to creatures on the one hand, and ascribing all man's acts to God, on the other.

God wills Man's Freedom to Disobey, but does not will Disobedience from a Māturīdī Doctrinal Statement (fourth/tenth century)

The Zoroastrians say that the world had two creators; one of them was good and created good things; he is Yazdān. The other was evil and created harmful things; he is Ahriman, and the creator of evil is purposeless and not to be connected with Yazdān. We answer that the Creator of evil would only be purposeless if there were no wisdom in His creation (but there is); the least of which is that it brings tyrants low. The attributes of God are not He, and not other than He, like the color of an object. The Qur'ān, the Word of God, is an eternal attribute, subsisting in God's essence. What is in the text is the Word of God, but the letters and sounds are created—for we do not say that the Word of God inheres in the text so that there can be any talk of "separating," since when a thing is known with God's knowledge the attribute of knowing is not thereby separated from Him.

The acts of God's servants are created by Him, be He exalted, and the choice is not delegated to them, contrary to the Qadarīs. If they say "If their acts are His creation, why should He punish them for them?" we reply: the reward and punishment occur on the use of the created act, not for the created act itself, and so the servant will be punished for the use of his potentiality, which is capable of both obedience and disobedience, and not for generating the potentiality.

The potentiality which befits evil does not befit good, according to the Ash'arīya, and that is compulsion (*jabr*), for if it does not befit good, then the creature is compelled to do evil. Here they permit an unbearable burdening. We refute their position with the Word of God, be He exalted: "God tasks not any soul beyond its scope" (2:286). If they say "Then is the prayer of the Prophet, in the same verse, infidelity? For he says, 'Impose not on us that we have no strength to bear,' as if one said 'Do not be unjust to us.' " We reply: "This prayer is for lightening burdens, and not a lack of piety. It is matched by God's own Word, exalted be He: 'Lay not on us such a burden.' " (2:286)

Sins occur by God's will (*irāda*) and wish (*mashī'a*) and ordinance (*qaḍā'*) and power (qadr) but not by His pleasure (*riḍa*) liking (*maḥabba*) and command (*amr*), according to His Word, exalted be He: "He whom God wills to lead astray, He maketh his bosom tight, narrow" (6:125) and His Word, exalted be He, "Yet ye will nothing, unless God wills it" (76:31). If the creature were able to act according to his own will, he would prevail over God's will, be He exalted. The Mu'tazila have held that God does not will to prevail over man, according to His Word, exalted be He: "I have not created the Jinn and man except to serve Me." (51:56): i.e. "I have not created them for disbelief," so He can never want it. We say, the meaning here is that He commands them to serve Him, and He has so commanded. It does not mean "God does not will wrong to His worshippers" (40:31). That is true, but there is no discussion of it, and it does not apply here. Again, their statement that if God wills sin, man is compelled to commit it, does not apply. Just as man cannot escape God's will, he cannot escape God's omniscience, and it constitutes no excuse for sin. If they ask "What then does it mean when God says, "Whatever of ill befalls thee it is from thyself" (3:73), we answer: "It means that evil may not be attributed directly to God, for considerations of decency, just as one cannot say (to Him) 'O Creator of pigs!' but it must be attributed to Him in a general way, for He says, 'Say, all comes from God' " (2:78).

God created unbelief and willed it, but He did not command anyone to disbelieve; rather He ordered the infidel to believe, but He did not will that upon him. If it is asked "Is God's will pleasing to Him or not?" we say: "It is pleasing." If they then ask, "And why should He punish what pleases Him?" we answer: "Rather, He punishes what is *not* pleasing—for His will and providence, and all His attributes, are pleasing to Him, but the act of the unbeliever is *not* pleasing to Him, is hateful to Him, and is punished by Him."[25]

The Ash'arīya dominated the teaching of Sunnī theology for centuries, and their predestinationism reinforced tendencies to resignation already apparent elsewhere by the third century of Islam.

It was believed by many—including philosophers and scientists—that the will of God was made operative on earth by the turning of the celestial spheres, and astrology was studied at almost every court in order to know destiny in advance.

The Brothers of Purity at Baṣra also taught the acceptance of God's will, under the aspect of fate, and justified it as true Islam.

On the Decree and the Determination and a Willing Acceptance of This, from the Treatises *of the Brothers of Purity (fourth/tenth century)*

Among the requisites of faith and the characteristics of believers is the willing acceptance of the Decree and the Determination, which is the contentment of the soul with whatever determinations (*maqādir*) befalls it. (These) are necessary results of the laws of the celestial bodies, while the Decree is the prior knowledge of God of what the laws of the celestial bodies make inevitable. It is said that contentment with the Decree is the minimal act of man which ascends to heaven, and it is the most noble of the requisites of faith and the most excellent of the characteristics of the believers.

Then know, my brother, that there is no one satisfied with the acrid, bitter determinations that befall him, except those who know the sacred character of the Law of God. One should be submissive to the judgement of the Law of God, satisfied of soul, like the submission of Socrates, the philosopher of the Greeks. It was said to him, "You are being killed unjustly. Do you want us to (ransom) you, or spirit you away?" Socrates answered, "I fear lest the Law of God should say to me tomorrow, 'Why did you flee from my judgement?' "

Before Socrates, one of the sons of Adam had submitted to the determinations, when his brother Cain said to him, "I will surely slay thee." Abel was satisfied with the Decree of God, and so he submitted to the determinations, which are the necessary results of the laws of the celestial bodies, content of soul.

Similarly Christ was satisfied with the decree of God and submitted to the determinations and surrendered his humanity to the Jews, content of soul, satisfied with the judgement of God.

Similarly the Prophet of God, blessings and peace be upon him, willingly acquiesced when, upon the Day of Uḥud, his excellent Helpers and noble Emigrants were slain, his banner broken, and there befell him of the determinations of the celestial bodies what befell him.

In like manner there is the acquiescence of 'Uthman ibn 'Affān [the Sunnī martyr.—Ed.], when they entered upon him to slay him and of al-Ḥusayn, may God be pleased with him, on the day of Karbalā. He knew that he was about to be killed, so he fought until he was slain, acquiescing in the Decree of God.[26]

Many mystics, too, preached contentment with occurrence, as the will of God.

On Contentment with God's Will
from A Garden for Postulants *(a Ṣūfī manual)*
by Ibn Yazdānyār (fifth/eleventh century)

Bishr al-Ḥāfī said "Contentment with God, when one has been afflicted by God in the body, is not to wish to be restored to health, and when He has healed him, not to wish to be taken unless it is his Lord who takes him, and when He has impoverished him, not to desire that He enrich him, but to be content with whatever his Lord does with him." And Fuḍayl ibn 'Iyāḍ said, "Ask for whatever is good, and do not exercise preference. How many a worshipper has preferred for himself that wherein lay his own destruction!" Sahl ibn 'Abdallāh says, "God created His creatures and did not veil them from Himself—but He made the veil their own will to dispose of themselves. Leave disposing to Him who is the Friend and Director, who preserves and watches over you."

Abū al-Ḥusayn al-Nūrī was asked about contentment, and said "Though I should be in the deepest abyss of Hellfire, still I should be more contented with God than one who is in the highest paradise." Shiblī said, on being asked about contentment, "Though Hell lay on my right eye, I would not ask God so much as to move it to my left eye."

They tell that in Baṣra there was once a man who was palsied and sick, with many griefs and calamities, and blind as well, yet he knew the greatest name of God. One of the people said to him, "If you would only ask God in prayer, He would cure you." And he said, "I am ashamed before my Lord to will other than He wills, for I want only what He desires."[27]

At least some of the Ṣūfī mystics found the idea that God is the ultimate source of evil, a demonic temptation to be overcome. For example, here is an anecdote about al-Jilānī, the great Ḥanbalī saint of Baghdad.

Satan's Argument
from The Opening of the Unseen
by 'Abd al-Qādir al-Jīlānī (d. A.H. 561/A.D. 1166)

Shaykh 'Abd al-Qādir al-Jīlānī, God be satisfied with him, said: "I saw Iblīs (Satan) the accursed one in a dream. I was standing in a great crowd, and I wanted to kill him. But he whom God has cursed said to me, 'Why would you kill me? What have I done? If God wills evil, I have no power to alter it for good and bring it to that; if He wills good, then I have no power to alter it for evil and bring it to that. So what is in my hands?' Now his appearance was like that of a depraved effeminate, his voice soft and his face hateful, with a mass of hair on his chin, and a contemptible aspect. Then he smiled in my face, a confused and cowardly grin. This occurred on the eve of Saturday the 12th of the Month of Pilgrimage, in 516 (1123)."[28]

The greatest of all Ash'arī theologians was al-Ghazālī. He shows the considerable development of al-Ash'arī's ideas in the school, and to them he added many ideas of the philosophers, and the rich beauty of Ṣūfī faith. In discussing the absolute sovereignty of God's power, he skillfully avoids the sins of imputing evil to God, or creation to man.

How God's Omnipotence does not Obviate Human Power to Disobey, from Right Proportion in Belief
by Abū Ḥāmid al–Ghazālī (d. A.H. *505/*A.D. *1111)*

The first attribute of God is power (qudra). We assert that the Creator of the World is powerful, because the world is a masterful work, well ordered, perfectly arranged, with many sorts of wonders and signs, all of which indicates power. To properly order the syllogism, we may say: "Every masterful work proceeds from a powerful agent; the world is a masterful work; therefore it proceeds from a powerful agent."

Is there any disputing of the two premises? If anyone asks, "Why do you say that the world is a masterful work?" we answer: "We mean by being 'masterful' its organization, systematic arrangement, and symmetry. One who examines even the members of his own body, external and internal, will perceive wonders whose perfection surpasses his accounting. This premise therefore is perceived by knowledge of the senses and observation so its denial is not possible." If anyone asks, "How do you know the second premise, that every masterful and well–ordered work has a powerful agent?" we reply: "This is perceived by the necessity of the mind. The intellect confirms it without apodictic proof, and an intelligent person cannot deny it. Even so, we shall furnish a proof, so as to cut the ground from under any denial or obstinacy."

We mean by His being powerful that the act proceeding from Him either proceeds from Him by itself, or because of a meaning distinct from it, and it is absurd to say it proceeds from Him by itself, because if that were the case, the act would be externally pre-existent (*qadīm*) along with the essence (*dhāt*). This proves that it proceeds from a meaning distinct from the essence. We call this distinguishable attribute, by which the act exists, power. The term "power" in language is nothing other than the attribute by which act is made possible for agent, and by it, the act occurs. This description is proven by the decisive distinction we mentioned, and by power we mean nothing other than this attribute which we have established.

If it is said, "But this argument could be turned against you regarding power because, if it is eternal, why do you say its object is not eternal?" we say: "The answer to this will follow when we deal with the properties of will, since we are dealing here with power, by which I mean all possible things. Now it is evident that the possible things are infinite, and therefore, there is no end to the objects of power. We mean by our saying that the possible things are infinite, that the creation of contingent things never comes to a point beyond which it would be rationally impossible for contingent things to occur. The possibility continues forever, and the power is wide enough to include all of it. The proof of the assertion, i.e. the all inclusive connection of power, is that it is already clear that the Creator is One. Either He has a particular power vis–a–vis each object of power—and the latter are infinite, so we thus establish an infinite progression of powers, which is absurd because of what we have already said about the absurdity of infinite devolutions—or, power should be one, so that despite its oneness it will be connected with all atoms and accidents in their multiplicity, because of something common to them all. However, there is no common element other than potentiality (*imkān*). Thus it necessarily follows that every possible thing is undoubtedly an object of power, occurring by power."

On the whole, if any atoms and accidents proceed from Him, then their like must necessarily also issue from Him, because power to do a thing is also power to do its like, since multiplicity of the objects of power is not impossible, and since power has only one mode of relationship to all movements and all colors, and thus power leads itself perpetually to the creation of one movement after another, one color after another, one atom after another. . . . By necessity we know that what is necessary for one thing is necessary for a like thing, and from this axiom three points arise.

1. If anyone asks "Do you say that a thing contrary to what is known could be an object of power?" we reply: "It is established that every possible is an object of power (hence could exist), and that the impossible is not. Let us, therefore, examine closely whether the contrary to what is known is possible or impossible! We shall not know that, until we know all the meanings of possible and impossible. You should know that there is equivocation in the terms. It is evident that a thing can be both possible in itself, and impossible in relation to other things, but it cannot be in itself both possible and impossible.

"For example, we may say that it is present in God's knowledge that He will cause Zayd to die on Saturday morning. One may ask then whether the creation of life for Zayd on the morning of Saturday is possible or impossible. The truth is that it is both: possible in itself, but impossible in consideration of the divine knowledge. Impossible in itself would be that which is unattainable in itself, like the bringing together of the colors black and white, and not something which would be impossible because it involved impossibility in something else. In the case of Zayd's life, his living is not impossible in terms of life itself, but in terms of knowledge itself, since otherwise knowledge would have to be transformed into ignorance, which is absurd."

2. Someone may say "You have claimed that the generality of power in its connection with things is possible. What do you have to say about objects of power for animals and other creatures? If you maintain that these fall within God's power, you shall have to affirm one of two things: a. That a single object of power is acted upon by two powerful agents, which is absurd; or b. That man and the animals do not have power, which is an obstinate negation of necessity, and negates the commands of the Divine Law, since it cannot demand what cannot be done. God can never demand of man what He knows man is incapable of."

In solving this problem, we may say that people have taken different positions on the issue. The Jabarīya denied the power of man, and so were forced even to deny any necessary difference between an involuntary tremor and a voluntary movement, and consequently had to admit that the Divine Law made unfulfillable demands.

The Mu'tazila claimed that all action issuing from man, animals, angels, jinn and devils is originated by them and created by them. They thus had necessarily to commit two abominable enormities. One was to deny what the pious forefathers had joined together on, viz: that there is no creator but God, and no originator beside Him. The second was to relate origin and creation to one who is ignorant of them, for a child or a kitten seeks the breast of its mother, and the spider weaves houses in strange form that baffle an architect, yet we know that the spider does not have access to knowledge of which geometricians are ignorant. Bees, too, form their honeycombs in hexagons, without any square or circular or octagonal forms. This is because the hexagon has the principle, unlike the circle or octagon, that if hexagons are placed in contiguity, no unemployed apertures are formed, and (unlike the square, which may be contiguous), encompasses the bodies of the bees, which are almost round. There are wonders of this sort in the works of animals which, if some were mentioned, would awe the hearts with the majesty and power of God Most High. May misery befall those deviators who think that they share with God in His creation. For the mighty Lord of Heaven alone possesses omnipotence.

Observe now how the People of the Sunna were guided to what is right, and neared the golden mean in their belief. The right, they say, is to affirm that there are two powers operating on one act, but with a single power relating to both agents; however, the two powers differ, as does the pattern of their connection, so that their concurrence on a single object is not absurd.[29]

In other moods, however, al-Ghazālī was capable of the most rigid determinism, which could lead him to deny human responsibility, and even simple human gratitude.

How God Alone is Your Benefactor
from Revivification of the Sciences of Religion
by Abū Ḥāmid al-Ghazālī

It is man's nature to love one who bestows benefits and possessions on him and is kind of speech to him and gives evil to those who are evil to him (but) benefits from human beings are not to be imagined, except in a metaphorical way, for the Benefactor is God alone. Let us suppose that a man has endowed you with all his treasures and empowered you to dispose of them as you will, and that you then think that these benefits came from that man. That would be a mistake, for the man's good action was only performed by means of himself and its possessions and his motivation to turn them over to you. But who was it who was gracious to His creature, and who created his possessions and his ability to act thus, and who created his will and his motivation? Inasmuch as God empowered his motives, he was overcome and compelled to give his wealth to you, for he was unable to oppose Him. The owner of the hand (that gave) was compelled as a water channel is compelled to let water run in it, so that if you believed him to be the benefactor, or thanked him as other than the means, you would be ignorant of the truth of the matter. For doing good cannot be expected of a man, except to himself. Created beings will not give up something that is theirs, except for some selfish motive. And a knowing man will not love any but God for doing good, for He alone is worthy of that.[30]

A world where all that occurs is by God's will is, as al-Ghazālī suggests, a world where everything that happens, in the realest sense of the word, is a miracle. Anything could, and did, happen. The world was a place of unending wonder, marvel, and delight, where the vast arabesques of God's will proliferated and blossomed, and all was order and harmony at the end.

It is not necessary to belabor this point, for it is one of the aspects of Islamic culture with which the rest of the world is most familiar.

The World as Field of Miracles

Conclusion of A Thousand and One Nights' Entertainment
(Compilation of many periods)

Now during this time Shahrazad had borne King Shahriyar three sons. On the thousand and first night, when she had finished her last tale, she rose and kissed the ground before him, saying, "Great King, for a thousand and one nights I have been recounting to you the fables of past ages and the legends of ancient kings. May I make so bold as to crave a favour of your majesty?"

The King replied, "Ask, and it shall be granted."

Shahrazad called out to the nurses, saying "Bring me my children."

Three little boys were instantly brought in; one walking, one crawling on all fours, and the third sucking at the breast of his nurse. Shahrazad ranged the little ones before the King and, again kissing the ground before him, said "Behold these three whom Allāh has granted to us. For their sake I implore you to spare my life. For if you destroy the mother of these infants, they will find none among women to love them as I would.'

The King embraced his three sons, and his eyes filled with tears as he answered, "I swear by Allāh, Shahrazad, that you were already pardoned before the coming of these children. I loved you because I found you chaste and tender, wise and eloquent. May Allāh bless you, and bless your father and mother, your ancestors, and all your descendants. O Shahrazad, this thousand and first night is brighter for us than the day!"

Shahrazad rejoiced; she kissed the King's hand and called down blessings upon him. . . .

The city was decked and lighted; and in the streets and market squares drums rattled, trumpets blared, and clarions sounded. The King lavished alms on the poor and the destitute, and all the people feasted at the King's expense for thirty days and thirty nights.

Shahriyar ruled over his subjects with justice, and lived happily with Shahrazad until they were visited by the Destroyer of all earthly pleasures, the Annihilator of men.

Now praise and glory be to Him who sits throned in eternity above the shifts of time; who, changing all things, remains Himself unchanged; who alone is the Paragon of all perfection. And blessing and peace be upon His chosen Messenger, the Prince of Apostles, our master Muḥammad, to whom we pray for an auspicious END.[31]

THE RESPONSE OF MAN

It would be fair to say that for the great majority of people who lived in Islamic civilization, the will of God was seen both as command and destiny, and they accepted living in a paradox. It is in the tension of parallel values such as this, or the related dualism of the Law and mysticism, that the inner life of a civilization is woven. The response men made to this tension to be sure took various forms.

The Shī'ī theologians of course still insisted that man had free will. Their history had proved to their satisfaction that the majority could be wrong, that individuals could make desperately bad choices, and that God had never in any way desired what had actually happened. In the long run, of course, evil could not triumph, but its day was real and bitter enough. Their statements on this—like that of 'Allāma al-Ḥillī below, with its commentary by Miqdād-i Fāḍil—closely parallel those of the Mu'tazila.

Shī'ism and Free Will
from The Eleventh Chapter *(Twelver Doctrinal Statement)*
by 'Allāma al-Ḥillī (d. A.H. *726/*A.D. *1326) with later commentary*

118–22: We are free agents, and necessity requires this. The belief of Abū al-Ḥasan al-Ash'arī and those who follow him, is that all actions take place by the Power of Allāh the Most High, and no action whatever belongs to the creature. And some of the Ash'arites say that the essence of the act is of Allāh, and the creature has *kasb,* which they explain as the action's being obedience or disobedience (that is, the moral quality of the act belongs to man, the act itself is Allāh's). And some of them say that its meaning is that when the creature determines to undertake some thing, Allāh the Most High creates the act thereupon. And the Mu'tazilites and Zaydites and Imāmites say that actions which proceed from the creature, and their qualities, and the kasb which they spoke of, *all* take place by the power and choice of the creature; and he is not forced (*majbūr*) to act as he does, but he can act and refrain from acting, and this is the reality, for several reasons:

1. First, we find a necessary difference between the issuing from us of an action which results from purpose and motive, like the descent from the roof by a ladder, and the issuing of an action of another sort, like falling from the roof either by constraint or accidentally. For we have power to refrain from the first, but not from the second.

2. If the creature were not the bringer-into-existence of his actions, then his responsibility (*taklīf*) would be impossible, otherwise he would be responsible for what he has no power to perform . . . because he would not have the power to do that for which he is responsible. For if he were responsible, the responsibility would be for something which he has no power to perform, and this is false, by the agreement of all. And when he is not responsible, he is not disobedient when he opposes (God's will), but by the agreement of all he *is* disobedient.

3. If the creature were not a bringer-into-existence of his actions, and did not have power over them, then Allāh would be the most unjust of unjust beings. For since the evil action proceeds from the Most High (not from man), it is impossible for the creature to be punished for it, for he has not performed it. But all agree that the Most High punishes. Then He would be unjust—but He is exalted far above that!

4. All the (Qur'ānic) verses of promise and threatening and blame and praise (prove this), and they are more than can be numbered.

123: (Evil is impossible for Him) because He has that which deters Him from it, which is knowledge of evil; and He has no motive, for the motive would be either the need (or the wisdom) of evil, both of which are excluded.

124: . . . The will to do evil is impossible for Him, for that will is evil.

79: As to the priority (pre-existence) or origin of (God's) speech: the Ash'arites said that the idea is prior, and the Ḥanbalites said that the letters were prior. And the Mu'tazilites said that the speech was an originated thing, and that is the reality.[32]

The word "Islam" can mean both "commitment" and "submission" to the will of God. One understanding is activist, vital; the other fatalistic and resigned. Faced by the apparent contradiction of a demand for action and a denial of its efficacy, the majority of the faithful responded with a simple and often heroic trust in God.

Trust God
from What is in It is in It
by Jalāl al-Dīn Rūmī (d. A.H. *623/*A.D. *1273)*

The philosophers deny ocular vision (of God), saying: If you see, it is possible that you will become satiated and weary, and this is not feasible. The Sunnī theologians say: it is in the moment when He appears single-colored. For in every instant He appears in a hundred colors. If He should reveal Himself a hundred times, not one will resemble another. You also at this very moment see God; every instant in His works and acts you see Him multicolored. Not one act of His resembles another act. In time of gladness is one epiphany, in time of weeping is another epiphany, in time of fear another, in time of hope another. Since the acts of God, and the epiphany of His acts and works, are infinitely various, not one being like another, therefore the epiphany of His Essence is likewise infinitely various as is the epiphany of His acts: judge of that by this analogy.

You yourself too, being a part of the Divine omnipotence, every moment take on a different form and are not constant in any one.

Once say "God," then stand firm under all calamities that rain upon you.[33]

On The Characteristics of Trust in God
from A Garden for Postulants
by Ibn Yazdānyār (fifth/eleventh century)

God has commanded trust (*tawakkul*) in Him, and conjoined it with faith, according to His Word: "Put all your trust in God, if you are believers." (5:23) Thus He has placed the real secret of faith in trust in Him, so trust in Him is God's bridle on earth, with which He strengthens the hearts of the faithful, and hunger is God's good cheer on earth, with which He satisfies the hearts of the righteous, while strong attachment is a sign of God on earth, which He places in the hearts of the longing.

Sahl ibn 'Abdallāh (d. 869 A.D.) says "The first stage of trust in God is for the worshipper to be before God as a corpse to the corpse–washer, who turns it about as he will, while it has no movement or disposition of its own." And Junayd said "Trust in God is not pursuit of gain or abandoning gain; it is simply the heart's resting on what God has promised it." Dhū al–Nūn al–Miṣrī (d. 861 A.D.) was asked about trust in God, and said, "It is divesting oneself of lords, and cutting one's secondary ties." Ruwaym (d. 915 A.D.) said "Trust in God is letting fall the vision of intermediate things, and depending upon the highest tie of all."

And trust in God is basing the heart on God, by suppressing one's cupidity for anything beside Him. Ibrāhīm ibn Adham (d. 777 A.D.) said "For one who trusts in God, it is the same if he reclines on the thighs of a lion, or on a soft cushion." And al–Daqqāq (d. 1015 A.D.) said "Trusting in God is holding life down to a day at a time, letting tomorrow drop from consideration."

Ibrāhīm al–Khawwāṣ (d. 903 A.D.) says: One of those who trusts in God was asked about trust, and said "It is faithfully believing that God is the Creator, the Sustainer, the Possessor of all things; the Giver and the Denier, the Harmer and the Benefitter, the Restrainer and the Releaser; and that there is no hastening what He delays, and no delaying what He hastens; that the worshipper cannot, either by moving or sitting still, increase his daily bread, for God has already undertaken to provide it, rather than any creature." A part of our sustenance, then, comes by our asking for it, and a part comes to us without our asking, and one of the people of gnosis would be ashamed to trust to God to take care of him in any special way; sufficiency for the creatures has already been established by God. So he trusts to Him only to take care of him in the next world, in those things for which He has not guaranteed him His care, such as death, and the desolation of the grave, and what comes after. Perform that trust, if you would trust in God, for it is the trust which many of those who trust forget.

Ibn-Masrūq (d. 911 A.D.) says, "He who leaves his own managing lives in peace." And al-Khawwāṣ says in his book *Trusting in God*: "Trusting is for the heart not to rely on wealth, or trade, or connections with any created thing, but to trust in God until one finds the same sweetness in God's forbidding a thing as in His giving it. And it is for the heart to take rest in what God has apportioned it in the Unseen, and made invisible to be disclosed when He chooses, and for it to let its security in the Unseen be as its security in what is in hand, for what is in the hand is exposed to unforseeable happenings, but what is with God is permanent, and in times (of exaltation) the heart can reach it. If the heart can attain this state, it will be strengthened for either the passing of the world or success in it, and for either being forbidden or being given."

Ibrāhīm ibn Shaybān (d. 941 A.D.) was asked what was the real essence of trust in God, and said, "That is a secret between God and His worshipper, so it is incumbent on the worshipper not to inform anyone of the secret except God." Yaḥya ibn Mu'adh al-Rāzī (d. 871 A.D.) said, "Trust is in three stages: the first is ceasing to complain, the second satisfaction with one's portion, and the third is love. The first is for the good, the second for the pious, and the third is for prophets." Shiblī (d. 945 A.D.) was once asked about trust in God, and said "One forgets about trusting in Him, when in audience with Him." Then he recited this verse:

> "How many of my needs I veil to Thee!
> For when we meet, I blush to mention them."

And Sahl ibn 'Abdallāh said "Whoever disparages action disparages the example of the Prophet, God bless him and give him peace; and whoever disparages trust in God disparages faith."[34]

Some responded to the legalism and determinism of official theology with antinomianism and skepticism. They were not often atheists, and many became ṣūfīs of a well-known stamp. One of their best-known spokesmen was the astronomer and mathematician 'Umar Khayyām (d. A.H. 744/A.D. 1132), who in his quatrains asks often poignant questions of the Ash'arī orthodoxy of his day. The following versions from a recent translation are much closer to the originals than the Victorian verses of Fitzgerald.

Questioning
from the Quatrains
by 'Umar Khayyām (d. A.H. *744/*AD. *1132)*

And these, the choicest and the best
Of lowly Earth's ingenious breed,
Mounted on speculation's steed
Still strive to gain Heaven's highest crest.
But Thou, sublime upon Thy throne,
Beholdest with indifferent eyes
Their reasons, reeling like Thy skies,
Defeated by the great Unknown.

Ah, that at Fortune's fickle lust
We waste and wither to no goal,
That in the wide inverted bowl
Of Heaven we are ground to dust.
Woe and alas, that as the eye
This instant flickers in its lid,
We, who were pleased in naught we did,
Unwilling born, unwilling die.

Lovers, and all in disarray,
Dishevelled, drunken and distraught
Where the fair idols dwell, and naught
But wine to worship, this glad day—
With selfhood to oblivion hurled
We stand emancipate, alone
Attached to God's eternal Throne
As at the dawning of the world.

A stark and solemn truth I say,
Not as in parables to preach:
We are but counters, all and each,
That Heaven moveth at its play.

We stir awhile, as if at will,
About the chessboard of the days,
Till in the box of death Time lays
Our pawns, to be forever still.

Best of all friends I ever had,
Give heed to this my counsel wise:
Think not on the unrooted skies,
Let not their swivelling make thee sad.
Best in contentment's quiet court
Choose thou thy corner and there squat,
Regarding with amusement what
The heavens contrive in their poor sport.[35]

Beyond trusting that all would be well, or mocking the accepted theology, there was for the few a third response, one that saw beyond the paradox of command and destiny to a unified vision. This was the vision of some of the Ṣūfī saints, who beheld the nexus of the Law of men and the Law of objects, and for whom the eternal life had already begun.

The Relativity of Obedience and Disobedience
from What is in It is in It
by Jalāl al-Dīn Rūmī (d. A.H. *623/*A.D. *1273)*

A prince orders a tent to be stitched. One man twists the rope, another strikes the pegs, another weaves the covering, another stitches, another rends, another sticks in the needle. Although to outward seeming they are diverse and different, from the standpoint of meaning they are united and doing the same job.

So it is with the affairs of this world. When you look into the matter, all are doing God's service, reprobate and righteous, sinner and obedient, devil and angel. For example, the king wishes to prove and make trial of his slaves by various means, so that the constant may be sorted out from the inconstant, the loyal from the disloyal, the faithful from the unfaithful.

A certain king ordered his slavegirl to adorn herself and offer herself to his slaves, so that their loyalty and disloyalty might be revealed. Though the girl's action appears outwardly sinful, in reality she is doing the king's service.

These true servants (the saints) have seen themselves in this world, not by proof and rote, but face to face and unveiled, that all men, good and evil alike, are obedient servants of God. "Nothing there is, that does not proclaim His praise." (17:46). Therefore, in regard to them this world itself is the resurrection, in that the resurrection means in reality that all are serving God and doing no other work but His service.[36]

It is a true saying, that all things in relation to God are good and perfect, only in relation to us it is not so. Fornication and purity, not praying and prayer, unbelief and Islam, polytheism and unitarianism—with God all these are good; in relation to us fornication and thieving, unbelief and polytheism are bad, while unitarianism and prayer and good works in relation to us are good. But in relation to God, all are good.[37]

NOTES

1. Ibn 'Abdūn. *Risāla fī al-Qaḍā' wa al-Ḥisba.* Edited by Lévy-Provençal. Cairo, 1955. pp. 3–5. (Editor's translation. A French translation by Professor Lévy-Provençal also exists.)
2. al-Ghazālī. *Naṣīhat al-Mulūk.* Translated by F. R. C. Bagley as "Counsels for Kings," (London, 1964) p. 61.
3. al-Ghazālī. *Iḥyā' 'Ulūm al-Dīn.* Cairo, 1939. Book XX, Chap. 6. (Editor's translation and abridgement.)
4. Rūmī. *Fīhi mā Fīhi.* Translated by A. J. Arberry as *Discourses of Rumi,* (London, 1961), pp. 13–14.
5. Ibn Qutayba. *'Uyūn al-Akhbār.* Berlin and Strassburg, 1900–1908. p. 87. (Editor's translation. Also translated by Margoliouth, *J.R.A.S.* 1910, 311–12.)
6. Ibn 'Abdūn. *op. cit.* pp. 14–15. (Editor's translation.)
7. Abū al-'Alā' Mawdūdī. *Islamic Law and Constitution.* Translated by Khurshid Ahmad. Lahore, 1960. pp. 120–22.
8. al-Māwardī. *al-Ahkām al-Sulṭānīya.* Cairo, 1909. pp. 64–80. (Editor's translation and abridgement.)
9. al-Nawawī. *Minhaj al-Tālibīn.* Batavia, 1884. pp. 205–44. (Editor's translation and abridgement.)
10. From Sūra 13:17 in A. J. Arberry, *The Qur'ān Interpreted,* (Oxford, 1964) pp. 241–42.
11. *Rasā'il Ikhwān al-Ṣafā.* Beirut, 1957. Vol. IV, pp. 76–78. (By courtesy of Lorne M. Kenny, translator.)
12. Ibn Taymīya. *Risālat al-Ḥisba fi al-Islām.* In *Majmu' al-Rasā'il al-Kubra.* Cairo, 1905. p. 66.
13. Ibn 'Abdūn. *op. cit.* pp. 16–17. (Editor's translation.)
14. Ibid. pp. 26–27. (Editor's translation.)
15. Ibid. pp. 44–46.
16. Ibid. p. 49.
17. Ibid. pp. 51–53.
18. Ibid. p. 55.
19. Ibid. p. 57.

20. Ibid. p. 59.
21. Ibid. pp. 60–61.
22. Ed. by Ritter. *Der Islam.* 1933, Vol. 21, pp. 67–83. By courtesy of David Ede, translator. (Editor's abridgement.)
23. 'Abd al-Jabbār al-Asadabādī. *Sharḥ al-Uṣūl al-Khamsa.* Cairo, 1965. pp. 457–83. (Editor's translation and abridgement.)
24. R. J. McCarthy, translator. *Kitāb al-Luma'.* Beirut, 1953. pp. 37, 63, 65, 99–100. (Here slightly abridged.)
25. Yörükän, editor. *Islam Akaidine Dair Eski Metinler.* Istanbul, 1953. Propositions 3, 7, 8, 10, 13, 14. (Editor's translation.)
26. *Rasā'il Ikhwān al-Ṣafā. ed. cit.* pp. 73–75. Translated by Lorne M. Kenny. (Editor's abridgement.)
27. Ibn Yazdānyār. *Rawḍat al-Murīdīn.* From unpublished mss. in Princeton, Paris, Berlin, Cairo, and Istanbul. (Editor's translation and abridgement.)
28. 'Abd al-Qādir al-Jīlānī. *Futūḥ al-Ghayb.* Cairo, 1913. Twenty-first discourse. (Editor's translation.)
29. al-Ghazālī. *al-Iqtiṣād fī al-I'tiqād.* Ankara, 1962. pp. 80ff. By courtesy of 'Abd al-Raḥmān Abū Zayd, translator. (Editor's abridgement.)
30. al-Ghazālī. *Iḥyā'.* Vol. IV, Bk. 26. (Translated also by editor in *Islam,* New York, 1961.)
31. N. J. Dawood. *Aladdin and Other Tales from the Thousand and One Nights.* Penguin Books, 1957. pp. 210ff.
32. *al-Bābu-l Ḥādī 'Ashar.* Translated by Wm. McE. Miller. London, 1958. (Sections here abridged.)
33. Rūmī. *Fīhi ma Fīhi.* Arberry translation. London, 1961. pp. 124–25.
34. Ibn Yazdānyār. *Rawḍat al-Murīdīn.* From the chapter on Tawakkul. (Editor's translation and abridgement.)
35. Translated by A. J. Arberry, in *Aspects of Islamic Civilization,* (London, 1964) pp. 290ff.
36. Rūmī. *Fīhi ma Fīhi.* Arberry translation. London, 1961, p. 58.
37. Ibid. p. 43.

The Expected Deliverer

CHAPTER 4

The Expected Deliverer

From the Qur'ān

He whom God guides, he is the rightly guided one; and those whom He leads astray—you will never find for them protectors, apart from Him. . . . (17:97)

That is God's guidance; He guides by it whom He will, and he whom He leads astray, no guide has he. (39:23)

That was one of God's wonders; he whom God guides, he is the guided one, and he whom He leads astray, you will find for him no protector, directing. (18:18)

ORIGINS OF THE MAHDĪ DOCTRINE

The Qur'ān does not use the word *mahdī* (guided one), but it does several times use *muhtadī*, a related word meaning "guided," or specifically "one who accepts guidance." Nonetheless, mahdī soon came to have a special meaning, as a person who was guided by God. Since thus he could do no wrong, a mahdī would clearly be a leader, a model, for others. We shall see that the word occurs often in certain ḥadīths, although there is some question as to whether they are genuinely Muḥammadan ḥadīths.

One of the first likely uses of mahdī as a title is in a context where it is clear that the person so designated was not the only mahdī: his father had been guided before him. It belongs to the story of the "Penitents" of al-Kūfa, who repented their failure to assist al-Ḥusayn and swore vengeance on his slayers: hence, to the early Shī'a.

The Penitents of Kūfa
by Abū Mikhnaf al-Azdī of Kūfa (d. A.H. *157/*A.D. *774)*
quoted in Ṭabarī's History of Prophets and Kings

Abū Mikhnaf says: "(In the year A.H. 65/A.D. 684, Sulaymān ibn Ṣurad took his followers) and came to the grave of al-Ḥusayn in the morning, and stayed that night and a day, praying there and begging God's mercy for him." He says "When the people arrived at the tomb of Ḥusayn, they cried aloud with one voice, and fell to weeping, and never was seen such a day, where most of it was weeping." And he adds: " 'Abd al-Raḥman ibn Jundub told me on the authority of 'Abd al-Raḥman ibn Ghazzīya, 'When we reached the grave of al-Ḥusayn—peace be upon him—the people all wept together, and I heard most of them wishing that they had been slain with him.' Then Sulaymān said 'O God, have mercy on Ḥusayn the Martyr, the son of the Martyr, the Mahdī, the son of the Mahdī, the believing son of the Believer! O God, we testify that we are of their religion and their way, the enemies of those who murdered them, and the friends of those who love them!' Then he left, and those who were with him went away."[1]

Once Ḥusayn was dead, his sympathisers seized power in Kūfa. However, his sons and those of his brother al-Ḥasan were still children, and hence unsuitable as leaders, by Arab standards. The man who became governor of Kūfa, al-Mukhtār, therefore claimed to be acting in the name of another son of 'Alī not by the Prophet's daughter: Muḥammad, called "ibn al-Ḥanafīya" after his mother.

Conveniently for Mukhtār, this Muḥammad, who seems to have been an unenthusiastic heir to the family misfortunes, was in Mecca, in the power of still another rebel against the Umawīs, the son of the Prophet's companion al-Zubayr.

Al-Mukhtār turned the resentment at Ḥusayn's death into a social revolution, calling for equality of non-Arabs with Arabs, and a more just distribution of the spoils. When ibn al-Ḥanafīya died or disappeared, Mukhtār gave out that he was only in a state of occultation (*ghayba*) and would someday return to bring victory to his followers.

At about the same time, traditions attributed to the Prophet were circulated, referring to a Mahdī who would come as a deliverer and vanquish the forces of iniquity. Ibn al-Ḥanafīya was identified by his followers with this figure.

Al-Mukhtār and Ibn al-Ḥanafīya
from Meadows of Gold and Mines of Gems
by Abū al-Ḥasan ʻAlī al-Masʻūdī (d. ca. A.H. *345*/A.D. *956)*

The Partisans (of the Prophet's family) gathered to al-Mukhtār and they made themselves masters in Kūfa. . . . He then wrote ʻAlī, son of al-Ḥusayn, asking him to accept the *bayʻa* and claim the Imamate, but ʻAlī [or more likely the child's guardians—Ed.] refused to accept this from him and denounced him. . . . When al-Mukhtār despaired of ʻAlī ibn al-Ḥusayn, he wrote to his paternal uncle Muḥammad ibn al-Ḥanafīya [who] went to Ibn ʻAbbās (ancestor of the ʻAbbāsī caliphs) and told him the story. Ibn ʻAbbās counselled him, "Do nothing, for you do not know what may come upon you from (the anti-caliph of the Ḥijāz) Ibn al-Zubayr." So he followed his advice, and kept quiet about al-Mukhtār's faults.

The forces of al-Mukhtār grew stronger in Kūfa, and people followed him. He made his claims proportionate to their rank and their spiritual and intellectual attainments. To some he preached the Imamate of Muḥammad ibn al-Ḥanafīya; to others he rejected that and announced that an angel came to him with revelations and gave him information of things unseen. He prosecuted the murderers of al-Ḥusayn, and killed them. . . .

Ibn Zubayr grew angry with those of the Hāshimī clan (that of the Prophet) who were in Mecca, and locked them in a narrow alley, with a great quantity of fuel, such that if a spark landed in it, not one of them would escape. Among them was Muḥammad ibn al-Ḥanafīya (and al-Mukhtār sent a force from Kūfa to release them.) They told him, "Permit us to deal with Ibn al-Zubayr," but Ibn al-Ḥanafīya refused, and left them for Ubulla, where he lived for some years until Ibn al-Zubayr was killed. Those who came to the rescue of Muḥammad ibn al-Ḥanafīya are the Kaysānī Shīʻīs, who hold that he was the Imām, but after that they differ: some there are who stop with his death, and some assert that he did not die, and is living in the mountains. This sect too is divided into sects. They are only called "Kaysānī" because they followed al-Mukhtār ibn ʻUbayd al-Thaqafī, whose name was Kaysān. . . .

Some claim that Ibn al-Ḥanafīya entered the valley of Raḍwa with a group of his disciples, and that nothing more is known of them to this day. Many *akhbārīs* (purveyors of information) mention that the poet Kuthayyir was a Kaysānī, and he held that Muḥammad ibn al-Ḥanafīya was the Mahdī who will fill the earth with justice as it is filled with oppression and tyranny . . . he said in verses, where he mentions Ibn al-Ḥanafīya:

The Imāms from Quraysh, the friends of Truth are four equals:
'Ali and three of his sons, they the grandsons undoubted.
The grandson heir to his faith and pious devotion (Ḥasan),
The grandson who disappeared at Karbalā (Ḥusayn),
The grandson unseen 'til he leads the horsemen preceded by banners,
Veiled to the sight for a time; in Raḍwa with honey and water.

Also on this, al-Sayyid al-Ḥimyarī, who was a Kaysānī says:

Oh, tell the Viceregent 'My life be your ransom!
Long in that mountain now grows your sojourn.
And they persecute the host of your friends,
All of us who call you Imām and Successor.
The peoples of Earth count seventy years since you left us,
But the son of Khawla (the Ḥanafī woman) has not tasted death,
And the earth has not covered his bones.'
Deep in the valley of Raḍwa he stays, and angels answer his speaking.[2]

This appears to have been the first instance of identification of a person as an expected deliverer. By the end of the first century A.H. many ḥadīths were circulating about a future figure, the Mahdī, who would put an end to the trials and divisions of the Community, and bring an age of gold. These ḥadīths are found along with eschatological material relating to the signs of the Hour (the end of time), and the second coming of Christ.

The ones we quote here are probably from the first two centuries. When the 'Abbāsīs began their revolution against the Umawīs in Khurāsān, their ensign was a black banner, so as to conform to the ḥadīth.

Ḥadīths on the Mahdī
from the Niches of Lamps
by al-Khaṭīb al-Tibrīzī (written A.H. *737*/A.D. *1337)*

Muslim: Jābir reported God's messenger as saying, "In the last days there will be a Caliph who will distribute wealth without reckoning it. . . ."

Tirmidhī: Abū Sa'īd al-Khudrī reported the Prophet as saying in the course of a story about the Mahdī that a man will come to him and say, "Give me, give me, Mahdī," and he will pour into his garment as much as he is able to carry.

Abū Dāwūd: Abū Sa'īd al-Khudrī reported God's messenger as saying: "The Mahdī will be of my stock and will have a broad forehead and a prominent nose. He will fill the earth with equity and justice as it was filled with oppression and tyranny, and will rule for seven years."

Abū Dāwūd: 'Abdallāh ibn Mas'ūd reported God's messenger as saying: "The world will not pass away before the Arabs are ruled by a man of my family whose name will be the same as mine." In another version, he said "If only one day of this world remained, God would lengthen that day until He raised upon it a man who belongs to me (or, to my family) whose name is the same as mine and whose father's name is the same as my father's name (i.e. 'Abdallāh), who will fill the earth with equity and justice as it had been filled with oppression and tyranny."

Abū Dāwūd: Umm Salama told that she heard God's messenger say, "The Mahdī will be of my family, of the descendants of Fāṭima."

Aḥmad ibn Ḥanbal and Bayhaqī: Thawbān reported God's messenger as saying, "When you see the black standards come forth from the direction of Khurāsān go to them, for God's Khalīfa the Mahdī will be among them."

Abū Dāwūd: Abū Isḥāq told that 'Alī looked at his son al-Ḥasan and said, "From his loins will come forth a man who will be called by your Prophet's name and resemble him in nature but not in appearance." He then mentioned the story about his filling the earth with Justice. Abū Dāwūd transmitted this but did not mention the story.

Abū Dāwūd: Umm Salama reported the Prophet as saying, "Disagreement will occur at the death of a Caliph and a man of the people of Medina will come forth flying to Mecca. Some of the people of Mecca will come to him, bring him out against his will, and swear allegiance to him between the corner (of the Ka'ba) and the Maqām (of Abraham.) An expeditionary force will be sent against him from Syria, but will be swallowed up in the desert between Mecca and Medina, and when the people see that, the high saints (*abdāl*) of Syria and the best people of Iraq will come to him and swear allegiance. Then will arise a man of Quraysh, whose maternal uncles belong to (the tribe of) Kalb and send against them an expeditionary force which will be overcome by them, and that is the expeditionary force of Kalb. He will then govern people by the sunna of their Prophet and establish Islam upon the earth. He (the Mahdī) will remain seven years, then die, and the Muslims will pray over him."

Al-Ḥākim: According to Abū Sa'īd, he also said, "Those who dwell in heaven and those who dwell on earth will be pleased with him. The sky will not cease to give any of its rain, but will pour it forth copiously, and the earth will not cease to produce any of its plants, but will bring them forth so that the the living will wish that the dead were alive, in that period of seven, eight, or nine years."

Muslim: Abū Hurayra reported God's messenger as saying, "When three things appear faith will not benefit anyone who has not previously believed or acquired any good from his faith: the rising of the sun in its place of setting, the *dajjāl* (antichrist), and the beast of the earth."

Bukhārī and Muslim: Anas reported God's messenger as saying, "There is no prophet who has not warned his people about the one-eyed liar. I tell you he is one-eyed, but your Lord (whom he will claim to be) is not one-eyed. On his forehead are the letters (*kāf, fā', rā'*, for *kufr*: infidelity)."

Bukhārī and Muslim: Abū Hurayra reported God's messenger as saying, "Let me tell you something about the dajjāl which no prophet has told his people. He is one-eyed, and will bring with him something like paradise and hell, but what he calls paradise will be hell."

Muslim: Anas reported God's messenger as saying, "The dajjāl will be followed by seventy thousand Jews of Isfahān wearing Persian shawls."[3]

Muslim: Abū Hurayra reported God's messenger as saying, "The last hour will not come before the Muslims fight with the Jews and the Muslims kill them, so that the Jews will hide behind stones and trees and the stone and the tree will say 'O Muslim, O servant of God, there is a Jew behind me; come and kill him.' The only exception will be the box-thorn, for it is one of the trees of the Jews."[4]

Tirmidhī and Abū Dāwūd: Mu'adh ibn Jabal reported that the Messenger of God said: "The greatest battle, the conquest of

Constantinople, and the appearance of the dajjāl will all come within seven months' time.[5]

Tirmidhī: from Nawwās ibn Sam'ān, who said: "The Messenger of God—God's blessing and peace be on him—mentioned the dajjāl. We asked how quickly he would go in the world, and he said, 'Like rain driven by the wind. He will come to the people and call them to him, and they will believe in him. He will command the sky, and it will give rain to the earth, and bring forth crops. At evening their herds will come to them with humps as high as can be, their udders full and flanks bulging. Then he will come to the people and summon them, but they will reject his words and he will go away. When they rise the next morning they will be destitute, with none of their wealth. He will pass by wastelands and tell them: "Bring out your treasures," and the treasures will follow him like swarms of bees. Then he will call a man in the fullness of his youth and strike him with a sword and cut him in two as one shoots at a target. Then he will call to him and he will come forward laughing, with his face shining. Just at that time God will send the Messiah son of Mary, who will descend at the white minaret in the east of Damascus wearing two garments dyed in saffron, placing his hands on the wings of two angels. When he lowers his head it will drip, and when he raises it up it will let fall drops like pearls. Every infidel who is touched by his breath shall die, and his breath will reach as far as he can see. He shall seek the dajjāl until he comes upon him at Ludd Gate, and kills him. The people whom God protected from him will then come to Jesus, who will wipe their faces and tell them the place they have in paradise. While this is happening God will tell Jesus, "I have brought forth servants of Mine with whom none may do combat, so collect My worshippers at Mount Sinai." Then God will send (the peoples of) Gog and Magog, "and they slide down every slope" (21:96). The first of them will pass Lake Tiberias and drink what is in it, and the last of them will pass and say, "There was once water here." They will march until they come to the Mount of Thickets, which is a mountain of Jerusalem, and say "We will slay those who are in heaven." Then they will shoot their arrows at the sky, and God will send them back covered with blood. The Prophet of God and his companions will remain confined until the head of an ox means more to them than a hundred gold pieces to one of you today. Then Jesus the Prophet of God and his companions will beg God, and

He will send insects upon their (Gog and Magog's) necks, and at morning they will be dead like one dead man. God will send birds with necks like camels necks, and they will carry them and throw them where God wills. Then the earth will be told "Bring forth thy fruits and return to thy fertility," and in those days a party shall eat from a pomegranate, and one cow will supply a whole tribe with milk. Then God will send a pleasant wind, and it will take the life of every believer and every Muslim. The bad people will remain screaming with hoarse cries like those of a donkey, and the Hour shall come upon them.' "[6]

Bukhārī and Muslim. Abū Hurayra related that the Messenger of God, the blessing of God and peace be upon him, said: "By Him in whose hand is my life, it is not to be doubted that the son of Mary shall descend among you, ruling with justice, and he shall break the Cross, and kill the swine, and exact the jizya tax, and wealth will increase until no one will accept it, and one ritual prayer seems better than the world and all that is in it." Then Abū Hurayra said, "You can read it in the Book if you like: 'And there shall not be one of the People of the Book who does not believe in him before his death' (4:159)."

Bukhārī and Muslim: Abū Hurayra reported that the Messenger of God said, "How will it be with you when the son of Mary descends among you, and your Imām is with you?"

Muslim: Jābir says that the Messenger of God, on whom be peace and blessing of God, said: "One party of my Community will not cease to struggle for truth victoriously up to the Day of Resurrection. Jesus son of Mary will come down, and their leader will say 'Come, lead us in prayer,' but he will say 'No, for verily some of you are commanders over others, because of God's grace to this community.' "[7]

Such ḥadīths set the terms for many later discussions of the Mahdī. He will come near the end of time. However the older meaning of mahdī—a guided person but not necessarily a unique or eschatological figure—continued for awhile. The pious adherents of 'Umar ibn 'Abd al-'Azīz, for example, considered him a mahdī, and the usage appears to have survived to some extent among the Zaydī Shī'īs, today found in the Yaman. Many of their Imāms have been called "the Mahdī."

The Zaydīs trace their origins to the leader of an unsuccessful Shī'ī revolt against the Umawīs. His story follows:

The Story of Zayd ibn 'Alī Zayn al-'Abidīn
from Meadows of Gold and Mines of Gems
by Abū al-Ḥasan 'Alī al-Mas'ūdī (d. ca. A.H. *345*/A.D. *956)*

In the reign of Caliph Hishām the Umawī in the year 121/739 (though some say it was 122) Zayd son of 'Alī Zayn al-'Abidīn the son of al-Ḥusayn ibn 'Alī was martyred. He had consulted his brother Muḥammad [the fifth Imām of the Twelver Shī'īs—Ed.] and his brother had told him "Do not (attempt a revolution) with the aid of the deceitful and treacherous people of Kūfa. That was where your great-grandfather 'Alī was killed and your uncle Ḥasan was wounded, and where the people of the family have been insulted."

Before this, Zayd had been to see Hishām at Ruṣāfa, and when he presented himself, he found no place to sit, and had to sit in the lowest part of the hall [This accorded neither with hospitality nor with his family's rank.—Ed.]; and he said "Commander of Believers, no one is either so great or so humble that he need not fear God." Hishām replied "Be quiet, you slave girl's bastard, you who cast eyes at the Caliphate!" Zayd replied "Commander of Believers, there is an answer to that, which you may hear or not, just as you choose." "Nay, speak!" said he. "The slavery of a mother does not impede the progress of a son," Zayd said. "The mother of Ishmael was the slave of Sara, and it did not keep God from choosing Ishmael as a prophet, and the father of the Arabs, and the ancestor of Muḥammad, the noblest of mankind—so do you tell me that, when I am also the son of 'Alī and Fāṭima?" With that, he rose and left. . . .

Then he went to Kūfa, and made an uprising against (Hishām's governor) Yūsuf ibn 'Umar al-Thaqafī. When the war broke out, Zayd's supporters laid down their arms, and he remained with a handful of men, fighting a terrible battle. He recited these words:

"Life without glory and glorious death
Have both, I think, a bitter taste.
But if it must be one or the other,
Then I'm going to death by the best way."

When night separated the two parties, Zayd retired covered with wounds. An arrow had struck him in the forehead, and they looked for someone to extract the arrowhead. A village cupper was brought from whom they hid Zayd's identity, but when he drew out the iron, Zayd expired on the spot. He was buried in a watercourse, and his grave was covered with grass, and the water allowed to run over it. But the surgeon told Yūsuf al–Thaqafī and showed him the grave. Yūsuf had the body dug up, and sent the head to Hishām and crucified the naked body. Upon this, one of the Umawī poets wrote:

> We nailed your Zayd on a palm–trunk (*jadh'a,* also: a lively youth).
> Well, I never saw a Mahdī who was stuck on one of those.[8]

The revolt of the 'Abbāsīs, as we have seen, contained distinct evocations of Mahdism. Change of dynasty did not mean that religious revolts in the name of the Mahdī ceased, however. In one of these, the descendants of al-Ḥasan were nearly extirpated (though one of them, Idrīs, escaped to Morocco and there founded the Idrīsī dynasty at Fez.)

The Revolt of Muḥammad ibn 'Abdallah al–Ḥasanī
from Al–Fakhrī
by Ibn al–Ṭiqtiqā' (written A.H. *702*/A.D. *1302)*

Toward the end of the Umawī dynasty, the leading Hāshimites (both the descendants of 'Alī and the descendants of al–'Abbās) met to discuss their situation and the treatment they received from the Umawīs, and agreed to make secret propaganda among the people, and to elect as their head Muḥammad ibn 'Abdallāh ibn al–Ḥasan ibn al–Ḥasan ibn 'Alī ibn Abī Ṭālib, who was called "The Pure Soul." He was one of the leading Hāshimīs and one of their best men in merit, nobility, and religious knowledge. . . . They all agreed to render homage to him, up to the leader of the Ḥusaynī branch of the 'Alawīs, Ja'far al–Ṣādiq [sixth Imām of the Twelvers. —Ed.] and he said to Muḥammad's father 'Abdallāh, who was called "*al–mahd*—the thoroughbred" [in distinction to the Ḥusaynīs, who had mixed their blood with non–Arabs.—Ed.] "Your son will never get it (meaning the Caliphate): no one will ever get it but the man in the yellow robe (meaning Manṣūr the 'Abbāsī.)" Manṣūr later said of this occasion, "At the time I was thinking to myself of whom I should appoint as my governors in the provinces. . . ." Then events took their course, and the empire passed to the 'Abbāsīs. . . . And al–Manṣūr demanded of 'Abdallāh, father of Muḥammad, that he turn over his two sons to him. But he said, "I have no knowledge of them," for they had concealed themselves in fear of al–Manṣūr. When the questioners persisted, he cried "How long will you go on? By God, if they were under my foot, I would not raise it for you. Great God! Shall I give you my two boys so you can murder them?" So Manṣūr arrested him and his relatives of the Ḥasanī family (and they died in his prisons.)

At the beginning of this affair, information had spread that Muḥammad was the promised Mahdī, and his father had confirmed this in the spirits of some parties of the people, for it is related that the Messenger, God's blessings and peace be upon him, said: "If only one day remained for the world, God would prolong that day until He had sent our Mahdī, or our Leader, and his name is like my name, and his father's name is like my father's." Now the Imāmī Shī'a repeat this, but they leave out "and his father's name is like my father's."

'Abdallāh "The Thoroughbred" would tell people about his son Muḥammad: "He is the Mahdī of whom good tidings are given: he is Muḥammad, son of 'Abdallāh."

And God caused the people to love Muḥammad, and they inclined to him and his desire to seek supreme power grew as the desire of the people for him grew. He went into hiding when the state fell to the 'Abbāsīs, fearing for himself, but when he learned what had happened to his father and his people, he took Medina. He revealed himself; the notables of the city rallied to him, and very few opposed him. Thus he gained control of Medina, and deposed its commandant, appointed a governor and a qāḍī, and broke down the doors of the prisons and set free those within. . . .

Then Manṣūr was standing and sitting (in his anxiety), and time passed. They each wrote and sent letters to the other which are accounted to be among the finest of documents, in which argumentation of every sort is employed.

At last Manṣūr ordered his nephew 'Isā ibn Mūsā to do battle, and 'Isā met him with a great army. The victory went to the forces of Manṣūr, and Muḥammad ibn 'Abdallāh was killed, and his head taken to Manṣūr. All this occurred in the year A.H. 145/A.D. 762. Then Muḥammad's brother Ibrāhīm, who is called "The Martyr of Bākhamra" [and who was also called "The Hādī," or "Guide"—Ed.], raised a revolt at Baṣra.

During the time he was hidden, Ibrāhīm used to mix with the army of Manṣūr incognito, and even eat at their mess, though Manṣūr had organised an intense search for him. Then he left Manṣūr's capital and went to Baṣra and appeared openly and called for support. Many followed him, and their numbers grew, so Manṣūr sent 'Isā ibn Mūsā against him when he returned from killing The Pure Soul.

'Isā came against him with fifteen thousand warriors. They came together at a village called Bākhamra, sixteen parasangs from Kūfa. Victory was with the army of Manṣūr, and Ibrāhīm was killed in the battle. . . . May God Most High have mercy on him![9]

Although Manṣūr gave his son and successor the name "al-Mahdī," in order to attract the charisma of the title to his dynasty, it was the Shī'īs who did most to keep the legend of the promised deliverer alive in the first centuries of Islam. Instead of the reign of justice and perfect Islam they had promised, the 'Abbāsīs instituted a persianized oriental despotism, with theocratic pretensions. In the context of the times, a religious revolution in the name of the expected Mahdī was the perfect answer, and it was the Shī'īs who had most to gain by making it. In the tenth century A.D. the Ismā'īlī Shī'īs made a great revolt under an Imām who claimed to be of the "Children of Fāṭima," a descendant of Ja'far al-Ṣadiq's son Ismā'īl, and they set up a state in Tunisia by driving out the 'Abbāsīs' hereditary prince–governors, the Aghlabī dynasty. The Aga Khans today trace their descent from the Fāṭimī Imāms, and 'Ubaydallāh the Mahdī is still considered by the Ismā'īlīs to have been the Expected One.

The following account was written by a scholar–member of the princely family of the Banu Ḥammād, who ruled eastern Algeria as viceroys of the Fāṭimīs after they moved to Cairo. He lived from A.H. 548/A.D. 1150 to A.H. 628/A.D. 1230.

'Ubaydallāh the Mahdī and the Rise of the Fāṭimīs
from History of the Kings of the 'Ubaydī Dynasty
by Ibn Ḥammād (d. A.H. *628/*A.D. *1230)*

The Mahdī 'Ubaydallāh: People have differed about his claim of descent from Ḥusayn the son of 'Alī—on both of whom be peace. Some admit his claim and recognise what he said. Others reject and deny what he adduced, and people will not cease to disagree about it except by a mercy of God. Now what he claimed was that he was 'Ubaydallāh ibn Muḥammad ibn al–Ḥusayn ibn Muḥammad ibn Ismā'īl ibn Ja'far al–Ṣādiq ibn Muḥammad ibn 'Alī Zayn al–

'Abidīn ibn al-Ḥusayn ibn 'Alī, but there is no way to prove what people have said, and I myself have no need to do so.

He was born in Salamīya in Syria, though some say it was Baghdad, in the year A.H. 260/A.D. 873–4. In A.H. 289/A.D. 902, he went to Egypt disguised as a merchant, in search of great adventures. The 'Abbāsīs were looking for him, sending letters to all the provincial capitals with his name and description, ordering that he be arrested as soon as he was discovered, but he was saved from the hands of the governors until he reached the oasis of Sijilmāsa (in Morocco), either by previous agreement or by chance, appearing there on Sunday the 7th of Dhū al-Hijja 296/27th of August A.D. 909. He and his son Abū al-Qāsim were both taken (by the Khārijī prince of the city) and shackled with irons.

During this time (his agent) Abū 'Abdallāh al-Ḥusayn ibn Aḥmad ibn Muḥammad—known as "the Muḥtasib," because he had been inspector of the spinners' bazaar at Baṣra—made an uprising. He was also called "The Teacher," because he used to teach people the doctrine of the esoteric Shī'īs (or Ismā'īlīs). When Abū 'Abdallāh had made his preparations, he raised an army and conquered cities and seized provinces. He constructed a city west of Constantine and called it "The House of the Hijra," and named his followers and partisans from among the Kutāma Berbers and others "The Believers." When he mounted, a herald would cry to his troops "To horse, O Cavaliers of God!" and on the cruppers of the horses was written "God's is the Kingdom." Among the Qur'ānic verses on his banners were "Certainly their host shall be routed and turn their backs" (54:45). . . . And on his seal was "Perfected are the words of thy Lord in Truth and Justice, no one shall change His words; He is the All-Hearing, the All-Aware" (6:115).

Then he subjected Africa (i.e. Tunisia and eastern Algeria) and possessed it by force of arms. The last of the House of Aghlab, the (hereditary) governors of the 'Abbāsīs, was Ziyādat Allāh, and when Abū 'Abdallāh the Shī'ī had seized all their kingdom he left Raqqāda their capital by night with all he could carry and fled to the East in A.H. 296/A.D. 909.

Abū 'Abdallāh settled in the Palace of the Lake, and ordered that the negro slave-guards of the Aghlabī be put to death. They were killed to the last man, and buried (ignominiously) face down.

He sent an army against Tripoli, and it brought back his brother

Abū al–'Abbās al–Makhtūm who had been imprisoned there, and the mother of 'Ubaydallāh's father, who was living there with her sorrows.

Then he set out with an enormous army of cavalry and foot–soldiers to Sijilmāsa and laid siege to it and took it and released 'Ubaydallāh (the Mahdī) and his son . . . he came out dressed in superbly beautiful robes, a flowing mantle, and Arab sandals, mounted on a thoroughbred mare, and was acclaimed as the Imām in Rabī' II A.H. 297/December A.D. 909.

'Ubaydallāh went to Africa (Tunisia) and settled in Raqqāda until the city of Mahdīya should be built at the place called "The Peninsula of the Grotto." He laid it out in the ascendancy of the sign of Leo, because it is a fixed constellation, so that it should be fixed, and because it was in the house of the Sun, which is the sign of kings. . . .

He built in it the palace known by his name, which stands still today, and built (facing it) a palace for his son Abū al–Qāsim. He also built the maritime arsenal which is found there today. . . .

He settled in Mahdīya in A.H. 308/A.D. 921. In A.H. 298/A.D. 911 he had put to death Abū 'Abdallāh his propagandist *(dā'ī)* with his brother Abū al–'Abbās, in the palace garden. . . .

Thus in the end he consolidated his power, and ruled over all Africa and Morocco, Tripolitania, Jerba, and Sicily. His son and heir Abū al–Qāsim made two expeditions against Egypt, in A.H. 301/A.D. 913, and A.H. 306/A.D. 918. (But the Fāṭimīs did not succeed in conquering Egypt until 969.)[10]

The Fāṭimī dynasty was no more successful at bringing forth the Kingdom of God on earth than the 'Abbāsīs had been. What they produced was a rival empire, with similar institutions. The Saljūqs (and the Crusaders) prevented them from taking Iraq and Syria, and in 1171 their state was brought to an end by Salāḥ al-Dīn the Ayyūbī.

But Mahdism as social and religious revolution, and as a reforming movement, had by now become a recurrent theme in Islamic history. The exalted claims of state theory coupled with the limitations of worldly power acted as a forcing–bed for extravagant reactions. If the Shī'īs were at first the most active in such movements, it was not because Sunnīs did not also accept the legend of the Mahdī. Around 955 A.D., a native of Jerusalem named Mutaḥḥar ibn Ṭāhir, who lived and wrote under the Sunnī Samānī dynasty in eastern Iran, summed up thus ideas about the Mahdī in his time.

The Campaign of the Mahdī
from The Beginning and History
by Mutaḥḥar ibn Tāḥir of Jerusalem (written ca. A.H. *344*/A.D. *955)*

The Campaign of the Mahdī: There have been diverse stories told about this, and sayings of the Prophet, on whom be God's blessing and peace, from 'Alī, Ibn 'Abbās, and others. . . . The best of these traditions is that transmitted by Ibn Mas'ūd, who relates that the Prophet said, "The world will not pass away until my community has been ruled by a man of my family whose name shall agree with mine. . . ." The Shī'a have many poems about this, and far-fetched writings. Yet Aḥmad ibn Muḥammad ibn al-Ḥajjāj, known as al-Sijzī, told me at Shīrjān in A.H. 325/A.D. 937, "Muḥammad ibn Aḥmad ibn Rashīd al-Iṣfahānī told me by a sound chain of authorities that the Prophet said 'Matters will only grow more difficult, and the world is only going to its end; people will only grow more hard-hearted, and rise only to do evil to each other, and there will be no Mahdī but Jesus, the son of Mary.' "

Those who accept the first of these two traditions differ: some say that the Mahdī was 'Alī ibn Alī Ṭālib, interpreting thus the statement, "You will find him a good guide, well guided." Others assert that the Mahdī was the 'Abbāsī Caliph Muḥammad ibn al-Manṣūr, titled "al-Mahdī," who was indeed a Muḥammad of the Prophet's family and who did in fact make efforts to make justice triumph and repel tyranny. It was said to Ta'ūs, " 'Umar ibn 'Abd al-'Azīz is the Mahdī of whom we have heard," but he said "No, for he has not yet attained perfect justice, but that one shall attain it." The Shī'a deny that the Mahdī can be anyone but a descendant of 'Alī, but they disagree, and some say that it was Muḥammad ibn al-Ḥanafīya and he did not die, but will rise and rule the Arabs with only a stick. As proof, they adduce the fact that 'Alī gave him his banner at the Battle of the Camel. Others say he must be a descendant of al-Ḥusayn, 'Alī's son by Fāṭima, because he exerted himself to get what was right, until he found martyrdom. Still others say that he must be a descendant of 'Alī's other son, al-Ḥasan. And they also disagree on his signs and physical appearance, for some say, "He must be the son of a slavegirl, brown-eyed, with flashing white teeth, and a mole on his cheek." Others say that he will be born at Medina and rise in Mecca, and the people will swear allegiance to him between Safā and Marwa. Still others assert that he shall rise at ʿAlamūt. And the Idrīsīs [should be: Fāṭimīs—Ed.] have given the name of "Mahdīya" to their capital in Africa (lit: "to Qayrawān") in their ambition that the Mahdī should be one of them. It is said that he shall cause oppression to cease among the people of the earth, and cause justice to flow upon them, and he shall cause the strong and the weak to be as equals, and spread Islam in the East and West, and he shall conquer Constantinople, and there shall not remain one who is not either a Muslim or pays the forfeit, and at that time the promise of God shall be fulfilled, to make him entirely victorious over religion. And they also differ about the length of his life, for some say he will live (sic) seven years, and others say nine, or twenty, or forty, or sixty.

There is a tradition from Abū Hurayra (that the Prophet said) "The last hour shall not strike until the travellers turn back from Rome, and it shall not strike until a man from Qaḥṭān (South Arabian stock) governs the people." People differ about this; it is reported that Ibn Sīrīn said, "The Qaḥṭānī is a righteous man, and it is he whom Jesus shall follow in the prayers, and he is the Mahdī," and that Kaʿb al-Aḥbār said, "The Mahdī will die, and afterward they will swear allegiance to the Qaḥṭānī" and that ʿAbdallāh ibn ʿUmar said, "It is a man who will rise after the children of ʿAbbās." Kaʿb al-Aḥbār said, "He shall not be inferior in justice to the Mahdī." Some commentators interpret the Qur'ānic verse "*Alif. Lām. Mīm.* The Greeks have been vanquished" (Qur. 30:1) as referring to something that is to be, and it is said that between the conquest of Constantinople and the rise of the False Messiah (al-dajjāl) there shall be a space of seven years.[11]

Apart from the Ismāʿīlīs, who believed that ʿUbaydallāh was the promised Mahdī, there were once many Shīʿī sects who believed that some leader of the Prophet's family was in ghayba (a period of temporary concealment) and would reappear as the promised Mahdī. Most of them are only remembered as curiosities.

However, we have already seen that the largest sect of the Shīʿa, the Twelvers, believe that their vanished twelfth Imām is in occultation. They believe that in the fullness of time he will come as the Mahdī, to fulfill the promise.

The section following is by one of the greatest early Twelver doctors.

The Mahdī of the Twelver Shī'īs
from the Treatise on Matters of Belief
by Abū Ja'far Ibn Babūya al-Qummī (d. A.H. *381/*A.D. *991)*

Our belief is that after His Prophet, the blessings of Allah be upon him, the proofs of Allah for the people are the Twelve Imāms, the first of them being the Prince of Believers 'Alī b. Abī Ṭālib, then al-Ḥasan, then al-Ḥusayn, then 'Alī b. al-Ḥusayn, then Muḥammad b. 'Alī, then Ja'far b. Muḥammad, then Mūsā b. Ja'far, then 'Alī b. Mūsā al-Riḍa, then Muḥammad b. 'Alī, then 'Alī b. Muḥammad, then al-Ḥasan b. 'Ali, then Muḥammad b. al-Ḥasan the Proof, who upholds the command of Allah, the *sāḥib al-zamān* (Lord of the Age), the Viceregent (*khalīfa*) of the Beneficent One in His earth, the one who is present in the earth but invisible (*ghā'ib*) to the eyes—the blessings of Allah on all of them. . . .

We believe that the earth cannot be without the Proof of Allah to His creatures—a leader either manifest and well-known, or hidden and obscure.

We believe that the Proof of Allah in His earth and His viceregent among His slaves in this age of ours is the Upholder (al-Qā'im), the Expected One (al-Muntaẓar), Muḥammad b. al-Ḥasan b. 'Ali b. Muḥammad b. 'Alī b. Mūsā b. Ja'far etc., on them be peace. He it is concerning whose name and descent the Prophet was informed by Allah the Mighty and Glorious, and he it is *who will fill the earth with justice and equity,* just *as now it is full of oppression and wrong.* And he it is through whom Allah will make His faith manifest "to supersede all religion, though the polytheists dislike it" (9:33, 48:28, 61:9). He it is whom Allah will make victorious over the whole world until from every place the call to prayer will be heard, and all religion will be to Allah, Exalted is He. He it is who is the Rightly Guided (mahdī), about whom the Prophet gave information that when he appears, Jesus son of Mary will descend upon the earth and pray behind him, and he who prays behind him is like one who prays behind the Prophet, because he is his viceregent.

And we believe that there can be no Qā'im other than him; he may live in the state of occultation (as long as he likes); and were he to live in the state of occultation for the space of the existence of this world, there would nevertheless be no Qā'im other than he. For, the Prophets and the Imāms have indicated him by his name and descent; him they appointed as their successor, and of him they gave glad tidings—the blessings of Allah on all of them.[12]

The period after the Mongol invasion of the 'Abbāsī state was again a time of toleration for the Shī'a, and the indefatigable Moorish traveller Ibn Baṭṭūṭa of the fourteenth century A.D. describes thus the cult of the Twelfth Imām as he found it in Iraq.

The Expectation of the Twelfth Imām in Iraq
from the Rare Works of Beholders in Exotic Cities and Marvelous Journeys
by Ibn Baṭṭūṭa of Tangier (written A.H. *756*/A.D. *1357)*

The inhabitants of Ḥilla are all Imāmīs (Shī'īs) of the 'Twelver' sect, and are divided into two factions, "the Kurds" and "men of the Two Mosques," and fighting is always going on. Near the principal bazaar in this town there is a mosque, over the door of which a silk curtain is suspended. They call this "The Sanctuary of the Master of the Age." It is one of their customs that every evening a hundred of the townspeople come out, carrying arms and with drawn swords in their hands, and go to the governor of the city after the afternoon prayer; they receive from him a horse or mule, saddled and bridled and (with this they go in procession) beating drums and playing fifes and trumpets in front of this animal. Fifty of them march ahead of it and the same number behind it, while others walk to right and left, and so they come to the Sanctuary of the Master of the Age. Then they stand at the door and say, "In the name of God, O Master of the Age, in the name of God come forth! Corruption is abroad and tyranny is rife. This is the hour for thy advent, that by thee God may divide the True from the False!" They continue to call in this way, sounding the trumpets and drums and fifes, until the hour of sunset prayer; for they assert that Muḥammad ibn al-Ḥasan al-'Askarī entered this mosque and disappeared from it, since he is, in their view, the "Expected Imām."[13]

Sāmarrā has fallen into ruins, so that nothing is left of it but a a fraction. It has an equable climate and is strikingly beautiful in spite of its decay and the effacement of its monuments. Here too there is a sanctuary of the 'Master of the Hour,' as at al-Ḥilla.[14]

The shrine at Sāmarrā is still in use, and contains the *sardāb* (cool-cellar) into which the Twelfth Imām is said to have disappeared so long ago. The following prayers to be said on visiting the shrine were written during the Ṣāfavī period (A.H. 1502–A.D. 1722) when Twelverism was made the state religion of Persia.

Prayers to be Said at the Shrine of the Twelfth Imām.
by Muḥammad Bāqir al-Majlisī (d. A.H. *1111/*A.D. *1700)*

At the sardāb a prayer of salutation is made to the Imām, as follows:

"I bear witness that thou art the established truth, that there can be no mistake or doubt, and that God's promise of thy coming is sure. But I am dismayed at thy tarrying so long, and do not have patience to wait for the distant time. It is not surprising that some have denied thee. I am waiting, however, for the day of thy coming. Thou art an intercessor who will not be questioned, and a master who will not be taken away. God has kept thee for the assistance of the Faith, a protection for believers, and a punishment for infidels and heretics. . . .

"O my leader, if I am living on the bright day of thy coming, with its glistening standard, then am I thy servant to command. May I have opportunity for martyrdom before thee! And O my leader, if I should die before thy coming, grant me thy intercession and that of thy pure fathers. . . ." [15]

On entering the sardāb where the Imām disappeared, he is to stand between the two doors, to grasp one of the doors, to cough "like one asking to enter," and to say slowly and from the heart . . .

"O God, Thou hast lengthened the period of our waiting! Those who oppose are ridiculing us, and further waiting is a sore trial. Show us the face of Thy blessed Friend during our time or after we have died. O God, as I trust Thee that I will return (at resurrection), hear my cry, hear my cry, hear my cry!

"O Master of the Age, I have left all friends for thee! I have left my native land to visit thee! Concealing my action from those of my home town, I have sought that thou mightest be my intercessor before my Sovereign and thy Sovereign, and before thy fathers, who are also my friends. Be thou my good fortune, and as thy bounty is ample, send good to me."[16]

THE MAHDĪ: CLAIMANTS TO THE TITLE

Mahdism became a recurrent theme of Islamic history because it spoke to the deepest and most perennial need of Muslims. One may of course compare it to Jewish Messianism and Apocalyptic Christianity, and surmise that these influenced it, but that will not help one to understand it in its Muslim context.

It should not be considered as exotic. The belief in the Mahdī came as a natural countertheme to the abuse of power and the recalcitrance of history in the Community committed to the will of God, and it developed in the internal logic of Islamic doctrine and practise. If (as some would say) there was no mention of a Mahdī in the prophetic period, then it became necessary for Muslims to invent the Mahdī. There is no doubt that belief in him became intensely real.

Many Muslim states were founded by claimants to the title of the Mahdī. One of these was the empire of the al-Muwaḥḥids ("Almohades"), or Unitarians, in North Africa. Its rulers were the Caliphs, or successors, of Ibn Tumart, an aspirant to Mahdism who claimed to be restoring the purity of Islam. For the warlike mountaineers who followed him, one of the advantages of the doctrine was that it gave them a justification for attacking any Muslims who disagreed with them.

The Mahdī Ibn Tumart and the Rise of the Muwaḥḥids
from The Admirable in Abridgement of the News of the West
by 'Abd al-Wāḥid al-Marrākushī (written A.H. *621*/A.D. *1224)*

In the year 515 (A.D. 1121), there arose in the Sūs district (of the Atlas) one Muḥammad ibn 'Abdallāh ibn Tumart, in the guise of one who commands to do good and rejects the reprehensible. This man Muḥammad was a native of Sūs, born in the village known as Ijilī (in the territory of the Banū) Wārghan, of the tribe named the Ḥargha, of the people known as the Isarghinan, which signifies "high-born," in the language of the Maṣmūda Berbers. A genealogy has been found for him, written in his own hand, tracing his descent from al-Ḥasan ibn al-Ḥasan, son of 'Alī. He had travelled in the course of the year 501 (A.D. 1107–1108) to the Orient to study, and went as far as Baghdad. There he met Abū Bakr al-Shāshī (d. A.H. 507; noted Shāfi'ī scholar), from whom he learned something of the principles of law and theology; he heard Ḥadīth from Mubārak ibn 'Abd al-Jabbār and others like him, and it is said that in Damascus he met al-Ghazālī at the time he was living as an ascetic there, but as to that, God knows best. . . .

He returned by way of Alexandria, where he attended the lectures of the jurist Abū Bakr al-Ṭurṭushī (d. A.H. 520). The call he made in that city to order the good and reject what is reprehensible led to incidents following which he took ship. I am told that he continued his habit of commanding and reprehending until the crew threw him into the sea, but for more than half a day he swam in the wake of the ship without incident, and when they perceived this they took him out, and he became great in their sight. They continued to treat him with consideration until he disembarked at Bijāya (Bougie) in North Africa. There he openly began to teach and preach, and people gathered to him and became sympathetic to him. When the prince of Bijāya became fearful of his influence, he ordered him to depart, and he departed toward the West, stopping in a village called Malāla, about one *farsakh* from Bijāya, where he met one 'Abd al-Mu'min ibn 'Alī, who was on his way to the Orient to study (and persuaded him to accompany him). Ibn Tumart stayed in Malāla some months, and then travelled to the West, accompanied by one of the inhabitants, a man named 'Abd al-Wāḥid, known to the Maṣmūda as 'Abd al-Wāḥid the Easterner, who was the first to follow him after 'Abd al-Mu'min, until they came to Tlemcen where (Ibn Tumart) stayed at a mosque outside it, known as al-'Ubbād. (There he was) active in his usual way, and did not leave until all the inhabitants, ruler and subject, venerated him, so that he departed having attracted the notables and won their hearts. From there he came to the city of Fez, where he exposed and developed the doctrines of the Ash'arīya school. Now we have already remarked that the people of the Maghrib had tasted little of this sort of knowledge, and they followed with great eagerness one who could expound it to them. The governor of the city then organized a debate between him and the (Mālikī) *fuqahā'*, in which he won the victory, for he had found a virgin field, and a people deprived of all speculative knowledge or anything but the application of legal rulings.

When the fuqahā' had heard his theology, they advised the governor of the city to exile him, lest he corrupt the minds of the common people. Exiled, he went to Marrākesh. . . .

When (a learned Andalusian) Mālik ibn Wuhayb heard Ibn Tumart, he counselled 'Ali ibn Yūsuf, the (Murābiṭ or Almoravid)

Commander of the Muslims to kill him, saying, "If he gets abroad in the land of the Maṣmūda with this, much evil will befall us from it." The Murābiṭ ruler hesitated to kill him, for religious scruples. He was in fact a virtuous man, but weak and devoid of energy, and in the latter part of his reign appeared a number of reprehensible things and hateful scandals, produced by the intrusion of women into affairs and the authority they assumed. . . .

Then Mālik counselled him to imprison Ibn Tumart for life, but he said "How shall we take one of the Muslims and imprison him without just cause?" Thus he and his companions went out and turned their steps to the Sūs, where he settled in a locality known as Tīnmal.

From this place he began his propaganda, and he is buried there. When he had settled, the notables of the Maṣmūda gathered around him and he began to teach them religious knowledge and invite them to good deeds, without however disclosing to them his goals or his thirst for power. He composed for them a treatise on the articles of faith in their own tongue, in which he was one of the most eloquent men of his time, and when they understood the refinements of this treatise, their veneration for him was much increased: their hearts were filled with love of him, and their bodies with obedience to him.

When he felt sure of them, he summoned them to either stand with him or not, in the guise of ordering the good and rejecting the reprehensible, and he absolutely forbade them to shed blood (in feuds). After some time of this, he charged those men whose minds he judged were ready for it to preach his mission and conciliate the chiefs of the tribes. He began to mention the Mahdī and make them desire his coming, and to gather the traditions which speak of him in the collections.

When he had fully impressed on them the excellence, the genealogy, and the qualities of the Mahdī, he claimed the title for himself, and said that he was Muḥammad ibn ʿAbdallāh, and openly declared that he was the sinless Mahdī. They took the oath of allegiance to him, and he said that he undertook the same engagements to them that the Prophet undertook to his companions.

Afterwards he wrote several treatises on religious knowledge for them, among these the book called *Aʿizz mā Yuṭlab*, and statements of belief in the principles of religion. In most questions he followed the school of al-Ashʿarī, except in the affirmation of the (uncreatedness of) the Divine Attributes, which he denied like the Mu'tazila, and a few other matters, and he inclined somewhat to the Shī'ī position, but he let nothing of this appear to the masses.

He grouped his disciples by categories, appointing from them the first ten to leave their homes and follow him. These were called the Collectivity (Jamā'a). The next category were the Fifty. Moreover, these categories included people from different tribes, not only one. These he called the Believers, saying "There are none on the face of the earth who believe with your faith; it is you whom the Prophet designated when he said 'There will always be in the West a group who know what is right, and whom no deviation will hurt, until God's command shall come.' By you God shall conquer Persia and Byzantium, and slay the Deceiver (dajjāl); from among you will come the prince who will make the Prayer with Jesus, son of Mary; and with you the power will remain until the Hour. . . ."

The obedience of the Maṣmūda to Ibn Tumart kept increasing; their enchantment with him grew, their respect for him was confirmed, so that at last they came to the point where if he had ordered one of them to murder his own father or brother or son, he would have hastened to do so without the least hesitation. This would have been facilitated by the natural lightness with which these people shed blood; this is a thing which is one of the inborn traits of their nature, and to which the climate of their region predisposes them . . . as to the alacrity with which they shed blood, I myself during my stay in the Sūs saw some astonishing examples.

In 517, he raised a considerable army of Maṣmūda, composed of men of Tīnmal and their allies from the Sūs, and told them: "March against these heretics and perverters of religion who call themselves the al-Murābiṭs, and call them to put away their evil habits, reform their morals, renounce heresy, and acknowledge the sinless Imām Mahdī. If they respond to your call, then they are your brothers; what they have will be yours, and what you owe they will owe. And if they do not, then fight them, for the Sunna makes it lawful for you."

He gave them as commander 'Abd al-Mu'min, saying "You are the Believers, and this is your Commander." The army then marched on Marrakesh, and the Murābiṭs met them not far from them at al-Buḥayra with a strong army of warriors of the Lamtūna [the original Murābiṭ tribe.—Ed.]. The battle took place, and the Maṣmūda were defeated with many losses. . . . When the news was brought to Ibn Tumart, he said "Did 'Abd al–Mu'min escape?" When they told him yes, he said "Then it is as if no one had fallen!"

After this, the Maṣmūda began raids on the territory of Marrakesh, cutting off provisions and communications, killing and pillaging without sparing anyone. A great number of people recognized their authority and joined them. Ibn Tumart thereupon gave himself over more and more to asceticism and simplicity, giving the appearance of a saint, and strictly applying the full provisions of the Law, following the first Muslim practise. . . .

All this strengthened their uprising and their veneration for him, as well as predictions he made which came true. Such was the case, favorable for him and his companions, since the affairs of the Murābiṭs were in decline, as we have mentioned earlier, and the dissolution of their empire was gaining, until Ibn Tumart died in A.H. 524/A.D. 1130, having laid the foundations of their affairs, organized the administration, and traced for them the path to follow.

His successor was 'Abd al–Mu'min . . . those who chiefly assisted his rise and obtained it for him were three of the Collectivity; 'Umar ibn 'Abdallāh al–Ṣanhājī, known as al–Aznaj; 'Umar Abū Ḥafṣ Intī, and 'Abdallāh ibn Sulaymān, of Tīnmal. The other members of the Collectivity agreed on this, as well as the Fifty and and the rest of the Muwaḥḥidīn.

After the death of Ibn Tumart, 'Abd al–Mu'min continued to conquer province after province and to subject the land, so that its people accepted his rule.

His last conquest of the lands of the Murābiṭs was the city of Marrakesh, their capital (where he put to death the young ruler) and when all the provinces of Morocco were submissive to 'Abd al–Mu'min, he turned his armies to the (Eastern areas of North Africa, and then to Spain.)[17]

The career of Ibn Tumart gives some explanation of how single–handed men were able to gain followings and build kingdoms, as Mahdīs. He certainly would not have been successful if he had not appeared as a reformer of morals, but his progress was greatly aided by the tribal rivalries he knew so well how to exploit. Mahdism provided the Maṣmūda with a religiously sanctioned device for seizing power from the Lamtūna. Similarly Abū 'Abdallāh the Ismā'īlī had raised the Kutāma Berbers of Kabylia against the Aghlabīs. One may observe as a general rule that Mahdist revolts have seldom achieved much political success where they were not based on existing tribal loyalties. But the function of Mahdism as a device for changing absolutist government, and as religious revolt within the Muslim Community, was recognized and dreaded. It is instructive to note how the pious Fīrūz Shāh of Dehli dealt with a man who claimed to be the Mahdī, and how he treated a man who was only revered as God.

Religious Pretenders in Dehli
from The Victories of Fīrūz Shāh
Fīrūz Shāh Tuhgluq (d. A.H. *790/*A.D. *1388)*

(*Item*) There was a sect which wore the garments of atheism, and having thrown off all restraint, led men astray. The name of their chief was Aḥmad Bahārī. He dwelt in the city, and a party of his followers called him God. They brought those people before me in bonds and chains, and informed me that he had presumptuously made himself a prophet, and said that there could be none of the grace of prophecy in any one who had not been admitted to his following. One of his disciples affirmed that God had appeared in Dehli, that is, Aḥmad Bahārī. When these facts were proved against them, I ordered them both to be confined and punished with chains. I admonished the others to repent and reform, and I banished them to other cities to put a stop to the influence of this wretched sect.

(*Item*) There was in Dehli a man named Rukn al-Dīn, who was called Mahdī, because he affirmed himself to be the Imām Mahdī who is to appear in the latter days, and to be possessed by knowledge by inspiration. He said that he had not read or studied under anyone, and that he knew the names of all things, a knowledge which no prophet had acquired since Adam. He pretended that the mystery of the science of letters (*ḥurūf*) had been revealed to him. . . . He led people astray in mystic practices, and perverted ideas by maintaining that he was Rukn al-Dīn, the prophet of God. The elders brought the facts of this case to my attention. When he was brought before me he was convicted of heresy and error. The doctors of the Law said that he was an infidel, and worthy of death, for having spread such false and pernicious doctrines among the people of Islam. If any delay were made in putting them down they would spread like a pestilence, and many Muslims would stray from the truth faith. A revolt would follow, and many would fall into perdition. I ordered that this vile fellow's rebellion and wickedness be made public to all men, high and low; and that in accordance with the decision of the doctors learned in the holy Law, the guilty should be brought to punishment. They killed him with some of his supporters and disciples, and the people rushing in tore him to pieces and broke his bones into fragments. Thus was his iniquity prevented. God in His mercy and favour made me, His humble creature, the instrument of putting down such wickedness, and abolishing such heresy, and guided me to effect a restoration of true religion. Thanks for this are due to the great and glorious God. Upon hearing or reading the facts here recorded, every well-wisher of His religion will admit that this sect was deservedly punished, and for this good action I hope to receive a future reward.[18]

There were Sunnī Mahdīs as well as Shī'ī Mahdīs. However, the Shī'a had bitter and sorrowful memories, and were excluded from power. The Zaydīs succeeded in building states in the third Islamic century (ninth century A.D.); the Ismā'īlīs, as we have seen, in A.H. 296/A.D. 909. But the Twelvers established real political power only with the Ṣāfavī dynasty, in A.D. 1502. (Those Shī'ī sects who failed to establish a political base did not, of course, survive as a rule.) One can see that the longing for a deliverer would be very strong among the Shī'a, while among Sunnīs, those who supported the rulers and received benefits from them would have had far less cause to hope for delivery. Only those who felt oppressed or repelled by the current Sunnī establishment would have felt the need to look for the Mahdī—e.g. overtaxed peasants, frustrated tribesmen, purist 'ulamā' and otherworldly Ṣūfīs.

Among some Sunnī 'ulamā' there was a tendency to either deny the Mahdī legend altogether, or to identify him with Jesus, who was to descend from heaven, and could thus not be easily confused with men like Ibn Tumart.

The great historian–qāḍī Ibn Khaldūn (d. A.H. 808/A.D. 1406) was a familiar of courts and emphatically an 'ālim of the establishment. In a magisterial discussion of the Mahdī doctrine, he inclines to consider the whole matter a Shī'ī conspiracy, but he is very cautious not to deny the doctrine outright, a move which could have involved him in a charge of heresy.

He does however criticise the ḥadīths on which the doctrine was based, and points out, quite correctly, that most of them can be faulted, by the standards of traditional Sunnī criticism.

An Examination of the Mahdī Doctrine from the Prolegomena
Ibn Khaldūn (d. A.H. *808/*A.D. *1406)*

Know that it has been generally bruited about among a substantial part of the people of Islam in every epoch, that at the end of time there must appear a man from the People of the House (of the Prophet) who will bring support to the religion and cause justice to triumph, so that the Muslims will follow him and he will assume power over all the Islamic lands. He will be called the Mahdī, and shortly after this, the dajjāl will emerge. After that, Jesus will come down and slay the dajjāl. According to another version, Jesus will descend with the Mahdī and assist him to kill the dajjāl, and then will let the Mahdī lead him in the ritual prayer.

All this is adduced from ḥadīths edited by leading men of religion, which have also been discussed by those who reject the story, and even refuted by other ḥadīths. The later Ṣūfīs have taken a different track in the matter of this Fāṭimī with a sort of reasoning based usually on the idea of personal revelation (*kashf*: literally, unveiling), which is the basis of their various mystical paths. We shall make clear what is sound in this, if so God wills.

Now, the joining together of all the learned of the Community has accepted as soundest the two Ḥadīth Collections of al-Bukhārī and Muslim, and in "joining together" is our greatest protection and best defense. There are no collections like their two *Ṣaḥīḥs* for reliability. . . .

The ḥadīth with the strangest chain of transmission is the one mentioned by Abū Bakr al-Iskāf, in his *Fawā'id al-Akhbār*: "He who says the story of the Mahdī is lies is an unbeliever, and he who says the Antichrist is not real is an unbeliever. And he (the Prophet) said something similar about the rising of the sun in the West, as I believe." Now Abū Bakr al-Iskāf is considered a forger of ḥadīths.

Al-Tirmidhī and Abū Dāwūd have both brought out this tradition, with chains of authority going back to 'Asim ibn Abī al-Najūd: "If no more than one day remained, God would lengthen that day until He sent a man of mine—or; of my House—whose name will be like mine, and whose father's name will be like my father's name."

As to this 'Aṣim, al-'Ijlī said, "There was some difference of opinion as to his reliability," and Ibn Khirāsh says, "His ḥadīths contain things unknown." Abū Ja'far al-'Uqaylī said "There was nothing wrong with him but a bad memory."

Abū Dāwūd brought out a tradition from 'Alī, as reported by Fiṭr ibn Khalīfa and others, that the Prophet—God's benediction and peace be on him—said, "If only one day of Time remained, God would still send a man of my House to fill the earth with justice." Al-'Ijlī says of Fiṭr, "He was fair in ḥadīth, but had some pro-Shī'ī bias." Ibn Ma'īn said, "He is reliable–as a Shī'ī." Aḥmad ibn 'Abdallāh ibn Yūnus says, "We used to pass by Fiṭr: he is rejected, and we wrote nothing he said. I used to pass by, and leave him like a dog." Abū Bakr ibn 'Ayyāsh says, "I only gave up transmitting ḥadīths from him because of his bad school of thought."

Abū Dāwūd also brought out a ḥadīth going back to 'Alī—God be well pleased in him—according to Hārūn ibn al-Mughīra according to 'Amr ibn Abī Qays, from Abū Isḥāq al-Sabi'ī, that 'Alī looked at his son al-Ḥasan and said "This son of mine is your chief. The Messenger, God bless him and give him peace, has said that from his loins will come forth a man who will be called by your Prophet's name, and resemble him in looks but not in character, who will fill the earth with justice." As to Hārūn, Abū Dāwūd says elsewhere, "He was an offspring of the Shī'a;" and al-Sulaymānī says, "There is opinion about him." As to 'Amr ibn Abī Qays, Abū Dāwūd said, "Nothing wrong with *him*, but his ḥadīths are faulty." As to Abū Isḥāq al-Sabī'ī, it is well established that he became confused at the end of his life.

Abū Dāwūd also publishes a ḥadīth on the authority of 'Alī ibn Nufayl, from Umm Salama, that she heard the Messenger of God, may God's blessing and peace be on him, say "The Mahdī will be one of the offspring of Fāṭima." Al-Ḥākim reports this as "Yes, the Mahdī is a fact, and will come from the sons of Fāṭima." Abū Ja'far al-'Uqaylī declared this a weak tradition, and said " 'Alī ibn Nufayl is not supported by anyone on this tradition, and it is known only through him."

It is also Abū Dāwūd who published the ḥadīth of Umm Salama: "There will be disagreements at the death of a caliph. A man of the people of Medina will leave, fleeing to Mecca, etcetera. . . ." This is said to be related on the authority of Qatāda, but Qatāda related ḥadīths he never heard from the authorities he cites, and such a man's traditions are only accepted when he states explicitly that he heard the tradition [and did not read it—Ed.]. Moreover, it is not stated that this relates to the Mahdī, even though Abū Dāwūd puts it in that section of his book.

There is the tradition of Abū Sa'id al-Khudrī . . . "The Mahdī is from me (the Prophet), with a bald forehead and an aquiline nose. He will fill the earth with equity . . . and rule seven years." This is transmitted through 'Imrān al-Qaṭṭan, and there is difference of opinion about using him as a source; Bukhārī would only use him as a secondary support. Yaḥya ibn Ma'īn said "He's not strong," and once said "He's not anything." Aḥmad ibn Ḥanbal said "I hope his ḥadīths may be sound." Yazīd ibn Ruzī'a said, "He was a Hurūrī Khārijī, and viewed it as suitable to put people of the Qibla to the sword."

Al-Ḥākim relates from . . . Abū al-Ṣiddīq al-Nājī from Abū Sa'īd al-Khudrī that God's Messenger, on whom be benediction and peace, said "The Hour will not strike until the earth is filled with injustice, wrong, and aggression. Then will come forth a man of my House who will fill it with equity and justice . . ."

Al-Ḥākim also relates a tradition of al-Khudrī, transmitted by Abū al-Ṣiddīq to Sulaymān ibn 'Ubayd, as follows: "At the end of my Community the Mahdī will emerge; God will pour copious rain upon him, and the earth will bring forth its vegetation. He will give wealth away with righteousness, the herds will increase, and the Community will become mighty. He will live for seven or eight (years)." Al-Ḥākim said these were both sound according to the criteria of Bukhārī and Muslim, yet neither collected them.

Ibn Māja has published in his book of traditions one coming from 'Abdallāh ibn Mas'ūd, transmitted by Ibn Abī Ziyād, from Ibrāhīm, from 'Alqama, from 'Abdallah, saying "While we were with the Messenger of God—God bless him and give him peace—some youths of the clan of Hāshim (the Prophet's clan) came forward. When he saw them, his eyes filled with tears, and his color changed. I remarked on this, and he said "For us, the people of the House, God has chosen the next world, and not this one. After me, they will suffer misfortunes, banishment and exile, until people come from the East with black banners. They will ask for goodness, but not be given it, so they will fight and be victorious. Then they will be offered what they had asked for, but they will not accept it. Finally, they will hand over the government to a man of my family, and he will fill the earth with equity as others have filled it with injustice. Let him of you who lives to see that go join them, even if you have to crawl over the snow."

Ḥadith scholars know this tradition as the "ḥadīth of the banners." The leading ones agree that it is weak. Wakī' ibn al-Jarrāḥ said "It is nothing," and so did Aḥmad ibn Ḥanbal. Abū Usāma said "If Yazīd swore fifty solemn oaths to me, I still could not believe it. Is this the way of Ibrahīm? Is it 'Alqama's way? Is it 'Abdallāh ibn Mas'ūd's way?" And al-Dhahabī says "It is unsound."

[Ibn Khaldūn gives similar criticisms of all the other ḥadīths on the Mahdī, pointing out that neither Bukhārī or Muslim so much as mention him by name.—Ed.]

These are the ḥadīths produced by leading figures on the matter of the Mahdī. As you have seen, very few of them are above attack. Those who disapprove of the Mahdī business hold by what Muḥammad ibn al-Khālid al-Jundī related (through a sound chain of authorities), from the Messenger of God: "There will be no Mahdī but Jesus, the son of Mary." But although Yaḥya ibn Ma'īn said that this Muḥammad ibn Khālid was reliable, al-Bayhaqī said "He is isolated with this tradition," and al-Ḥākim says that he was an unknown person.

It has been said that "no Mahdī but Jesus" means no one spoke in the cradle (*mahd*) but Jesus," but that can be refuted with the story of Jurayj, and similar miraculous events.

As for the Ṣūfīs, the early ones did not go into anything of this sort. Their doctrine was all of striving and spiritual conditions.

The doctrine of the Imāmīs and the Rāfiḍīs [rejecters of the first three Caliphs—Ed.] among the Shi'a was that 'Alī had a preferred status, and was the Imām and legatee of the Prophet, God bless him and give him peace, and they dissociated themselves from "al-Shaykhayn" (the Two Elders, Abū Bakr and 'Umar.) Then they began their doctrine of the "Sinless Imām." The Ismā'īlīs among them asserted the divine nature of their Imām, by a sort of incarnationism, while others asserted the return of the Imām from the dead, by transmigration, and still others expected the return of the people of the Prophet's family to power, using ḥadīths such as these we have mentioned, and others.

Then there also came to be discussed among the later Ṣūfīs the belief in personal revelation (kashf) and what is beyond the (veil of) the senses. Many of them went on to talk of incarnation and union with God, so that many came to share the doctrine of the Imāmīs and the Rāfiḍīs of the divine nature of the Imāms, and the incarnation of the Godhead in them. They also came to believe in the "Pole" (quṭb) and the High Saints (abdāl), as if in imitation of extremist Shī'ī doctrines. Thus they became saturated with Shī'ī theories; hence they base their habit of the patched mantle on a story that 'Alī invested Ḥasan al-Baṣrī with such a mantle, and took an oath from him. Their preference for 'Alī among the Companions smells strongly of pro-Shī'ī tendencies. And thus, books of the later Ṣūfīs came to be affected by the writings of the Ismā'īlīs, and like them to speak of the Expected Fāṭimī.

Those of the Ṣūfīs who speak most of the Fāṭimī are Ibn al-'Arabī, Ibn Qusayy, 'Abd al-Ḥaqq ibn Saba'īn and Ibn Abī Wāṭīl. Thus they argue that Prophecy is followed by Caliphate, and Caliphate by temporal power, and that in turn by tyranny, pride, and vanity, in a degenerative cycle. Prophecy and truth will then be revived by sainthood (wilāya), then by its caliphs, and then by the dajjāl, who will take the place of royal authority and the rule of power.

In his book *'Anqā' Mughrib,* Ibn al-'Arabī calls (the Mahdī) "The Seal of the Saints." Ibn Abī Wāṭīl quotes him thus: "This expected Imām is of the people of the House and the children of Fāṭima, and his appearance will be when *kh – f – j* years have followed the Hijra;" that is, in A.H. 683/A.D. 1284–85. Another theory is that the dajjāl will emerge in A.H. 743/A.D. 1343. Ibn Abī Wāṭīl says "The Expected Saint, Muḥammad the Mahdī and Seal of the Saints is no prophet: he is a saint, sent by his spirit and his Friend." He adds "(The Philosopher) Al-Kindī mentioned that this saint would say the noon-prayer with the people, restore Islam, make it triumph, conquer the Iberian Peninsula, march to Rome, and conquer it. He will conquer Constantinople, and the East, and the kingdom of the earth will be his. The Muslims will be pious, Islam will be exalted, and true monotheism will appear . . . And the Prophet, God bless him and give him peace, said: '. . . He who will kill Caesar and spend his treasures in God's cause is the Expected One, when he conquers Constantinople. Happy the Commander, and happy the army of that day!' "

With such talk as this, they specify the time, the man, and the place, but the time passes, and there is not a trace of any of it. Then they go on to build a new theory, based on linguistic meanings, imaginary things, and astrological predictions. In such as this they spend their lives, the first of them to the last.

This is all we have received from the discussions of these Ṣūfīs, and all that the ḥadīth scholars adduce concerning the Mahdī. The truth is that no religious or political propaganda can be successful unless there is also present the power of group loyalties to support it and provide a defense against those who would reject it. If it is correct that a Mahdī is to appear, then the only way for his mission to succeed is for him to be one of the Bedouin, and for God to unite their hearts to follow him, until effective power is his. Any other way, such as a Fāṭimī to make propaganda for his cause just anywhere, without group loyalties and effective power, simply relying on his descent from the Prophet, will never be feasible or successful.

The vulgar sort of people, the great masses who do not depend on reason to guide them, assume that he will appear in some faraway area, such as the Zāb in Africa or the Sūs in Morocco. Many weakminded people make their way to the Ribāṭ of Māssa in Sūs, to take on a cause that the soul in its delusion tempts them believe will succeed, and many of them have been killed.

Our shaykh Muḥammad ibn Ibrahīm al-Abilī told me that in the beginning of the eighth/fourteenth century, at the time of Sulṭan Yūsuf ibn Ya'qūb the Marīnī, a mystagogue called al-Tuwayzirī came forth at Ribāṭ Māssa, asserting that he was the Fāṭimī. Many of the people of the Sūs followed him and the chiefs of the Maṣmūda Berbers feared for their power. Then one of them sent a man to kill him as he was sleeping, and his power was dissolved.

Similarly there appeared among the Ghumāra in the nineties of the seventh/twelfth century a man called 'Abbās who claimed to be the Fāṭimī. The great mass of the Ghumāra followed him, and he forced his way into the city of Fez and set fire to the market, and then went off to the area of Muzamma where he was killed by stealth, and his affair came to nothing. There are many examples of this sort.

In quite recent times there have been movements in the Maghrib calling for Truth and the Sunna, but not making claims for the Fāṭimī or anyone else. At times, individuals occupy themselves with implementing the Sunna and changing what is reprehensible, and thus gain a following. Most of them busy themselves with the safety of the roads, since that is where most of the corruption of the Arabs there is found, due to their way of living. However, the religious coloring cannot be firmly established, since by repentance the Bedouins mean only giving up raiding and plundering. The leaders differ from them by the firm rooting of religion and saintliness in their souls, unlike their following. But if the leader dies, his influence dissolves, and their group-loyalty is dissipated.[19]

One Mahdist movement which did not actually attempt to create a state, but still obtained a considerable notoriety as a reforming sect, appeared in Muslim India in the sixteenth century. A certain Sayyid (descendant of the Prophet) Muḥammad of Jaunpūr who was born in A.H. 847/A.D. 1443, following studies in the Law and mysticism, obtained a reputation for holiness and proclaimed himself a Mahdī after pilgrimage to Mecca, around A.D 1499. Little enough is really known about him, but his memory and his sayings were preserved by his followers. These Mahdavīs, as they were called, kept a militant Ṣūfī form of communal life, and in their emphasis on the ḥisba, they showed a characteristic aspect of Mahdism. The Muslim state existed to "enjoin the good and reject the reprehensible." But (perhaps because of its specific form), in most times and in most places it clearly fell far short of expectations. Hence a deliverer was needed. Hence historical Mahdīs busied themselves with the ḥisba.

The Mahdavīs were an intolerant and ingrown group, but they appear to have been one of the earliest stirrings among the Indian Muslims of the legalism and exclusivism which finally triumphed in the later seventeenth century with the reign of Emperor Awrangzīb.

In a letter he is believed to have written to the Sulṭān of Gujarāt, he declared, "I have proclaimed myself Mahdī by the command of God. You should investigate this claim; if I am right, you must obey me, if I am wrong you must admonish me, and if I do not understand and accept the truth, you must kill me. I declare to you that wherever I go I shall proclaim and preach the truth about myself and point out the (right) path to the people, or, in the view of the worldly 'ulamā', 'mislead the people.' "[20]

Sayings of Sayyid Muḥammad of Jaunpūr (d. A.H. 910/A.D. 1504)
from the Book of Equity
by Walī ibn Yūsuf (sixteenth century A.D.)

Haḍrat Mahdī (a follower writes) "always enjoined that we should entrust ourselves to God utterly; that we should not indulge in idle talk with anyone; and that we should not desire anything. Depend on God only and do not be obliged to any of His creatures even for the smallest thing."

Hadrat Mahdī said, "God will not ask you whether you are the son of Aḥmad or of Mahdī. He will ask about the works done with love. Therefore, my brother, seek what God has commanded, and do not presume that because you are a member of the Dā'ira (circle or brotherhood) you will attain salvation for the Mahdī's sake."

Haḍrat Mahdī said, "God sent the Mahdī at a time when the purpose and aim of the Faith had been nullified by three things: (social) custom, (personal) habit, and innovations."

Haḍrat Mahdī said, "It is hard for anyone who has a slave girl or a slave in the house to remain (firm) in the faith."

Haḍrat Mahdī said, "Whoever reads much disgraces himself by desiring the world, and if he does not desire the world, he becomes puffed up with pride."[20a]

The Mahdavī movement produced other leaders in India. The following accounts are abridged from the History of 'Abd al-Qādir Badā'ūnī (died about 1615), an *'ālim* and litterateur at the court of the Emperor Akbar, who employed him in translating Hindu works such as the *Mahabharata* into Persian. Badā'ūnī was sympathetic to the Mahdavīs, and decidedly hostile to Akbar's "Universal Toleration" and interest in other faiths. In his history he wildly charged that Akbar had apostatised from Islam and was trying to found a new world religion.

Mahdist Leaders in India
from Selections from Histories
by 'Abd al-Qādir al-Badā'ūnī (d. ca. A.H. *1024*/A.D. *1615)*

Another important incident was the affair of Shaykh 'Alā'ī Mahdī of Bayāna, which closely resembled the affair of (the martyred saint) Sīdī Mawla. The father of the aforesaid Shaykh 'Alā'ī, named Ḥasan, was one of the great shaykhs of the country of Bengal, and took up his abode in the province of Bayāna in A.H. *935*/A.D. *1528–29.* Shaykh 'Alā'ī was the most orthodox of Ḥasan's sons, and devoted himself to the acquirement of exoteric and esoteric sciences, and to the improvement of his character, and in a short time having read all the routine works, engaged in tuition and instruction. After the death of his revered father, he set himself to follow the paths of obedience (to God) and austerity, firmly occupying the prayer–carpets of the (Ṣufī) Shaykhs, and used to instruct seekers of the right way. Nevertheless he still retained a residue of evidence of worldly desires: "the last thing to leave the head of the just is the love of glory." He was unwilling that any other shaykh of the city should share his dignity, so that on a festival, from excessive jealousy and envy he caused one of the contemplative and ascetic Ṣūfī shaykhs to descend [i.e., threw him out.—Ed.] from his litter.

In the meantime Mīyan 'Abdallāh, a Niyāzī Afghan who was a noted lieutenant of (St.) Salīm Chīshtī of Fātiḥpūr, and had performed pilgrimage, took part with Mīr Sayyid (Muḥammad) of Jaunpūr, may God sanctify his holy resting place, who claimed to be the promised Mahdī, and adopting also the manners of a Mahdī on his return from the Hijāz made his dwelling at Bayāna in a grove far from men on the borders of a tank, and when the times of prayer came round he used to gather together laborers who passed that way and encourage or compel them to form an assembly for prayer, so that the reward of prayer in an assembly (rather than alone) should not escape him.

When Shaykh 'Alā'ī saw his conduct, he was greatly pleased, and said to his own followers, "This is religion and true faith, whereas ours is only idolatry and infidelity." Giving up his claims as a shaykh, trampling underfoot his self-esteem and conceit, he devoted himself to the poor, and abandoning his benefice and his alms–house and dervish–convent, he entered the valley of self-abnegation, and bestowed even his books upon the poor, saying to his wife, "If thou canst endure poverty, come with me in God's name, but if not, take thy portion and go thy ways." Of her own accord, she was highly pleased with this determination. He then approached Mīyān 'Abdallāh with respectful submission, and learned from him the *dhikr* service of that (Mahdavī) sect.

The true meanings of the Qur'ān were easily revealed to him, and three hundred householders, abandoning all source of gain, spent their time with him, apportioning to each an equal share of what was given them by Providence. Shaykh 'Alā'i had such marvellous power of attraction that almost all who heard him elected to join that assembly and never troubled themselves again about work or worldly gain. In spite of this they kept arms and implements of war always by them, and whenever they saw any irreligious or forbidden action in the city or market they called the offenders to account by main force, admitting no investigation by the governor, but aiding every magistrate who acted in conformity with their principles. Thus fathers left their sons and wives their husbands, and entered the charmed circle of the Mahdī. When Mīyān 'Abdallāh saw that Shaykh 'Alā'ī was losing (good repute) among rich and poor, he was much vexed, and speaking with gentleness said, "Truth nowadays has become more bitter than colocynth. It were better for you to quit this vale (of iniquity), and either retire or perform the pilgrimage."

Shaykh 'Alā'ī, retaining the conduct which he always had, then set out for (the parts of) Gujarāt accompanied by six or seven hundred families. At this time, my late father took me to do homage to him, and by reason of my tender years, his form has remained in my memory as a dream or as a vision. In consequence of certain opposition which arose, he turned back in the middle of his journey and returned to Bayāna.

When Islām Shāh took possession of the throne in Agra, he summoned Shaykh 'Alā'ī, who came to the court accompanied by a party of select companions all in mail and fully armed, and paying no heed to kingly ceremony greeted the assembly (only) with *Salām 'alaykum.* Islām Shāh acknowledged this with indignation and displeasure.

Makhdūm al-Mulk Mawlāna 'Abdallāh of Sulṭānpūr had fully persuaded him that Shaykh 'Alā'ī was a revolutionary who laid claim to being the Mahdī, and was deserving of death. In accordance with his custom, Shaykh 'Alā'ī expounded a few verses from the Qur'ān and delivered such a profitable discourse, in most elegant language, of criticism of the world and description of the Judgement and contemptuous remarks regarding the learned men of their time and all their faults and failings, that it had the most profound effect upon Islām Shāh and the Amīrs there present, notwithstanding their hardness of heart, bringing tears to their eyes. Islām Shāh then retired, and personally sent out refreshments from the palace to the Shaykh and his companions. The Shaykh however refused to touch the food himself, and when they asked him why, he said, "Your food is not proper for Muslims, because you have possessed more than was yours by the Law." Islām Shāh notwithstanding repressed his anger, and referred the inquiry and the decision to the 'ulamā'.

Shaykh 'Alā'ī vanquished everyone of them in argument, and when Mīr Sayyid Rafī' al-Dīn cited traditions relating to the appearance of the promised Mahdī, the Shaykh would say, "You are a Shāfi'ī in religion and we are Ḥanafīs, your traditions are different from ours; how can we accept your interpretations on this question?"

In the meantime tidings reached Islām Shāh daily: "Today such and such an officer has gone over to the following of the Shaykh." At last he gave orders for the Shaykh's expulsion, ordering him to leave the kingdom (of Dehli) and go to the Dakkan. Shaykh 'Alā'ī had for years desired to travel in the Dakkan and see how the Mahdavī ideas were progressing there, and on hearing this good news he started without delay. At Hindīya, on the frontier, the governor of that place embraced his tenets, and more than half his army sided with him. This news aroused Islām Shāh's indignation, and orders were given summoning the Shaykh.

Just at this juncture Islām Shāh had left Agra for the Panjāb, and when he arrived opposite Bayāna, he ordered the governor of the place, Mīyān Bahwa Luhānī, to produce Shaykh 'Abdallāh Niyāzī, the mentor of Shaykh 'Alā'ī. The governor warned the Shaykh to flee, but he said "I had better interview him now, since whatever is predestined will come to pass." Accordingly he set out and met Islām Shāh as he was about to march, and greeted him with "Salām 'Alaykum." On the instant, the governor seized him by the nape of the neck and bent him down, saying "My friend the Shaykh, this is the way they salute kings." The Shaykh looked savagely at him, and replied "The salutation that the Companions and the Prophet, may the peace and blessing of God be upon him and all his family, used to make was this very form; I know no other." Islām Shāh, with evident aversion, said "Is this the master of Shaykh 'Alā'ī?" Mawlāna 'Abdallāh of Sulṭānpūr, who was lying in wait for him, said "The very man." By order of Islām Shāh he was at once beaten and left for dead. When he was nursed back to health (by his followers) he left Bayāna, and used to say "This was the fruit of consorting with argumentative people." Finally he came to Sirhind, gave up all connections with the Mahdavīs, and moreover turned those of that party from that faith, dealing with all Muslims according to the orthodox school. In A.H. *993*/A.D. *1585* the Emperor Akbar gave him a grant of land in Sirhind, and in the year A.H. 1000, he bade farewell to this transitory world at the age of 90 or thereabouts.

After Islām Shāh returned to Agra, Mullā 'Abdallāh Sulṭānpūrī prevailed on him to send for Shaykh 'Alā'ī from Hindīya, as there was great probability of disturbance in the kingdom. Recognising that there was no one among the learned men of Dehli and Agra capable of settling the dispute, Islām Shāh directed Shaykh 'Alā'ī to be sent to Bihār to the learned Shaykh Budh, in whom he had the utmost confidence. The sons of Shaykh Budh impressed on him that Mawlāna 'Abdallāh was the Ṣadr al–Ṣudūr (Chief 'Alim) and, whether he would or not (for he was very infirm and aged), wrote a letter saying, "Mawlāna 'Abdallāh is one of the most learned men of the day. His decision (will be) the right decision." When Shaykh 'Alā'ī arrived at Islām Shāh's camp, the king read the sealed letter of Shaykh Budh (which arrived with him), and calling Shaykh 'Alā'ī to him said in a low tone, "Only say to me in my own ear that you are penitent for having made this claim (of Mahdīhood.) You shall then be accorded complete liberty." Shaykh 'Alā'ī however refused to pay any heed to him, and in despair Islām Shāh said to Mullā 'Abdallāh, "I leave him in your hands," and gave orders for him to receive a certain number of stripes in his presence. Shaykh 'Alā'ī had a wound in his neck, the result of an operation for pestilence which raged that year throughout the whole of Hindustān, and in addition was suffering from fatigue and had hardly a breath left in him, so that at the end of the third stroke his lofty soul quitted its humble frame. And after his death they tied his delicate body to the feet of an elephant and trampled him to pieces in the camp, and forbade the burial of his body. At that very time a vehement whirlwind arose with so great violence that people thought the last day had arrived, and great lamentation was heard throughout the whole camp. And they say that in the night so many flowers were scattered over the body of the Shaykh that it was, so to speak, entombed in flowers. After this event the power of Islām Shāh lasted barely two years.[21]

Another expectation of the Mahdī was that he would launch a holy war to "make Islam victorious," and as we have seen, several Mahdist states were created by such wars.

In the bad and confused days between the decline of Mongol power in Iraq and the rise of the Ṣāfavī empire in Iran at the beginning of the sixteenth century A.D., a small state was built by a Sayyid or descendant of the Prophet, among the Arabs of lower Iraq and Khuzīstān. Although it was not much more than a robber–principality, it was a factor in the final expulsion of the Mongols.

The Sayyid was preaching a heresy of Twelver Shīʿism, and his son was yet more heretical, but the dynasty they founded, that of the Mushaʿshaʿī Sayyids, later abandoned their heterodox ideas and became the hereditary princes of Khuzīstān under the Ṣafavī Shāhs. This account was written by a Persian ʿālim historian put to death by Jahāngīr in A.H. 1019/A.D. 1610.

On the Mushaʿshaʿī Sayyids of Khuzīstān
from The Sessions of the Believers
Nūr Allāh Shūshtarī (d. A.H. *1019/*A.D. *1610)*

Sayyid Muḥammad ibn Sayyid Falāh ibn Haybat Allāh traced his descent from the Imām Mūsā al-Kāẓim, on whom be peace, and his place of origin was Wāsiṭ. He began as a student of Shaykh Aḥmad ibn Fahd, who was one of the greatest Ṣūfīs and greatest Twelver Shīʿī mujtahids (interpreters of the Law.) The reverend Shaykh had a book on the occult sciences, and when he was near death, he gave this book to one of his servants to throw it into the Euphrates. However, the Sayyid took it from him by a trick, and by means of the occult sciences made all the bedouins of the country of Khuzīstān his followers. He taught them a *dhikr* composed of the name of ʿAlī, which if repeated he said would teach them how to be true partisans of the Prophet's family, while their bodies became hard as stone, capable of dangerous feats, such as pressing a sharp sword against their bellies and making the blade bend, and other strange things. His fame became widespread, and he gave himself the title of the Mahdī, appearing in the year A.H. 828/A.D, 1425, and he gained the ascendancy in all of Khuzīstān, including Shushtar, Dizfūl and Huwayza. A partial biography of Sayyid Muḥammad which has been written by a recent scholar of Iraq, in the *Tarīkh-i Ghiyāthī* adduces that "Sayyid Muḥammad appeared in the year 820 A.H., and claimed to be the Mahdī, and astrological conjunctions which appeared in that year indicated his appearance (while under the same conjunction it happened that Ispand Mīrzā, son of Qara Yūsuf the Blacksheep Turcoman, who was ruler of Iraq, summoned the Shīʿī fuqahā' to debate with the fuqahā' [legalists] of Baghdad, and heard their views, and since the Shīʿīs prevailed, the Mīrzā chose the Shīʿī *madhhab* [school] and stamped coins with the names of the Twelve Imams.) He was of the line of Imām Mūsā al-Kāẓim, peace be upon him, and at one time sought assiduously for knowledge in the madrasa of Ḥilla, in the service of Shaykh Aḥmad ibn Fahd al-Ḥillī, who was the Mujtahid of the Shī'a. In those days it used to run on the tongue of Sayyid Muḥammad that he would soon manifest himself, and that he would be the appointed Mahdī. Finally these words came to the Shaykh, and he denied Sayyid Muḥammad's words and reprimanded him, for such statements were contrary to the doctrine of the Twelver Shī'a.

"The Sayyid learned all traditional and rational subjects, and was a mystic and ascetic, having visions, and what he told of his future manifestation came to him in visions. When among his own people and tribe, he would tell them that he would conquer the whole world, and that he was the appointed Mahdī, and would distribute the lands and provinces to his tribe and companions. When these words came again to the Shaykh Aḥmad ibn Fahd, he delivered a *fatwa* stating that he should be put to death, and wrote something to the Amīr Manṣūr ibn Qayyān declaring that the Sayyid's blood was lawful (to shed). When this letter came to Amīr Manṣūr, he seized Sayyid Muḥammad intending to put him to death, but he said, 'I am a Sunnī Sayyid and a Ṣūfī, and because of this the Shī'īs have become my enemies and aim to kill me.' He then brought out a copy of the Glorious Qur'ān and swore an oath upon it, and said other things, until Amīr Manṣūr set him free. When he was free of bonds, he returned to the area of Kasīd, and as the first group to follow him from the tribe of Ma'dān in those parts was the subtribe of the Banu Salāma (Sons of Security) he took this as a good omen. Afterwards, other tribes of bedouins joined him from the Tigris region near Baghdad. He told them that he was the Mahdī, and performed several extraordinary things among them (and by terrorism and battles with the local rulers he made himself a power.)"

He sent six thousand men to plunder Wāsiṭ, and its ruler was at first defeated, but then won the victory and killed eight hundred of the Musha'sha'īs, while on the road home many more perished. When this setback reached Sayyid Muḥammad, he went to Huwayza in Khūzistān and destroyed the villages around the city, killing all whom he saw. This event occurred the first of Ramaḍān A.H. 845/A.D. 1442. . . .

Later on they returned to Huwayza and busied themselves besieging it. When the news of the siege came to Ispand Mīrzā son of Qara Yūsuf Qaraqoyūnlu, the Black-Sheep Sulṭān of Baghdad, he gathered his army and set out to Huwayza. When he arrived at Wāsiṭ, the officers of Huwayza, one of whom was Amīr of the Muzara'a, and another Amīr of the Banu Mughayzal, asked that they might go with him to help Huwayza and free the people in the fortress from the hand of the Musha'sha'ī. . . . (After a battle) Sayyid Muḥammad left the neighborhood of Huwayza, to a place there called Ṭawīla. Mīrza Ispand entered the fortress of Huwayza and his army settled in the town and seized much wealth from the people of Huwayza. Then they moved to Ṭawīla and killed many of the Musha'sha'īs. Sayyid Muḥammad sent an envoy with rich gifts and presents and goods which he had seized to Ispand Mīrzā, and asked for pardon, adding such a word in his message that Ispand Mīrzā was very content, and sent a bow and quiver and boatloads of rice to Sayyid Muḥammad. Then he marched most of the garrison of Huwayza away, and Sayyid Muḥammad fell upon those whom Ispand Mīrzā had left in charge there, and then the Musha-'sha'īs seized boatloads of clothing and provisions belonging to Ispand Mīrzā which he had sent upriver from Baṣra to Wāsiṭ, and killed every person on the boats. When this news came to Ispand Mīrzā, he retreated from Baṣra to Baghdad, and sent an army to Wāsiṭ but it achieved no decisive results, and finally most of the Arab tribes of those parts came over to Sayyid Muḥammad, and his prestige and power increased, and Ramahīya came under his power and he built himself a castle there. When Pīr Budāgh left Baghdad for Shīrāz, and no more Mongol rulers were left in all the lands of the Iraq Arabs, Mawla 'Alī, son of Sayyid Muḥammad, besieged Wāsiṭ and cut down all its palm groves. In this siege most of the people there died of starvation, so that the inhabitants agreed with Amīr Afandī, Pīr Budāgh's governor, to go to Baṣra, and Wāsiṭ passed into ruin. This was in A.H. 858/A.D. 1454. After that Mawla 'Alī went to the Holy City of Najaf (the tomb of 'Alī) and plundered the pilgrim caravans, killing all the pilgrims. From there he went to the area around Baghdad and stayed there nine days, plundering, killing, and capturing people. After that Jahān Shāh Mīrzā Qaraqoyūnlu sent aid to the people of Baghdad, and Mawla 'Alī went back to Huwayza. He then gathered an army and besieged the citadel of Bihbihān (in Fars), and while he was engaged in this an arrow struck him and he immediately died. This was in A.H. 861/A.D. 1457 . . . and Sayyid Muḥammad died on a Wednesday in A.H. 870/A.D. 1465–6. In his father's latter days,

Mawla 'Alī had seized the reins from Sayyid Muḥammad, pleasing these people and teaching them to believe that the purified soul of our lord the Prince of Believers ('Alī), on whom be peace, was reincarnated in him, and since that holy presence was living (in him), the bedouins might plunder Iraq and raid the holy tombs (of the Imāms.) His father was unable to better things, and when the rulers of those parts rebuked him, he used to reply that he was powerless. . . . After him ruled his (other) son, Sulṭān Muḥsin.[22]

Among the Ottoman Turks, Mahdism seems to have been a rare occurrence. There were religious revolts among the Turks, but they were usually led by antinomian dervish elements, and while they had messianic and eschatological aspects, they did not appear as attempts to establish a "more Islamic" society. One must surmise that among Turks at least there was a degree of satisfaction with the "Islamicness" of the Ottoman state. When Mahdist revolts did occur, they were usually among the non–Turkish Muslims of the empire and came at a time when its power had begun to wane perceptibly. The Mahdī here mentioned appeared in Anatolia, but among the Kurds. Probably the fact that this was after the millenium of Islam, in A.H. 1077/A.D. 1666, when expectation was heightened, should also be considered. At any event it does not seem to have been a serious uprising.

An Anatolian Mahdī
from The Silaḥdar's History
by Silaḥdar Meḥmet Aga (d. A.H. *1136*/A.D. *1724)*

It was submitted to the Imperial Court by the former *beylerbeyi* of Mosul, Pahlavān 'Alī Pasha son of Ḥajjī Pīr, that a certain shaykh and descendant of the Prophet among the 'ulamā' of the Kurds in the province of 'Ammādīya named 'Abdallāh due to excessive affection had claimed "My son Meḥmet (Muḥammad) is the Mahdī," and gathered a group of Kurds around him. The more this group increased, the more probable became the possibility that they might cause dissension and disorder. The aforementioned 'Alī Pasha, together with the governor of 'Ammādīya, after having secured a fatwa, marched against them and after heavy slaughter defeated the said Kurds. Sayyid 'Abdallāh, who was responsible for this society, escaped and was captured by 'Alī Pasha, while his son was apprehended in a cave by the Wālī of Diyarbakr, Wazīr Shaytān Ibrāhīm Pasha.

An Imperial Firmān was issued that they be made present at the Exalted Court. While the Sulṭān was hunting at Vize, Meḥmet Mahdī after prostrating himself in the Exalted Presence was asked about his case, and entirely denying any claim to Mahdīhood, he begged for forgiveness with sensible and reasonable responses.

As he was a mature boy and there was room for pity, in imperial clemency he was given employment among the pages of the Treasury of the Inner Palace.

As to his father Sayyid Shaykh 'Abdallāh, he was brought within a month, on the second Thursday of Dhū al-Ḥijja the Month of Pilgrimage, and was received at the 'Ammādīya Kiosk on the shores of the Tunja. The Shaykh al-Islam and Vānī Effendi were brought to this place. They conversed with the Shaykh, at times in Arabic and at times in Kurdish, and testified that in the foregoing events he had been wronged and hurt. Thereupon his heart was made glad by the mercy of the king of kings. He was honored with dervish robes as a mark of respect and granted a convent (*tekkīya*) in Istanbul, with adequate duties. As for the governor of Mosul, he was deposed in anger.[23]

In the nineteenth century, when the decay of Islamic Civilization was apparent and the aggressiveness of the industrializing Western powers convinced Muslims that Islam was in danger, a spate of Mahdīs appeared. Many of these manifestations were rather pathetic little popular affairs.

A Mahdī in Tunisia

from Presentation of the Men of the Age, with an Account of the Kings of Tunisia and the Treaty of Protection
by Ibn Abī al-Ḍiyāf (d. A.H. *1291*/A.D. *1874)*

In these days (of 1860) there appeared in the Khumīr mountains a man claiming to be from Baghdad, whose name was Muḥammad ibn 'Abdallāh of the Prophet's family. The temptation occurred to him that he was the awaited Imām Mahdī, and some of the eminent men of the area began to gather about him as moths gather about a lamp. Inspired by some crack-brained fancy, he then mentioned that he wanted a holy war in God's service.

When this reached the consul of the French, Leon Roche, he asked the Bey to remove this man from the Algerian border, and the Bey wrote to his brother at Maḥalla about the affair. He sent people to bring him from Khumīr, and he came willingly. He did not refuse, and those around him did not prevent it. He said to the Bey of Maḥalla "The Arabs of Khumīr asked me to go on holy war in God's service: I am far from home, and I have held off for your permission, and the upshot of it is that you should give me a mount and a saddle." Then the Bey of Maḥalla sent him to his brother (in Tunis) who imprisoned him.

When he next sat in Judgement, he ordered the man to be brought before him, and when he saw him said to him "What led you to do such a thing?" and gave orders to put him to death.

When he was led to the place of execution, in front of the Bardo Gate, they offered him water, as is the custom, but he said "I am fasting, because I want to meet my Lord as a servant, for I am a wronged man." They cut off his head, may God have mercy on him. This was on Thursday the 13th of Ṣafar/August 30, 1860.[24]

An Egyptian Mahdī

from The True Information of the States of the Seas
by Ismāʿīl Sarhang (d. A.H. *1343*/A.D. *1925)*

There appeared in the first part of the reign of Khedive Ismāʿīl Pasha (1863–1880) in the village of Qāw in the Mudīrīya of Girgā in Upper Egypt a man called Aḥmad al-Ṭayyib, who came from the south. He claimed that he was a *sharīf* (descendant of the Prophet) of the line of Jaʿfar, and pretended to learning and sainthood and visions. Many turned to him within a short time, and he began to attack the government and its actions and to accuse the rulers of straying from the Religion. Now it happened that a Copt had bought a slave girl there, and tried to baptize her. When she opposed this, he treated her harshly.

When Aḥmad al-Ṭayyib learned of this, he took it on himself to free the slave girl, and a rabble from the mudīrīyas of Girgā and Asyūt followed him. When the slave girl had been set free as he desired, he did not stop there but went further and claimed that he was the Mahdī. It became a momentous matter, and the government began to fear a serious uprising. The Khedive ordered armed forces to be sent against him of two battalions and two field pieces. . . . They travelled to Qāw by the Nile steamers, and when they arrived they were joined by a body of irregulars (*bashibozuqs*). All of them then went after Shaykh Aḥmad al-Ṭayyib and his flock, and a confused battle broke out at the tenth hour of the day. After an hour the revolutionists were surrounded and their leader was killed by one of the bashibozuqs. With that, the insurrection ceased altogether. The soldiers remained there another three days to preserve the peace. Many of the revolutionists had been killed, their houses destroyed and their possessions carried off. A good number of them were exiled to the Mediterranean coast for life, and the Khedive pardoned the rest.[25]

MAHDISM IN AFRICA

We have seen that Mahdism had strongly influenced the course of Islamic civilization. In modern times, it continued to play an important role in the history of Muslims, particularly in Africa, where it served to deflect or modify the course of Western imperialism. Mahdism has also played a vital part in the development of "modern" states, more or less organised along national principles.

Expectation of the Mahdī played a part in the complex movements of the peoples of the sub–Sahara who had once controlled the caravan routes, were partly islamised, and now saw the Europeans diverting African trade to the coastal ports. The following document was circulated in support of an important reformer of West African Islam in the nineteenth century, al–Ḥājj 'Umar ibn Sa'īd, who from 1852 to 1864 built up a sizable kingdom that reached from northern Guinea and Senegal (where it encountered the French) to Timbuktu. The document purports to be from the Sharīf of Mecca, the greatest Muslim authority known to the pilgrims from Africa, and asserts that Ḥājj 'Umar is carrying out jihād to prepare for the day of the Mahdī, whose viceroy he will be. Its warnings of calamities to come appears to be an echo in distant West Africa of the malaise in all the Muslim world at that period. The document is in such poor Arabic that as its editor points out, it does not seem likely that it actually came from the Sharīf in Mecca, but rather seems to have been prepared by one of Ḥājj 'Umar's followers.

A Mahdist Document from Guinea from the mid–nineteenth century A.D.

This is a dispatch from 'Abd al–Muṭṭalib the Sharīf, who is the Sulṭān of Makka, to your country, where the Qur'ān is read. "In the name of God, the Beneficent, the Merciful! O God, bless Muḥammad and his family and give them peace! Praise to God; blessing and peace be upon the best of God's creation, Muḥammad the Messenger of God! God bless and preserve him!

"After which: from the Sharīf to al–Ḥājj 'Umar ibn Sa'īd Fūtī al-Fulānī. 'May God have mercy on you: convey this message to the entire Community of Muḥammad, may God bless him and give him peace! Truly the Hour is very close, for the Mahdī has appeared in the world; he will come to you. You have heard the news: (allegiance has not yet been sworn to him?) Only three years remain to him before (the sending?) His ministers have already come; these three have made manifest their jihād – al-Shaykh Ibrāhīm Sharīf al-Dīn in the South, Shaykh 'Abd al-Bāqī in the North, and Shaykh al-Ḥājj 'Umar ibn Sa'īd in the West, and the Mahdī in the East. (This is so) because the people of Makka live amongst the Turks and the Turks were kings of the lands of the East. . . .'

"Travelling one day between Makka and al-Madīna, we found a great enclosed garden whose length was sixteen days' (journey) and which was eleven days' journey in width. There was no one inside it; within it we found high buildings, of which only God knows the length, until it (reached?) Madīna the Illuminated. We asked about the garden and the buildings which were in the middle of it, and were told that the buildings contained nobody. They were reserved for the Mahdī, whose time had come.

" 'Abd al-Muṭṭalib says: 'O Community of Muḥammad . . . you have heard this stupendous news: Obey the Prophet: do not seek your own advantage; do not be envious, O Community. Fear God: do not quarrel (among yourselves); do not break up your religion, O Community. You have heard the word, which has come from God: "Help one another (in works of) piety and reverence; do not aid each other in sin and enmity." And fear God, O Community of Muḥammad; after this will come a year with plague and affliction; in it death, hunger, and lions will be abundant. Do not take risks, O servants of God! Fear your Lord, be generous with alms, invocations, prayer, and zakāt, for the Community of Muḥammad can only ward off misfortune, plague, and catastrophe with alms and congregational prayers, and by reading the Qur'ān.

"Some people have asked me about Shaykh 'Umar ibn Sa'id Fūtī and the interval between him and the Mahdī. (The Mahdī) shall reign from *f. r. j. d.* to the land of India, and 'Abd al-Bāqī will rule from the land or Rūm (Anatolia) to Daylam, and Shaykh 'Umar will rule from the land of Sawakin (on Red Sea, to West?) For the Mahdī is (a Sharīf.) Ibrāhīm will rule from *j. l. k.* or Fung, God knows best; they say he is a Sudānī, and Shaykh 'Umar is a

Turudu (Tukolor scholar), and 'Abd al-Bāqī an Arab. There is nothing for a messenger but to give information. The mission is for Shaykh al-Ḥājj 'Umar; we shall return to Makka.

"I have wished to say this, O servants of God. The Community of the generous Muḥammad is noble. Be generous to the Shaykh, the Ḥājj, and to the orphan and the poor who are with you. May God have mercy on us and on you, O Community: fear God and do not be envious. O God, bless Muḥammad and his family and give them peace!"

This concludes the dispatch issued by the hand of 'Abd al-Muṭṭalib the Sharīf, the Sulṭān of Makka which is the House of God. It was copied by Muḥammad Tūrk (sic), who wrote it for the sake of God and the Prophet. Praise to God, Lord of the Worlds.[26]

In Libya in the nineteenth century, the powerful Sanūsī brotherhood, imbued in part with fundamentalist reform doctrines found among the Waḥḥābīs of Arabia, was preaching from its oasis headquarters to the peoples of the Sahara and expanding into the sub-Sahara. The son of the founder and second head of the order from 1859 to 1902 was Sayyid al-Mahdī al-Sanūsī. Although he made no explicit claim to be the promised Mahdī, there is no doubt that thousands of his followers believed that he was. It fell to the Sanūsīs to organise resistance to the Italians in the early twentieth century. The Sanūsīs have been the cohesive force in modern Libya, and Sayyid Mahdī's son Idrīs became the first king of independent Libya in 1951.

In the eastern Sudān, a Mahdist uprising among the tribes collided headlong with British expansion in 1883 and made "the Mahdī of Sudan" a well known figure. Muḥammad Aḥmad ibn 'Abdallāh was a Ṣūfī shaykh, apparently convinced of his own mission and able to convince others. Like the Waḥḥābīs of Arabia, he considered the Turks and their nominal vassals the Egyptians—both trying to hastily borrow Western techniques to shore up their tottering power—as worldly apostates to Islam, unbelievers. He would himself rebuild Islamic power, but with moral reform and jihād. Inevitably this drew Britain into the Sudān, even though she had to reconquer the country from the Mahdī's dervishes with great effort and destruction of life. The Sudanese were totally defeated, but the foundations of their nationalism had been laid by the Mahdī and his anṣār. The brotherhood he founded has been a main force in Sudanese life and has made his descendants both religiously and politically prominent.

An interesting letter has been preserved from the Mahdī of Sudān to Sayyid Mahdī the Sanūsī, proposing an alliance between them.

The Sanūsī, a more sophisticated 'ālim who believed in a less violent propagation of righteousness, ignored the letter.

A Letter of the Mahdī of Sudan to Sayyid Mahdī the Sanūsī from the Correspondence of Muḥammad Aḥmad ibn 'Abdallāh (dated A.H. *1300*/A.D. *1883)*

In the name of God, the Compassionate, the Merciful, from the poor servant of his Lord al-Mahdī ibn al-Sayyid 'Abdallāh, to his beloved in God the Khalīfa Muḥammad al-Mahdī ibn al-Sanūsī. May God help him, amen.

Most beloved and true believer in the law of the Prophet and honorable guide of God's worshippers: know, beloved, that I and my helpers were expecting you to revive true religion before Mahdīhood was inspired in me, who am but an humble servant. I wrote to you but you did not answer me, therefore I conclude my letter did not reach you. . . .

I was told by the lord of existence, Muḥammad, that I am the expected Mahdī, and he placed me on his throne several times in the presence of the four caliphs, the poles (*aqṭāb*) and al-Khiḍr; he also girded me with his sword in the presence of the saints, the aqṭāb, the angels, and al-Khiḍr. I was told that none could gain a victory over me, having received the sword of victory from him. He told me that God had made a mark in proof of my Mahdīhood which is a mole on my right cheek, and also another sign, which is a flag of dazzling white carried by 'Izrā'īl (the angel of death) which appears during the battle. On the appearance of this flag the hearts of my followers are strengthened, and fear enters the hearts of my enemies so that none can oppose me, for it is God's will that they should fail. The Prophet also said to me, "You are created from the light issuing from the center of my heart."

He therefore for whom happiness is decreed should believe that I am the expected Mahdī. Those who disbelieved pretend to know that everything is subject to the will of God, but the Almighty's will was to inspire me with Mahdism, I, his humble servant Muḥammad the Mahdī. . . . When I was receiving the instructions of God and His Prophet, I was always thinking of you, and was informed by the Prophet that you are one of my wazīrs or ministers. Whilst I was awaiting your arrival I was informed by al-Khiḍr concerning your belief and your present life; subsequently a vision took place in which the Prophet and his special disciples, who are also my helpers, were present. Then one of my helpers took his place on the chair of Abū Bakr al-Ṣiddīq, and another on the chair of ʻUmar, but the chair of ʻUthmān was left empty, and concerning this the Prophet said, "This chair is for the son of Sanūsī, and is kept for him until he comes forward sooner or later." He then seated one of my helpers on the chair of ʻAlī. May God bless them all. . . .

The lord of existence, Muḥammad, said that he who doubts my Mahdīhood is a renegade from God and His Prophet, and he exhorted me to fight against the Turks, those who would not believe in my Mahdīhood, and those who unite with them in fighting against me. He called them infidels, and worse that that, for they were endeavouring to extinguish the light of God. He announced to me the good news that my followers would rank as his followers, and that those of lowest degree would have the same rank as Shaykh ʻAbd al-Qādir al-Jīlānī. . . . All that I have told you of my Mahdīhood has been revealed to me by the lord of existence when I was wide awake and in good health. I was not asleep, or hallucinated, or drunk with wine, nor mad, but I was in full possession of all my mental faculties. Follow the example of the Prophet, obey his orders, and shun what he forbids.

"Setting forth" (the Hijra) is a sacred duty, described as such in all the holy books and laws. He who cares for the faith, and has compassion toward his religion, complies with this call and unites with us in spreading God's religion.

Let it be known to you that I am a lineal descendant of the Prophet. My father is a Ḥusaynī, both on his father's and mother's side, and my mother is a Ḥusaynī on her father's side and an ʻAbbāsī on her mother's side. . . .

As soon as you receive my letter, you are either to fight for the cause of God in your own provinces, marching down to Egypt and its neighbourhood, or you are to make the Hijra to us, but the Hijra is preferable; you cannot be ignorant of its advantages. Whatever you decide, send us an answer, informing us whether you decide to fight or make the Hijra.

A hint is sufficient to a personage like you.

Dated Rajab 1300/May 1883.[27]

Another East African Mahdī appeared in 1899, among the Somalī tribesmen of the Horn of Africa. Muḥammad ʻAbdallāh Ḥasan was a Ṣūfī shaykh, who tried to unite the quarrelling Somalī tribes in a holy war against the British infidels and their Italian allies. For a long time his violent raids on the British and their supporters could not be defeated, but the development of the airplane and the perennial divisions of the tribes made it possible to drive him out of his last stronghold in March 1920, and he died soon after, in November. The wars of the "Mad Mullah of Somaliland," as he was called, caused great sufferings in his country, but he was a new kind of hero–leader, striving for a greater than tribal social system, and he will always be remembered by the Somalīs. He was also a master of the heroic tribal poetry, which he used to justify his actions and curse his enemies. His poems are still highly appreciated, and even in translation retain a scalding, bitter power. Here he answers the British:

Mahdism in Somalia
Poems of Muḥammad 'Abdallāh Ḥasan
The "Mullah of Somaliland" A.H. *1338*/A.D. *1920)*

I had no issue with the Italians until you summoned them to your aid.
It was you who intrigued and plotted with them;
It was you who said "Join us in the war against the Dervishes."
And they did not say "Leave us, and stop conspiring with us;"
Did you never tire of these evil machinations?
. . . .
It is you who lead to pasture these weaker infidels;
Can I distinguish between you and your livestock?
As to the raiders of whom you talk, I also have a complaint.
It is you who oppressed them and seized their beasts,
It is you who took for yourselves their houses and property,
It is you who spoilt their settlements and defiled them with ordure,
It is you who reduced them to eating the tortoise and beast of prey;
This degradation you brought upon them.
If they (in turn) become beasts of prey and loot you,
And steal small things from the clearings between your huts,
Then they were driven to this by hunger and famine;
Do not complain to me and I will not complain to you.[28]

Here he addresses a chief of the Ogādēn clan, who has promised to join him, and abandon alliances with the British and Ethiopians. In the symbolic description of a journey home, he foresees the long hardships, and eventual peace.

When in the early morning, at dawn, you rise and mount your stallion,
Apart from the sand and dust that rises up around you, the columns of dust,

The road which you will follow is not one on which people lose their way,
And indeed it is straight from here to Huraan.
Nevertheless, what the Haud is known for is hardship and lack of water.
The present season is the time of the light Kalul rains.
God who fills our water-ponds will not make you thirst.
Bush thick and impenetrable, scorched ḥagar trees, the hot air rising from them,
Hot wind and heat, which will lick you like a flame,
A mantle of air and a shade-giving tree will shelter you;
The swelling of feet pricked by thorns, a thorny thicket, plants prickly and spiny,
Charred plants, hot stumps of burned trees, the hot air rising from them,
The burnt branches and tree trunks through which you pass will not harm you.
A bull rhinoceros, ready to jump, a male lion, angry and roaring in attack,
The goring with the head, the clutching of claws, the biting fang,
The giraffe's rocking gait, the kicking of the leg, the elephant flying,
The hyena's attack, the beasts of prey, open–mouthed, panting for meat,
. . . .
Creeping beasts, evil reptiles, venomous, bearing poison;
The robbers who roam, the raiders, the fugitives, the thieves;
The small bustard with its piteous cry, the great bustard whose heart trembles;
The heat of the rainless season, the desolate terrain, losing the way;
I invoke the saints who keep the straight path, and the riches of the Sūra Yāsīn,
May God, day and night, turn danger from you,
Before you, on each side and behind, everywhere, may the peace of God be upon you.
From the time of Abel we have enjoyed the riches of the Faith;
God does not refuse my prayers for grace;
When I curse a person God cuts his tendon.
Whatever you expect from me, you will receive.
Come to me! You will be drenched in God's munificence.[29]

NEW SECTS

Mahdīs of the nineteenth century were also responsible for heterodox movements within the Muslim Community which have had repercussions outside it, in Africa and North America.

One of these was the Bābī movement in Persia. One Sayyid 'Alī Muḥammad of Shīrāz, a student of theology, was first hailed by certain Twelver mystics as the Bāb, or Door, by which mankind would be united with the Hidden Imām. On a pilgrimage to Mecca in 1844, he seems to have declared that he himself would be the Mahdī, al–Qā'im. A wave of conversions and religious enthusiasm ensued in Persia, and in July 1850 the Bāb was shot by firing squad at Tabrīz with some of his followers. After a Bābī made an attempt on the life of the Shāh, a frightful persecution of the sect took place. The leaders were killed or exiled, and the movement divided. The majority followed Bahā' Allāh at Haifa in Palestine, who had declared that he was the one "whom God shall make manifest" mentioned by the Bāb. A minority followed Bahā' Allāh's half-brother, Subḥ–i 'Azal, in Cyprus. Under the leadership of Bahā' Allāh the original gnostic Shī'ī doctrine and the sense of release from an old dispensation that had characterised Bābism were given a new universalist turn, and the Bahā'īs actively propagated a new world religion with many adherents outside Iran, in North America and Africa. The selection is taken from a Bahā'ī book, and emphasizes that the Bāb was preparing the way for Bahā' Allāh. There is no doubt that it appeared different at the time.

The Appearance of the Bāb in Persia
from The New History
by Mīrzā Ḥusayn (written A.H. *1298*/A.D. *1880)*

On the 2nd of Muḥarram A.H. 1233 (November 12, 1817) was born our Great Master His Holiness Bahā' Ullāh (to whom be Glory!) His original name was Mīrzā Ḥusayn 'Alī, son of one of the Ministers of the Royal Court of Persia in Tehran, the metropolis of the Persians.

When he reached twenty–seven years of age, there appeared His Holiness the Harbinger, whose noble name was Mīrzā 'Alī Muḥammad, and who is entitled the Bāb and the First Point (Nuqṭa–i 'Ulā), who declared himself to be the Promised Qā'im (He who shall arise) and the Mahdī whose advent is expected in Islām. This event occurred . . . (May 24, 1844).

From the very beginning of his Manifestation, the Bāb began to give good tidings of the imminence of some Great Event and the advent of some Promised Benefactor, of whom he made mention in his writings with great emphasis, whom he describes as "He whom God shall make manifest," or "He who shall appear," which expression is contained in most of his writings. He lays great stress on His celebration, description, and Manifestation, while he himself, notwithstanding his claim to the highest of stations, reckons himself only a servant in relation to Him so mentioned and described.[30]

MAHDISM IN INDIA

The Aḥmadīya Muslims are another sect which was produced by the arrival of an expected deliverer. For them the promised one was Mīrzā Ghulām Aḥmad of Qāḍiyān in the Panjāb of India. After some ten years of religious activity as an independent scholar and Ṣūfī, he announced in 1891 that he was both Christ and the Mahdī. This raised great opposition, but a community developed and after his death in 1908 it followed his khalīfa until 1914. At this time a division occurred, between the majority, the so-called Qādiyānīs, and a rather modernist westernized minority, the Lahorīs. Each has tended to go its own way: the Qāḍiyānīs teach that Ghūlām Muḥammad was a prophet, and that other Muslims who rejected him are therefore infidels, and the Lahore group regards him merely as a restorer and renewer of Islam.

Ghūlām Aḥmad's ideas have been well characterised as "a late Indian Ṣūfī version of Islam activated by modern–Western infiltrations."[31] The threat of Christian missions has been met with the riposte that Christians completely misunderstood Jesus (so as not even to recognise him when he reappeared), and by a vigorous, well–planned mission activity in Europe, America, and Africa with particular attention to Negros, as victims of Western Christianity. Both groups have been effective in winning converts. The work of Aḥmadī missionaries among American Negros in turn activated the so–called Black Muslim group, who follow still another new prophet. Here is a Qādiyānī document presented to the Niẓām of Haydarabad (at that time a Sunnī) by the present head of the sect, the son of Ghūlām Aḥmad, justifying their teaching in terms of Islamic eschatological doctrine.

The Aḥmadīya Muslims and Eschatology
from Ahmadiyyat or the True Islam
by Mīrzā Bashīr al–Dīn (written 1924 A.D.*)*

I shall now try to disprove the notion that since the Dajjāl has not yet made his disappearance, it is not still time for the Messiah to appear. I would say in reply that the Dajjāl has already appeared, but people have failed to recognise him. The meaning of the word

Dajjāl is, according to the Arabic lexicons, a counterfeiter. It may now be clear to your Highness that by the peril of the Dajjāl it meant nothing but the menace of those societies whose ministers are busy endeavouring in a thousand ways to win the world to their preposterous doctrines. That the Dajjāl would be blind of one eye signifies that his spiritual eye would be blind. Such figurative meanings are not farfetched, rather they are supported by the Ḥadīth. The same view is also corroborated by the Ḥadīth "He will break the Cross," that is, the Promised Messiah will refute the Christian creed with arguments and signs so that at last the cross will be broken, meaning that most people will accept Islam, and Christianity will lose its influence.[32]

In *Ahmadiyyat or The True Islam,* Mīrzā Bashīr al-Dīn addresses a cosmopolitan audience. He points out that every major religion has the idea of a promised deliverer.

Our belief is that all these things are to be found in the Holy Founder of the Aḥmadiyya movement, Hazrat Mirza Ghulam Ahmad (on whom be peace and blessings of God) whom God raised for the reformation of the present age. He claimed to be the Messiah for the Christians, the Mahdī for the Muslims, Krishna or the *Neha Kalank Avatar* for the Hindus, and Mesio Darbahmi (the Saoshyant) for the Zorastrians. In short he was the Promised Prophet of every nation and was appointed to collect all mankind under the banner of one faith. In him were centered the hopes and expectations of all nations; he is the Dome of Peace under which every nation may worship its Maker; he is the opening through which all nations may obtain a vision of their Lord; and he is the center at which meet all the radii of the circle. It is ordained therefore, that the world shall find peace and rest only through him.[33]

The expectation of the Mahdī fostered by the African tarīqas or brotherhoods has assisted the rise of many claimants to the title even in recent times. Mūsā Amīnu ibn Muḥammad al-Amīn was a Songhay Murābiṭ, or dervish shaykh, in West Africa. After travels to Ghana, Morocco, and Upper Volta, he settled at Wani on the Niger. On March 26, 1949, he declared a "jihād," and with a few followers killed a French colonial administrator. The next day he was wounded and left to die by French troops. His diary tells of sixty-two dream-revelations, in which the symbolism is striking.

A Modern African Mahdī
from his diary,
by Mūsa Amīnu (d. A.H. *1368*/A.D. *1949)*

In the name of God the Merciful, the Compassionate, I wish to tell what I saw between waking and sleeping, and repeat the words of God. 'Ubāda ibn Sāmit asked the Prophet about "good news in this world," and the Messenger told him, "They are the good dreams which a Believer has." Tirmidhī transmitted it. According to Bukhārī and Muslim, the Messenger of God said, "At the end of the world, the dreams of believers will not lie. They constitute one of the forty–six parts of prophecy." They also relate that he said, "Whoever sees me in his sleep sees me as if waking, and the devil will not be able to resemble me. . . ."

1. I saw the Prophet in Rabī' II, in the early part of Saturday night. I was seated with our Shaykh Ḥāmallāh on a carpet before the Prophet. 'Alī was seated behind us. The archangel Gabriel, with Abū Bakr and 'Umar (and others whom I did not recognise) were seated at the right hand of the Prophet. At his left there were Michael and perhaps 'Uthmān and many other persons. In front of the Prophet someone was reciting his praises. The Prophet said, "I am the Messenger of God; here is Gabriel at my right hand and Michael at my left, and these are my Companions. What do you say to that?" This is what I saw in my dream, and God is Most Knowing!

3. On Friday night the 24th of the Month of Pilgrimage, I saw myself enter Mecca with a great crowd. After the rites of the Pilgrimage we came upon the tomb of the Prophet. On it, there were two pouches full of musk. I took them and put them in my pocket.

6. On Monday night the 6th of Jumāda, I saw myself enter Medina. I asked the way to the tomb of the Prophet. A man took me by the hand and led me. I passed my hand through the grill into the tomb enclosure, and it seemed that I touched *his* hand. After that I passed my hand over my face and body.

8. I saw the Prophet. He was on a gray horse, followed by his grandsons Ḥasan and Ḥusayn and an innumerable multitude. I ran to him, and seized the bridle of his horse. I placed my hand on the forehead of the animal, then passed it over my face and said, "God is most great, and this is the Messenger of God." And then

the Prophet removed the turban of al-Ḥasan and placed it on my head. May God be praised!

9. The (French) Administrator of Dori and impious men put me under house arrest, and the district guards and spies rummaged my effects, but without finding anything. I was sad and filled with thoughts, when sleep came upon me. Our master Shaykh Ḥāmallāh [a modern "reformer" of the Tijānī order—Ed.] appeared to me with Gabriel. He clasped my hand and smiled at me. Gabriel saluted me also, saying "God will save you from these people."

10. When I was imprisoned at Wahiguya, I saw our lord 'Alī. He came to shake my hand. Then our queen Fāṭima came. She made me sit upon her knees, and said, weeping, "This is my oppressed son." The next day, she caused me to leave that prison. May God be praised!

13. Our Shaykh Ḥāmallāh, leader of those who are saved, appeared to me, clasped my hand and embraced me. He took a paper, red ink, and a pen, and drew a fourfold seal, and handed it to me. I took it and put it in my pocket. Praise be to God, Lord of the Worlds!

18. I saw the Prophet; he was in a pretty little automobile, and I was with him. I heard a Voice which said, "You are the Caliph of God in His Kingdom, you are the Mahdī of Muḥammad, beyond a doubt. Shaykh Ḥāmallāh came before the Mahdī, but he is not himself the Mahdī. You must go to Bāb al-Huda, to join Jesus the son of Mary!" This was in 1945.

19. Another time the Voice said, "You are the Caliph of God, on the earth as it is in heaven." It continued to speak to me until the end of the year. Each time, it changed the phrase. . . . "Peace be to you, O Mahdī Muḥammad." But at that time I paid no attention to the Voice, which I heard without seeing anyone. It told me, "You are the Caliph of God in His Kingdom, you are the Mahdī Muḥammad, do not doubt it. Shaykh Ḥāmallāh is the one who must come before the Mahdī. . . ."

25. Another time, I saw the Shaykh come to me. He entered the zāwiya (house of the order) and found me standing, reciting the profession of faith. I held a rod gleaming with whiteness, and our Shaykh held a large torch in his hand. He was accompanied by an overseer (muqaddam). He passed his torch over the wall of the *zāwiya*, and the light of it illumined the East and the West. . . . As

I was going to the house for a carpet to spread beneath the feet of our Shaykh, there came from the East an automobile, white as the full moon and shining like the sun. This car was made like the Ka'ba. It came very fast, and entered our zāwiya. I went to it very quickly while our Shaykh remained still, and I made the circumambulation. It then opened, showing a closed white cup. I took it. Someone asked, "What is this cup that Mūsā holds?" Someone else replied, "No one knows what it contains; only Mūsā has the key to it, and he will open it on Friday."

26. Another time I received a visit from our Shaykh Ḥāmallāh and Shaykh Aḥmad Tijānī. . . . I hastened to greet them. Our Shaykh was holding a luminous rod. When they saw me, both greeted me, and our Shaykh handed me his rod, saying "God gives it to you." I took it. Then they said "We wish to build a city here." I followed them to the zāwiya, reciting the profession of faith. Before the door stood a horse, saddled and bridled. Its height was extraordinary.

56. I saw the Messenger of God. He told me "Mūsā, you are my true son. Your religion must triumph over every other, and the power of the Christians must end, that only the authority of Islam may remain, and that you destroy that city. Fear not, for I am always with you."

60. I saw the Prophet. He embraced me, clasped my hand, and said "Have you transmitted God's message to men?" I laughed for joy, and said "Surely, O Messenger of God!" I told him that the people were complaining of poverty, drought, and famine. He replied "It is a good for them, if they but knew it." This was in 1949.

61. Good and joyful news: my destiny will be achieved in 1949. I have learned this on Friday the 20th of February 1949. God be praised!

62. A Voice from God gave me good tidings in this verse: "The last of the evildoers shall be exterminated." God be praised. This was in 1949.[34]

The more urbane Sunnī of today is inclined to deprecate Mahdism of the traditional type, although as we have seen in discussing the Perfect Ruler there is an element of Messianism in modern political thinking. It would be naive to think that an idea of such long influence could vanish overnight, particularly in times like ours, when so much appears to have gone awry, and it is quite possible that Mahdism will play an important role in the future upheavals of Muslim society.

The thought of the Western-educated Indian Muslim poet philosopher Sir Muḥammad Iqbāl had a great influence, and he is considered one of the fathers of Pakistan. Steeped in Persian mysticism, he was also influenced by the ideas of Bergson and Nietzsche. Iqbāl's vision of the promised deliverer is at once modern, mystical, and dynamic. He will arise when by struggle and faith the Muslim Community evolves the Superman who can be the Viceregent of God on earth. The seed of the Superman is the individual Self.

Divine Viceregency
from The Secrets of the Self
by Muḥammad Iqbāl (written 1915 A.D.*)*

If thou canst rule thy camel (body), thou wilt rule the world,
And wear on thine head the crown of Solomon.
Thou wilt be the glory of the world while the world lasts,
And thou wilt reign in the kingdom incorruptible.
'Tis sweet to be God's viceregent in the world,
And exercise sway over the elements.
God's viceregent is as the soul of the universe,
His being is the shadow of the Greatest Name.
He knows the mysteries of part and whole,
He executes the command of Allah in the world.
His genius abounds with life and desires to manifest itself:
He will bring another world into existence
. . . .
To the human race he brings both a glad message and a warning,
He comes both as a soldier and as a marshal and prince
. . . .
Our handful of earth has reached the zenith,
For that champion will come forth from this dust!
There sleeps amid the ashes of our Today
The flame of a world-consuming Morrow
. . . .
Appear, O rider of Destiny!
Appear, O light of the dark realm of change!
Illumine the scene of existence;
Dwell in the blackness of our eyes!
Silence the noise of the nations,
Imparadise our ears with thy music!
Arise and tune the harp of brotherhood!

Give us back the cup of wine of love!
. . . .
Mankind is the cornfield and thou art the harvest,
Thou art the goal of life's caravan.
The leaves are scattered by autumn's fury:
Oh, do thou pass over our gardens as the Spring!
Receive from our downcast brows
The homage of little children and of young men and old!
It is to thee that we owe our dignity
And silently undergo the pains of life.[35]

Another modern view of Mahdism is here advanced by the Pakistani neo–fundamentalist journalist Abū al–'Alā' Mawdūdī. Regarded as an 'ālim by his followers, he owes much of his popularity to a lucid Urdu style, which makes complex matters seem very simple. Since the creation of Pakistan, he and his party have played an important role in the debates on the meaning of "Islamic State", and they were also involved in the riots with the Mahdist Qādiyānīs. The renewal of Islam is a much discussed topic in Pakistan, and Mawdūdī has been accused of trying to be a Renewer and a Mahdī. He disclaims this. For him and his followers, the earth can only begin being filled with justice and equity when the present westernized ruling class is ousted, and the ancient Law is the constitution of Pakistan. He believes there will be a Mahdī, but takes a common sense approach to the nature of his manifestation.

The Coming Mahdī
from A Short History of the Revivalist Movement in Islam
by Abū al–'Alā al–Mawdūdī (written ca. 1960)

Those Muslims who believe in the coming of al–Imām al–Mahdī are not very different in their misconceptions from those who do not believe in such an event at all. They seem to think that the Mahdī will suddenly emerge, one day, rosary in hand, from some madrasa or (khānqāh) and will forthwith proclaim himself to be the Mahdī; bay'a will be performed and jihād declared. All the ascetics gone into seclusion and all the living orthodox people of the old type will gather round him under his banner. Swords will be used merely as a token, for the battle will be fought and fields won by spiritual powers and by the use of charms and sacred words. His mere glance will be enough to undo infidels and mere curses sufficient to demolish tanks and aeroplanes. But as far as I have studied this subject I have found the matter to be just the reverse. In my opinion the coming one will be a most enlightened Leader of his age possessing an unusually deep insight in all the current branches of knowledge and all the major problems of life. As regards statesmanship, political sagacity and strategic skill in war he will take the whole world by surprise and prove the most modern of all the moderns. But I am afraid that the people who will be the first so called to raise hue and cry against his "innovations" will be the 'Ulamā' and the Ṣūfīs. I also do not expect that his bodily features will be any different from the common man so as to render him easily recognizable. . . . Most probably he will not be aware of his being the promised Mahdī. People, however, will recognize him after his death from his works to be the one who was to establish "Caliphate after the pattern of prophethood" as mentioned in the prophecies. As I indicated above, none but a Prophet has any right to start his work with a claim. "Mahdī–ism" is not something to be claimed, it is rather something to be achieved. People who put forward such claims and those who readily accept them, in fact, betray a serious lack of knowledge and a degraded mentality. . . . If the expectation that Islam eventually will dominate the world of thought, culture and politics is genuine, then the coming of a Great Leader is also certain. People who look askance at the idea surprise me by their lack of common sense. When leaders of iniquity like Lenin and Hitler can appear on the stage of this world, why should the appearance of a Leader of Goodness only be regarded as remote and uncertain?[36]

NOTES

1 Ṭabarī. *Tarīkh*. Cairo, 1963, new edition. Vol. V, p. 589.

2. Mas'ūdī. *Murūj al-Dhahab*. Paris, 1869. With French translation. Vol. V. pp. 171–83. (Editor's translation and abridgement.)

3. *Mishkāt al-Masābīh*. English translation by Robson. Lahore 1961. p. 1137ff.

4. Ibid. p. 1130.

5. *Mishkāt*. Calcutta edition, 1932. Vol. IV, p. 32. (Editor's translation and abridgement.)

6. Ibid. p. 55ff.

7. Ibid. p. 81ff.

8. Mas'ūdī. *op cit*. Vol. V, pp. 467–71. (Editor's translation and abridgement.)

9. Ibn Ṭiqṭiqā'. *al-Fakhrī*. Cairo, 1927. pp. 119–22. (Editors' translation and abridgement.)

10. Ibn Ḥammād. *Akhbār Mulūk Banī 'Ubayd*. Algiers, 1927. With a French translation. pp. 6–12. (Editor's translation.)

11. Muṭahhar ibn Ṭahir al-Maqdisī. *al-Bad' wa al-Ta'rīkh*. Paris 1899–1919. With a French translation. Vol. II, p. 180. (Editor's translation.)

12. Ibn Babūya. Translated by A. A. Fyzee, as *A Shi'ite Creed*, (London, 1942) pp. 95–99. (Here abridged.)

13. Ibn Baṭṭūṭa. *al-Rihla*. translated by H. A. R. Gibb, Cambridge University Press, 1958. Vol. II, p. 324ff.

14. Ibid. p. 326.

15. D. M. Donaldson. *The Shī'ī Religion*. London, 1933. p. 247.

16. Ibid. p. 249.

17. Marrākushī. *al-Mu'jib fī Talkhīs Akhbār al-Maghrib*. Cairo, 1949. pp. 178–204. (Editor's translation and abridgement.)

18. *Futūḥāt-i Fīrūz Shāhī*. In Elliot and Dawson, *History of India*. London, 1867–77. pp. 378–79.

19. Ibn Khaldūn. *Muqaddima*. Edited by 'Alī 'Abd al-Wāhid Wāfī. Cairo 1958. pp. 725–59. (Editor's translation and abridgement.)

20. Mujeeb, Muḥammad. *The Indian Muslims*. London 1966. pp. 103–106. (Translations of Mahdavī documents are by Professor Mujeeb.)

20a. Ibid.

21. Badā'ūnī. *Muntakhab al-Tavārīkh*. English translation by Ranking, Calcutta, 1895. Vol. III. pp. 507–25. (Here abridged.)

22. Nūr Allāh Shūshtarī. *Majālis al-Mu'minīn*. Teheran, 1956. Vol. II, pp. 395–400. (Editor's translation and abridgement.)

23. Silahdār Aga. *Ta'rīkh*. Istanbul, 1928. Vol. I, pp. 434–45. (Courtesy of Ruşen Sezer, translator.)

24. Ibn Abī al-Ḍiyāf. *Ithāf Ahl al-Zamān bi Akhbār Mulūk Tūnis wa Ahd al-Amān*. Tunis 1964. Vol. V, p. 39. (Editor's translation.)

25. Ismā'īl Sarhang. *Ḥaqā'iq al-Akhbār min Duwal al-Biḥar*. Cairo A.H. 1314/ A.D. 1896. p. 281. (Editor's translation.)

26. Martin, Bradford G., editor and translator. "A Mahdist Document from Futa Jallon," *Bulletin de l'Institut Français d'Afrique Noire*. Vol. 6 (1963), pp. 69–72.

27. Wingate, Sir Reginald. *Mahdiism and the Egyptian Sudan*. London, 1891. pp. 69–72.

28. B. W. Andrzewski and I. M. Lewis. *Somali Poetry, an Introduction*. Oxford 1964. p. 78. Abridged.

29. Ibid., p. 102, here abridged.

30. Mīrzā Ḥusayn. *Ta'rīkh-i Jadīd*. Translated by E. G. Browne in *The New History of the Bāb*. Cambridge 1893. pp. 2–3.

31. In *Encyclopedia of Islam* 2, "Ahmadiyya."

32. Mīrzā Bashīr al-Dīn Maḥmūd Aḥmad. *Ahmadiyyat or The True Islam*. Washington, D. C., 1951. p. 11.

33. Mīrzā Bashīr al-Dīn Maḥmūd Aḥmad, *Tuhfat al-Mulūk*. In English translation. Qāḍiyān. No date. pp. 63–65.

34. Vincent Monteil. *l'Islam Noir*. Paris 1964. pp. 297–306.

35. Sir Muḥammad Iqbāl. *The Secrets of the Self*. Lahore, 1955. p. 78ff. (Translated by R. A. Nicholson, and first published in London, 1920.)

36. Abū al-'Alā' Mawdūdī. *A Short History of the Revivalist Movement in Islam*. Lahore, 1963. pp. 40ff.

Struggle: Jihad

CHAPTER 5

Struggle: Jihad

From The Qur'ān:

O you who believe, if you come upon the unbelievers preparing for battle, then turn not your backs upon them. And he who turns his back upon that day, except he be withdrawing to do battle or moving to join with another force, is loaded with God's anger, and his refuge is Hell—an evil destination. You did not slay them, but God slew them, and when you cast, not you cast but God cast, that He might confer a fine benefit upon the believers. Surely God is All-Hearing, All-Knowing. That for you, and God foils the unbelievers' guile.

And if you but seek the victory, then victory has already come upon you. And if you cease (pursuit), that is better for you, but if you turn back, then We shall turn back (from you), and your force will avail you nothing though it be multiplied. Truly God is with the believers. (8: 15–19).

Say to those who disbelieve, if they cease He will forgive them what has passed, but if they turn again, then usages of the ancients are past! And fight them until there is no temptation, and religion is entirely unto God. And if they give over, God shall surely see what they are doing, but if they turn again, then know that God is your Protector—best Protector, and best Helper! (8: 38–40).

Those who believed and emigrated, and struggled with their possessions and their lives in God's way, and those who gave refuge and help are friends one to another. And those who believed but did not emigrate, you have no tie with them until they emigrate to you. Yet if they seek aid from you in the name of the religion, then it is for you to aid them, except against a people between whom and you there is a covenant, and God sees the things you do! (8: 72).

And give good tidings to the unbelievers of a painful torment, except those idolators with whom you have made a covenant and they failed you in nothing and supported no one against you. With these fulfill their pact until its term: surely God loves them who fear Him. Then when the forbidden months are past, slay the idolators wherever you find them; seize them, confine them, and wait for them in every ambush. Then if they repent and perform the ritual prayer and pay the poor-tax, let them go their ways; surely God is forgiving, compassionate. (9: 3–5).

Do you reckon giving water to pilgrims and inhabiting the Holy Mosque like to him who believes in God and the Last Day and struggles in God's path? They are not equal in the sight of God, and God guides not the people who do wrong. Those who believed and emigrated and struggled in God's path with their possessions and their lives are greater in rank with God; those—they are the triumphant. (9: 19–20).

O you who believe, bow down and prostrate yourselves and worship your Lord and do good; so may you prosper. And struggle for God as He deserves to be struggled for, for He has chosen you, and laid no hardship on you in your religion, the creed of your father Abraham. (22: 77).

O you who believe, why do you say that which you do not? Very hateful it is to God that you say what you do not do. God loves those who battle in His way, as if they were one building solidly constructed. (61: 2–4).

O you who believe, shall I direct you to a commerce that will save you from a painful torment? You shall believe in God and in His messenger and struggle in God's way with your goods and your lives. That is best for you, did you but know it. (61: 10–11).

Prescribed for you is fighting, though it be hateful to you; and it may happen that you hate a thing and it is best for you, and happen that you love a thing which is bad for you; God knows, and you do not know.

They will question you about the holy month and fighting in it. Say "Fighting in it is a serious matter, but to block God's way, and rejection of Him and the Holy Mosque, and expelling its people—that is graver in God's sight, and persecution is graver than killing." They will not cease to fight you until they turn you from your religion, if they can, and whosoever among you turns from his religion and dies rejecting, their works have failed in this world and the next. Such are the inhabitants of the Fire, and therein shall they dwell forever. (2: 216–217).

O you who believe, fight those who are near to you of unbelievers, and let them find in you a harshness, and know that God is with those that fear Him. (9: 123).

Whoever struggles has only struggled to his own gain: surely God can dispense with all the worlds. And those who believe and do righteous deeds We shall acquit of their bad deeds and recompense them for the best of what they did. (29: 6–7).

And if a wound befell you, a wound like it befell the people before you. Such days We deal among men in turn, that God may know who are believers, and to take witnesses (martyrs) from among you—God loves not wrongdoers—and that God may test the believers and efface the unbelievers. Or did you suppose that you would enter Paradise without God knowing who among you has struggled and who endures? (3: 141–142).

We shall assuredly try you until We know who are the strugglers among you, and the patient, and try your tidings. (47: 31).

The verses of the Qur'ān commending struggle against non–believers were revealed after the emigration to Medina. The Prophet permitted his followers to continue the old nomadic pattern of raids for booty against enemies.

While at one level this was only a continuation of pre–Islamic Arabian practise, a profound transformation was involved. The raids were given an aura of religion, were only against non–Muslims, and served to enlarge the territory under Muslim control, while Muslims who died in battle achieved the status of martyrs. The effect was to consecrate the Muslim Community to a religious struggle with an unbelieving world. The following account of the battle of Nakhla, the first raid on the Meccans in which blood was shed, is abridged from the biography of the Prophet by Ibn Hishām of Baṣra.

The Battle of Nakhla
from The Way of the Prophet
by Ibn Isḥāq (d. ca. A.H. *151/*A.D. *768)*
in the rescension of Ibn Hishām of Baṣra (d. ca. A.H. *218/*A.D. *833)*

The Messenger of God sent 'Abdallāh b. Jaḥsh in (the sacred month of) Rajab with eight of the Emigrants and none of the Medinans. With him were Abū Hudhayfa of the 'Abd Shams clan,

'Ukkāsha b. Miḥṣan of Clan Asad b. Khuzayma, 'Utba b. Ghazwān of the clan of Nawfal, Sa'd b. Abī Waqqāṣ of Clan Zuhra, 'Amir b. Rabī'a of 'Adī, Wāqid b. 'Abdallāh of the clan of Tamīm, Khālid b. Bukayr of Clan Asad b. Layth, and Suḥayl b. Bayḍā' of the Banu Ḥārith b. Fihar. The Messenger wrote something for 'Abdallāh and ordered him not to look at it until he had journeyed south for two days, and then do what he was ordered to do, but not to force any of his companions.

When 'Abdallāh opened the letter, this is what it said: "Proceed until you reach Nakhla between Mecca and al-Ṭā'if. Lie in wait there for Quraysh and find out for us what they are doing." So he went on, as did all his companions, not one of them falling back, until Sa'd b. Abī Waqqāṣ and 'Utba b. Ghazwān lost their camel, so they stayed behind to look for it. The rest went on to Nakhla. A caravan of Quraysh carrying raisins and leather and other merchandise passed by them. Guarding it were only 'Amr b. al-Ḥaḍramī of Kinda, and two of Clan Makhzūm and another man. The caravan was afraid of them, but 'Ukkāsha showed himself, and as he had shaved his head, they said, "They are pilgrims. We have nothing to fear." The raiders took counsel among themselves, for this was the last day of Rajab, and they said, "Tonight they will enter the sacred territory (about Mecca) and be safe, yet if we kill them outside, it will be in a forbidden month," so they feared to advance on them. Then they took courage, and agreed to do whatever they could do, and take what they had. Then Wāqid shot an arrow at 'Amr b. al-Ḥaḍramī and killed him. Two men surrendered, and one escaped. 'Abdallāh and his companions took the caravan and the prisoners and came to Medina. This was before God had assigned a fifth of the booty to the Messenger of God. The rest they agreed to divide among themselves.

When they came to the Messenger, he said, "I did not order you to fight in the sacred month," and he impounded the caravan and the prisoners, and refused to take anything. When he said that, the raiders despaired, thinking they were doomed. They were reproached by their brother Muslims, and when there had been much talk about it, God sent down these verses: "They will question you about the sacred month and fighting in it. Say: 'Fighting in it is a serious matter, but blocking God's way, and rejection of Him, and the Holy Mosque, and expelling its people—that is graver in God's sight, and persecution is graver than killing. They will not cease to fight you until they turn you from your religion, if they can, and whosoever among you turns from his religion and dies rejecting, their works have failed in this world and the next. Such are the inhabitants of the Fire, and therein shall they dwell forever.' " (2: 217).

When the Qur'ān had come down on that, and God had relieved the anxiety of the Muslims, the Messenger took the caravan and held the prisoners for ransom. As to the men who made the raid, God sent down: "Those who believed and emigrated and struggled in the Way of God, such may hope for God's mercy, for God is forgiving, merciful." That is, God gave them the highest hopes in that verse.[1]

The word for religious struggle is jihād. Like other great religious traditions of Western Asia, Islam has seen the world as the theatre of a battle between opposing forces. The Community of Believers committed to doing God's will must struggle to enlarge the kingdom of God. In the early period of Islamic expansion, struggle tended to be viewed fairly simply as a war with those who rejected God's will. There are many ḥadīths on the attitude of the Prophet as to the merit of such struggle.

Ḥadīths on Jihād

from the Niches of Lamps
by al-Khaṭīb al-Tibrīzī (written A.H. *737*/A.D. *1337)*

Muslim, from Salmān al-Fārsī: I heard the Messenger of God say, "To keep guard a day and a night in the way of God is better than a month's fasting and watching by night."

Bukhārī and Muslim, from Zayd ibn Khālid: The Messenger of God said, "Whoever equips a warrior in the way of God has himself fought, and he who supplies the needs of the family of a warrior has himself fought."

Tirmidhī and Ibn Mājā, from Abū Miqdam ibn Ma'dī: The Messenger of God said, "A martyr has six privileges with God. He is forgiven his sins on the shedding of the first drop of his blood; he is shown his place in paradise; he is redeemed from the torments of the grave; he is made secure from the fear of hell and a crown of glory is placed on his head of which one ruby is worth more than the world and all that is in it; he will marry seventy-two of the *hūrīs* with black eyes; and his intercession will be accepted for seventy of his kinsmen."

Muslim, from Abū Mūsā: The Apostle of God said, "The doors of paradise are under the shadow of swords."

Bukhārī, from Ḥasnā' bint Mu'āwiya: My uncle said to us: "I said to the Prophet, 'Who is already in paradise (i.e. before the judgement day)?' He said, 'A prophet is already in paradise, a martyr is in paradise, a newborn child is in paradise, and a child buried alive is in paradise.' "

Abū Dāwūd, from 'Abdallāh ibn 'Amr: When the Messenger of God obtained plunder he used to call Bilāl, and Bilāl would call the people, and then they would bring the plunder they had taken. The Prophet would take his fifth and divide the remainder. One day after that there came a man bringing a halter made of hair, and he said, "Messenger of God, this is a part of that which we took in plunder." He answered, "Did you hear Bilāl call three times?" "Yes," he said. He asked, "What prevented you from bringing it then?" And the man made some excuse. The Prophet said, "Go on now; you will bring it on the Day of Resurrection, for I shall never accept it from you."[2]

By the time the Prophet made his final attack on Mecca, he had disarmed all but the most rabid opposition by an able combination of economic and military persuasion. The former leader of Quraysh, Abū Sufyān of the Umawī clan, was now Muḥammad's father-in-law, a recent convert and a secret ally. The account is abridged from that given by the 'Abbāsī historian al-Balādhurī, who died around A.H. 279/A.D. 892.

The Capture of Mecca
from The Conquest of the Lands
by Aḥmad ibn Yaḥya al-Balādhurī (d. A.H. 274/A.D. 829)

From 'Abdallāh ibn Rabaḥ: A number of deputations came to call on Mu'āwiya (in Syria). It was in Ramaḍān, and I, Ibn Rabāḥ, therefore prepared (the evening) meal and invited them. Then Abū Hurayra asked, "Shall I, O Anṣār (Medinans), amuse you with a narrative concerning you?" And he went on to describe the conquest of Mecca. . . .

"The Prophet advanced until he came to Mecca. At the head of one of the two wings of the (camel-mounted) army, he sent al-Zubayr; at the head of the other Khālid ibn al-Walīd, and of the infantry, Abu 'Ubayda. . . . The Prophet was at the head of his (horse-mounted) cavalry detachment. On seeing me, he said, 'Abu

Hurayra, summon the Anṣār, and let no one come but my Anṣār.' I summoned them, and they came around. In the meantime, Quraysh had gathered their mob and followers, saying, 'Let us send these ahead. If they win, we shall join them, and if defeated, we shall give whatever is demanded.' 'Do ye see,' said the Prophet, 'The mob of Quraysh?' 'We do,' answered the Anṣār. He then made a sign as if to say 'Kill them.' To this the Prophet added, 'Meet me at aṣ-Ṣafā.' Accordingly we set out, each man killing whoever he wanted to kill, until Abū Sufyān (leader of Quraysh) came to the Prophet saying, 'O Prophet of Allah, the majority of Quraysh is annihilated. There is no more Quraysh after this day.' The Prophet thereupon announced 'He who enters the house of Abū Sufyān is safe, he who closes his own door is safe, and he who lays down his arms is safe.' On this the Anṣār remarked one to the other, 'The man is moved by love to his relatives and compassion on his clan.' 'Nay,' said the Prophet, 'I am the slave of Allah, and His prophet. I have migrated to Allah, and to you. My life is your life; my death is your death.' Hearing this, the Anṣār began to weep, saying 'By Allah, we said what we said only in our anxiety to spare the Prophet of Allah!' The Prophet proceeded to the (black) stone and laid hold to it. He then made a circuit of the House (of God: the Ka'ba) and came, with a bow in his hand held at its curved part, to an idol at the side of the Ka'ba. He began to stab the eye of the idol saying, 'Truth has come and falsehood has vanished; it is the property of falsehood to vanish.' When the circuit was done, he came to (the mount of) aṣ-Ṣafā, climbed it until he could see the House, and raised his hands praising Allah and praying.

"On the day of the conquest the Prophet asked the Quraysh, 'What think ye?' to which they replied, 'What we think is good, and what we say is good. A noble brother thou art, and the son of a noble brother. Thou hast succeeded.' The Prophet then said, 'My answer is that given by my brother Joseph (son of Jacob) 'No blame be on you this day. Allah will forgive you; for He is the most merciful of the merciful.' " (12:92).[3]

From all these texts, we can begin to make a few more generalizations. The Prophet of Islam, much like the Arabs who heard him, must have seen the world as a generally inimical place, one in which harsh struggle was necessary for moral as well as material survival.

Thus, self-defense is not merely permitted in Islam, it is absolutely mandatory, and the spiritual rewards given for it are very great. One who dies defending himself, or enlarging the Community, dies a martyr and goes immediately to the eternal joy of paradise. Violence is not preferred, but in view of the nature of the world, it is not to be shunned either. And finally, because struggle is a moral activity, even violence must be conducted by rules.

In the days just following the Prophet's death, Abū Bakr dispatched a column of warriors ordered up by Muḥammad himself against Mu'ta in Syria. It was the statement of a program of expansion to a community already growing rebellious. The speech placed in his mouth by tradition contains many of the basic propositions of the Law of War.

Abū Bakr's Injunctions on the Jihād
from History of Prophets and Kings
by Muḥammad ibn Jarīr al-Ṭabarī (d. A.H. *310*/A.D. *923)*

Abu Bakr went out (with the army) and he was walking, while Usāma (the leader) rode. 'Abd al-Raḥman ibn 'Awf was leading Abū Bakr's mount. Then Usāma said to him, "Successor of God's Messenger; you will either mount, or I shall dismount." He replied, "By God you shall not dismount, and I will not mount. I must get my feet a little dusty in the path of God, for a *ghāzī* (raider) with every step he takes has seven hundred merits credited to him and he is raised seven hundred degrees, while seven hundred sins are forgiven him!" When he had walked enough, he said to Usāma "If you see fit to let 'Umar (stay in Medina and) help me, please do so." And Usāma gave him leave. Then he said "O ye people! Stand, while I give you ten words of advice, and learn them from me. Do not act treacherously; do not act disloyally; do not act neglectfully. Do not mutilate; do not kill little children or old men, or women; do not cut off the heads of the palm-trees or burn them; do not cut down the fruit trees; do not slaughter a sheep or a cow or a camel, except for food. You will pass by people who devote their lives in cloisters; leave them and their devotions alone. You will come upon people who bring you platters in which are various sorts of food; if you eat any of it, mention the name of God over it. You will meet with people who have laid bare the tops of their heads, and left something like strips of cloth around it: smite them a good one with your swords. Go forth now in the name of God, and may He give you death by a wound or an epidemic!" [*Cf.* Ḥadīth: "The passing of my Community is in wounds or pestilence," *i.e.* not a death of ease.—Ed.][4]

After this, Abū Bakr had to subdue the rebellious tribes who refused to pay their taxes, and were called "Apostates." When they had been forced into obedience, he turned the Arabs toward Syria, where the predominantly monophysite Christian population was hostile to its Byzantine Orthodox rulers.

The Conquest of Syria
from The Conquest of the Lands
by Aḥmad ibn Yaḥya al-Balādhurī (d. ca. A.H. *279/*A.D. *892)*

When Abū Bakr was done with the case of those who apostatized, he saw fit to direct his troops against Syria. To this effect, he wrote to the people of Mecca, al-Ṭā'if, al-Yaman, and all the Arabs in Najd and al-Hijāz calling them for a holy war and arousing their desire in it and in the obtainable booty from the Greeks (Byzantines). Accordingly, people, including those actuated by greed as well as those (in) hope of divine remuneration flocked to al-Madīna. It is reported on the authority of al-Wāqidī that Abū Bakr assigned 'Amr (ibn al-'Āṣ) to Palestine, Shuraḥbīl (ibn Ḥasana) and Yazīd (ibn Abī Sufyān) to Damascus saying, "When ye all fight together, your commander is the one in whose province ye are fighting." It is also reported that to 'Amr he gave oral instructions to lead the prayers in case the armies are united, and to have each commander lead the prayer in his own army when the armies are separate. . . . (At first) each commander had 3,000 men under his leadership, but Abū Bakr kept sending reinforcements until the total (for the three) was increased to 24,000.

According to a tradition the first conflict of the Muslims was the battle of al-'Araba before which no fighting at all took place since they left the Hijāz. . . .

On his arrival in the first district of Palestine, 'Amr sent to Abū Bakr informing him of the great number of the enemy. Abū Bakr thereupon wrote to Khālid ibn al-Walīd—who was at that time (campaigning) in al-'Irāq—directing him to go to Syria. . . . Whenever the Muslims met for a battle, they would choose (Khālid) as their chief for his valor and strategy. . . .

When Khālid received Abū Bakr's letter at al-Ḥīra, he set out at the head of 800 men in Rabī' al-Thānī in the year A.H. 13/A.D. 634. He made an incursion on Qurāqir which was a spring belonging to the Kalb tribe, and thence crossed the desert to Suwa, a spring held conjointly by the Kalb and some men of the Bahrā. . . . When

Khālid wanted to cross the desert, he gave the camels all they could drink and (muzzled them) lest they should ruminate and get thirsty again. The quantity of water he carried along, though big, was exhausted on the way. So Khālid had to slay the camels one after the other and drink with his men the water from their bellies. . . . He came to Marj Rāhiṭ and led an incursion against (the Ghassānī Arabs) on their Easter day—they being Christians. He took some captive and killed others. Khālid arrived at Thanīyat in (the oasis of) Damascus, and encamped at the East gate. . . .

The Muslims conquered all the region of Ḥaurān and subdued it. The battle of Ajnādayn ensued. About 100,000 Greeks took part. (the Emperor) Heraclius was in Ḥimṣ (Emesa, north of Damascus.) Against this army, the Muslims fought a violent battle, and Khālid particularly distinguished himself. At last, by Allah's help, the enemies of Allah were routed and shattered into pieces. Those (Muslims) who suffered martyrdom on this day (included many notable people). When the news came to Heraclius, his heart was filled with cowardice and he was confounded. Consequently, he took to flight to Antioch from Ḥimṣ. This battle of Ajnādayn took place on Monday twelve days before the end of Jumāda al-Awwal, year 13/634 (though other dates are also given). . . .

(After this many parts of Greater Syria were occupied). The Greeks met in great numbers and were reinforced by Heraclius. The Muslims encountered them at Marj aṣ-Ṣuffar on their way to Damascus on the first day of the year 14 (February 25, 635). The battle that ensued was so violent that blood flowed along with water and turned the wheels of the mill. Of the Muslims about 4,000 were wounded. At last the unbelievers took flight and were dispersed, disregarding everything until they came to Damascus and Jerusalem. On that day Khālid ibn Sa'īd ibn al-'Āṣ fell a martyr. The evening (before) he was married to Umm Ḥakīm, daughter of al-Ḥārith ibn Hishām al-Makhzūmī. Hearing the news of his death, Umm Ḥakīm pulled out the post of the tent and fought with it. On that day, according to report, she killed seven, and her face was still covered with the ointment perfumed with saffron (used on a wedding night).

When the Muslims were done at al-Marj, they returned to Damascus. This took place fourteen days before the end of Muḥarram, year 14. (The oasis) and its churches the Muslims took by force.

The inhabitants of Damascus closed the gate of the city. Khālid and some 5,000 men camped (outside) the East gate. . . .

The bishop who had provided Khālid with food at the beginning of the siege was wont to stand on the wall. Once Khālid called him, and when he came, Khālid greeted him and talked with him. The bishop one day said, "Thy case is prospering and thou hast a promise to fulfill for me; let us make terms for this city." Thereupon, Khālid wrote: "In the name of Allah, the Compassionate, the Merciful. This is what Khālid would grant to the inhabitants of Damascus, if he enters therein: he promises to give them security for their lives, property and churches. Their city–wall shall not be demolished; neither shall any Muslim be quartered in their houses. Thereunto we give to them the pact of Allah and the protection of His prophet and the Believers. So long as they pay the (tribute), nothing but good shall befall them."

One night a friend of the bishop came to Khālid and informed him that it was a feast for the inhabitants and that they had blocked the gate with stones and left it unguarded. Occupants of the convent, by which Khālid's army camped, brought him two ladders. The gate was guarded only by one or two men. The Muslims cooperated and opened the door . . . The conquest was effected in Rajab, year 14.

Heraclius gathered large bodies of Greeks, Syrians, Mesopotamians and Armenians numbering about 200,000 under the command of one of his choice men. (He) sent as a vanguard Jabala ibn al–Aiham (the Ghassānī prince) at the head of the Arabs of Syria resolving to fight the Muslims. By Allah's help, some 70,000 (Byzantines) were put to death, and their remnants took flight. When Heraclius received the news he fled from Antioch to Constantinople, and as he passed ad–Darb he said: "Peace unto thee, O Syria, and what an excellent country this is for the enemy!"—referring to the numerous pastures in Syria.

When Heraclius massed his troops against the Muslims, and the Muslims heard that they were coming to meet them, they refunded to the inhabitants of Ḥimṣ the (tribute) they had taken from them, saying, "We are too busy to support and protect you. Take care of yourselves." But the people of Ḥimṣ replied, "We like your rule and justice far better than the state of oppression and tyranny in which we were. The army of Heraclius we shall indeed, with your (governor's) help, repulse from the city." The Jews rose and said "We swear by the Torah, no governor of Heraclius shall enter the city of Ḥimṣ unless we are first vanquished and exhausted." Saying this, they closed the gates of the city and guarded them. The inhabitants of the other cities—Christian and Jew—that had capitulated did the same. . . . When by Allah's help the unbelievers were defeated and the Muslims won, they opened the gates of their cities, went out with the singers and music-players . . . and paid the (tribute).[5]

The texts leave us little doubt that the early Muslims regarded struggle, or jihād, primarily as holy war: as divinely commended violence. And, as a religious activity, it was subject to the Law just as were prayer, sacrifice, or pilgrimage. The Mālikī legalist Ibn Abī Zayd of Qayrawān, North Africa, who died in A.H. 386/A.D. 996, states briefly a model Sunnī view.

The Laws of Holy War *from the (Mālikī)* Legal Treatise *of Ibn Abī Zayd al-Qayrawānī (d.* A.H. *386/*A.D. *996)*

The jihād is a religious duty which some of the people may perform on behalf of the others. For us Mālikīs it is obligatory not to fight the enemy until he has been summoned to God's religion, if he does not himself force the battle. He then may become a Muslim or pay the tribute, and if he does not, he may be fought. The Jizya tax however is not accepted from the non-Muslims unless they live where our Muslim rule can reach; but if they are too far away from us for that, the tribute is not accepted unless they move to our territory. If they do not move they may be fought.

To flee from the enemy is one of the grave sins, if his numbers are double those of the Muslims or less. If they are more than double, there is no wrong in fleeing.

The enemy may be combatted under any ruler, whether he is pious or immoral.

There is no wrong in killing prisoners who are non-Arabs; but no one may be killed if he has been given safe-conduct (*amān*), and promises to such people may not be broken. Women and children may not be killed, and the slaying of monks and rabbis is to be avoided unless they have taken part in the fighting. Similarly a woman may be put to death if she fought. A safe conduct given by the least of Muslims is as valid as any other's. Similarly a Muslim woman or child who has reached the age of reason may give a safe conduct, although some say the Imām must ratify it.

Whatever is taken as plunder by the Muslims in war, the Imām takes the fifth of it, and the remaining four-fifths are divided among all the army. To divide this in the enemy territory is more worthy.

Only that which has been seized by the cavalry or taken in actual fighting is divided into fifths and distributed. There is no wrong in consuming food or fodder taken as booty before it is divided, if one is in need of it. The division is only made to those who were present at the fighting, or performing some task for the jihād by working. A portion is given to the man who became ill or the horse who became lame in the campaign. Two portions are given for a horse and one for a rider (thus a mounted man receives thrice the amount of booty given to a foot-soldier). Nothing is given to a slave, a woman, or a boy, unless the boy did not abstain from fighting, by the prior agreement of the Imām. In this case, he is given his share. There is no share for a hired servant, unless he actually took part in the fighting.

An enemy who becomes a Muslim, while holding property he took earlier from Muslims, is allowed to keep it. And when the Muslims capture something formerly belonging to a Muslim from the enemy, the previous owner may not have it without first paying its price. . . .

No gifts may be made of the booty, except from the (Imām's) fifth at the discretion of the Imām, and it may not occur before the formal division. The spoils of the enemy dead are subject to the same rules.

To serve in a frontier fort (ribāṭ) is a highly meritorious act, in proportion to the danger to which the people of that frontier are exposed, and the care they must take against the enemy. A son may not take part in an expedition without the permission of his parents, unless the enemy has attacked the city by surprise. In that case, there is a strict obligation (on all) to defend themselves, and parents are not asked permission about such a matter.[6]

The Law of the Shī'a is different only in a few details, and in its method of exposition. The much fuller treatment of the Twelver Shī'ī doctor Najm al-Dīn al-Muḥaqqiq of Ḥilla in Iraq, who died in A.H. 676/A.D.1278, is here abridged from the "Book of Jihād" in his work *The Ordinances* (Sharā'i') *of Islam*. It can serve both as contrast and elucidation to the earlier Sunnī writer.

Shī'ī Jihād Law
from the (Twelver) Ordinances of Islam
by Najm al-Dīn al-Muḥaqqiq al-Ḥillī (d. A.H. *676/*A.D. *1278)*

Jihād is a religious obligation for every legally responsible free adult male who is sound of body. It is not a duty for a child, an insane person, a woman, an infirm or old man, or a slave. It is a *fard 'alā al-kifāya* (i.e. must be performed for the Community by a number sufficient to see that the job is done), on condition that the Imām, on whom be peace, is present or has delegated someone to lead the Jihād. [When the Imām is "hidden," the religious scholars declare the war and the ruler leads it.—Ed.]

It does not become an individual, personal obligation unless the Imām orders an individual to perform it for the general good [as in a dream or vision.—Ed.], or the number of those performing it is too small to repulse the enemy except by a general effort, or if one has taken it upon himself by a vow, or the like.

Fighting in self-defense is obligatory, even if one is among normally inimical people who are attacked so that one assists them by defending oneself, and this is not jihād (but self-defense.) [The point here is that a Shī'ī in non-Shī'ī territory may find it expedient to help the inhabitants.—Ed.]. This also applies to anyone who fears for himself, his family, and his possessions, if it seems possible that he may succeed (by taking up arms).

Four things that are legal impediments to jihād are: blindness; crippling such as paralysis; any weakness that prevents one from mounting and galloping; and poverty which prevents one from caring for himself or his family during the campaign, or paying for the necessary equipment (and this of course differs according to the circumstances).

If a man has an unpaid debt, it is not for his creditor to forbid him to go. Parents may forbid one to participate in a campaign, if one has not been ordered to (by the Imām).

If the legal impediment should appear only after the fighting has begun, it is ineffective, unless it is such as to disable one for duties.

If a poor man is given the wherewithal to go on jihād, it becomes an obligation for him to go—unless it is given to him as a salary; then he is not obligated to go. One who is unable physically but has the means to go must delegate another. Some say this is merely commendable, not obligatory.

Raiding during the holy months is forbidden, unless the enemy begins the fight or sees no sacredness in the holy months (*i.e.*non–Muslims).

Although it used to be forbidden to fight in the sacred territory, that is abrogated. (9–15: "Slay the unbelievers wheresoever you find them.")

One is obligated to emigrate from the territory of polytheists, if he is prevented there from openly practising Islam, if he is able to do it. This hijra lasts as long as unbelief prevails there.

Manning the forts for the protection of the frontiers is commendable even in the absence of the Imām, since it does not necessarily involve fighting, but is for protection and for a show of force.

People against whom jihād should be carried out are three categories:

1) Those who rebel against the Imām; 2) protected minorities such as Jews, Christians and Zoroastrians, if they violate the conditions of protection; and 3) whoever is hostile, among the various kinds of unbelievers. The Muslims must bring all of these into submission, either by subjecting them or converting them to Islam. If they begin hostilities, it is obligatory to fight them. Otherwise, it is only necessary to fight them according to one's ability to do so, but it should be at least once a year. If the general welfare requires it, it is permissible to make a peace treaty with them, but no one has the power to do this except the Imām or his deputy.

It is worthiest to begin by attacking those who are most accessible, unless some less accessible pose the greater threat. If the enemy's numbers are great, and those of the Muslims small, it is necessary to postpone the war until the Muslims' numbers are sufficient to allow them to attack. Then war becomes obligatory. One may not begin it without first inviting them to become Muslims. This invitation is made by the Imām or by his delegate. The obligation to formulate the appeal does not apply, if they already know the principles of Islam.

It is permissible to fight the enemy by any means which will lead to victory, but it is reprehensible to cut down the trees, and throw fire, or cut off the water, unless it is necessary (for victory); and it is forbidden to throw poison. Some however say that this is only reprehensible.

If the enemy hides behind women and children or Muslim prisoners, one should withhold the attack, if fighting has not already broken out. If a prisoner was killed because this was necessary for the jihād, the killer does not have to pay the blood-money. It is not permissible to kill the insane, the children, or the women of the enemy, even if they helped him, unless one is compelled to do so.

It is forbidden to make an example of the prisoners, or to use treachery [such as concluding an agreement one intends to break—Ed.]. It is forbidden to attack by night or before noon, unless it is necessary.

(When a battle is being decided by single combat), if the companions of the enemy champion seek to help him, he has lost his claim to safe-conduct. But if they do it of their own accord and he forbids them, he has kept his agreement. If he does not forbid them it becomes lawful to attack both him and them.

The Dhimma: Only the Imām or his delegate gives the protected status of the dhimma in general and in particular to the enemy. Faithful observance of the dhimma is necessary, so long as it is not an agreement contrary to the Law. If the agreement was made under compulsion, it need not be kept. As for the formula, one may say "I protect you," or "I take you under protection," or "You are under the dhimma of Islam," or any expression that clearly gives that meaning. But if one says, "May no harm befall you," or "Don't be frightened," that does not constitute protection, since there is nothing in it indicating a safe-conduct. If the enemy asks for it after he is already a prisoner, and is given it, it is not valid. If any Muslim declares that he has extended protection to a polytheist in the time when it was legally permissible, however, it is valid.

When an enemy declares that a Muslim extended him protection, and the Muslim denies it, the Muslim's word is accepted. If an enemy receives protection and permission to live under Muslim rule (*fī dār al-Islām*), his possessions enter into protection with him. If a Muslim makes a slave of a prisoner, he becomes possessor of his possessions as well, by virtue of slavery. A Muslim who enters a hostile territory on safe-conduct and steals something must return it, whether the owner is in Islamic or in hostile territory.

Prisoners: Women prisoners become property (i.e. slaves) the moment they are captured, even if the fighting is still going on. This also applies to boys under the age of puberty. Males above the age of puberty must be put to death, if fighting is still going on and they refuse to become Muslims. The Imām may choose whether to cut off their heads, or if he likes he may cut off their hands and feet and let them bleed until they die.

If they were made prisoner after the fighting is over, they are not killed, and the Imām may choose between showing favor, holding them for ransom, or making slaves of them. Even if they become Muslims upon being made prisoner, this law still applies.

If a prisoner is unable to walk, it is not obligatory to put him to death, since one does not know what the Imām has decided to do with him, and if he should become a Muslim, killing him would be pointless. It is necessary to give a prisoner food and water even if one wishes to kill him (later). It is reprehensible to put him to death by torture, or to carry his head away.

It is obligatory to bury the martyred (Muslim dead) but not the enemy. If there is doubt as to which is which, then those who are circumcised should be buried.

Booty is in three categories: Movables, such as gold, silver, and furnishings; Non–movables, such as land and buildings; and Slave–captives, such as women and children.

It is not permitted to make use of anything in the first category before being assigned it at the division of the spoils, except fodder and food. Those things which a Muslim may not possess, such as wine and pork, must be destroyed. Wine may be converted to vinegar.

All cultivated land becomes the property of all the Muslims and those who conquered it in general. Its disposition is reserved for the Imām. No one may take it as a private domain, but what it produces may be given by the Imām to projects of general benefit for all. Uncultivated land becomes the special property of the Imām, and no one can develop it without his permission, if he is present. If anyone develops it and cultivates it in a period of the Imām's absence, it becomes that man's property.

(After the Imām's fifth is set aside) the remaining four–fifths are divided among the combatants and those present at the fighting, even if they did not fight, including the child born after the pillage but before the division of spoils. A foot soldier is given one share, and the horseman two shares. Some say three, but the first opinion is more apparent. There is no share given for camels, mules, and asses.

Rules for the people of the Dhimma: The jizya, or protection tax may be taken from those who stay in their own religion. These are Jews, Christians, and those who have a kind of scripture, who are Zoroastrians. From any but these, nothing except conversion to Islam is acceptable.[7]

Ismāʻīlī Shiʻī official and legal statements on the theme of struggle follow the pattern. However, the Ismāʻīlīs, who preached a Neo–Platonic interpretation of Islam, were in close sympathy with mystical thought. In a passage from a medieval Fāṭimī creed, another secondary but highly important meaning of jihād is mentioned. Beyond lawful killing, plundering and enslaving to expand the territory of Islam, there is the expansion of the interior kingdom of God, by war against whatever in one's own nature is opposed to His sovereignity.

An Ismāʻīlī Definition of Jihād
from the Crown of Creeds
by ʻAlī ibn Muḥammad ibn al–Walīd (ca. 1200 A.D.*)*

Religious (struggle: jihād) is obligatory against the people who turn away from religion [hence often Sunnīs.—Ed.] When one is called to discharge this duty, he is bound (*mukallaf*) to take it up under the guidance of the right Imām or whoever the latter chooses or commissions. If the Mu'min [believer, hence especially a true Shīʻī.—Ed.] loses his life discharging the duty of jihād, he acquires special nearness to God. Apart from ordinary wars of religion, jihād can have yet another form. This is the struggle against one's own vices and sensuality, which make him deviate from the right path prescribed by the (Law: *sharʻ*). This spiritual war against oneself is only permitted to those who have the necessary qualifications of *ʻilm* and *ʻamal*; i.e. theoretical education and practical religious training.[8]

Islam came late into the world and found it occupied by other faiths. It was the jihād that built the Muslim empire and expanded it for centuries.

Enlargement of the Muslim patrimony by force naturally implied also that force must be used wherever necessary to keep it from diminishing. Those who failed to remain Muslims, or did not act like Muslims, or protected groups who rebelled, all had to be brought back into submission.

Whether war against other Muslims was a jihād was a moot point for the Sunnīs; less of one for the Shī'īs. The Shāfi'ī theorist al-Māwardī does not call such wars jihād, but he clearly believes that they are necessary and good.

On Wars in the General Interest
from the Governing Statutes
by al-Māwardī (d. A.H. *450/*A.D. *1058)*

Aside from jihād against polytheists, there are three categories of fighting: fighting against apostates, fighting against rebels, and fighting against refractory forces (*al-muḥāribīn*).

The first category is against those who have been ruled by Islam and apostatized, whether they were born in Islam or converted to it. If they apostatize by joining any other religion, they may not still profess Islam, for profession of the truth entails following its precepts. The Prophet, on whom be God's blessing and peace, said, "Whoever changes his religion (i.e. Islam), kill him." Since apostatizing from the religion of truth to any other religion entails their death, their situation is then one of two matters: They are isolated in Muslim territory, not constituting a separate territory, so that there is no need for us to do battle with them to bring them under our power. Then one should clarify matters for them, with argument and proof, until the Truth becomes clear to them and then accept their repentance, though Mālik (eponym of the Mālikī school) says, "I do not accept the repentance of anyone who has been in something which obliges him to hide the facts, such as *zandaqa* (Manicheeism and Mazdakism), unless he himself initiates it."

Whoever persists in apostacy, whether man or woman, must be put to death bound, and by the sword, though Ibn Surayj, the pupil of al-Shāfi'ī, says they should be beaten to death with a stick, because that is slower than the sword, and may lead them to repent. His body is not washed when he is dead, no prayers are said, and he is buried, not in the cemetery of the Muslims, because he left them, nor in that of the polytheists, because he was a Muslim. His property goes to the public treasury of the Muslims as booty, and may not be inherited by any of his kin.

If the apostates reside in a special territory apart from the Muslims, then one must do battle with them. After having tried to persuade them to Islam, then one should observe the rules used in fighting a people of non–Muslim territory (*Dār al–Ḥarb*), attacking by surprise or when they sleep, and in open battle, and frontally or from the rear. The captured should be put to death if they do not repent, and it is not permitted to make slaves of them though children born after the parents' apostacy may, according to some, be enslaved.

The territory of apostates differs from that of non–Muslims in four ways: it is not permitted to make a truce with them; one may not accept money to leave them in their apostacy; it is not permitted to make slaves of them; and the booty becomes a Community property. However, Abū Ḥanīfa says their apostacy transforms their land into a hostile territory, so that one may plunder it and enslave their wives and children.

If a group denies their obligation to pay the zakāt to a just Imām, then their denial renders them also apostates, and they are treated as such. Refusal to submit to him, while acknowledging an obligation to pay, only renders them rebels.

Fighting rebels: When a party of the Muslims opposes the Collectivity and form a distinct (heretical) school, but do not leave the appearance of obedience to the rule of the Imām, and do not dwell apart in a territory of their own, but as separate individuals who may be apprehended, they are left alone, and the laws apply equally to what is due to them and from them. If they make a show of their doctrines when mixing with the people of justice, then the Imām should expose to them the corruptness of their doctrine and the vanity of their heresy . . . he may apply discretionary punishment to those who display bad conduct, but he should not put them to death, and there is no divinely fixed punishment (ḥadd). It is related that the Prophet, on whom be peace and God's blessing, said: "It is not permitted to shed the blood of a Muslim except for one of three: apostacy, adultery by a married man, and murder unprovoked by murder."

If a group of dissidents lives withdrawn in a territory of their own, where they are not in contact with the Collectivity, so long as they observe their obligations and do not rebel one may not make war on them. If this party however throws off obedience and their obligations and do not take an imām or chief of their own, the tax-money they withhold is illegally gained, and the sentences (of their qāḍīs) are void and not legally binding. If they do take an imām of their own, their laws are not suspended, and their taxes are considered as paid, but in both cases it is still compulsory to fight them and return them to obedience, for God—blessed be He and exalted—has said, "And if two parties of the Believers fight against each other, mend matters between them; then if one party rebels against the other, fight the rebellious one until it returns to God's command; and if it returns, then set things right between them equitably, and be just, for God loves those who do justice." (49: 9–11). There are eight differences between battle with rebels and battle with polytheists or apostates: 1) The goal should be to gain them, not to kill them. 2) They should be attacked frontally, and one should not fall on them from behind. 3) Their wounded may not be put to death, as is legal with the others. 4) Those captured may not be put to death. 5) They may not be plundered or their families enslaved. The Prophet is related to have said, "Islamic territory has a forbidden character, while territory of polytheism has a permitted character." 6) One may not use polytheist confederates or tolerated non-Muslims against them, although this is permissible against enemies of Islam and apostates. 7) One may not make a truce with them or reach a financial settlement, as with polytheists. If there is a truce, it is not obligatory to observe it. 8) One may not use mangonels or burn their dwellings or cut their palms or fruit trees, because it is in Islamic territory, though the People of Justice are allowed to use all necessary means to save their own lives. After the fighting, their property is restored to them, but whatever is destroyed in the fighting is their loss. Their dead are buried, with Muslims prayers and ablutions. (According to the Shāfi'ī school) the rebel may not inherit from the orthodox Muslim he has killed, and vice versa, although Abū Yūsuf (of the Ḥanafī school) says "I let each inherit from the other because each kills according to his interpretation (of the Law)."

Fighting refractory groups and bandits: If a group of corrupt people unite to carry weapons, cut the roads, seize property, commit murder, and impede communications, then they are the refractory, of whom God—be He exalted—says, "The recompense of those who are refractory to God and His Messenger, and hasten about the land to do corruption there, is that they be killed, or crucified, or their hands and feet shall be alternately cut off, or they shall be banished from the land." [Though legalists differ in their interpretation of this verse.—Ed.]

We hold that if they persist in refractory uprisings, they must be fought in general like rebels, with these five exceptions. 1) They may be attacked frontally or from behind. 2) One may aim at killing any who have committed murder. 3) One may imprison them in order to look into their case. 4) Any taxes they have collected are looked upon as money stolen, and those who paid the tax are still liable to taxation.

When it is known what crimes each has committed, then whoever has murdered and stolen property shall be killed and then crucified after death. However, Mālik ibn Anas says that they should be crucified living, and then pierced through with lances until they die. This death is legally mandatory, and there can be no pardon. Crucifixion should last three days. It is not legal to leave the body up after that period.

Whoever has killed, but not taken property, should be killed, but not crucified, and then washed and prayed over. Mālik says the one who leads the funeral prayers should not be the one who condemned him to death.

Whoever stole without killing should have his alternate hand and foot cut off—the right hand because he stole, and the left foot, for notoriety. Whoever of them has wounded someone but not killed or taken property shall have the same wound inflicted on him, in retaliation. Some say this retaliation is prescribed, and not remissible; others allow the victim or his next of kin to pardon or take payment of money, if they choose. Those of the refractory group who only participated in terrorism and made up one of the band, without killing or stealing, shall be punished at the discretion of the judge, and reprimanded or put in prison, since that is one of the forms of discretionary punishment.[9]

JIHĀD AS AN INSTRUMENT OF CONVERSION

Forced conversion was of course forbidden by the Qur'ān. Yet it was praiseworthy to call non-Muslims to embrace Islam before attacking them, even though according to most legal thinkers it was not always necessary. The following section is from the *Great*

Book of Campaigns of al-Shaybānī (d. A.H. 189/A.D. 805) a great Ḥanafī who was the successor of Abū Yūsuf as Chief Justice under Harūn al-Rashīd. The text in brackets is the commentary of Muḥammad al-Sarakhsī, a Ḥanafī scholar who wrote in A.H. 480/A.D. 1087.

On Calling to Islam in Battle
from the Great Book of Campaigns
by al-Shaybānī (d. A.H. *189/*A.D. *805), with a commentary*
from 1087 A.D. *by al-Sarakhsī.*

When the Muslims encounter polytheists whom Islam has never reached before, it is not necessary to fight them, until they have been called upon to accept Islam. [According to God's Word, exalted be He: "We use not to chastise, until We have sent a messenger." (17:15). And this the Prophet advised the commanders of his armies, saying, "Call them first to the testimonial that there is no god but God," for they often think that we attack them in greed for their possessions and to carry off their women and children, whereas if they knew that we attack them in service to God, they might respond without any necessity for fighting. In expounding. Islam to them, they should be called to the path of God with wisdom and kindly exhortation, at least in the beginning.]

Even if news of Islam has come to them, but they still do not know that we are permitted to accept the jizya tribute from them, we should not attack them until we have called on them to pay the tribute. God, be He exalted, says, "Until they pay the jizya out of hand, and have been humbled." (9:29) [Here there is a necessity for some Muslim rulers, who should be bound by this in their actions, and if they do not know, it should be explained to them.]

Unless they are a people from whom jizya may not be accepted, such as apostates and Arabs who worship idols. From these, nothing may be accepted except Islam or the sword. . . .

'Aṭa ibn Yasār relates that the Prophet, God bless him and give him peace, sent 'Alī on a mission and 'Alī said, "How shall I act with them?" He replied, "When you alight in their territory, do not attack them until they attack you: if they attack, do not fight until one of your men is killed, and even then do not attack until you make them see what they have done. Then say, "Will you say now, 'There is no god but God?' If they say yes, say 'Will you do the ritual prayers?' If they say yes, say 'Will you pay the poor tax on what you own?' If they say yes, then ask nothing else of them, by God, though He should guide to their hand a man dearer to you than all that the sun rises and sets on." [It is known that all this causes no problems. It was mentioned by way of kindness, not as legal necessity.]

'Abd al-Raḥman ibn 'A'idh is quoted as saying, "The Messenger of God whenever sending anyone on a mission would say, 'Be kind to the people and treat them gently, and do not change until after you have called them to Islam, for there are no people in the land, whether dwellers in tents or mud huts, that you should not bring to me as Muslims. I like that better than your bringing me their women and children and killing their menfolk.' "

Abū 'Uthmān al-Nahdī says, "We used to call them and let them alone." That is, we used sometimes to call them and sometimes not to call them, and attack them. That indicates that all this is good, to call them again and again when their conversion is desired, but if it is not desired, then there is no harm in attacking them without any call to Islam. [It is related that the Prophet, God's peace and blessing be upon him, fell upon the Banu Muṣṭaliq at dawn as they were watering their flocks, and slew their warriors and captured their women and children, and one of the captives was Juwayriya bint al-Ḥārith (who became one of the Prophet's wives), and he ordered Usāma to raid Ubna early in the morning and set fire to it, all without any call to Islam.]

It is mentioned that al-Ḥasan said "There need be no call to the Byzantines (to accept Islam), for they were called long ago." [That is, the call came to them before our time, for Jesus, on whom be peace, revealed to them that Muḥammad—God's blessing be on him, and peace—would come after him, and ordered them to believe in him when he was sent, according to God's Word: "(Jesus said), 'I give good tidings of a Messenger who shall come after me, whose name shall be Aḥmad.' " (61:6) Truly in God is our assistance.][10]

MYSTICAL INTERPRETATIONS OF STRUGGLE

We have seen that it is the Ṣūfī mystics who have most emphasized interior struggle: to conquer one's Self is better than the taking of a city, for to them it is self-ishness that most opposes commitment to God.

One of al-Ghazālī's teachers, the orthodox Ṣūfī theorist al-Qushayrī of Nīshāpūr, writes thus of spiritual struggle.

On Spiritual Struggle
from Treatise on the Knowledge of Mysticism
by al-Qushayrī (d. A.H. *466/*A.D. *1074)*

God, be He exalted, says "Those who struggle in Our cause We shall surely guide in Our ways, for God is with those who do good." Abū Sa'īd al-Khudrī related that the Messenger of God—God bless him and give him peace!—was once asked what was the most meritorious jihād, and replied, "A just word in the presence of a tyrannical ruler," and (as he spoke) a tear stood in Abū Sa'īd's eye.

Also I once heard Ustādh Abū 'Alī al-Daqqāq say, "If one bedecks his outer life with striving, God will bedeck his inner self with witnessing." God—exalted be He—has said that those who struggle in His cause He will guide in His ways, and one who does not struggle from the very beginning will find no candle in the Way of the mystics.

Al-Sulamī said that his grandfather heard Abū 'Amr ibn Najīd say, "Whoever is generous with his Self attaches no importance to his religion."

Know then that the basis of striving and possession of it is weaning the Self from what it is accustomed to, and bearing the Self contrary to its desires generally, for the Self has two characteristics which prevent it from the good: indulgence in lusts, and abstinence from obedience. When these two come together and passions mount it, it must be curbed with the bridle of fear of God, and if it is stubborn when conformity is demanded, then it must be gentled, for there is no contest with a more satisfying result than that with an anger whose power has been broken by good character and whose flames have been put out with gentleness. Though the Self finds the wine of laxness sweet, it also becomes obedient when its virtues are displayed and it is well-groomed for the eye of the beholder, and it is necessary to break that in it, and to punish it with a humiliation that will remind it how low is its rank, how vile are its origins, and how foul are its actions.

The struggle of common people consists in fulfilling actions; that of the elect in purifying their interior conditions. The sufferings of hunger and sleeplessness are relatively easy to sustain, but working upon one's character and winnowing its chaff is hard and difficult work. Among the obscure diseases of the Self is its tendency to relish praise. One who has taken a draught of that will carry the heavens and the earths on the tip of his eyelash, and the proof of it is that when he is deprived of that drink, his state will turn to laziness and futility. There was once a shaykh who used to pray at his mosque in the front rank of the worshippers for many years, but one day he was not among the early arrivals at the mosque, and had to say his prayers in the last row. After that he was not seen at all for a time, and people asked him the reason. He replied, "I have been saying all the prayers I prayed in the years when I believed that I was being faithful to God, for on the day I came late to the mosque where people could not see me, I felt a kind of discomfiture, and then I realized that my zeal, all my life long, had only been for their observation when I prayed."

Muḥammad ibn Ḥusayn told me he had heard that Dhū al-Nūn al-Miṣrī had said, "God honors none of His servants with any honor greater than that of beholding how humble is his Self, and He humbles none of them more than by concealing from him his humiliation." The same man told me that Ibrahīm al-Khawwāṣ had once said, "Nothing has ever frightened me but I rode it." Shaykh Abū 'Abd al-Raḥman told me he once heard al-Nasrābādhī say, "Your prison is your Self, and when you go beyond it, you find eternal rest." Abū al-Ḥusayn al-Warrāq once said, "The best rule of our novitiate at the mosque of Abū 'Uthmān al-Hīrī was that we ate up whatever was given to us and did not go to sleep owning anything, and if we received hateful treatment from anyone, we did not seek revenge, but apologised and humbled ourselves to him; and if disdain for anyone entered our hearts, we undertook to do him service and treat him kindly, until that disdain went away."

Abū Ḥafṣ said, "The Self is darkness, and its light is the inner heart (*sirr*). The light of the lamp is grace (*tawfīq*) and whoever has an inner heart unillumined by grace from his Lord is all in darkness." It is for this that the shaykhs say, "He who has no inner heart (i.e. conscience) is poor indeed."

Abū Sulaymān said, "I have never been pleased by anything from myself, or set any store by it."

Dhū al-Nūn the Egyptian said, "Corruption has only come to mankind because of six things: weak intention in the works of the hereafter; their bodies becoming the hostages of their lusts; being overpowered by long hopes despite short lives; prefering to please creatures rather than the Creator; following their own desires and putting behind them the path of their Prophet—God bless him and give him peace—and taking for an excuse the little slips of the first Muslims while burying the memory of their many good deeds."[11]

The identification of struggle with the Self as a holy war is here graphically expounded in a sermon of the great Baghdad saint, 'Abd al-Qādir al-Jilānī.

On Struggling with the Self, and a Description of That
from The Opening of the Unseen
by Shaykh 'Abd al-Qādir al-Jilānī (d. A.H. *561*/A.D. *1166)*

Each time you struggle against your lower self (*nafs*) and overcome it and slay it with the sword of opposition, God restores it to life and it contends with you again, and demands of you desires and delights, whether forbidden or permissible, so that you must return to struggle and compete with it in order to carry off the everlasting reward. This is the meaning of the Prophet's saying —God bless him and give him peace—"We have returned from the lesser jihād (war) to the greater jihād (self-control)." He meant by this struggle with the Self, because it is always there, and because of its continuation in lusts and pleasures and its obstinate persistence in rebellion.

And this is the meaning of God's Word—blessed be He, and glorified!—"And serve your Lord, until the Certainty comes to you." In this, God ordered His prophet to worship, and that is opposition to the Self, for the lower self turns away from all service of God, and desires its opposite: to serve itself—until the certainty comes, which is Death.

If anyone says, "And how could the Prophet's self turn away from service of God, when he, God bless him and give him peace, knew no desires of his own: 'He speaks not of his own desire; this is (not other than) a revelation revealed'?" (53:3). The answer is first that God, blessed and glorified be He, told His prophet this in order to establish the Law thus and make it generally known among the Community until the Hour should come, and secondly that God, blessed be He and glorified, gave His prophet power over his lower self and his desires so that these should not compel him and incite him to struggle, unlike his Community, and thus the (ordinary) believer is perpetually engaged in this struggle until death comes to him and he meets his Lord with sword drawn and dyed with the blood of selfhood and selfish desire, and then He gives him what He has guaranteed him in paradise, according to His Word: "But as for him who feared his Lord's Station, and denied his Self its desires, surely paradise shall be his refuge." (79: 40).

And then He renews for them each day at every hour and each moment, every sort of blessing, and gives them always new robes of honor and adornments, until there is no end or measure or spending of (His gifts); just as in the world He renewed each day, each hour, and every moment, the struggle against the Self and its desires.

As for the rejecter of God (*kāfir*), the hypocrite and the rebel—since they gave over struggling against the Self and its desires in the world, but followed them, and agreed with Satan and postured freely in various rebellions of infidelity and idolatry and what else beside, until death found them without Islam or repentance—God causes them to enter hellfire, prepared for unbelievers according to His Word . . . and "As often as their skins are wholly burned, We shall give them in exchange other skins, that they may taste the Chastisement." (4:59) Thus the people of Hell have their skins and flesh constantly made new, so that torment and pain may reach them, while the people of Paradise have continually renewed their ease, that desire and delight may be redoubled. And the reason for all this is in their struggle against the Self, and the fact that they did not make peace with it in the worldly abode. And this is the meaning of the saying of the Prophet, on whom be blessing and peace: "The world is the seedbed of the hereafter."[12]

JIHĀD IN INDIA

The next great wave of Islamic expansion after the early Arab conquests came in the eleventh century A.D., initiated by Turks in Central Asia, India, and Anatolia. One of the most celebrated of all Ghāzīs, or warriors for Islam, was Maḥmūd, the Turkish ruler of Ghazna in Afghanistan, the first ruler to be called "Sulṭān" (by his followers, not by the Caliph), who in A.D. 1000 began to raid the Hindu kingdoms of Northern India. The selection is abridged from a court chronicle typical in style of these works after the tenth century; rich in hyperbole and high-flown eulogies.

Maḥmūd of Ghazna in Northern India
from the History of Yamīn al-Dawla
by Abū al-Ḥasan al-'Utbī (written in A.H. *412/*A.D. *1021)*

Sultān Mahmūd first designed in his heart to go to Sijīstān, but subsequently preferred to engage first in a holy war against Hind, and he distributed arms prior to convening a council on the subject, in order to secure a blessing on his designs of exalting the standard of religion, of widening the plain of right, of illuminating the words of truth and of strengthening the power of justice. He departed toward the country of Hind, in full reliance on the aid of God, who guiding by His light and His power, bestowed dignity upon him and gave him his victory in all his expeditions. On his reaching Peshawar, he pitched his tent outside the city. There he received intelligence of the bold resolve of Jaipal, the enemy of God and King of Hind, to offer opposition, and of his rapid advance towards meeting his fate in the field of battle. . . .

The Sulṭān would not allow him to postpone the conflict, and the friends of God commenced the action, setting upon the enemy with sword, arrow, and spear, and the Hindus, being greatly alarmed, began to kindle the flame of fight. The elephants moved on from their posts, and line advanced against line, shooting their arrows at one another as boys escaped from school at eventime shoot at a target for a wager. Swords flashed like lightning amid the blackness of clouds, and fountains of blood flowed like the fall of shooting stars. The friends of God defeated their obstinate opponents and quickly put them to a complete rout. Noon had not yet arrived when the Muslims had wreaked their vengeance on the infidel enemies of God, killing 15,000 of them, spreading them like a carpet on the ground, food for beasts and birds of prey. Fifteen elephants fell on the field of battle, as their legs, pierced with arrows, became motionless, and their trunks were cut by the swords of the valiant heroes.

The enemy of God, Jaipal, his children and grandchildren and nephews, and the chief men of his tribe, were taken prisoners and strongly bound with ropes were carried before the Sulṭān as the evildoers on whose faces the fumes of infidelity are evident will be bound and carried to Hell. Some had their arms tied behind their backs, some were seized by the cheek, some were driven by blows on the neck. . . . God also bestowed on His friends booty beyond all bounds and all calculation, including five hundred thousand slaves, beautiful men and women. The Sulṭān returned victorious to his camp, having plundered immensely, and thankful to God, the Lord of the Universe. For the Almighty had given them victory over a province of the country of Hind broader and longer and more fertile than Khurāsān. This splendid and celebrated action took place on Thursday the 8th of Muḥarram, 392 (27 November, 1001).

After the victory, the Sulṭān directed that the polluted infidel, Jaipal, should be paraded about, so that his sons and chieftains might see him in that condition of shame and that the fear of Islam might fly abroad through the country of the infidels. He then entered into conditions of peace with him, after demanding fifty elephants, and took from him as hostages his son and grandson, till he should fulfill the conditions imposed on him.

The infidel returned to his own country and remained there. . . .

There is a custom among these men that if any one is taken prisoner by an enemy, as Jaipal was by the Muslims, it is not lawful for him to continue to reign. When Jaipal, therefore, saw that he was captive in the prison of old age and degradation, he thought death by cremation preferable to shame and dishonor. So he commenced with shaving his hair off, and then threw himself upon the fire until he was burnt.[13]

Maḥmūd's family, the Ghaznavīs, were succeeded by the Afghan Ghūrī dynasty, who continued to raid the Indian kingdoms. In the early thirteenth century, one of their Mamlūks succeeded in establishing the Sulṭānate of Dehli, a self–sustaining base of Muslim power in India. The Sulṭāns of Dehli continued the wars of expansion. Under the redoubtable 'Alā' al–Dīn Khāljī (d. A.H. 715/A.D. 1315), most of India was conquered or forced to pay tribute. He destroyed many temples. This prose account of his campaign against Barmatpūr was written by Amīr Khusraw. (d. A.D. 1325), the famous courtier–poet of Dehli.

'Alā al–Dīn Khaljī's Campaign Against Barmatpur
from The Treasuries of Victory
by Amīr Khusraw of Dehli (d. A.H. 725/A.D. 1325)

Next the Muslims came with a body of holy warriors to destroy the holy temple in which the idols were kept. They saw a building, old and strong as the infidelity of Satan, and enchanting like the allurements of worldly life. In truth this towering edifice testified to the fact that the earth is the infidel's paradise. It rose from the earth, a structure scratching the eyes of the stars and piercing the people of the Sun. Its roofs and walls were inlaid with sparkling rubies and emeralds, and after gazing at them, red and yellow spots came into the spectator's eyes. God be praised that all of these gems have been brought into the treasury of the 'Shadow of God!' [i.e. the Sulṭān.—Ed.]

The foundations of this golden temple, which was the holy place of the Hindus, were dug up with the greatest care. The "ears" of the building were opened by the sound of the spade. At its call the sword also raised its "head" from the scabbard; and the heads of the Brahmans and idol-worshippers came dancing from their necks to their feet at the flashes of the sword. The golden bricks rolled down and brought with them the plaster of sandalwood; the yellow gold became red with blood, and the white sandal turned scarlet. . . . Where mire used to be created by rose-water and musk, there was now a mud of blood and dirt; the stench of blood was emitted by ground once fragrant with musk and by this smell the men of Faith were intoxicated and the men of Infidelity ruined. The stone idols, called "Ling-i Mahadeo," which for long had been established in that place, on which the women of the unbelievers used to rub their secret parts; these, up to that time, the kick of the horse of Islam had not attempted to break. The Muslims destroyed all the *lingas.* Deō Narāin fell down, and the other gods, who had fixed their seats there, raised their feet and jumped so high that at one leap they reached the fort of Lanka, and in that affright the lingas themselves would have fled, had they any legs to stand on. . . . Wherever there was any treasure in that desolated building, the ground was sifted as a sieve and the treasure discovered. No part of gold remained with the *gabrs* except its dust, no jewels (principles) except the 'principle' of fire.[14]

USES OF JIHĀD

It was always in the interest of a Muslim ruler to be able to identify his own wars against other Muslims as jihād. No one made more consistent use of the technique than Tīmūr-i Lenk, the Turkish Muslim Lord of Samarkand in Central Asia, who devasted the Islamic East under the banner of "holy war."

At the end of the fourteenth century, he visited the Muslims of Dehli with a terrible "jihād," and sacked and destroyed it on the pretense that the country was still full of infidels (who, however, were paying tribute). Most of the people here referred to by his son's court historian as "infidel Hindus" (i.e. Indians) were in fact Muslim inhabitants of a great Muslim city.

Tīmūr in Dehli
from the Victory Book
of Sharaf al-Dīn 'Alī Yazdī (written A.H. *828/*A.D. *1425)*

Just at that time, A.H. 800/A.D. 1398, Tīmūr had resolved to assemble forces from all his dominions, and to march against China, with the intent of destroying the idol temples, and of raising mosques in their places. He had previously heard that the standards of the faith of Islam had been raised in Dehli and other places, and that its profession of faith was impressed upon the coins, but that the country in general was polluted by the inhabitants being infidels and idolators. Impelled by the desire of waging a religious war, he resolved to march against Multan and Dehli. He consulted with his nobles and chiefs, and they concurred in the propriety of making the invasion.

(After many battles and sieges his army crossed the Indus.) On the same day Amīr Jahān Shāh and other Amīrs represented to Tīmūr that from the time he crossed the Indus, 100,000 Hindu prisoners more or less had been taken and were kept in the camp. It was to be feared that in the day of battle with the forces of Dehli they might join the enemy. Tīmūr considered the point, and deeming the advice of his officers to be wise, he gave orders for all the Hindu prisoners to be put to death. Every one who neglected to comply with this command was to be executed, and his wives, children, and goods were to become the property of the informer.

In pursuance of this order 100,000 infidel Hindus were put to the sword. Mawlānā Nāṣir al-Dīn, a most distinguished ecclesiastic, had fifteen Hindus in his train, and he who had never killed a sheep was obliged to kill these fifteen Hindus. Tīmūr also issued an order that one man out of every ten should be left in camp to guard the wives and children of the prisoners and the captured cattle.

On the same day Tīmūr resolved upon marching to Dehli, and setting off after mid-day prayer he encamped on the banks of the Jumna. The astrologers and sooth-sayers disputed whether the stars and presages were favorable. Tīmūr placed no reliance in their predictions, but put his trust in God, without whose pleasure nothing happens. . . . He crossed the river Jumna.

When he saw the opposing forces he alighted from his horse, and turning the face of supplication to heaven he offered his prayers, and begged for victory over his enemy. It was not long before a sign was given of the acceptance of this prayer. . . .

When by the favor of God the enemy was defeated and put to flight, Tīmūr advanced to the gate of Dehli. He carefully examined the walls and bastions of that noble city, and then retired to the Ḥawz-i Khāṣṣ. This is a reservoir constructed by Sultān Firūz Shāh, so large that an arrow cannot be shot from one side to the other. It is filled by rain in the rainy season and the people of Dehli obtain water from it all the year round. The tomb of Fīrūz Shāh is by its side. Tīmūr encamped there. . . . On hearing the reports (of the battle) he was moved to tears, and gave thanks to God who had distinguished him by such valiant sons and such faithful servants.

In the darkness of the night Sulṭān Maḥmūd of Dehli left the city and fled. Orders were given to officers to take possession of the gate of the city and prevent the escape of anyone. On the 8th of Rabīʿ al-Thānī (Dec. 17, 1398), Tīmūr hoisted his victorious flag on the walls of Dehli. He then took his seat in the ʿIdgāh (a sanctuary outside the walls) and held his court, and the *sayyids*, qāḍīs, nobles and great men who were in the city hastened to pay their homage to him. Mawlāna Nāṣir al-Dīn was ordered to go with other learned doctors to the mosque (on Friday) and proclaim the name of the Ṣāḥib-Kirān (lord of the fortunate stars), Amīr Tīmūr Gūrkhān, in the khuṭba.

On the 16th of the month a number of soldiers collected at the gate of Dehli and derided the inhabitants. When Tīmūr heard of this, he directed some of the *amīrs* to put a stop to it. But it was the divine pleasure to ruin the city and to punish the inhabitants, and that was brought about in this way. . . . Orders had been issued to arrest every nobleman who had fought against Tīmūr, and in execution of this they were scattered about the city. When parties and bands of soldiers were going about the city, numbers of Hindus in the cities of Dehli, Sīrī, Jahānpanāh and Old Dehlī seeing the violence of the soldiers, assaulted them. Many of the infidels set fire to their goods and effects, and threw themselves, their wives and children, into the flames. The soldiers grew more eager for plunder and destruction. Notwithstanding the boldness and the struggles of the Hindus, the officers in charge kept the gates closed. . . . But that Friday night there were about 15,000 men in the city who were engaged from early eve till morning in plundering and burning the houses. In many places the impure infidel *gabrs* made resistance. In the morning the soldiers who were outside went to the city. . . .On that Sunday, the 17th of the month, the whole place was pillaged, and several palaces destroyed. On the 18th, like plundering went on. Every soldier obtained more than twenty persons as slaves, and some brought as many as fifty or a hundred men women and children as slaves out of the city. The other plunder and spoils were immense beyond all computation. Most of the women wore bracelets of gold or silver on their wrists and legs. . . . On the 19th of the month Old Dehli was thought of, for many infidel Hindus had fled and taken refuge in the great mosque, where they prepared to defend themselves . . . 500 trusty men proceeded against them, and falling upon them with the sword dispatched them to hell. High towers were built with the heads of the Hindus, and their bodies became the food of ravenous beasts and birds. On the same day all Old Dehli was plundered. Such of the inhabitants as escaped alive were made prisoners. For several days in succession the prisoners were brought out of the city. Several thousand craftsmen were brought out, and were divided among the princes, amīrs and agās, and some were reserved for those who were maintaining the royal authority in other parts. Tīmūr had formed the design of building a great mosque in Samarkand, his capital, and he now gave orders that all the stone masons should be reserved for that pious work.[15]

OTTOMAN EXPANSION AND JIHĀD

At the beginning of the fourteenth century, where the Saljūq Sultanate of Anatolia bordered the shrunken Byzantine Empire weakened by the attack of the Fourth Crusade, a dynasty of ghāzī march–lords calling themselves "The Family of 'Uthman" began to build a mighty patrimony by jihād.

Although their progress in the Balkans was slowed by the disastrous defeat inflicted on them in Anatolia in 1402 by Tīmūr (for the Ottoman soldiers lacked will to fight fellow–Muslims), in ten years the 'Uthmanlu were expanding their borders again. By 1453, Muḥammad II (Turkish : Mehmet), the "Conqueror," was able to take the "impregnable" city of Constantinople and extinguish the Byzantine Empire.

In the Western world, which first betrayed and looted Constantinople, and then abandoned it in its need, there has been a tendency to shed romantic tears for the conquest. For people who do, the following telling of it must seem tendentious and offensive.

However, time and distance can lend the conquests of the Turks the same indulgent covering we cast over the bloody deeds of the ancient Hebrews; one can today perceive that this prose poem, composed long after the events, in the Ottoman courtly style of the sixteenth century, to celebrate the triumph of the faith of heroic ancestors, is nobly epic and even beautiful.

The Conquest of Constantinople
from the Crown of Histories
by Khoja Sa'd al-Dīn (d. A.H. *1008/*A.D. *1599)*

Though Sulṭān Murād Khān II had determined upon this conquest, the Issuer of Decrees to the clime of existence delivered not the key of this achievement into the hand of his might; and, his ascension to the Holy Spheres being decreed, he left as a bequest to his most illustrious successor (Mehmet II) the erection of the standards of the jihād for the capture of that city, by the addition of which to the Defended (Ottoman) Dominions, he might protect the prosperity of the people of Islam, and break the backs of the wretched misbelievers.

After he had set forth (from Bursa) in the direction of Adrianople the blockading of the Strait of (Gallipoli) by ships of the misbelievers was represented to him, and immediately he proceeded (to the Bosphorus). . . . Disembarking on the (European) side, he said to Khalīl Pasha (Jandarluzāda, his wazīr), "It were good that a fortress be erected on this shore, so that the path of the vessels of the infidels may be blocked!" Five thousand masons toiled to complete that building (Rumeli Hisar), and the heaven-assisted troops exerted their strength in the arrangement of materials.

In four months or (some say) forty days, its completion was effected. It had become a lofty walled castle. . . . In its towers and on its ramparts they placed cannons like dragons, each opening its mouth to shower sparks of fire, and scatter venom in the hour of strife and tumult. In this manner the Pādishāh, the asylum of the world, closed the way of the vessels of the enemy and cauterised the liver of that blind-hearted emperor. (This) was effected in the year 855 (A.D. 1451).

Aq Chāyli Oghlu Muḥammad Beg, by command of the Sulṭān,

devastated the environs of Constantinople, driving off cattle and flocks and making prisoner the misbelievers that he found without the walls, and so he satiated the hearts of the ghāzīs with spoils beyond computation and leave was given to the army, the asylum of victory, until the days of Spring, and the Sulṭān honored Adrianople by his arrival fraught with prosperity, and prepared all the appliances of war.

Verse:

Now had passed the bitter cold and snow of winter,
And the vernal season at length had come . . .
The lovely rose had discovered its beauty,
The sad nightingale had begun to wail,
The fields had decked themselves with their green vestment
That the king of the earth might his camp o'er them spread,
And that, in his council devising wise measures,
He might find to the conquest of Istāmbōl a path.
The violet had in its hands grasped the bow,
The iris had girded its saber on its thigh . . .
The tulip had donned its leaves crimson as the West,
The peony had over its shoulder flung its mace,
The red rose had drawn its shield over its visage . . .
The carnation had planted its lance in the turf—
All those who saw, shouted "Bravo!" and "Well done!"
The scouts were the zephyrs; the narcissus the watch,
The lily in front bore aloft its white banner,
And the pageant through that standard perfect became;
Praying, the plane tree extended its arms,
Saying thus, "O Allah, drive away all misfortune,
To the king of the horizons grant his hope and his victory,
And do Thou facilitate the capture of Istāmbōl!"

The successful king looked on the array of the rank–adorning amīrs; on the cypress–tall vezirs . . . on the glittering of the crescents on the flags and standards, and entered the path of gratitude to the Creator, and regarded with affection his victory–guided army.

He exhorted those furious, blood–lapping lions of the forest of valour; telling them of the universality of the command "Strive!" (5:39) and of the purport of the Divine promises in the verses concerning the Holy War; how it were most fitting to complete the achievements performed in the exaltation of the banners of Islam, by the addition of the city of Constantinople to the realms of the Unitarians . . . how the Prophet foretold that that vast city, that lofty fortress, would be subdued by the exertions of his followers, and become the abode of the people of the Faith, and the resort of the Unitarians. Having inclined the hearts of the Champions of the Faith to partake of the honey of martyrdom, he turned the rein of the steed of his fortune in the direction of Constantinople.

The 'ulamā', the shaykhs and the sayyids, in conformity with the ancient custom rode by the rein of that Sulṭān of lofty glory. . . . Although many pure souls were present, and legions of the Mystics (dervishes) were the advance guard of the troops, still from among the Possessors of Hidden Power and the Lords of Visible Signs [Saints.–Ed.] . . . the Truth–beholding Shaykh Aq Shams ud–Dīn and Aq Biyiq Deda were conspicuous in the offering of prayers to implore the aid of the Giver of all gifts.

The imperial army encompassed the fortifications on the land side. Then they attacked that protected city, the greatest of all strongholds, with such dread fury and determination that the footsteps of the defenders went astray.

As the ill–fated emperor saw that to oppose him would be but a vain dream, he sent a message of submission, entreating that the Sulṭān accept all his castles and possessions, leaving to him only Istāmbōl, and that he would enroll him in the list of tributary Christian princes and accept the appointed tribute.

The justice–dispensing prince, regarding not the words of the message, reminded him of the saying, "Either the sword or al–Islām," and demanded the surrender of the city. When the ill–fated Emperor was thus disappointed of his hope, he employed himself in preparing to scorch the ranks of the defenders of the Faith with cannons and muskets, and rend them with bombs filled with naphtha.

From morn to eve the tumult of battle had lasted. . . . The Janissaries and the *'azabs* (young men levies) made the gates and walls of the city torn like the hearts of hapless lovers. The stones and cannon–balls of the cruel misbelievers overthrew the existence of many a champion of the Faith; and the martyrs in their gore–stained garments gave to the field of battle the aspect of a garden of tulips. . . .

(Since the way to the Golden Horn was blocked by a chain, the Turks carried ships overland to the Golden Horn from the Bosphorus, and thus attacked the city's sea walls.)

The understanding of the impure emperor passed away when

he was told the sea side had also been breached, yet as his mind was distracted, he confided to the Frank (Western Christian) soldiers the defense of the breaches made in the land walls by the Adrianople Gate. The (Byzantine) imperial guards were offended that this was entrusted to aliens, and this was a cause of derangement to good order. . . .

As soon as it became certain that confusion and dissension had smitten the ranks of those wretches, the battlement–overthrowing heroes, regarding as worthless the merchandise of their lives, rushed upon the breaches by the Adrianople gate. . . .

From morn until eve, and from dusk until dawn, intent on battle, they united the greatest of meritorious works—holy warfare and passing the night in prayer; and in the stream of the blood of martyrdom they cleansed their garments from the soil of sin. . . .

(The Frankish captain was mortally wounded, and the Franks sought their ships.)

At the same instant, the ghāzīs, knowing the breaches to be the gate of victory, rushed upon them. Then was the naked scimitar busy, and lance and spear–head grew used to licking the blood of the obstinate. . . .

The blind–hearted emperor became aware that they had found a path to within the walls. He delayed not a second, but with anguish of soul rushed from his palace, north of the Adrianople gate, and he encountered a small number of the heroes, who were busy, with minds at ease, collecting plunder. Their poverty set light to the fire of hate in his dark bosom, and with the sickle of his sabre he reaped the harvest of their lives. . . . One feeble wounded ʿazab was lying on the ground suffering the life dissolving torment of his wounds. That monarch of evil custom, raising his sword against that helpless one who was soon to be a wanderer from existence, thought to destroy the last spark of his being. Then that helpless one, struggling with but half his life, through the aid of the Granter of Desires, tore down that enemy of the Faith and brought down upon his head the damasked blade of the Jihād. He cut off his head and confounded the emperor's followers.

The hosts began to enter the city. For three days and nights, there was with (the Sulṭān's) permission, a general sack; and the victorious troops entwined the arm of possession around the neck of their desires, and binding the lustre of their hearts to the locks of the damsels, beautiful as hūrīs, by the sight of the sweetly smiling fair ones they made the eye of their hopes the participator of their good fortune. Silver and gold, which are to vain covetousness a source of trial, but to the obscure in the world the means of distinction and exaltation, became the capital of the traffickers in the market of undying life. . . .

On the third day, the *chawūshes* of the lofty court made known the command, irresistible as destiny, requiring the restoration of tranquillity and serenity; and they published the imperial will regarding the ghāzīs taking repose. . . .

That strong and lofty city, from being the Dār al–Harb (hostile territory), became the Dār al–Zarb (city of the mint: hence, the capital), and from being the nest of the owl of error, was turned into the capital of glory and honor. . . . For the evil–voiced clash of the bells of the shameless misbelievers was substituted the Musulman call to prayer, the sweet five–times–repeated chant of the Faith of glorious rites, and the ears of the people of jihād were filled with the melody of the *adhān*. The churches were emptied of their vile idols and by the erection of Islāmī mihrabs and pulpits, many monasteries and chapels became the envy of the Gardens of Paradise.

On the first Friday, prayers were recited in Aya Sofīya, and in the Sulṭān's name was the Khuṭba read. Thus that ancient edifice was illumined by the rays of the Orthodox Faith, and perfumed with the breath of the odours of the Noble Law: and as the hearts of the Unitarians were filled with joy so that most desirable of fanes was filled with the people of Islam, and its delight–reflecting interior, by being burnished with the Declaration of Unity, became brilliant as a polished mirror.[16]

Ottoman Islam was always marked by the mystic, militant fervour of the Islamic frontier. It is interesting to compare a contemporary document of the fifteenth century to the sixteenth century court chronicle of Khoja Efendi we have just read. The author of the selection, 'Ashiqpashazāda, was born around 1400. He was a dervish and jihād fighter, under Mehmet I, Murat II, and Mehmet II, and is one of the earliest Ottoman historians. He writes after the changeover to imperial society, in a zestful, folk–tale style, nostalgic for times already legendary, when piety and worth were measured in terms of bravery and loyalty. Here he describes the conquest of the little Greek "empire" of Trebizond on the Black Sea, soon after the fall of Constantinople.

Mehmet Fātiḥ's Campaigns Against Koyulhisar and Trebizond
from Histories of the Family of 'Uthman
by Dervish Aḥmad 'Ashiqpashazāda (d. ca. A.H. *889/*A.D. *1484)*

How Sulṭān Mehmet Khān Ghāzī took Koyulhisar, and what happened: Before Sulṭān Mehmet (II) took the field against Koyulhisar, it had a prince, whose name was Ḥusayn Bey. One day this Ḥusayn Bey rode out into the open country to hunt, and there while he was hunting, Uzun Ḥasan (ruler of the Whitesheep Turcomans) took him prisoner and carried him off to his castle. And willy–nilly, Ḥusayn Bey had to turn over his stronghold to him.

When the Hūnkyār (Ottoman Sulṭān) heard this, that Uzun Ḥasan had taken Koyulhisar by a trick, then the Hūnkyār gave the command to the Beylerbey of Rumelia, Ḥamza Bey. He gave him soldiers and he took levies of unmarried men from the country, saying: "March against Koyulhisar. Fight so that you conquer the Castle, and if it is not to be taken, then fall upon the villages of its province, and lay waste and burn, so that for a long time they cannot be built up again."

When Ḥamza Bey heard the command of the Hūnkyār, he ordered the army up and marched against that castle. For many days there were many battles; then finally they saw that the castle was not to be captured. But they saw that the country was still there, and so they raided it and laid waste to it.

Perchance some of the young men levies come to an Armenian village, where they find Armenian men and women; then they despoil every part of it. On these women and men they practise forbidden things—these young men commit really sore deviations. At this, the Armenian priests went to Uzun Ḥasan and cried, "Under our former ruler, such shameful things never befell us, and yet he was but a petty prince. And now that we are under such a mighty ruler as yourself, such unbecoming things happen to our people!"

After he had raided the country, Ḥamza Bey went back to his own region, and some years passed after these occurrences. And after Sulṭān Mehmet Khān the Ghāzī had conquered Sinope, he marched thither and camped before Koyulhisar. On every side, he set cannon. After some days, when a few cannonballs touched the castle, the minds of the people inside were bewildered and their wits were lost. They immediately surrendered the castle. By the command of the Padishāh, the castle was taken over and his own kullar (household troops) were placed in it.

Question: "O dervish (i.e. 'Ashiqpashazāda), why did these young men commit such forbidden deeds? Are such things proper for the soldiers of the House of 'Uthman?"

If anyone asks that, here is the answer: "My dear, the soldiers of the House of 'Uthman are many groups; there are a dozen kinds. Each of them vexes some particular kind of people. Wherever these young men levies go, there is nothing forbidden, because they go there in the pay of the Padishāh. Wherever they come in, according to their pleasure they harm those who practice deceit and trickery against their Padishāh. So it will be, until every clime where the Ottomans go shall be obedient and submissive to the Padishāh."

How Sulṭān Meḥmet Khān marched against Trebizond and conquered it. After he had conquered Koyulhisar, he marched from there to Erzincan. Uzan Ḥasan sent his mother in the escort of the Prince of Gemişgezek, who was called Kurd Shaykh Ḥasan, as an ambassadress to Sulṭān Mehmet Khān. They went there, and near Mt. Bulgar Dagh they met him. Very fine gifts indeed they brought him. The Padishāh accepted their gifts, and treated them with much honor. . . . The mother of Uzun Ḥasan, who was called Sara Hatun, he treated as his own mother, and he called Shaykh Ḥasan "Father." He took them both with him, and marched toward Trebizond. When they had come to the summit of Mt. Bulgar Dagh, they began to descend toward Trebizond. On this mountain, the Padishāh went most of the way on foot. And so he marched down to Trebizond.

He had taken the mother of Uzun Ḥasan with him, and as they marched down, Sara Hatun spoke to Sulṭān Mehmet. "Ah, son, why should you bear all this trouble for this Trebizond?" The Padishāh answered her, "Mother, this trouble is not for Trebizond; we bear this trouble for the religion of Islam, so that in the next world, when we arrive before the Lord God, we may not be ashamed. For in our hands lies the Sword of Islam, and if we should not take this trouble on ourselves, then it would be a lie to call us Ghāzī."

And as they marched down to the citadel, Sara Hatun pleaded with Sulṭān Mehmet for Trebizond. "This belongs to my daughter–

in–law (Uzun Ḥasan had married a princess of Trebizond); spare it, for my sake, my son!" said she. But as to this, the Sulṭān gave no answer at all.

After this he waited, until the ships from Sinope came over the sea. When the ships came, after a short time the battle was joined by sea and by land. Immediately, those in the citadel begged for quarter, but in a stroke of the hand they were captured.

And so they took Trebizond. They brought the Padishāh all that was worthy of a Padishāh. The king of Trebizond and his nobles and many useful infidels they put on the ships and sent to Istanbul. In the meantime, the ghāzīs raided several regions of the country, and despoiled it to their heart's content. The Sulṭān gave many a fine piece from the precious things he had taken from the citadel to the mother of Uzun Ḥasan, and sent her with marks of respect back to her son.

As the Padishāh always put in order every stronghold, so too he did in Trebizond. Inside it, mosques and madrasas were set up, and Muslim families were brought in. The houses of the unbelievers which stood empty were given to the Muslims as their property, and the citadel was strongly fortified. Then the Padishāh returned in glory. . . . This conquest occurred in the year 865 after the Hijra (A.D. 1461).[17]

JIHĀD IN AFRICA

Islam entered the Sudan, the savannah belt below the Sahara in Africa, as a result of trade relations with North Africa, and spread chiefly by peaceful conversion of the ruling houses and warriors and merchants in the Negro kingdoms.

With the change from caravan routes to sea routes for African trade in the fifteenth century, a period of decadence began. While Muslims continued to rule, a popular accomodation with pagan and fetishistic practices was tolerated.

The Fulānī cattle-raising tribes, which had begun to settle among the Hausas of Northern Nigeria in the eighteenth century, were virile, ambitious, and ready to follow a leader.

Shaykh Usuman dan Fodio (or 'Uthmān ibn Fūdiyu), a devout Muslim, began a jihād against the Hausa kings in Gobir, which fell to him in 1804. He then took the caliphal title of Commander of Believers, and set up a state which looked forward to the imminent coming of the Mahdī. The jihād spread, and resulted in a rooting out of African pagan practises, a much higher level of Islamic orthopraxy among the peoples of the area, and their integration in a single Muslim society. Not unnaturally, Hausa Muslim scholars complained that the jihād had been against people who might have had faults, but who were still Muslims. Here Muḥammad Bello, Usuman's son, who ruled the new caliphate from Sokoto, answers them in a detailed defense.

A Defense of the Fulānī Jihād
from Expenditure of the Easeful
by Muḥammad Bello (d. A.H. *1253/*A.D. *1837)*

Now the reasons which justified this holy war were two. First, in order to repel attacks upon ourselves, our families, and our faith. I have told you of every battle and the place where it was fought. The beginning was the stand we made when we repulsed the army of the Sarkin (Prince) of Gobir at the time when he was oppressing us. He began the fight, he rose up and attacked us, and all his brother chiefs consented and made alliance against us. Then we rose up and repelled them from us until God gave us the victory over all their towns (and) all the heathen were destroyed.

And the second reason for our jihād was that they were heathens, the people of Hausa. Our jihād tore up the trees of the heathen and destroyed their thickets and made Muslims of most of the people of this land, and gave Muslims power over the length and breadth of the country. In our wars we slew whom we slew and drove out whom we drove out. Thereupon their neighbours came forth to help them, (and) we fought them. For we indeed to this day have never begun war, even though it were right to begin it. That is our character and those that know us know that this is so.

A further reason was to strengthen Islam. For to make war on the heathen from the beginning, if one has the power, is declared a duty (and) it is a duty to make war on (Muslims) who have reverted to heathenism, if one has the power.

The Hausa chiefs, their people and their *mallams* [from Arabic mu'allam; one who has been instructed in religion.—Ed.] were evildoers. Though they called themselves Muslims and made the confession of faith and prayed and fasted, yet with these acts they joined that which none but heathen would do, such as sacrifices to stones and trees. . . .

Our Mallam Jibidu son of 'Umaru says, "What happened in the countries of the Soudan was the mingling of heathen and Muslim practices. The Hausa chiefs did not begin it themselves nor did they make the change. It was something they inherited for we do not hear that they were ever free of this mingling of practises. They are in fact as they were when they first received the revelation of prayer and fasting and confession of faith. The ignorant imagine that they are Muslims but they are not so."

What we have stated on the Hausa chiefs is the truth, for we have had dealings with them and know their character. The master of the house knows what is in it. God is all knowing.

But now in our times these countries have become Muslim, for God has taken away their corrupt practises and left what is good by the blessing of Shehu (i. e. Shaykh Usuman), who is God's gift to this land, for he has enriched it with many blessings; he has given it a surpassing glory. For they heard him and obeyed, those that were stubborn in heart and found not salvation, for he saved them and they obeyed him by force. God laid open these countries to him. He established justice, prayer became constant, zakāt was given, the jihād was carried on, knowledge was spread abroad, strife was put down, the disobedient were punished, extortioners brought to justice, the roads made safe and the faith made secure in the world. In truth Shehu became the expounder of the Law to the Muslim chiefs, (and) he was firm in purifying the faith. God takes pleasure in his servants even to the end of time.

If you think (Usuman's) greatness exaggerated, remember that he is near the greatest time of all, that he is the mighty helper. Every *mallam* was like a star, but Shehu was like the moon to them. Yet he is not to be called the Mahdī. There are no words in language that shall tell his glory.

Here it is right that we should discuss the question of slavery in these lands. We have said (before) that the people were of three kinds. First the pure Muslims, but these were very few at the time of Shehu's coming. The second are those that mingled pagan and Muslim practices. The third are those heathens who have never entered Islam. These were subjects of the chiefs of Sudan and are called Maguzawa. You will know that captives if they are Maguzawa are to be enslaved, for they are heathen. Let their women and children be taken and their property divided. The mallams are in complete agreement here.

But as to those who have become open apostates, or say they are Muslim, we tell you they are heathen because they practise that which none but heathen would do. As to these, if they are captured seek to make them repent. If they repent, let them go. If they do not repent, slay them, for they are heathen. But as to whether they may be enslaved the mallams are in dispute. Mallam Khalīl in his *Mukhtasar* says "If a people becomes apostate and fights against Muslims, let it receive the punishment of the apostate," i.e. if a person is grown up seek to make him repent; if he is a child compel him to become a Muslim and set aside his property, but let not the women be taken. The immense majority of mallams agree with this. There are only a few who hold the contrary opinion.

Mallam Ashango says, "They are like heathen, let war be made upon them, and enslave them and their children and women." He says he would swear by his life that it was on this point that Abū Bakr and 'Umar contended with in regard to the Arabs who had apostatized. Abū Bakr slew their leaders and enslaved their women and children and divided them with their property.[18]

JIHĀD IN MODERN TIMES

Secularism in modern Muslim countries is often thought of as being inimical to Islam. In fact, of course, it can be rooted in deeply Islamic attitudes. For the Turks who united under Mustafa Kemal Ataturk to drive the Greek and Allied invasion out of Anatolia after World War I, the war of liberation was a jihād, just as the struggle against Zionist colonization has been for the Arabs. The Turkish uprising led to a rejection of the moribund Ottoman Sultanate and Islamic establishment, because they had proved unable and unwilling to defend the Muslim patrimony, and the secularist father of modern Turkey was given an official title.

Mustafa Kemal is Given the Title of Ghāzī
from History of the Turkish Republic
(Istanbul, 1931)

On the day that the Grand National Assembly chose him as commander-in-chief of the Turkish armies, Mustafa Kemal announced to the Turkish nation and to the world at large that he had full confidence in the eventual defeat of her enemies. How clearly he read the future, the victory at Sakarya had already testified. The Turkish nation did not hesitate to award this greatest of her sons, in whom were manifested all her own qualities, the reward of which he was worthy: the Grand National Assembly conferred upon the victor of Sakarya the title of Ghāzī, and the rank of fieldmarshal, on the nineteenth of September 1921.

The government of the Padishāh, as we have seen, had already expelled the Ghāzī from military service, and shamelessly referring to him as "Mister Mustafa Kemal," had even sentenced this prodigious man to death, on May 11, 1920. Since then, he had held no official rank of any sort. Now, however, the Turkish nation conferred upon him the highest military rank in Turkey, and the most honored title given to warriors in the eastern world.[19]

In the minds of Muslims who struggle against colonialism today, then, their exertion is a holy war. The emphasis on the holy necessity of self–defense is a main reason for the attractiveness of a version of Islam to the Black Muslims. There is a concomitant tendency to *restrict* jihād to self–defense, and to argue, unhistorically enough, that Muslims have never known any other kind. This is particularly true in the modernist Aḥmadīya movement. Jihād for the expansion of Islam, it argues, is a figment in the minds of anti–Muslim propagandists.

An Aḥmadīya Interpretation of Jihād
from Islam's Contribution to World Peace
by S. A. Haque (Lahore Aḥmadīya, no date.)

Allegations have at times been made to the effect that Islam preached jihād and its followers revelled in wars. . . . The conception of the institution of jihād as conveyed by the non–Muslim propagandists is so distorted that we cannot blame anybody who has not made an independent study of Islam if he entertains the acutest repulsion against this religion. The word jihād has been derived from *jihd,* which means to exert yourself to the utmost. This term is used in Arabic in different connections, but all convey the same sense. In fact it denotes a state of mind in which after undergoing untold sufferings, a man is forced to resort in self–defense to measures not necessarily warlike. In daily life we find people saying that they wish to carry on a jihād against drinking and smoking or against foreign goods. But this does not mean that they intend making a war on anybody. Thus by inculcating the spirit of jihād Islam rendered a great service to humanity. It substituted jihād for *ḥarb* which means warfare pure and simple. . . . It is an institution which enjoins on every Muslim to sacrifice his all for the protection of the weak and oppressed whether Muslims or not. He is in duty bound to see that oppression and injustice, in whatever form, are stopped. It is on this account that one who goes to jihād is called Ghāzī and holds a position far superior to one who has spent his whole life in prayer and meditation. I wish and pray that the entire world may accept this teaching of jihād so that a lasting peace may be concluded in the world under which no man will be allowed to play the tyrant in any form. This will be heaven on earth.[20]

Muslim apologists today find themselves discomfited by the traditional view of jihād in a world where lip service to the Christian ideal of non-violence is admired. The same arguments made by the heterodox Aḥmadīya are advanced by orthodox Sunnī Muslims. The following selection is quoted from an official publication of the Egyptian Ministry of Waqfs, written by a prominent legal scholar in the United Arab Republic.

A Modernist Defense of Jihād
from The Concept of War in Islam
by Shaykh Abū Zahra (contemporary)

The historical instances dating back to the time of the Prophet reaffirm that war in Islam was waged with the sole object of self–defence, and that relations between the Muslims and other people were based on peace.

This is clear from the fact that the Prophet never threatened war against his opponents unless they transgressed, or prepared an aggression.

The Prophet lived for thirteen years among the unbelievers of Quraysh. He had been calling on them, throughout this period, to believe in the unity of the Creator, purge themselves of the sins of Ignorance, and the oppression of bigotry . . . they besieged his home and laid in wait for him, but the Almighty failed [*sic*] their plot and saved the Prophet. The Prophet fled from his home and emigrated. Before him, his companions had emigrated and safely got away with their faith which they loved. At that moment God sent down the injunction to fight.

Fighting was restricted to Quraysh because they were the first to spark it off, and perpetuated their aggression by continually harming the outnumbered Muslims who were detained in Mecca. . . .

The faithful therefore had the right to repulse their aggression: "God will render his followers victorious and is full of strength, exalted in might."

When the Prophet migrated to Medina, he did not permit the killing of the Jews. He lived in peace with them and signed a pact of good neighbourhood with them which gave them rights and obligations. . . . In the third year, the Jews betrayed the Muslims when they were engaged in the conquest of Uḥud. Again the Jews betrayed the Muslims in the fourth year in the battle of al-Aḥzāb where all the Arabs gathered to uproot Islam from its homeland. It therefore was imperative to break the pledge, in accordance with the Qur'ānic verse.

As regards the Christians, the Prophet did not fight them until they killed the faithful in Syria. Even then, he did not fight all the Christians. He fought the Byzantines, while remaining on good terms with the Christian Arabs. He fought the Byzantines, not as Christians, but as aggressors.

Dār al-Ḥarb and Dār al-Islam: The term "world of war" was invented by the jurists who classified people into three groups: "World of Islam," whose members were predominantly Muslims, and inside which the rules and enactments of Islam were put into force.

The second group are those with whom an agreement had been signed. This world embraced all non-Muslims who had signed a pact with Muslims.

The third group was "Dār al-Ḥarb," or world of war.

This division was dictated by events and was not derived from legislation. As Islam gathered strength and spread in all directions, the vanguard of the faithful fought those who had attacked them, and emancipated neighbouring peoples from their despotic rulers. Consequently all the non-Muslim rulers made preparations to crush the Muslims. They opposed Islam because it liberated peoples, defended freedom and established human equality; none of which was compatible with the prevalent absolutism of monarchs.

The Kings launched a concerted attack on the Muslims on all fronts. The Muslims had to resist them, in accordance with the scriptural text.

This in no way contradicts the established rule, that war in Islam is prohibited unless in reply to aggression.[21]

NOTES

1. Ibn Hishām's rescension: *Sīrat al-Nabī.* Cairo 1963. pp. 435–39. (Editor's translation and abridgement.)

2. Tibrīzī, *Mishkāt al-Masābīh*; Karachi: 1948 edition. Selected from the book on jihād. (Editor's translation.)

3. al-Balādhurī. *Futūh al-Buldān.* pp. 64–68 in P. K. Hitti's translation, titled *Origins of the Islamic State.* (Reprint edition, 1966). (Here abridged.)

4. al-Ṭabarī. *Tarīkh.* New Cairo edition, Vol. III. 1962, p. 226–227. (Editor's translation.)

5. Balādhuri, *op cit.* pp. 165–211, abridged. (Professor Hitti's translation.)

6. Ibn Abī Zayd. *Risāla* (Algiers 1945, w. French paraphrase.), pp. 163–167. (Editor's translation.)

7. Ja'far ibn Sa'īd Najm al-Dīn al-Hilli, *Sharā'i' al-Islām fī fiqh al-Islām al-Ja'farī* (Beirut, no date), *kitāb al-jihād.* (Editor's translation. This work has also a translation to French, by Querry, made in 1872.)

8. From W. Iwanow, *A Creed of the Fatimids* (Bombay, n.d.), pp. 50–53.

9. al-Māwardī, *al-Aḥkām al-Sulṭānīya.* Cairo ed. 1960, pp. 55–64. (Editor's translation and abridgement.)

10. Al-Shaybānī. *Kitāb al-Siyar al-Kabīr.* Cairo 1958, Vol. I, pp. 75–80. (Editor's translation and abridgement.)

11. Al-Qushayrī, *al-Risāla fī 'Ilm al-Taṣawwuf.* Cairo, 1957. p. 47ff. (Editor's translation.)

12. *Futūḥ al-Ghayb,* on margin of Shaṭṭanawfī's *Bahjat al-Asrār* (Cairo, A.H. 1330/A.D. 1912), pp. 143–146. (Editor's translation, with reference to Walther Braune's German translation, Berlin 1933.)

13. 'Utbī, *Tarīkh -ī Yamīnī,* translated in Elliot and Dowson's *History of India,* Vol. II, p. 21ff. (London, 1877). Here abridged.

14. *Khazā'inul Futūḥ,* translated by Muḥammad Habīb (Madras, 1931) p. 100ff. Here abridged.

15. Yazdī, *Zafar-Nāma,* translation in Elliot and Dowson, *op. cit.* Vol. III, pp. 497–504. Abridged.

16. Khoja Sa'd al-Dīn, *Tāj al-Tawarīkh,* trans. by E. J. W. Gibb (Glasgow, 1879) pp. 9–36. Here abridged.

17. 'Ashiqpashazāda, Atsiz edition, pp. 159–161. (Here abridged. The editor gratefully acknowledges the help of Mr. Ruşen Sezer in the translation.)

18. *Infāk al-Maysūr.* Translated by F. J. Arnett. Kano, 1922. pp. 122–26, and here abridged.

19. *Tarih Turkiye Cumhuriyeti.* Istanbul, 1931. p. 101. (Translation of Mr. Ruşen Sezer.)

20. S. A. Haque. *Islam's Contribution to the Peace of the World.* Lahore Ahmadiya. p. 37–48, here abridged.

21. Shaykh Abū Zahra. *The Concept of War in Islam.* Cairo, Ministry of Waqfs. No date. p. 12–13.

The Friends of God

CHAPTER 6

The Friends of God

From the Qur'ān:

God is the Friend of those who believe in Him; He brings them out of the shadows into the Light. (2:257)

Or have they taken to them friends apart from Him? But God—He is the Friend; He brings the dead to life, and He is powerful over every thing. (42:9)

He it is who sends down the rain after they have despaired, and He unfolds His mercy; He is the Friend, the All-praised. (42:28)

Surely the friends of God—no fear shall come upon them, nor shall they grieve. Those who believed and feared Him—for them are good tidings in the life of the lower world and in the hereafter. There is no changing in the Words of God; that is the mighty triumph. (10:63–65)

On that, friendship is only unto God, the Truth; He is best Rewarder, best in the issue. (18:44)

Your friend is only God, and His messenger, and the believers, who perform the prayer and pay the zakāt, bowing down. He who takes as friend God and His messenger and those who have believed—the party of God, they are the victors. (5:55)

Theirs is the Abode of Peace with their Lord; He is their Friend for what they were doing. (6:127)

O Thou, Creator of the heavens and the earth, Thou art my Friend in this world and the next. Do Thou receive me as one committed, and join me with the righteous. (12:101)

We indeed created man, and We know what his self whispers

within him; and we are nearer to him than his jugular vein. (50:16)

When the earth shall be shaken, and the mountains are crumbled, and become as dust scattered, and you are three bands—Companions of the Right—(who are they, of the Right Hand?), Companions of the Left—(who are they, the Sinister?), and the Winners of the Race, the Farrunners; those who shall be brought near, in the Garden of Delights. (56:4–12)

The Qur'ān repeatedly suggests that a more intimate relationship than that of Lord and slave can exist between God and His servants. He is the *Friend,* He loves those who do His will, and there are men who are His friends. The word used, *walī,* comes from a root meaning "to be near, or adjacent." Beside meaning "friend," it carries a sense of being able to act on another's behalf. It has frequently been translated by orientalists as "Saint," but it is worthwhile to keep the basic meaning in mind. The *Awliyā'* are the friends of God, who have become near to Him.

Ḥadīths on the Friends of God

Bukhārī, from Abū Hurayra: The Messenger of God, God's blessing and peace be upon him, said: "When God loves one of His servants, He cries to Gabriel, 'God loves such a one: love him too,' and Gabriel loves that man. Then Gabriel cries to the inhabitants of Paradise, 'God loves so–and–so: love him too,' and the inhabitants of Paradise love that man, and his conduct also is rendered agreeable to the people of the earth."[1]

Al-Sarrāj (from Ibrahīm ibn Adham): The Messenger of God, God bless him and give him peace, said "God says, 'My servant continues to draw near to Me by acts of supererogation until I love him; and when I love him, I am his eye by which he sees, his ear by which he hears, his tongue by which he speaks, and his hand by which he grasps.' "[2]

EARLY FRIENDS OF GOD

It was clear to Muslims, of course, that the prophets, God's chosen messengers, were "near" Him. The first generation of Muslims, as we have seen, were men of action, engaged in building an empire, and they tended to remember Muḥammad first of all as a soldier and statesman (it is significant that the first episodes of his life to be written down were his military campaigns and legal statements). As a more settled society grew up, men thought more of private example in the Prophet's life.

Yet among the Prophet's Companions there were those who were conspicuous for their asceticism and disregard of worldly matters. In one of them, 'Imrān ibn Ḥuṣayn, who settled at Baṣra and suffered a lingering death from disease, it is perhaps appropriate to see, as Louis Massignon says, "the first flowering of the interior life in Islam." Baṣra, his adopted city, became famous for its ascetics and mystics, many of whom gave evidence of the effect of his personal example. By a life of humility and patience, like his, ordinary men could draw near to God.

'Imrān ibn Ḥuṣayn
from The Great Generations
by Ibn Sa'd (d. A.H. *231/*A.D. *847)*

'Imrān ibn Ḥuṣayn said, "My right hand never touched my private parts after it gave the bay'a to the Messenger of God, God bless him and give him peace." 'Ubayd Allah ibn Ziyād (Umawī viceroy of Iraq) made him a qāḍī, and two men brought a quarrel to him. The evidence was against one of them, and he gave judgement against him. Then the man said "You have given judgement against me wrongly; for by God, it was false." 'Imrān said "O only God!" and sprang up and burst in on 'Ubayd Allah ibn Ziyād saying, "Divest me of the qāḍīship!" 'Ubayd Allah said, "Easy now, Abū Nujayd!" But he said "No, for by the only God, I shall not judge between two men while I serve God."

Muḥammad ibn Sīrīn (who knew many of the great early Muslims) said, "No more excellent companion of the Prophet ever came to Baṣra than 'Imrān ibn Ḥuṣayn."

It is related that 'Imrān once said, "I wish that I were ashes, scattered by the winds."

Ḥujayr ibn Rabi'a reports that 'Imrān ibn Ḥuṣayn sent him to the Banu 'Adī so that he should come to them at the afternoon prayer in the mosque, to tell them, " 'Imrān ibn Ḥuṣayn, the friend of God's apostle, has sent me to greet you with Peace, to say that he is a sincere adviser to you, and to swear by the only God that for his part, he would rather be a mutilated Abyssinian slave herding goats in the mountain hollows [all highly unattractive for an Arab of the time.—Ed.] until death struck him down, than throw one lance at either party of the Muslims either to hit or to miss: may his father and mother be your ransom!" Then they raised up their heads, and said "Let us alone, boy—by God we would not invite such dregs of God's apostle to participate in anything!" The next day was the Day of the Camel (when 'Alī fought against Talḥa, Zubayr, and 'A'isha at Baṣra), and many a one of them, by God, was killed, and seventy among them who could recite all of the Qur'ān.

Muḥammad ibn Sīrīn reports: " 'Imrān ibn Ḥuṣayn was afflicted with dropsy for thirty years, and during the whole time cauterization was indicated, but he refused it [because he could find no religious authorization for it—Ed.], up until two years before his death." And Qatāda says "The angels used to salute 'Imrān ibn Ḥuṣayn on either side after the ritual prayers up until he was cauterized, and then they stopped."

Ḥasan al-Baṣrī (his student) relates that 'Imrān used to say, "I got burned; it was no success and I did not prosper for it." Muṭarrif says that 'Imrān said, "I used to perceive him [sic] saying, 'Peace be upon you,' but when they cauterized me, the greeting stopped." I said, "Did he stand by your feet or by your face?" "Why, by my face," he said. I told him, "I do not think that you will die until it has been repeated." Later on, he told me, "I perceive that the salutation has come back," and only a little later, he died.

Ḥasan of Baṣra said that 'Imrān suffered terribly, so that people began to find it repugnant, and one of them said, "What we see here prevents us from coming to visit you more often." But he replied, "Truly, since it has pleased God to send it, it is very pleasing to me."

His daughter said, "When the end drew near, he said 'Wrap me in the bedclothes and my turban when I am dead, and when you come back from the cemetery, slaughter animals and make a feast.' "

Some of his pupils relate that he once came out to them in a figured robe of silk [usually disapproved of by early Muslims—Ed.], which they never saw on him before or after that, saying "God's messenger, may God give him peace and blessing, once said 'When God has graced His servant with a thing, He likes to see that grace displayed.' " He related traditions from 'Umar and Abū Bakr, and died in Baṣra in the year 52 (672 A.D.), in the Caliphate of Mu'āwiya.[3]

Ibrahīm ibn Adham
from The Generations of the Ṣūfīs
by Abū 'Abd al-Raḥman al-Sulamī (d. A.H. *412/*A.D. *1020)*

One of them is Ibrahīm ibn Adham, called Abū Isḥāq, of the people of Balkh, in Bactria. He was the descendant of kings and had great wealth. One day he went out hunting, and a voice spoke to him, and he was wakened from his heedlessness, so that he left the path of worldly allurements and turned to that of people of asceticism and piety, and left for Mecca, where he became friends with Sufyān al-Thawrī (d. A.H. 160/777 A.D.) and Fuḍayl ibn 'Iyād (d. A.H. 187/A.H. 803). Then he went to Syria and labored, and ate from the work of his hands, until he died there (date unknown). He reported various ḥadīths. One of them is from Ibn 'Abbās: The Prophet—God bless him and give him peace!—used to prostrate himself in prayer while winding his turban.

(A sound chain of authorities reports that) he said this about his conversion: "My father was one of the princes of Khurāsān, and I was a youth, and rode to the chase. I went out one day on a horse I had, with my dog along, and started a hare or a fox. While I was pursuing it, I heard a voice from an unseen speaker, saying 'Ibrahīm, were you created for this? Is it this you were commanded to do?' I felt terrified, and stopped. Then I started up again, spurring my horse. I heard it again, and did as I had before, three times. Then I heard the voice—and this time it came from the horn of my saddle, by God!—'Not for this were you created! It is not this you were commanded to do!' Then I got down off my horse, and coming across one of my father's shepherds, I took his woolen tunic and put it on. I gave him the mare and all I had with me in exchange, and set out for Mecca."

The earliest sources have Ibrahīm state that he learned true knowledge of God from a solitary Syrian monk. The fifth century A.H. hagiographer al-Sulamī, perhaps finding such a statement unseemly in a Muslim walī, adds the following material to the story we have just read.

"While I was in the desert, I came across a man walking, who had no water or provisions with him. When evening came, and he prayed the sunset prayer, he would move his lips in some words I did not understand. Then in my scrip there would be food, and drink in my bottle, and I would eat and drink. He was with me for some days, and taught me the Greatest Name of God. Then he departed from me and I remained alone. One day when I was utterly lonely in my solitude, I called on God with it, and then I felt someone holding me about the waist, saying 'Ask, and it shall be given!' I was frightened at these words, and he said 'No harm, no fear! I am your brother Khiḍr. It was my brother David who taught you the greatest name of God. Never use it against anyone for whom you have a grudge, for it will be his destruction in this world and the next. Pray only that God may give courage to your cowardice, and strengthen your weakness, and console your loneliness, and renew in you, every hour, your desire for Him.' Then he went away, leaving me by myself."[4]

By the end of the sixth century A.H., the Persian Farīd al-Dīn al-'Aṭṭār, a great lover of miracles, could add the following flourishes to the story:

Ibrahīm ibn Adham
from Memorial of the Saints
by Farīd al-Dīn al-'Aṭṭār (d. ca. A.H. *617/*A.D. *1220)*

One day Ibrahīm was seated on the bank of the Tigris stitching his threadbare robe. His needle fell into the river.

"You gave up such a mighty kingdom. What did you get in return?" someone asked him.

"Give me back my needle," cried Ibrahīm, pointing to the river. A thousand fishes put up their heads from the water, each with a golden needle in its mouth.

"I want my own needle," said Ibrahīm. A feeble little fish held up Ibrahīm's needle in its mouth.

"This is the least thing I have gotten by abandoning the kingdom of Balkh," said Ibrahīm. "The rest you know nothing of."[5]

When Ibrahīm left Balkh, he left behind him a son at the breast. When the boy grew up, he set out on the pilgrimage to Mecca with his mother, hoping to see his father. As the caravan entered Mecca, Ibrahīm told his ascetic associates, "There are women and children entering the city on this pilgrimage. Mind your eyes!"

All accepted his counsel. As Ibrahīm was making the circumambulation of the Ka'ba, a handsome boy approached him, and Ibrahīm looked at him keenly. His friends noted this and were astonished, but waited until they had finished the circumambulation.

"God have mercy on you!" they then said to Ibrahīm. "You bade us not to glance at any woman or child, and then you yourself gazed at a handsome lad."

"Did you see?" Ibrahīm exclaimed.

"We saw," they replied.

"When I left Balkh," Ibrahīm told them, "I abandoned there a suckling son. I know that the lad is that son."

Next day one of the companions went out before Ibrahīm to look for the caravan from Balkh. Coming upon it, he observed in the midst of the caravan a tent pitched all of brocade. In the tent a throne was set, and the boy was seated on the throne, reciting the Qur'ān and weeping. Ibrahīm's friend asked if he might enter. "Where do you come from?" he enquired. "From Balkh," the boy replied. "Whose son are you?" The boy put his hand to his face and began to weep.

"I have never seen my father," he said, laying aside the Qur'ān. "Not until yesterday, and I do not know whether it was he or not. I am afraid that if I speak he will run away, as he ran away from us before. My father is Ibrahīm ibn Adham, the King of Balkh."

The man took him to bring him to Ibrahīm. His mother rose and went along with him. Ibrahīm spied from afar his friend with the boy and his mother. As soon as the woman saw him, she cried aloud and could control herself no longer. "This is your father."

An indescribable tumult arose. All the bystanders and friends of Ibrahīm burst into tears. As soon as the boy recovered himself he saluted his father. Ibrahīm returned his greeting and took him to his breast. "What religion do you follow?" he asked.

"The religion of Islam," answered his son. "Praise be to God!" cried Ibrahīm. "Do you know the Qur'ān? Have you studied the faith?" "Yes," his son answered.

Then Ibrahīm would have departed, but the boy would not let go of him. His mother wailed aloud. Turning his face to heaven, Ibrahīm cried, "O God, succour me!"

The boy immediately expired in his embrace. "What happened, Ibrahīm?" his companions cried out.

"When I took him to my breast," Ibrahīm explained, "love for him stirred in my heart. A voice spoke to me, 'Ibrahīm, you claim to love Me, and you love another along with Me. You charge your companions not to look upon any strange woman or child, and you have attached your heart to that woman and child.' When I heard this call, I prayed, 'Lord of Glory, come to my succour! He will so occupy my heart that I shall forget to love Thee. Either take away his life or mine.' His death was the answer to my prayer."[6]

This unedifying little tale must have been suggested to 'Aṭṭar's poetic imagination by Ibrahīm's name, "Abraham, father of Isaac," as one of the spiritual ancestors of the Ṣūfīs, the people of God. Its spirit of self-abnegation and total devotion, however, suits well a man who is said to have prayed: "O God, Thou knowest that Paradise weighs not so much with me as the wing of a gnat. If Thou befriendest me by Thy recollection, and sustainest me with Thy love, and makest it easy for me to obey Thee, then give Thou Thy Paradise to whomsoever Thou wilt."[7]

The Compact of Friendship
from the Book of Stayings
by Muḥammad 'Abd al-Jabbār al-Niffarī (written circa A.H. *349/* A.D. *960)*

Around A.H. 349/A.D. 960, a visionary of Iraq, Muḥammad 'Abd al-Jabbār of Niffar (the ancient Nippur) set down some of his personal revelations in states of ecstacy. His writing shows a deep awareness of the Friendship of God, and seems to spring from genuine experiences. He called his book the *Mawāqif,* or "Stayings," for before every mystical state or *hāl,* it was believed, there was a staying point, a mawqif, of preparation.

Here, al-Niffarī states the conditions of real friendship with God. It is not enough to fulfill the Law or to be an ascetic; these are intermediate things. True conversion is to God alone.

He stayed me, and said to me:

"I did not fashion thee in order that thou mightest obey science [i. e. ḥadīth and the Law.—Ed.], and I did not train thee that thou mightest stand at the gate of other than Me, and I did not teach thee that thou mightest make My instruction a path whereon to pass to sleep's forgetfulness thereof, and I did not take thee as a companion that thou mightest enquire of Me what might expel thee from My companionship.

"I have not appeared to thee in thy youth that I may afflict thee in thy old age.

"Know who thou art: for thy knowledge of who thou art is thy sanctuary which cannot fail.

"I have charged thee that thou mightest know who thou art. Thou art My friend, and I am thy Friend.

"Listen to the compact of thy friendship: Thou shalt not interpret against Me with thy knowledge, nor invoke Me on account of thyself. When thou goest forth, go forth unto me; when thou enterest in, enter in unto Me. When thou sleepest, sleep in resignation unto Me. When thou awakest, awake in fullest confidence on Me.

"In what degree thou imposest on thyself labouring for Me, there falleth from thee thy labouring for thyself; and in what degree there falleth from thee thy labouring for thyself, My standing shall be through thee, and My Self-subsistence shall be for thee. . . .

'The night belongs to Me, not to the scriptures that are recited: yea, the night belongs to Me, not to lauds and praises.

"The night belongs to Me, not to invocation. The secret of invocation is need, and the secret of need is self, and the secret of self is desire. . . .

"How regardest thou the heavens and the earth, and how regardest thou the sun and the moon? And how regardest thou everything that is regarded by thy eye or regarded by thy heart? Surely this; that thou regardest it as appearing from Me, and that thou regardest the realities of its gnoses, which celebrate My praise, and say '*There is naught like unto Him.*'

"If thy quality departs not from this vision, thou endurest the loss of thy quality and of the incitements of thy quality; and (then) it is said before Me, 'Lo, so and so.' Then say I to My angels, 'So and so is My friend.' And I shall proclaim thee through Myself, and inscribe My friendship on thy brow, and cause thee to witness that I am with thee, wherever thou mayest be. And I shall say to thee, 'Speak,' and thou shalt speak; and 'Intercede,' and it shall be so. . . ."[8]

The Iraqī Niffarī seems to show the influence of an earlier mystic of Khurāsān, Abū Yazīd al-Bisṭāmī (d. A.H. 275/A.D. 875), who fearlessly derived the ultimate consequences of such a doctrine. If the Friend of God abandons all intermediate things, all secondary causes, what must follow? His very identity, it would seem, must be annihilated: God alone is the final reality. To truly be converted to God means just that; no less. At last one must know that what one thought was his own identity has become God's; was indeed, in some sense, from eternity. And Abū Yazīd repeatedly states this dangerous final consequence. Dangerous, because it clashed head-on with the Law, with the doctrine of createdness, and of servanthood. If the essence of all things is divine, the legalists demanded, where is Satan? What is wrong? Where are the laws of an ordered Muslim society? What is authority? Abū Yazīd was not called to account in his own lifetime for divulging his mystical experience, but some mystics who said no more than he had said were later crucified, burned, or beheaded. Such perceptions at last gave rise to a school of Ṣūfīs who taught the *Waḥdat al-Wujūd*, the Unity of Existence, in a Divine Whole.

Abū Yazīd al-Bisṭāmī (d. A.H. *261/*AD. *875)*
from Light on the Sayings of Abū Yazīd.
by Abū al-Faḍl Muḥammad al-Sahlajī (d. A.H. *476/*A.D. *984)*

Abū Yazīd related: "I vanished into almightiness, and forded the seas of dominion and the veils of godhead, until I came to the Throne; and behold, it was empty. So I cast myself upon it, saying, 'Master, where shall I seek Thee?' Then He unveiled, and I saw that I was I, and I was I, turning back into what I sought; and I myself, not other than I, was where I was going."

He also related the following: "When He brought me to the brink of the Divine Unity I divorced myself and took myself to my Lord, calling upon Him to succour me. 'Master,' I cried, 'I beseech Thee as one to whom nothing else remains.' When He had recognized the sincerity of my prayer, and how I had despaired of myself, the first token that came to me proving that He had answered this prayer was that He called me to forget myself utterly, and to forget all creatures and dominions. So I was stripped of all cares, and remained without any care. Then I went on traversing one kingdom after another; whenever I came to them I said to them, 'Stand, and let me pass.' So I would make them stand, and I would pass until I had reached them all. So He drew me near, appointing for me a way to Him nearer than soul to body. Then He said, 'Abū Yazīd, all of them are My creatures, except thee.' I replied, 'So I am Thou, and Thou art I, and I am Thou.' "[9]

Ḥārith ibn Asad al-Muḥāsibī, the saintly ascetic of Baṣra who moved to Baghdad and there became, as al-Sulamī says, "the teacher of most of the Baghdad Ṣūfīs," describes in detail the reward reserved in Paradise for the friends of God in his "Book of Imagining" (*Kitāb al-Tawahhum*). While its full-blooded imagery may strike other tastes as too physical, and even gross, it is a careful construction from literalist reading of Qur'ān and Ḥadīth texts, and served as the source for almost all subsequent description of Paradise, including that of al-Ghazālī.

As a man who practised rigid self-denial in life, al-Muḥāsibī describes with obvious relish the uncircumscribed joys God is to give His friends in the next world, but he makes it clear that by far the greatest happiness that awaits them is the indescribable happiness of

well explained by al-Hujwīrī, a Persian Ṣūfī shaykh who settled in Lahore, in Northern India, and who is still venerated there as a friend of God. He wrote the earliest detailed treatise on Ṣūfism in Persian, the *Kashf al-Maḥjūb*) "Uncovering of the Veiled"), around A.H. 450/ A.D. 1057.

Sūfism is Founded on Wilāya
from the Uncovering of the Veiled
by Abū al-Ḥasan 'Ali al-Hujwīrī (written ca. A.H. *450/*A.D. *1057)*

You must know that the principle and foundation of Ṣūfism and knowledge of God rests on saintship (wilāya), the reality of which is unanimously affirmed by the Shaykhs, though every one has expressed himself in different language. . . . God may confer on one a "friendship" (wilāya) that enables him to persevere in obedience to Him and keeps him free from sin, and on another a "friendship" that empowers him to loose and bind and makes his prayers answered and his aspirations effectual. . . . God has saints (awliyā') whom He has specially chosen to be the governors of His kingdom. . . . Such have been in past ages, and are now, and shall be hereafter . . . because God has exalted this Community above all others and has promised to preserve the religion of Muḥammad. Inasmuch as the traditional and intellectual proofs of this religion are to be found among the divines ('ulamā'), it follows that the visible proof is to be found among the saints and the elect of God. . . . God, then, has caused the prophetic evidence (*burhān-i nabawī*) to remain down to the present day, and has made the saints the means whereby it is manifested. . . . He has made the saints the governors of the universe; they have become entirely devoted to His business. . . . Through the blessing of their advent the rain falls from heaven, and through the purity of their lives the plants spring up from earth, and through their spiritual influence the Muslims gain victories over the unbelievers. Among them are four thousand who are concealed and do not know one another and are not aware of the excellence of their state, but in all circumstances are hidden from themselves and from mankind. . . . But of those who have power to loose and to bind and are the officers of the Divine Court there are three hundred, called Akhyār, and forty, called Abdāl, and seven, called Abrār, and four, called Awtād, and three, called Nuqabā', and one called Quṭb (Pole) or Ghawth (Help). All these know one another and cannot act save by mutual consent. . . . Abū

Isḥāq al–Isfarā'īnī and some of the ancients hold that a saint is ignorant of his saintship, while Abū Bakr ibn Fūrak and others of the past generation hold that he is conscious of it. I ask the former party, what loss or evil does a saint suffer by knowing himself? If they allege that he is conceited when he knows himself to be a saint, I answer that Divine protection is a necessary condition of saintship, and one who is protected from evil cannot fall into self conceit. (But) it is a very common notion that a saint to whom extraordinary miracles are vouchsafed does not know himself to be a saint, or these miracles to be miracles. . . . The Mu'tazila (Rationalists), however, deny special privileges and miracles, which constitute the essentials of saintship. They maintain that all Muslims are friends of God when they are obedient to Him, and that anyone who fulfills the ordinances of the Faith . . . is a "friend."

Abū 'Alī al–Jūzajānī says: "The Saint is annihilated in his own state and subsistent in the contemplation of the Truth: he cannot tell anything concerning himself, nor can he rest with anyone except God."[14]

I have already said that the saints are not preserved from sin (ma'ṣūm), for that belongs to the prophets; but they are protected (*maḥfūẓ*) from any evil that involves denial of their saintship, and the denial of saintship depends on apostacy, not on sin. There is controversy here, but there is a consensus of opinion among Muslims that even a great sin does not put one outside the pole of faith. . . . Therefore, since the saintship of knowledge of God (*ma'rifa*) which is the foundation of all miracles (*karamāt*) vouchsafed by Divine grace is not lost through sin, it is impossible that what is inferior to it (namely the miracles) should disappear because of sin. . . . A miracle will not be manifested to a saint unless he is in a state of absence from himself, and bewilderment, and his faculties are entirely under the control of God. . . . I heard the Master and Imām Abū al–Qāsim Qushayrī say, "Once I asked Ṭābarānī about the beginning of his spiritual experience. He told me that on one occasion he wanted a stone from the river–bed at Sarakhs. Every stone that he touched turned into a gem, and he threw them all away." This is because gems were of less value to him, since he had no desire for them.[15]

It is well known among Ṣūfīs that every night the Awtād must go around the whole universe, and if there be any place on which their eyes have not fallen, next day some imperfection will appear in that place, and they must inform the Quṭb, in order that he may fix his attention on that weak spot, and that by his blessing the imperfection may be removed.[16]

The whole community of orthodox Muslims and all the Ṣūfī shaykhs agree that the prophets and such of the saints as are guarded from sin (maḥfūẓ) are superior to the angels. The opposite view is held by the Mu'tazila, who argue that the angels are of more exalted rank, of more subtle constitution, and more obedient to God (but) the angels are without lust, covetousness, and evil; they are instinctively obedient to God. . . . Therefore, one whose nature has all these characteristics, and who (still) turns back from sin and contends against the Devil is in reality superior to the Angel who is not the battlefield of lust, and need not have recourse to deeds and instruments.[17]

'Imrān ibn Ḥuṣayn, like the other early pietists, refused to be a qādī, as if feeling no responsibility for the administration of justice or of the social order. Al–Tirmidhī says that the incognito forty *Abdāl* are the real successors of the Prophet in the Umma. Hujwīrī puts it that the friends of God are God's governors given to the Community, and the *visible proofs of Islam*. Here, clearly, there is little or no regard to orthodox concern for the continuation of caliphate or of kingship, with the administration of public aspects of the Law, or with the ḥisba; only occasionally with the struggle to enlarge the physical territories of Islam (the Shaykhs tried usually to make more real Muslims). Here is a kingdom not of this world. The Ṣūfīs knew it; many later saints who possessed little more than the clothes they wore were given titles such as "Sulṭān," Malik," "Shāh".

It is a vision of the nature of the Islamic Community that either contradicts the official version, or treats it as ephemeral and irrelevant. It is individualistic, and indeed subversive. How is it to be related to Islamic civilization, and why did the 'ulamā', custodians of community law and values, come to tolerate the Ṣūfīs (though as we shall see, continuing to treat them with reserve)? And why did the sulṭāns, exponents of the power state, come to build and endow convents for Ṣūfīs, and shrines for the Friends of God?

Apart from the appeal of personal holiness among the saints to the rulers, the shaykhs had the ear of the people, and were thus to be conciliated whenever possible, in order to attach them and their adherents to the ruling powers. The traditional and intellectual proofs of Islam could be found with the 'ulamā', Hujwīrī states, and the visible proof, for the great mass of the believers, was found in the lives of saints and their followers, and in the miracles of holy men. It was an essential characteristic of friends of God that they should be able to perform miracles. We may consider here the treatment of this subject given by Abū Bakr al-Kalābādhī.

The Doctrine of the Miracles of the Friends of God
from An Introduction to the Exponents of Mysticism
by Abū Bakr al-Kalābādhī (d. A.H. *390/1000* A.D.*)*

The Ṣufīs are agreed in affirming the miracles of the (friends of God), even though they may enter the category of marvels, such as walking on water, talking with beasts, (miraculous journeys), or producing an object in another place or at another time: all these examples are also spoken of in the scriptures. . . . As miracles were vouchsafed in the time of the Prophet to testify to the truth (of his claims), so they have happened at other times for a similar reason. Abū Bakr al-Warrāq said, "A prophet is not a prophet because of some marvel, but because God has sent him and made revelation to him. . . . It is a duty to accept the claim of a messenger even if one does not see any marvel proceeding from him." They are agreed that God strengthens the truthful (claimant) by means of a marvel, whereas the false man cannot have the same property, for that would imply that God is unable to distinguish the truthful from the false. As for the man who is a true (friend of God), but not a prophet, he does not lay claim to be a prophet, or anything that is false or untrue: he only invites men to accept what is true and truthful. If God displays miraculous power in him, this in no way impugns the prophet's office but reinforces it.

Some of the Ṣūfīs maintain that God may cause His enemies to see in their own persons certain extraordinary powers and they imagine that they are miracles which they have merited by their actions . . . supposing themselves to be superior to other men; they despise God's servants, and behave arrogantly to them, for they do not suspect what God is plotting.

As for (friends) however, when any miraculous dispensation is accorded them by God, they are all the more humble, submissive, fearful and lowly toward God, and the more contemptuous of themselves.

Prophets, then, are accorded marvels, saints miracles, and enemies (of God) deceptions.[18]

The yearning of the masses for holy men and miracles which would verify the faith of the Community was answered not only by extraordinary occurrences, but also often by the tricks of charlatans seeking to exploit this hunger. One of the masterpieces of Arabic literature, the elegant *Maqāmāt* of al-Harīrī, who died in A.H. 516/A.D. 1122 in the Saljūq period, concerns a witty rogue, Abū Zayd, who frequently practises a spurious holiness in order to make a good living. A Mu'tazilī qāḍī of Iraq, al-Tanūkhī, who lived under the Buwayhī Shī'ī dictators and died in A.H. 384/A.D. 994, retails with relish the following story. As a Mu'tazilī rationalist, al-Tanūkhī was inclined to hostility toward saints and miracles.

The Story of a Trickster
from the Ruminations of Colloquy
by al-Maḥāsin ibn 'Ali al-Tanūkhī (d. A.H. *384/*A.D. *994)*

An accomplished person went from Baghdad to Ḥims in Syria with his wife, saying to her: "This is a foolish and wealthy town, and I want your help to bring off a (great coup)." He told her to remain in her place and not come near him, only each day to take two thirds of a *raṭl* of raisins and the same quantity of almond paste, knead them together, and place it at midday on a clean tile in a certain lavatory near the mosque. He then produced a tunic and breeches of wool [*ṣūf*, hence the word "Ṣūfī."—Ed.] and a veil to put over his head, and took his station at a certain pillar in the mosque where most of the people passed. Here he remained praying the whole day and night, except at the times wherein ritual prayer is forbidden, and when he sat down, he kept counting his (rosary) beads and did not utter a word. When he began to attract attention, it was noticed that he never ceased praying and never tasted food. The people were astonished, as he never left the mosque except at midday, when he went to the lavatory, where the paste had changed colour and looked like discolored dung. This he would eat (in seclusion) to support life, and drink as much water as he needed when he (made his ablutions). It was supposed that he maintained a complete fast for the whole period; extraordinary, and admirable. However hard they tried to get him into conversation, he took no notice, and so he won their profound respect; and indeed when he went for purification, they rubbed their hands on the place he had been occupying and carried away the dust; and they brought him the sick that he might lay his hands on them. After a year had passed, he met his wife at the lavatory, and told her to come on Friday, when people were praying, to seize hold of him and say: " 'You enemy of God, you scoundrel, after killing my son in Baghdad, have you come here to play the devotee?' You are not to let me go, but pretend you want to slay me to avenge your son. The people will gather, but I will see that you come to no harm. I shall admit that I have killed him, and have come here to do penance. You are to demand that I be brought to the magistrate for execution; the people will offer to pay the blood–money, but you are not to accept less than ten times the legal amount, or what you judge they will pay over that. When the bidding has reached (the highest possible amount), collect it and leave the town at once for the Baghdad road; I will escape and follow you."

The next day the woman came to the mosque, buffeted him on the face, and recited what he had taught her. The people of the town rose up wishing to kill her, saying: "Enemy of God, this is one of the chief saints, one of the maintainers of the world, the Pole of the time." He signalled to them not to hurt her, then rolled for a long time on the ground, and spoke (for the first time). They were delighted to hear his voice, and he said: "The reason I have been living among you is to do penance. I was a man who erred, and ruined himself murdering this woman's son; but I have repented and come here to practise devotion. I was thinking of looking for her, and I have been praying God to accept my penance and put me in her power that I might expiate my crime. At last my prayer is answered, and God has accepted my penance. Suffer her therefore to slay me; and I commit you to the care of God." Cries and lamentations arose, and the woman walked to the door of the mosque, to go to the palace of the governor that he might order the execution. Then the shaykhs said: "Citizens, why have you forgotten to remedy this disaster and protect your country by the presence of this saint? Ask her to accept the blood money, which we shall pay out of our purses." The woman said: "I refuse. One hair of my son's head was worth more than the legal amount!" They went on bidding until they had reached ten times the amount; then she said: "Collect it, and when I have seen it, if I feel that I can accept it and acquit the murderer, I will do so." The congregation went on collecting money until they had a hundred thousand dirhams, but she said: "I shall take nothing but the death of my son's murderer; so deeply has it affected my soul!" Thereupon, men and women began to fling down cloaks and coats and jewellery, any one who was unable to pay a part of the ransom feeling like an outcast from society. At last she took what was offered, acquitted the man, and went off. He remained in the mosque a few days—long enough for her to get a safe distance—and then decamped one night. When he was sought, he could not be found, nor was he heard of until a long time after, when they discovered that the whole affair had been a plot.[19]

THE SHĪ'A AND THE FRIENDS OF GOD.

The Mū'tazila, we have noticed, had close contacts with the Shi'a. It is perhaps partly as a result of Mu'tazilī influence that Shī'īs were at first slow to accept the cult of Ṣūfī saints. The underlying reason for this reserve, however, was that for the Shi'a the function of the friends of God was already fulfilled by the Imāms and their descendants, and not because of hostility to the doctrine of sainthood. Indeed, wilāya was of basic importance to them, since they often added to the profession "There is no god but God, and Muḥammad is His messenger," the words "and 'Alī is the walī of God." The visible proofs of Islam, as some of the Shī'ī statements of doctrine say, are the Imāms.

If one considers this question from the point of view of *function,* he will also see that saints were essential for the Sunnīs, but not for Shī'īs, because of their differing attitudes toward history, the actual Community, and the ruler. For the Sunnīs, troubled by the gap between theory and practise, yet still certain that the Community could not err, the awliyā' were God's contacts with an imperfect world, and the evidence of His continuing mercy to the Believers. For the Shī'īs, as we have seen, it was a basic tenet that something had already gone dreadfully wrong with history, and only the Mahdī could set it right. They might well have chosen to regard miracles and the hierarchy of saints with the skeptical eye of the Mu'tazilīs, yet in fact, they did not. The Imāms were friends of God, and the 'Alawīya, the descendants of 'Alī, were a sacred trust to the Community, to whom loyalty and devotion were due. Non–'Alawī saints there were, but they were less prominent than among the Sunnīs.

The Ṣāfavī dynasty was founded early in the sixteenth century A.D. by a family of hereditary saints claiming descent from 'Alī who were at first venerated by Sunnīs and Shī'īs alike. Even the most rigid Sunnī could cheerfully concede that the Shī'ī Imāms had been saints. Thus the Sunnī Ṣūfī shaykh Hujwīrī:

Concerning Ṣūfī Imāms who belonged to the House of the Prophet from the Uncovering of the Veiled
by Abū al–Ḥasan 'Alī al–Hujwīrī (written ca. A.H. *450*/A.D. *1057)*

'Alī is a model for the Ṣūfīs in regard to the truths of outward expressions and the subtleties of inward meanings. . . .

Al-Ḥasan: I have read in the Anecdotes that when Ḥasan ibn 'Alī was seated at the door of his house in Kūfa, a bedouin came up and reviled him and his father and mother. Ḥasan said, "O Bedouin, perhaps you are hungry or thirsty, or what ails you?" The bedouin took no heed, but continued to abuse him. Ḥasan ordered his slave to bring a purse of silver, and gave it to the fellow, saying "O Bedouin, excuse me, for there is nothing more in the house; had there been more, I should not have grudged it to you." On hearing this, the bedouin exclaimed: "I bear witness that thou art the grandson of the Apostle of God. I came hither to make trial of thy mildness." Such are the true saints and shaykhs who care not whether they are praised or blamed, and listen calmly to abuse.

Ḥusayn ibn 'Alī: He is the martyr of Karbalā, and all Ṣūfīs agree that he was in the right. So long as the Truth was apparent, he followed it, but when it was lost he drew the sword and never rested until he sacrificed his dear life for God's sake. The Apostle distinguished him by many tokens of favour. 'Umar ibn al-Khaṭṭāb related that one day he saw the Apostle crawling on his knees, while Ḥusayn rode on his back holding a string, of which the other end was in the Apostle's mouth. 'Umar said "What an excellent camel thou hast, O father of 'Abdallāh." [A teasing "grown-up" name for the little boy.—Ed.] The Apostle replied "What an excellent rider is he, O 'Umar!"

Abū Muḥammad Ja'far al-Ṣādiq [the sixth Imām.—Ed.] is celebrated among the Ṣūfī shaykhs for the subtlety of his discourse and his acquaintance with spiritual truths, and he has written famous books in explanation of Ṣūfism.[20]

To the frequently made allegation that the Shī'ā had produced few walīs or great Ṣūfīs, a Shī'ī apologist retorts as follows.

The Relations of the Ṣūfīs with the Shī'a
from The Book of the Deficiency
by 'Abd al-Jalīl al-Qazvīnī al-Razī (written A.H. *560*/A.D. *1165)*

As for ascetics, devotees, people of guidance and admonition, all of these believed in the Justice (of God; i.e. were Mu'tazilīs), professing the righteous school; and were innocent of any belief in God's tyranny (i.e. predestination) or the like of that, such as 'Umar (ibn 'Abd al-'Azīz ?) and 'Ubayd, and Wāṣil ibn 'Aṭā, and Ḥasan

Baṣrī, Shaykh Abū Bakr Shiblī and Junayd, and the Shaykh of the Age, Abū Yazīd Bisṭāmī and Abū Sa'īd ibn Abī al-Khayr, and they also had a very good opinion of the Shī'a. A part of this group who were beyond any doubt believing Shī'a in school as well as in principles are Ma'rūf al-Karkhī, Yaḥya ibn Mu'adh al-Rāzī, Ṭā'ūs al-Yamanī, Bahlūl Majnūn, Mālik ibn Dīnār, and Manṣūr ibn 'Ammār, so that the story has even come down that on the same night Manṣūr ibn 'Ammār was buried, one of his disciples saw him in a dream walking among the gardens of paradise, in the most splendid array, and said to him "O Manṣūr, how have you come already to the Hūrīs, the Palaces, and the Light?" And he answered, "By the prayers of the night vigils, and the love of 'Alī ibn Abī Ṭālib." And there are so many others apart from these that if we mentioned them all, this would be a very long book.[21]

In modern times, the relation of Shī'ī doctrine to the friends of God has been well and economically summed up by a Persian Shī'ī scholar, Professor Seyyid Hoseyn Nasr.

Shī'ī Doctrine and Wilāya
from Ideals and Realities of Islam
by Seyyid Hoseyn Nasr (written 1966)

In general the word "wilāyah" means sainthood and the saint is called Walī Allāh, "the friend of God." But in the specific context of Shī'ism it refers not only to the saintly life in general, but to the very function of interpreting the esoteric dimension of the revelation (i.e. to the Shī'ī Imāmate). The person whose duty it is to fulfil in every age the function of wilāyah is the Imām, whose figure is so central in Shī'ism. . . . The Imām is, in fact, the sustainer and interpreter *par excellence* of the revelation. His duty is threefold: to rule over the Community of Muslims as the representative of the Prophet; to interpret the religious sciences and the Law to men, especially their inner meaning, and to guide men in the spiritual life. All of these functions the Imām is able to perform because of the "Light" within him. The relation of the Imāms is not only a carnal one, but, most of all, a spiritual connection based on the passing of this "Light" from one Imām to another, by virtue of which each becomes 'ma'ṣūm' (preserved from error). . . .

The Imāms are also the intermediaries between man and God.

To ask for their succour in life is to appeal to the channel God has placed before men so as to enable man to return to Him. They are, in this sense, the extension of the personality of the Prophet. Their tombs as well as those of their descendants, the *imāmzādas* in Persian, are visited by pilgrims and are the centres of religious life. Shī'ites from all over the world make pilgrimage to the tombs of 'Alī in Najaf, of Ḥusayn in Karbalā, of the seventh and ninth Imams in Kazimain, of Imām Riḍā in Mashhad, of his sister Hazrat Ma'ṣūma in Qūm, of the sister of Imām Ḥusayn and his daughter and many other sites. In the popular daily life of the Shī'ah these sites fulfil the same functions as those of the great saints in the Sunnī world. . . . Of course often the two categories of sacred places merge. For example in the Shī'ite world the tombs of Ṣūfī saints who are considered the spiritual progeny of the Imāms are visited frequently, and in the Sunnī world the tombs of the Imāms and their descendants are very often visited as the tombs of great saints.[22]

SUFISM AND THE CULT OF SAINTS

'Abd al-Qādir al Jilānī, often called *al-Ghawth al-'Aẓam*, "the greatest Help, or Pole," who died in 1166 A.D. is the eponym of one of the most widespread of all Ṣūfī orders, the Qādirīya, and is said to have been one of the greatest workers of miracles among the friends of God. He was no intoxicated charlatan, but a teacher whose sobriety and gentleness impressed his own age, and about whom even the most skeptical saw inexplicable occurrences. There are many pious little books which tell in stupefying detail of his great wonders and miracles. However, the account which follows contains not only some of the most credible items about his life, but was compiled by a critic with no brief for the cult of saints, the Shāfi'ī legalist and biographer al-Dhahabī of Damascus, who died in 1348 or 1352 A.D.

Al-Dhahabī deliberately limited his biography of 'Abd al-Qādir to what he felt could not be denied. In this reserved biography of essentials, it is possible to discern quite another figure from the great miracle worker who confidently spoke by divine inspiration. It is the figure of an inarticulate young fundamentalist telepathic-sensitive from the Persian hill country, who came to the great city of Baghdad to study theology and the Law, and there discovered that he could overhear people's thoughts. Almost driven insane by the voices and his doubts, he at last discovered friends and a measure of peace among the Ṣūfīs of the city. He became a great spiritual leader, and a "Proof of Islam" for many.

'Abd al-Qādir al-Jilānī
from the History of Islam
by Shams al-Dīn al-Dhahabī (d. A.H. *748*/A.D. *1348)*

'Abd al-Qādir, Shaykh Abū Muḥammad al-Jilānī, the Ḥanbalī, the ascetic, endowed with miraculous powers and standing, and head of the Ḥanbalīs. He was born in Jilān (south of the Caspian sea in Iran) in the year A.H. 471/A.D. 1078–79, and came to Baghdad as a young man (about 18) and studied the Law and listened to Ḥadīth, and ḥadīths were later recited on his authority. He was the Imām of his time, the Pole of his age, and Shaykh of the shaykhs of that period, without fear of rebuttal.

Ibn al-Sama'āni said: "He was from Jilān, the Imām of the Ḥanbalīs and their shaykh in his time: an orthodox lawyer, reciting God's praises often, constantly meditating, and readily moved to tears. He studied the Law with the Qādī al-Mukharrimī and was a companion of Shaykh Ḥammād al-Dabbās. He used to live at the Azaj Gate in the madrasa they built for him. One day I passed to say farewell to a friend, and as we were going, someone said, 'Would you like to visit 'Abd al-Qādir for his blessing?' so we went, and entered his madrasa while it was still early. He came out and sat with his disciples, and they finished a reading of the Qur'ān. When it was over, I wanted to go, but he made me sit, and said 'Wait until we are finished with the lesson.' He then read a lecture to his students, of which I understood nothing; but what is more surprising than that, is that his disciples then rose and repeated his lecture, so perhaps they understood it, while we understood neither the terms nor the expressions."

Abū al-Faraj ibn al-Jawzī (an enemy of Ṣūfīs) said, "Abū Sa'd al-Mukharrimī the Ḥanbalī Qāḍī had built a fine school at the Azaj Gate, and it passed into the charge of 'Abd al-Qādir, who used to address the people with the tongue of preachment. He got a name for asceticism, and started a mumbo-jumbo all his own. The school became too small for the people who came, so he took to sitting at the wall of Baghdad, with his back against a tower. Great crowds used to get religion in one single session. Then the school was rebuilt and enlarged—the more vulgar sort of people being fanatically set on it. So he stayed there, preaching and teaching, until he died."

I should say that Ibn al-Jawzī's bitterness did not allow him to say more in his biographical notice than that, because of the hatred in his heart. We seek refuge in God from our passions!

Shaykh Muwaffaq said "We came to know him at the end of his life—he lodged us in his madrasa and looked after us. . . . He used often to send us food from his own house, and prayed the obligatory prayers with us, acting as Imām, and there were only two of us studying with him at that time. We stayed with him one month and nine days, and then he died. We said the funeral prayers over him by night, in his school. I never heard more talk of miracles about any one than about him, and I never saw anyone whom people venerated more for the sake of religion."

The late Shaykh Abū Bakr al-'Imād said, "I had been reading about the metaphysics of religion (*uṣūl al-dīn*), and certain doubts (about fundamental Ḥanbalism) crept into my mind, so I decided to go to the lesson of Shaykh 'Abd al-Qādir, since people said he addressed himself to the inmost thoughts. So I went to his lecture room, and the first words I heard were, 'Our faith is the faith of the pious ancestors and the Companions of the Prophet.' I said to myself, 'He's just said that by chance.' He went on, and then turned to the part of the room where I was, and repeated it. I said to myself, 'A preacher sometimes turns to this side, and sometimes to that.' Then he turned to me a third time, and said 'Abū Bakr! Abū Bakr! Get up, for your father has come!" Now my father had been away, so I rose and hastened to our house, and there my father was."

A similar story was told by the grammarian Abū al-Baqā': "I attended the lecture of Shaykh 'Abd al-Qādir, and there in front of him the students were reading with the wrong accents. I said to myself, 'I wonder why the Shaykh finds no fault with this?' Thereupon the Shaykh said, 'And here comes a man who has read a few chapters of the Law, to find fault!' I said to myself, 'Perhaps he means someone else,' whereupon he said, 'We mean *you*.' I repented in my heart for having criticised the Shaykh, and he said, 'God has accepted your repentance.' "

I heard our shaykh Ibn Taymīya say that he heard Shaykh Aḥmad al-Farūthī say that he heard our shaykh Shihāb al-Dīn al-Suhrawardī say "I intended to busy myself with scholasticism and the metaphysics of religion, but I said to myself, 'I will first seek the advice of Shaykh 'Abd al-Qādir,' and he said, before I could utter a word, ' 'Umar, that is no preparation for the grave! It's no preparation for the grave!' And so I abandoned the matter."

'Abdallāh ibn Abī al-Ḥasan Jubbā'ī wrote to me in his own hand as follows: "Shaykh 'Abd al-Qādir told me, 'My lower self one day worried me for a lust, but I resisted it, going down street after street to get away to the desert. While I was walking, I saw a scrap of writing which had been thrown in the street—and there on it was: "What have the strong to do with lusts? Lusts were only created for the weak, that they might strengthen themselves with them, to serve Me." And when I read it, that lust departed from my heart.' He also told me that he used to sustain himself with wild carobs and lettuce from the bank of the Tigris. . . ."

(He also) wrote me as follows: "Shaykh 'Abd al Qādir told me, 'I was in the desert, repeating my Law lesson, in a grinding state of poverty, and a speaker whom I did not see said, "Borrow what will sustain you, while you are studying the Law." I said "How shall I borrow, when I am so poor that I will never pay?" He answered "Borrow, and we shall undertake the payment." So I went to a greengrocer and said to him, "Will you deal with me on the condition that whenever God eases my way, I shall pay you, and if I die, you consider that I have paid my debt? Will you give me each day a loaf of bread and some herbs?" He burst into tears, and said "Sir, I am at your service!" So I took from him for a time, until I could endure it no longer.' Then I *think* that he told me, "A voice told me, 'Go to such and such a place, and whatever you find on the seat, take it and give it to the greengrocer.' When I came there, I saw a large gold-piece—so I took it and gave it to the grocer."

He also said, "Once I had a fit of madness, and was taken to the asylum, and a series of esctacies seized me, until I died. They brought a shroud and put me in the washing chamber—and then it passed, and I rose, and it came to my mind to leave Baghdad, because of my constant disturbances there, and I went to the Halba Gate. Someone there said to me, 'Where are you going?' and he gave me such a shove that it knocked me over. 'Go back,' he said, 'for you can do the people good.' 'I went to keep my religion sound,' I said, and he answered, 'It is granted,' although I still did not see the person. Then a new series of ecstacies came over me, and I wished that someone would make clear this matter for me. As I was passing by al-Zafarīya, a man opened his door and said, ' 'Abd al-Qādir!

What did you ask for yesterday?' Now it had slipped my mind, so I was silent, and he became furious with me and slammed his door in my face. . . . Now this was Ḥammād al-Dabbās (the Ṣūfī). I came to know him later, and he cleared up all that had upset me. If ever I absented myself from him in pursuit of Law and Ḥadīth, he used to say when I came back, 'What brought you to us Ṣūfīs? You are a legalist; go to the lawyers!' And I had no answer. One Friday I went out with him and the others to the Mosque, on a very cold day. When we got to the bridge, the Qāḍī (al-Mukharrimī) pushed me into the water. I said to myself, 'This is my Friday ablution. Let it be in God's name!' I had on a wool robe, and in the sleeve were manuscripts, so I raised up my sleeve that they not be destroyed. The others left me and walked on. I squeezed out the robe and followed them, but I suffered severely from the cold. The Shaykh used to treat me harshly and cuff me, and when I would come in hungry, he would say, 'A lot of bread and pastry came for us today, but we ate it all up, not caring for your company.' This caught on among his disciples, and they began to say, 'You're a legalist! What are you doing with us?' But when the Shaykh saw them annoying me, he took my part, and told them, 'You hounds! What are you teasing him for? By God, there's none of you like him. I only keep after him in order to prove him, and I find him solid as a mountain!'

"After awhile there came a man from Hamadān named Yūsuf al-Hamadānī, who was called 'the Pole.' He stayed at a Ṣūfī establishment, and when I heard of him I went to his ribāṭ. I did not see him, and asked about him, and was told that he was in the cool cellar. So I went down to see him, and when he saw me he rose and made me sit down, and looked me over carefully, and then told me all about myself, and solved many problems for me. Then he said, 'You must speak to the people.' I told him, 'Master, I am a foreigner, simple and inarticulate: what should I say to the fine people of Baghdad?' He told me 'You have committed the Law and its principles to memory, and know the disputed questions and the vocabulary, and the explanation of the Qur'ān. You need no more, in order to speak. Mount the chair and speak to the people, for I see in you a cutting that will grow into a palmtree.' "

Shaykh 'Abd al-Qādir also told me (al-Jubbā'ī), "I used to receive commands when I was sleeping and when I was awake, and things too great for speaking would crowd upon my heart until I nearly choked, and could not keep silent. First two or three would sit and listen to my words; then people heard of me and came to me in crowds, until there might be seventy thousand at one sitting."

He also told me, "I would like to be in the deserts and waste places, as I was at first, not seeing people, and not being seen." Then he added, "Still, God wished some benefit to mankind through me —and indeed, more than five hundred people have been converted to Islam at my hands, and more than a hundred thousand rogues and robbers have been brought to repentance. And that is a great blessing."

He also told me, "Great burdens come down on me, so heavy that a mountain would be crushed. Then I lie on my side on the ground, and recite the verse, 'Verily in difficulty, there is help,' (94:5–6) and when I raise my head, they have been lifted from me."

He said to me, "When a child is born to me, I take it in my arms and say 'This is born to die,' and then remove it from my heart. Then if it dies, its death makes no impression on me at all."

Ibn al-Najjār said, " 'Abd al-Qādir's son 'Abd al-Razzāq told me 'Forty-nine children were born to my father; twenty-seven males, and the rest females.' "

He says: " 'Abdallāh ibn abī al-Ḥasan al-Jubbā'ī said, 'I used to hear *Ḥilyat al-Awliyā'* (Lives of the Saints) read before Ibn Nāṣir, and my heart was softened, and I said, "I should like to cut myself off from people, and busy myself with devotions." Then one day I prayed behind Shaykh 'Abd al-Qādir, and when he had prayed, we sat down. He then looked at me, and said, "If you want seclusion, then before it study the Law and hear the shaykhs' lectures and learn some literature; otherwise you will remain just what you are, an unfledged chick." ' "

Abū al-Thanā' al-Naḥramalkī told me that he had heard it said that no fly ever alighted on the garments of Shaykh 'Abd al-Qādir, "So I said, 'I don't know about that.' So we went one Friday morning and attended his lecture. Then he turned to us and said, 'What should the flies want with me, when I have neither the syrup of this world nor the honey of the next?' "

The Shaykh of the Ṣūfīs, 'Umar ibn Muḥammad al-Suhrawardī said, "I used to study law, when I was a boy, and it came into my mind to read some speculative theology [*kalām*, detested by the Ḥanbalīs.—Ed.], and I decided to do so, without telling anyone about it. Now it happened that I went to pray once with my uncle, Shaykh Abū al-Najīb, and Shaykh 'Abd al-Qādir was there. So my uncle asked him to pray for me, and mentioned that I was studying the Law. I rose and kissed Shaykh 'Abd al-Qādir's hand, and he seized my hand, and said to me, 'Repent of what you are planning, and you will prosper.' Then he was silent, and dropped my hand. But I did not change my plan to busy myself with speculative theology, until all my affairs had gone awry, and life grew weary to me. Then I knew that this was because I had disobeyed the Shaykh."

Abū Muḥammad Ibn al-Akhḍar said, "I used to enter the presence of Shaykh 'Abd al-Qādir in mid-winter, when it was very cold, and he would be wearing a single tunic, with a skullcap on his head, and those around him would be fanning him, while all the time the sweat ran from his body as if it were exceedingly hot."

(An informant says): My maternal uncle Khaṣṣ Bey told me this story: "Shaykh 'Abd al-Qādir was holding a session one Sunday, and I went to bed planning to attend the next morning. Now it happened that I had a nocturnal emission, since it was a night of the full moon. I said to myself, 'I don't want to miss this session, so when I finish there, I can perform the Great Ablution.' [obligatory purification after seminal emission.—Ed.] I went to his madrasa, and he was already in the pulpit. After awhile, his eye fell on me, and he said 'Zubayr, do you come to our session when you are polluted, and in need of cold water?' "

And Muẓaffar al-Ḥarbī, a righteous man, related, "I used to spend the night in the madrasa of Shaykh 'Abd al-Qādir, in order to attend the early morning session. One night I went up to sleep on the roof of the school, as it was extremely hot. I was longing for some fresh dates, and I said, 'O God, if only I had five dates!' Now the Shaykh had a trap-door onto the roof, and he opened it and came out with five fresh dates in his hand, and said 'Here, Muẓaffar (although he did not know me by name), take what you have sought.' And there were many other things of this sort."

I should say that Shaykh 'Abd al-Qādir had no equal, and was a man of very wide renown: a leader in both learning and practical life. Shaykh Nūr al-Dīn al-Shaṭṭanawfī the Reader (of al-Azhar) has composed a long work, in three volumes, on his life and what is told about it, in which he has produced an equal weight of milk and cud, mixing truth with falsehood, for he wrote it on the authority of people of no morality. Thus they told him that the Shaykh once took thirteen steps in the air from his pulpit, and moreover that he was once preaching, and no one was moved, so he said, 'You are not moved, and show no pleasure. Lamps, show *your* delight!' And they say that the lamps moved and the dishes danced. All the same, stories of his miracles are attested by many credible witnesses, and there was no one after him who was his equal. He died on the tenth of Rabīʿ al-Akhir in A.H. 561/A.D. 1166, at the age of ninety, and his funeral was attended by a countless multitude. Al-Jubbā'ī relates that Shaykh ʿAbd al-Qādir used to say, "People screen you from yourself, and your Self screens you from God."[23]

The greatest popularization of Ṣūfī ideals and of the cult of saints—living and dead—was carried out by the Ṣūfī brotherhoods, or *ṭarīqas* (paths). This was even more true in the social disorganization introduced by the Mongol invasions of the thirteenth century A.D. Thus the teaching and example of Shaykh ʿAbd al-Qādir were commemorated and propagated by the Qādirī path, and it is frequently said that he thus founded the oldest existing widespread brotherhood of dervishes following a common master (others would point to the Chīshtī *ṭarīqa*, whose beginnings cannot be fixed with certainty, and in any case, ṭarīqas usually came into being after the death of the eponym.) Nonetheless, the growth of great brotherhoods was the final step in institutionalizing the theme of the friends of God.

It is notable that while Islam is traditionally strongly communal, the effort to achieve personal nearness to God—the interior aspect of Islam—was for centuries individual: the occupation of a single soul, sometimes seeking the companionship of a few like spirits, but reaching only a limited circle, and doing so usually by virtue of another function (reciting Ḥadīth, teaching the Law, etc).

In the vital eleven decades between 945 and 1055 A.D., which coincide with the Buwayhīs in Iraq and the late fourth and early fifth centuries A.H., Ṣūfīs began to organize. Certain Ṣūfīs began to try to give more ethical content to already long-existing groupings called the *fityān* (from *fatā*, which can perhaps best be translated as "Young man").

In some Arabic dialects, the word fatā still means "a tough;" "a bully." Traces of the old fityān can still be found in the Persian Zūrkhāna, the House of Strength, where men of the urban artisan class gather to perform physical exercises, wrestle, and listen to patriotic poetry. The fityān appear to have developed in Muslim cities as a response to the arbitrary behavior of the rulers' private armies, and to fill the vacuum created by the sketchiness of municipal governing institutions. Inevitably, these groupings tended to degenerate into gangs of young toughs. Yet the mutual loyalty and generous enthusiasms of the fityān seem to have won the sympathy of some of the Ṣūfīs, who lived close to the common people, and they attempted to infuse *futūwa*, "Young–manliness," with moral qualities such as concern for the weak, courtesy, self–sacrifice.

In the end, they succeeded well; for on the one hand, futūwa when taken up by the military elite came to have the value of "knightliness;" unmarried artisans formed fraternal organizations emphasizing the virtues; and Ṣūfīs themselves began to band in mutual–assistance groups with a common residence. So far, this had been almost totally an urban phenomenon; but on the frontiers, futūwa blended with the *ghāzī* tradition.

The selection that follows is from a Ṣūfī manual written around 1030 A.D. After a discussion of the Ṣūfī virtues, the author added a chapter on futūwa, in which he tried to consider what the word really should mean. Properly understood, he felt, it was a virtue which would bring one closer to God.

On Futūwa and Manly Virtue (Murūwa)
from A Garden for Postulants
by Ibn Yazdānyār (eleventh century)

As for Young–manliness, God has mentioned it in the Qur'ān, and adorned His intimate, Abraham, with it, saying "They said, 'we heard a young man (fatā) making mention of them, and he was called Abraham' " (Qur. 21:60). God calls him fatā because he parted with his Self and his possessions, his family and his children, giving all things to Him to Whom all things belong. After this, God tells us of His friends, using the same word—these are the Companions of the Cave (the Seven Sleepers)—how they were young men who believed in their Lord without any mediator, and were given guidance most bountifully, and how He gave them shelter in His most bounteous care. In this way, those who cleave to the way of futūwa are in the special care and governance of God. Also, He says "Surely God bids to justice and good–doing and giving to kinsmen." (Qur: 16:90). And 'Alī ibn Abī Ṭālib said, "Justice is giving each his due, and good–doing is showing special regard to one's brethren."

Someone asked one of the fityān, "What is the basic principle of your school?" He replied, "Three things are basic: following God's commands and prohibitions, accepting to perform our obligations, and solicitude for God's creatures." One of the shaykhs said, "A fatā is one in whose interior is no pretence; in whose exterior is no affection or hypocrisy, and whose own breast would not reveal to him what is between him and God, much less any other creature."

Abū al-'Abbās ibn 'Aṭā' said, "Virtue is really twofold—there is the virtue of religion, and personal virtue. Religious virtue is a pure conscience in all that is between one and God, and personal virtue is a good will in all that is between one and his brethren."

One of the fityān was asked, "On what principle is your way founded?" and replied, "On three good habits. We do not demand what is due to us personally from any man; we demand all mens' rights from ourselves; and we shortchange our Selves in all that we give them."

Another fatā was asked what was futūwa, and replied, "It is to look like the devil, while practising the deeds of the Abrār (saints)." Another, when asked said, "It is to be liberal with your brother with your own goods, and not to desire his; to be just with him, and not seek that he be so to you; to bear his rudeness, and not be rude to him; to find much however little he gives, and find little however much you give him."

Someone said to Muḥammad ibn al-Munkadir: "What, then, is futūwa?" and he answered, "It is finding the delight of this world." They asked, "And what shall one find delightful about this world?" He answered, "Doing good for one's brethren."

It is said that the first thing in Young-manliness is a bright face, the second thing affectionate behaving, and the third is assisting people in their need. One of them was asked "What is manly virtue?" and replied in these verses:

> "Indeed I feel shame when I feel in need,
> Lest my Friend and my brethren should learn I am poor."

Sufyān al-Thawrī was asked what was futūwa, and answered, "It is compassion for the faults of one's brethren." Manṣūr the Legalist says in this connection:

> "Suppose I have injured you, just as you claim:
> Where then is forgiveness, in brotherhood's name?
> And suppose that you hurt me, because I have hurt you:
> What's superior then about your manly virtue?"

So the important obligations of Young-manliness are truthfulness, loyalty, modesty, good moral character, generosity of spirit, amiability to one's brethren, avoiding listening to ugly things about comrades, generosity in compacts, quitting rancour and duplicity, being God's auxiliary and Satan's adversary, and being liberal to one's brethren with one's own possessions and position without expecting them to show gratitude for this; frequenting the excellent and avoiding the wicked, and similar things. We ask God to bestow on us high moral character and to provide for us the use of the ways of futūwa, and to forgive us that state wherein we now are: the squandering of our opportunities. Truly He is near, and swift to answer.[24]

THE FRIENDS OF GOD IN ANATOLIA

The greatest service of the friends of God to Islamic civilization was certainly their work of conversion of the masses in the older lands of Islam; of barbarian tribes in the border areas; and finally, of the peoples of the newly conquered lands in Anatolia, Africa and India following the new wave of expansion that began in the fifth century A.H. (eleventh century A.D.). It was they who "captured hearts" for Islam, when others captured lands and slaves.

Among the best remembered of them in Turkey is Jalāl al-Dīn Rūmī, a Khurasānī of genius, whose father had emigrated just before the devastation of Khurasān by Genghiz Khan in 1220 A.D. After 1228, Jalāl al-Dīn lived and taught at the capital of the Anatolian, or Rūmī, Saljūq Sultanate at Konya, and did more than anyone to bequeath the legacy of cultivated East Persian Ṣūfism to Turkey.

Mawlānā ("Our master;" in Turkish *Mevlana*) spoke Turkish, but his major works, prose and poetry, were all in Persian. In his memory his devoted son and disciples founded the Mevlevī ṭarīqa, the order of "whirling dervishes," which later came to have immense influence in the Ottoman Empire and was as a consequence suppressed in the Turkish Republic. Mevlana's tomb is still a center of pilgrimage, and the poetry and music of the Mevlevī order have helped form the religious and aesthetic imagination of the Turkish Muslims.

Jalāl al-Dīn had the gift of being able to address himself to all men, high or low, Muslim or Christian. In this selection from his greatest work, the *Mathnavī,* he considers one of the apparent paradoxes of man's relation to God. The legalists—with good grounds in Qur'ān and Ḥadīth—have emphasized the master-slave relationship. Man was created that he might serve and obey. Many fundamentalist 'ulamā' denied that man could know or love God in any sense more profound than that in which a worm might know and love sunlight. On the other hand, the basic principle of Ṣūfism was that man could become the *friend* of God. How? Can a slave be the friend of his owner? And if he could, would not the relationship be rather irrelevant?

Jalāl al-Dīn takes as his analogy the celebrated love between the mighty Maḥmūd of Ghazna and his slave Ayāz, a former Turcoman shepherd-boy, to show that both aspects of the relation are fully compatible, even in the most mundane terms. With a characteristic Ṣūfī consideration of God's Oneness and of the unforgivable sin of idolatry, he shows also that it is still wrong to attribute to any created thing a perfection that is the Lord's alone.

The Love of a King and a Slave
from The Rhyming Couplets
by Jalāl al-Dīn Rūmī (d. A.H. *623/*A.D. *1273)*

Instigated by spiritual insight, Ayāz hung up his sheepskin jacket and rustic shoes. Every day he would enter his private chamber and remind himself, "These are the shoes you once wore; regard not your present elevation."

His enemies told King Maḥmūd, "He has a chamber apart where he keeps gold and silver and a crock of jewels. He lets no one into it; he keeps the door always locked."

"Go," the king commanded. "Open the door and enter the chamber. Whatever you find shall be yours. . . . Expose his secret to all the courtiers."

The trusty officers proceeded to the door of the chamber and began their quest for treasure. . . . Inspired by greed and manifold foolish eagerness, the raiders at last burst open the door of the chamber. . . . Nothing was there but a torn pair of shoes and a sheepskin jacket.

"There must be some treacle in this place," they assured themselves. "These clod hoppers are only a blind . . . (let us) try digging and tunnelling."

The very holes shouted at them, "We are but empty holes!" So they became ashamed of their evil thoughts, and returned to the king, grimy and pale of face and ashamed.

"King of the world," they cried every one of them, "if you shed our blood, it is but lawful and just. If you forgive us, it is grace and favour."

"No," answered the king. "I will not determine. That is for Ayāz. Ayāz, pass judgement upon the sinners."

"King, the command is wholly yours," Ayāz replied. . . . "Had I forsaken the rustic shoes and sheepskin jacket, I should never have sown such seeds of reproach."

"Ayāz, what mean these marks of affection for an old shoe?" the king demanded. "You have made of your shoe your religion and cult. . . . You have mingled your soul's love with two ancient objects which you have hung up in your chamber."

One day the king hastened to his council–chamber, where he found all his ministers assembled. He brought forth a lustrous pearl, and placed it in the palm of the vizier. . . . "What is it worth?" he asked. "It is worth more than a hundred ass–loads of gold," the vizier replied. "Break it," ordered the king.

"How should I break it?" cried the vizier. "I am a well–wisher of your treasury and wealth. How should I deem it right?"

"Admirable!" the king exclaimed, bestowing on him a robe of honour and taking back the pearl. Then, after an interval he put it in the hand of a chamberlain. "What would this be worth?" he demanded. "Half a kingdom—God guard it from destruction!" the chamberlain answered. "Break it," the king ordered. "King," said the chamberlain, "it would be a great pity indeed to break it. Pass over its value, and consider its lustre and (beauty). How should my hand move to shatter it? How should I be the enemy of the king's treasury?"

The king gave him a robe of honor and increased his allowances, (praising) the chamberlain's intelligence.

After another interval, the king handed the pearl once again to the (Chief Qāḍī). The latter spoke to the same effect, as did all the other ministers.

"Now, Ayāz, will you say what this fine and lustrous pearl is worth?"

"More than I can tell," responded Ayāz.

"Break it into little pieces at once," the king commanded. Ayāz speedily ground the pearl into powder. Thereupon a great cry and clamour arose from the courtiers.

"Illustrious princes," Ayāz countered, "which is more precious —the king's command, or the pearl? In the name of God, which is worthier in your eyes—the Sulṭān's command, or this excellent gem? I will never turn my face to a stone, like an idolater. That soul has indeed lost the pearl of great price, that prefers a coloured pebble and relegates my king."

The king signalled to the veteran executioner, as if to say "Remove those wretches!" Thereupon the affectionate Ayāz leaped up, prostrated himself and spoke with his hand to his throat.

"Sovereign before whom the heavens themselves stand in wonder, storehouse of pardon, the heedlessness and impudence of these sinners derives from the abundance of your clemency. Pardon them, you in whose coffer all pardon is contained!

"Yet who am I, that I should beg you to forgive, you who are the sovereign, and the quintessence of the Divine fiat? Should I instruct you, or remind you of the rules of graciousness? What is there that is not known to you? Yet inasmuch as you yourself have brought me forth from the form to the reality, it is you yourself who make this intercession. . . . You were the inspirer of this prayer at the first; be also the hope of its fulfilment at the last, that I may boast that the king of the world pardoned sinners for the sake of his slave!"[25]

Another ṭarīqa of great importance in the Ottoman empire was that of the Bektāshīs, who were so syncretistic in their encounters with other religious systems that there has been some doubt as to whether being a Bektāshī involved being a Muslim at all.

If the Mevlevīs perpetuated high Khurasānī Ṣūfism among the Turks, the Bektāshīs perpetuated a folk–Ṣūfism of the frontiers, learned from Khurasānī itinerants and spread by wandering Turkish *Bābās* and minstrels among the shamanist tribes of Central Asia. The Saljūq invasions brought the migration of tribal Turks and their antinomian dervish teachers to Anatolia, and the Bektāshīs were their true heirs. They venerated the Imāms of the Twelver Shī'īs, laughed at the Law, and taught that real beliefs should be concealed, but that the true goal of faith was to realize that one was One with God. Apparently from contacts with Christians, they adopted the forms of communion, confession, confirmation, and a celibate clergy, as well as a trinitarian theology (the Unity of 'Alī, God, and Muḥammad). Women were fully accepted at their rites and participated unveiled. The Bektāshīs also fostered a fervent lyrical mystical poetry among the masses, and were responsible for the conversion of most of the Albanian and Bosnian Muslims of Europe.

The peculiar power of the Bektāshīs at court came from the fact that by the later fifteenth century they had charge of the religious formation of most of the *kapi–kullari*, or "slaves" of the Porte: the levies of Christian boys who furnished the padishāh's pages and household troops and could rise to the highest posts of the government; and the slavegirls who after a period of training in the palace would enter the imperial harem, or be given as wives and concubines to officials.

The following stories of walīs were written by a fervent seventeenth century Bektāshī, Evliya (Awliyā') Chelebi, son of a Bektāshī court jeweller and a *kapi–kulu* mother from the Caucasus. Evliya was enrolled as a page in the palace, enjoyed the favor of Murād IV, one of the last conqueror–sultans, and was able to indulge a passion for travels. His memoirs are an often more interesting than truthful but still invaluable source on seventeenth century Ottoman society.

We may begin with the story of Hajjī Bektāsh, the shaykh for whom the ṭariqa was named, and who the Bektāshīs claimed had been a contemporary of the earliest Ottomans. In fact, Hajjī Bektāsh was probably involved in the dervish Bābā'ī revolt against the Saljūqs of Rūm which took place much earlier, in 1240.

Hajjī Bektāsh, the Great Saint
from the Travel–Book
by Evliya Chelebī (d. A.H. *1095*/A.D. *1684)*

When young [Hajjī Bektāsh] never mixed with other boys, but sought retirement and scorned all worldly pursuits. He refused to accept the dignity of Sulṭān which was offered him by his father, who died a prince in Khurasān. Forty years long he did nothing but pray and fast, and arrived at such a degree of perfection, that in the night, during his sleep, his soul migrated into the world of spirits, and he became filled with the mystic science of spirits, and divine knowledge. One day the men of Khurasān asked him to perform a miracle as a proof of his sanctity; he then performed many miracles, and was acknowledged by all the great men of Khurasān to be their superior. My ancestor, the Pole of poles, the Sulṭān of learning, the fountainhead of science, the chief of the Shaykhs of Khurasān, Khwājā Aḥmad Yasavī ibn Muḥammad al–Ḥanafī (d. 1166 A.D.), was his (shaykh), and hinted that he had received from him even the gift of direction to bliss (*irshād*) and of true dervishship, which Gabriel brought from Paradise, with its symbols; the crown, the habit, the (prayer) carpet, the lamp, the *tabla* (drum), and the banner, to Muḥammad—God bless him and give him peace!—the true fountainhead of dervishship. The Prophet delivered irshād to Imām 'Alī, from whom it came to his son Ḥusayn, who bequeathed it to Imām Zayn al–'Abidīn, who left it to Ibrahīm al–Mukarram, who when in the prison of Marwān handed over to Abū Muslim the symbols of dervishship. From him they came to the Imām Muḥammad Bāqir, then to his son Imām Ja'far, and to his son Mūsa al–Kādhim, and from him to Aḥmad Yasavī, who never consented (to give them) until Hajjī Bektāsh made his appearance, who became by the possession of (them) the Pole of poles.

Hajjī Bektāsh of Khurasān was the (descendant) of Ibrahīm al-Mukarram and there is no doubt of his direct lineage from the Prophet. While yet a boy he was distinguished for his devotion, and was entrusted to the care of Luqmān, one of the disciples of Aḥmad Yasavī, from whom he learned the exoteric and esoteric sciences. Luqmān had been invested with the religious habit of Imām Ja'far by the hand of Abū Yazīd al-Bisṭāmī. With this habit Luqmān invested Hajjī Bektāsh. This is the crown or turban which has twelve folds in remembrance of the twelve Imāms, and the white *'abbā*, with sleeves like a jubba, which is worn by dervishes of the order of Bektāsh. By the order of Aḥmad Yasavī he accompanied Muḥammad Bukhāra Saltik with seven hundred men, Shams al-Dīn Tabrīzī, Muḥyī al-Dīn al-'Arabī, Kāri Aḥmad Sulṭān, and other pious men and saints into Rūm (Anatolia), where the Ottoman dynasty took its rise.

Hajjī Bektāsh instituted the new militia called Yenīcherī (Janissaries) and having established his seven hundred disciples in the towns conquered by Sulṭān Orhān, he sent Muḥammad Bukhāra Sari Saltik into Dobruja, Wallachia, Moldavia, Poland and Russia. The seven hundred convents of dervishes, Bektāshī, which actually exist in Turkey are derived from the seven hundred disciples of Hajjī Bektāsh.[26]

Evliya also tells the legend of Sari Saltik, whom the Bektāshīs identified with the popular Byzantine St. Nicholas. The story has also appropriated some of the details of the legend of St. George, and is a good example of Bektāshī syncretism. Sari Saltik was invoked as a warrior and protector-saint.

Sari Saltik Sulṭān
from the Travel Book
by Evliya Chelebī (d. A.H. *1095/*A.D. *1684)*

To him is ascribed the convent of Kilghra Sulṭān. Having been made a dervish in the town of Yasu (in Turkestan) by Aḥmad Yasavī, Sari Saltik came with Hajjī Bektāsh and three hundred faqīrs to Sulṭān Orhān, and was sent after the conquest of Bursa into Russia and Poland, Bohemia and Dobruja. Hajjī Bektāsh gave him a wooden sword, a prayer-carpet, a banner, a drum, kettle-drum and trumpet. . . . At Danzig he conversed with Svety Nicola the patriarch whom he killed, adopted his habit, and by this means converted many thousands to Islam. . . . He travelled many years under the name of Sari Saltik, but his proper name is Muḥammad Bukhāra, and he settled afterwards at Paravadī. The king of the Dobruja (in Bulgaria) requested a miracle from Sari Saltik in confirmation of his mission. There was then in Dobruja a terrible dragon, to which even the two daughters of the king were allotted as food. Sari Saltik agreed to deliver the two girls, on condition that they with their father would embrace Islam. He went to the column to which they were tied as victims for the dragon, accompanied by his seventy dervishes, who were beating the drum and swinging the banner; untied the princesses, and then waited with his wooden sword. . . . The dragon coming near, Sari Saltik addressed it with the verse of the Qur'ān beginning "Greeting on Noah in both worlds," and cut off three of his heads, so that the dragon fled with the remaining four. . . . He cut off the remainder with his wooden sword, and followed the dragon into his den. The beheaded dragon began to press him into the rock, which gave way so wonderfully as to receive the Saint's body, which place with the marks of his hands and feet is still actually shown. The dragon having exhausted his strength fell to the ground dead, and the Saint now led the two girls to their father in safety. A cursed monk, who had picked up the tongues and ears of the three heads (at the column) had laid them before the king, boasting that he had killed the dragon. . . . The monk persisting in his boast, the Saint proposed as a proof, to be boiled with the monk in a cauldron, and though the monk did not like this kind of trial, yet by order of the king he was forced to undergo it. . . . Both were put into a cauldron heated by an immense fire. . . . The cauldron being opened, Sari Saltik was found sweating, and saying "*Ya Hayy*!" (O Living One!); and of the monk nothing remained but black coals and burnt bones. The king instantly embraced Islam, with seven thousand of his subjects. . . . His name was 'Alī Mukhtār. In the same year Sari Saltik made his will, whereby he commanded seven coffins to be made, because seven kings were to contend for his body after his death. This happened. . . . Seven kings claimed to have the true body, which was found in every one of the seven coffins when they were opened. . . . Of these seven burial places of the Saint, three are in the Ottoman Empire, from which he is called Bābā Sulṭān at Bābādagh, Sari Saltik Sulṭān at Bābā Eskissi, and (at Kilghra) Kilghra Sulṭān; in Christian Countries he is generally called St.

Nicholas, is much revered, and Christian monks beg for alms under his auspices. . . .

The convent (at Kilghra) is situated on a cape which extends into the Black Sea like the proboscis of an elephant. . . . The convent was built by 'Alī Mukhtār; the wooden sword of the Saint (and other relics) are kept here. Numerous cells surround it, occupied by learned dervishes who reside here on their (sheepskin prayer–hides), all true Sunnīs and faithful believers, more than one hundred. . . . The windows all look toward the sea. The magnificent kitchen, like that of Kay Ka'us, is worth seeing; day and night the fire is kept up on the stove for passengers and strangers; they have no endowments, but live on alms. They are all purified by mystic divine love.[27]

Journey to a Rural Cult–Center
from the Travel Book
by Evliya Chelebī (d. A.H *1095*/A.D. *1684)*

We arrived, at the end of twelve hours, at Chaghir Kanli Sulṭān, who was a great Shaykh in the time of Meḥmet II. His tomb is adorned. . . . It is a reverential place, where prayers are put up to heaven. I visited it, and read the Sūra Yā Sīn there. Through the sanctity of this saint the country abounds in cattle. Two *chiftliks* are exempted by Imperial diploma from all taxes; the village consists of three hundred houses, with a mosque and a convent, the dervishes of which go bareheaded and barefooted and wear their hair long. The people carry wooden clubs in their hands, and some of them crooked sticks. The Pasha asked from whence they dated their immunity, and they invited him to visit their place of devotion (*samā' khāna*). We followed them to a large place where a great fire of more forty wagon-loads of wood was lighted, and forty (animals) were sacrificed. They assigned a place for the Pasha at a distance from the fire, and began to dance around it, beating their drums and flutes and crying "*Hu*" (He!) and "*Allāh*!" This being continued for an hour, about one hundred of these dervishes, naked, took their children by the hand and entered the fire, the flames of which towered like the pile of Nimrod, crying "O All–Constant! O All-Vivifying!" At the end of half an hour, they came out of the fire, without the least hurt except the singeing of their hair and beards; some of them retiring to their cells instead of coming before the Pasha, who remained much astonished. They then gave him a feast. . . . It was surprising that they were enabled to prepare such a feast in so short a time, as the Pasha had arrived suddenly, and by a by–road. The Pasha confirmed their immunities, and gave them a present of one hundred ducats.[28]

IBN AL 'ARABĪ AND THE CONCEPT OF WILĀYA

A discussion of Ṣūfism or of wilāya can hardly dispense with reference to the Spanish Arab master, Muḥyī al–Dīn Ibn al–'Arabī of Murcia, the greatest mystical sage of Islam, who died in Damascus in A.H. 638/A.D. 1240. His formulation of the esoteric doctrines of the Ṣūfīs was so powerful and compelling that it tended to dominate all those who came after him, just as his debt to al–Tirmidhī and indeed to all the great theorists who preceded him is quite obvious. In a sense, he is their systematizer and spokesman. At the same time, he seems to carry their ideas to a much higher level of explicitness, and provided students with an almost dangerously voluminous body of texts. That is not to say that these texts cannot often be very complex and even baffling.

As regards Union with God, Ibn al–'Arabī holds it to be impossible, for God is transcendant; but the mystic friend can realize that he is already one with God. The Spiritual Reality of Muḥammad (God's act of making Himself known) is the pre–existent Logos, by which all things were made. It finds its complete hypostasis in the Perfect Man (e.g. a great Walī); and the Perfect Man (manifestation of God's desire to be known, loved, and loving) is the *cause* of all things. Thus, though there is a deep relation between Prophecy and Sainthood, there is a distinction. The following passages are taken from Ibn al–'Arabī's essential work, the *Fuṣūṣ al–Ḥikam* (Bezels of Wisdom).

The Wisdom of Seth
from Bezels of Wisdom
by Muḥyī al–Dīn Ibn al–'Arabī (d. A.H. *638/*A.D. *1240)*

Let us turn now to (divine) gifts. We may say that these are either essential or nominal. As for those that are essential, these never come except by a divine overflowing; and an outpouring from the Essence can never come about except in the form of a preparation of the one in whom this overflowing shall be received. Other than thus it may not be.

Thus, the one receiving the outpouring can not see other than his own image in the Mirror of God. He still does not behold God Himself, even though knowing that he beholds his own image only in Him, much like a mirror in ocular experience: when you see an image in it, you do not see it itself, although you know that you only saw the images or your own reflection by looking into it. . . . This is as far as knowledge (of God) can attain, and the rest is as we have gone into it and explained it in our book, *The Revelations of Mecca.* If you have perceived this, you have perceived the utter limit to which a created being can attain. Do not seek or fatigue your soul to go higher than that, for after that in principle there can be nothing except pure Nonexistence. Thus God is the Mirror in which you behold yourself, and you are a mirror in which He beholds His names and their principles, which are not other than He Himself, so that the mater becomes confused and obscure.

Some of us are ignorant of knowledge of God, and say "To know that one cannot know Knowledge is knowledge." There are those among us also who know, and cannot pronounce such a thing, which is the last word, but to him is given the knowledge of silence, rather than that of not knowing, and such a one is most knowing of God. . . .

Every prophet from Adam to the Last Prophet (Muḥammad) receives light from the niche of the Seal of the Prophets, even though his clay was formed after theirs, since in reality he was present always, according to his word—God bless him and give him peace: "I was a prophet when Adam was between water and clay," while other prophets only became prophets at the time that they were sent. Similarly the Seal of the Saints was a Friend of God when Adam was between water and clay, and other saints only became such after they fulfilled the conditions of nearness to God, by taking on Divine qualities, those expressed in the Divine Names "The Friend, the Praiseworthy."

The Seal of the Prophets, by virtue of his friendship with God, thus participates in the Seal of the Saints just as the other prophets do in him. He is at once friend, messenger, and prophet. The Seal of the Saints is the friend and the heir, who partakes of the Source, and contemplates the hierarchies. He is one of the virtues of the Seal of the Prophets, Muḥammad, on whom be peace and God's blessing; foremost of the Collectivity and lord of the sons of Adam by opening the gates of intercession. . . .

As for the gifts of the names of God, know that the gift of God's mercy to His creatures comes altogether from the Divine Names, whether it is a pure mercy (like that of the joy of lawful pleasures in this world, such as a delicious daily bread, for which there will be no blame on the Day of Resurrection), which comes from the name "The Merciful," and is the merciful gift; or whether it is a mixed mercy, like that of a hateful medicine which brings with it rest. Such are the divine gifts, which are only received at the hands of one of those guardians of the Temple, who are the Divine Names. . . .

Although the Divine Names are illimitable in number—since they are only known by what comes about through them, which is itself infinite—still they go back to a definite number of principles, the "mother–names," or presences of the Names. In truth, there is only One Reality, which receives all these relations and constructions which are called, from it, the Divine Names. And this Reality also grants that each of these Names it infinitely manifests shall have a reality which is separate from every other name. It is this reality which distinguishes it from other names, rather than that which it has in common with the others, just as the divine gifts are all distinguishable from one another by their individuality, even though they all derive from a common source—since it is evident that this one is not that one. The reason for all this is the distinction of the names. In the Divine Presence, there is absolutely nothing that repeats itself—and that is a fundamental truth.

This knowledge is the knowledge of the prophet Seth, on whom be peace! It is his spirit which communicates this to every spirit that may receive of it, except the spirit of the Seal, to whom knowledge comes directly from God, without the intermediacy of any other spirit. Nay more, it is through the spirit of the Seal that the matter comes to every spirit (via Seth), even though the Seal does not himself realize it so long as he is in a corporeal body. In his reality, and by his function, he knows in a direct and essential way all that he may be unconscious of as a corporeal being. He is the knower unknowing—for one may attribute to him qualities which appear to be contrary, like his Source, who is his Essence, the Terrible and Beautiful, the Transcendant and Imminent, the First and the Last. Thus he knows, and does not know; perceives, and does not perceive; and witnesses unseeing.

By that knowledge Seth receives his name, for it means "the Gift of God." In his hand is the key of the Divine gift in all its variety and relatedness, and he was the first pure gift that God made to Adam, and He made it through Adam, for the child is the secret of his generator; he came forth from him and came unto him and every gift in creation is like this one: no one receives anything from God which does not come from himself, however distinct their forms may seem. But not everyone knows that; only he who is of the People of God. Therefore when you see one who knows that, prop yourself upon him; for such a one is an essence of purity, a quintessence of the elected from among the commonality of God's people.

Whenever a contemplative contemplates a form that communicates to him something he did not know before, that form is of his own essence, and not other; from the tree of his soul he cultivates the fruit of his own knowledge, just as his reflection in a polished surface is not other than him, even though the place or the presence in which he beholds himself is communicated to him with the inversion proper to its relative place. None can know the particulars of this, except one who knows God.

It is in the footsteps of Seth that the lastborn of the human race shall be born, the seal of the begotten, who shall gather together all the mysteries of Seth. A sister shall be born with him, but he shall be born after her, with his head between her legs. His birthplace shall be in China, and his language that of his locale. Sterility shall spread among men and women, and marriage without children shall be common. He shall call them to God, but they will not respond. When God has taken him and the last believers of his age, the rest shall be as brutes, not knowing good from evil, acting according to the law of nature: desire devoid of intelligence or moral law; and then the Hour shall come upon them.[29]

On the Difference Between Prophecy and Sainthood
from Bezels of Wisdom
by Muḥyī al-Dīn Ibn al-ʿArabī (d. A.H. *638/*A.D. *1240)*

On the difference between prophecy and sainthood: Know that wilāya is the general all-embracing sphere, and so does not end, whereas institution of prophetic law as well as prophetic mission ended with Muḥammad, God bless him and give him peace, and there will be no messenger after him who either institutes a law or operates within a given law, nor any prophet either who gives a law. . . .

Now the servant desires not to be a partner with his Lord in His Names, and God does not call Himself "Messenger" or "Prophet," but He does call Himself "Friend." (Hence one who is a walī is is entitled to be known with one of the Names of God.) This Name remains forever among mankind in this world and the hereafter, whereas names which are peculiar to man as apart from God, such as "prophet," "messenger," have not remained after prophethood came to an end.

Nonetheless, God has shown special kindness to His servants, and allowed a general sort of prophethood, unaccompanied by institution of a new law, to remain with them (and this is wilāya) just as he has allowed law-giving, in the sense of interpretation of the Law, to remain. Thus it is said, "The 'ulamā' are the inheritors of the prophets."

When you observe that a prophet has spoken of things apart from the Law, this is in his capacity as a friend of God and a gnostic. His state as a Knower is more complete and perfect than his function as a messenger or giver of Law, and if you hear one of the People of God say, or are told that he said that sainthood is higher than prophethood, he means no more than we have said. And if he says that the Walī is loftier than the Prophet or the Messenger, he means it about (different aspects of) one and the same person. The Prophet, on whom be God's blessing and peace, was more perfect as being a Friend of God, than as being a messenger. It is not the case, however, that a saint who follows a prophet is greater than the prophet he follows, for the follower can never attain what the one he follows has attained. . . .[30]

For Ibn al-'Arabī, all the saints and prophets, as "perfect men," subsist in the Reality of Muḥammad, which corresponds to the "First Reality" of Plotinus.

The Reality of Muḥammad
from Bezels of Wisdom
by Muḥyī al-Dīn Ibn al-'Arabī (d. A.H. *638/*A.D. *1240)*

The true nature of his wisdom was singularity, because he is the most perfect of the human race (which is the image of God), and for this reason the whole order of creation began with him and was sealed. He "was a Prophet when Adam was still between water and clay" (ḥadīth). Then he was born in his created form as the Seal of the Prophets. He is the first of the three unique emanations, and was the most perfect symbol of his Lord, and knowledge of his Lord is the result of perfectly knowing oneself, which is why he, peace be upon him, said "He who knows himself knows his Lord."

[ḥadīth: as Logos, Muḥammad had perfect knowledge of himself and of God.—Ed.][31]

THE FRIENDS OF GOD IN INDIA

We have seen in the theme of struggle the exultantly destructive side of the Muslims of Dehli in their encounter with Hindu civilization. Yet there was another, and most important aspect: the Ṣūfī saints who bound up where the ghazīs wounded, and won the hearts of many Hindus. At the same time, the shaykhs had the devoted support of the Muslim military elite, and one of the qualities most admired in Fīrūz Shāh Tughluq was his reverential treatment of the saints.

The most important ṭarīqa of Dehli was that of the Chishtīs (from Chisht, in Eastern Iran). The first of these shaykhs in India, Khwājā Mu'īn al-Dīn, had known 'Abd al-Qādir Jilānī, revered the memory of al-Hujwīrī, and settled at Ajmer, where he died in 1236 A.D. A great extension of the order came later, with Shaykh Farīd al-Dīn (d. 1260), who is still revered by Hindus and Sikhs as well as Muslims, and under whom the order developed adherents through all North India.

Under Shaykh Farīd's greatest disciple, Niẓām al-Dīn Awliyā', the order became a very powerful instrument of spiritual culture, and—due to its influence—really a state within the state. The didactic historian Baranī (d. ca. A.H. 758/A.D. 1357), a great partisan of the Chishtīs, describes in these somewhat exaggerated terms the effect of Niẓām al-Dīn's religious revival on the luxury-loving camp-town of Dehli.

Shaykh Niẓām al-Dīn Chishtī
from History of Fīrūz Shāh
by Ziyā' al-Dīn Baranī (d. ca. A.H.*758*/A.D. *1357)*

Shaykh Niẓām al-Dīn had opened wide the doors of discipleship and admitted (all sorts of people into his discipline), nobles and plebians, rich and poor, learned and illiterate citizens and villagers, soldiers and warriors, free-men and slaves, and all these people refrained from many improper things, because they considered themselves disciples of the Shaykh; if any of them committed a sin, he confessed it and vowed allegiance anew.

The general public showed an inclination to religion and prayer; men and women, young and old, shop-keepers and servants, children and slaves, all came to say their (regular) prayers. Most of those who frequented the Shaykh's company regularly said their (supererogatory) Chasht and Ishrāq prayers. Many platforms with thatched roofs over them were constructed on the way from the city to Ghiyāthpūr; wells were dug, water–vessels (for ablution) were kept, carpets were spread, and a servant and a (Qur'ān reader) were stationed at every platform so that people going to the Shaykh might have no difficulty in performing their supererogatory prayers.

Owing to regard for the Shaykh's discipleship all talk of sinful acts disappeared among the people. . . . (Even) at the Sulṭān's court many amīrs, clerks, guards and royal slaves had become the Shaykh's disciples, said their Chasht and Ishrāq prayers and fasted on the 13th, 14th, and 15th of every lunar month, as well as during the first ten days of Dhū al–Ḥijja (the Month of Pilgrimage). There was no quarter of the city where a gathering of the pious was not held every month or twenty days, with mystical songs that moved men to tears. Many disciples performed the *tarāwīḥ* (night) prayers (of Ramaḍān) in their houses or in the mosques. Those who were persevering passed the whole night standing in prayer throughout the month of Ramaḍān, on Fridays, and during the days of the Ḥajj. . . . Some of the disciples had by now reached eminent spiritual power through this education.

Owing to the influence of the Saint, most of the Muslims of this country took on an inclination to mysticism, and came to have faith in him. This faith was shared by Sulṭān 'Alā al–Dīn (Khiljī) and his family. The hearts of men having become virtuous by good actions, the very name of wine and gambling never came to men's lips, and sins and abominable vices seemed as bad to people as infidelity. Out of regard for one another the Muslims refrained from open usury and backbiting, while the shopkeepers, from fear of God, gave up speaking lies, using false weights, and deceiving the ignorant. . . . People asked the booksellers for books on devotion. No handkerchief was seen without a tooth–cleaner (*miswāk*) or a comb [both prescribed by Sunna.—Ed.] tied to it. Due to the great number of purchasers, the price of water and of leather vessels went up. In short, God had created the Shaykh as the peer of Shaykh Junayd and Shaykh Abū Yazīd in these later days and adorned him with that divine love which cannot be understood by human wisdom. The virtues of a Shaykh—and the art of leading men (in the mystic path)—found their fulfilment and their consummation in him.[32]

The great Chishtī Shaykhs did not write books, but an interesting document of Niẓām al-Dīn in Arabic has survived, in which he appoints one of his disciples, Shams al-Dīn Yaḥya, as his khalīfa, or deputy, for another khānqāh. It is dated A.H. 724/A.D. 1323, and contains the *silsila,* (chain) by which the shaykh received and deputed his own authority; always important to the Ṣūfīs.

A Chishtī Deed of Appointment
by Niẓām al-Dīn Chishtī (written in A.H. *724*/A.D. *1324)*

In the Name of God, the Merciful, the Compassionate. Praise be to God who disposed the aspiration of His friends from secondary things to existent things by self-reproach, beneficently restricting their cares to the One, the Tender. Among them passes the chalice of love at early morning and at nightfall, brimming from the generosity of their Beloved. When night enfolds them their hearts are kindled with the fires of longing, their eyes pour tears abundantly and the inner heart enjoys secret confidences. They walk round the Pavilions of Power in thought, and never does there cease to be one among them who is empowered with the splendour of gnosis. His trace appears in the lands, and his light shines upon the horizons. His tongue speaks with truth, while he prays to God for mankind, that He will lead them from the darkness unto light and bring them near to the forgiving Lord. Benediction be upon Muḥammad, bringer of the most beautiful Law and the resplendent Path, the Messenger of Mercy, distinguished as the viceregent of his Lord by the oath of allegiance; and blessing on the rightly-guided successors, who attained to every lofty station, and on his family who called upon their Lord morning and evening.

As for what follows: to call upon the One, the Omniscient, is one of the highest pillars of Islam, the firmest handhold on faith, as has come down from the Prophet, on whom be peace: "By Him in whose hand is Muḥammad's life, if you wished I would assuredly swear to you that the servants of God dearest to Him are those who cause His servants to love God, and cause Him to love His servants on earth by good counsel and command." And God has praised His servants who say, "Our Lord, give us coolness to our eyes in our wives and children, and make us as an imām to the God-fearing" (25:73). God has made it obligatory to follow the lord of apostles, the rider of the conspicuous steed, with His Word, exalted and glorified be He: "Say, this is my way. I call to God with sure knowledge, and whoever follows after me. To God be glory! And I am not of the idolators" (12:108). And following him can only be by minding his words and following his actions, averting one's soul from all that exists save God, in devotion to the Adored.

Now our most noble son, pious, learned, wellpleasing, and dedicated to the Lord of all being; Shams al-Milla wa-l-Dīn Muḥammad ibn Yaḥya, may God the One make his light effulgent upon people of firm faith and piety; since he has made his way to us, and put on the dervish cloak of disciplehood at our hands and taken on the full share of our companionship; and since he has undertaken to follow the Lord of created beings and fill his time with obedience and turn his heart from the promptings of his Self and its thoughts, and turn from the lower world and its contingencies, not leaning upon the children of this world or its rulers; since he has restricted himself to God in all things and the holy light has illumined in his heart heavenly secrets so that the door of understanding of divine instruction be made open to him; it is permitted for him to grant the dervish habit to disciples and guide them to the stations of those confirmed in faith, as it was granted to me by him whose favors spread throughout the land, the splendour of whose miracles perfumed the horizons, that wanderer in the realms of holiness whose thoughts declared the love of his Merciful Lord, he who was Pole of the earth and the sage of this world, our Shaykh Farīd of Truth, of Law, and of Religion, after he had bestowed the favour of his regard on me and clothed me with the habit, may God make fragrant his memory and appoint the fold of Paradise as his abode. And he received the dervish cloak from the King of Shaykhs and Sulṭān of the Way, that inspirer of the love of the Overpowering Lord, the Pole of the Community and true religion, Shaykh Bakhtiyārūshī, who received it from the Moon of Gnostics and Aid of the Community and Religion Ḥasan al-Sijzī, who received it from the Proof of Truth to men, 'Uthmān al-Harūnī, and he from the Speaker of the Word, the Pilgrim Sharīf al-Zandānī, and he from God's Shadow upon men Mawdūd al-Chishtī, and he from the King of Shaykhs of the People of Certitude, Naṣīr al-Milla wa-l-Dīn Yūsuf al-Chishtī, and he from the Stay of the Pious and Example of the Elect Abū Aḥmad al-Chishtī, and he from the Lamp of the Godfearing, Abū Isḥāq al-Chishtī, and he from the Sun of the Poor, 'Alī Dīnawarī, and he from that most generous of the Faithful, Hubayra al-Baṣrī, and he from the Crown of the Righteous and Proof of the Lovers of God Hudhayfa al-Mar'ashī, and he from the Sultan of Seekers and Proof of Finders, the Renouncer of Kingship and Power Ibrahīm ibn Adham, and he from the Pole of Sanctity, excellent and virtuous and perceptive of all excellence Fuḍayl ibn 'Iyāḍ, and he from the Pole of the World and Exalted Shaykh 'Abd al-Wāḥid ibn Zayd, and he from the Chieftain of the second generation after the Prophet, that Imām of the Learned, Ḥasan al-Basrī, and he from the Prince of Believers, last of links to which is traced the dervish cloak of every Seeker, 'Alī ibn Ṭālib, whose face God has saved. May God keep holy their secrets, and preserve their lights until the Day of Resurrection. And 'Alī received it from the Master of Messengers and Seal of the Prophets, the Model in following the Lord of all being, Muḥammad the Chosen one, God bless him and give him peace, with all those who trace their descent from him and are guided by his example.

Whoever has not reached us, but reaches (Mawlānā Shams al-Dīn); we have made him our successor, and his powerful hand is the deputy of our hand, and following his judgement in this world and the next is a mark of veneration for us; for we have exalted him, and humbled him who regards not the worth of him we have regarded. God is the Favourer and Guide, who alone is sought for aid, and in Him is our trust.

This writ was issued at the lofty direction of Niẓām al-Dīn Muḥammad ibn Aḥmad—God exalt him and preserve him from every shortcoming and guard him—by the hand of the weak slave who hopes for the Divine grace, Ḥusayn ibn Muḥammad al-'Alawī al-Kermānī, on the twentieth day of the Month of Pilgrimage in 724.[33]

THE LIGHT OF DEHLI

Niẓam al-Dīn's true successor was Shaykh Naṣīr al-Dīn, who was called "The Lamp of Dehli." In his lifetime, Sulṭān Muḥammad ibn Tughluq (partly under the influence of a legalist student of Ibn Taymīya, and partly to curb the power of the Ṣūfī orders in his kingdoms), turned against the Shaykhs, humiliated them, expelled them to the provinces, and forced many of them to accept state employment or benefices, thus breaking their treasured independence. Naṣīr al-Dīn died in A.H. 757/A.D. 1356, appointing no successor, and directing that the relics he had received from his predecessors be buried with him.

After him, the central leadership broke down, just as the central political authority of Dehli was breaking down. Shaykhs of the ṭarīqa in the provinces found it comfortable to appoint their sons as successors, and receive comfortable livings from the rulers.

Naṣīr al-Dīn wrote no book, but a record of his sayings and seances was kept by a disciple, Ḥamīd Qalandar, and was revised by the Shaykh himself. This charmingly written collection, the *Khayr al-Majālis,* or "Best of Assemblies," shows the technique of the shaykhs in winning souls, by the use of parables, striking stories, and an amiable reception of all visitors. Jalāl al-Dīn Rūmī had put the same winsome method to effective use in Anatolia.

An Assembly of Shaykh Naṣīr al-Dīn (d. A.H. *757/*A.D. *1356)*
from the Best of Assemblies
by Ḥamīd Qalandar (written A.H. *756/*A.D. *1355)*

The Second Assembly: When next I had the happiness of waiting on the Master of blessed memory, he was speaking about the Day of Resurrection. "The Resurrection is near at hand: already 755 years have passed," he said. When he said this, his blessed face turned white, and those present fainted. At this time, he signalled for sweetmeats to be passed to his friends, but the lives of those present had become so bitter from fear of the Resurrection that no one took any notice of the sweets, and the Master told the servant, "Take them away, and bring them at another time." We did not know whether we were in heaven or on earth; whether it was day or night; and in this state a third of the night passed away, and not a breath came from anyone there, until an 'alim came in and said in a loud voice, "Peace!" Then some of those present came to themselves, while others remained drowned in the state of terror of the Resurrection.

The Master—God bless his memory!—then gently inquired about the spiritual condition of the jurist. He declared, "I have to be at Court every day, and at every judgement they are asking for my opinion, so I have no time!" The Shaykh's blessed words were, "There is no harm in going to Court, if one can be of help to the people." Then he told this story: A certain dervish was travelling in the desert, when a shaykh met him and said, "When you arrive in that city, ask for the house of 'Abdallāh the Doorkeeper, in such and such a quarter. When you see him, give him my Salām, and say that he is to recite the Fātiḥa for the preservation of my faith." However, he did not tell his name. On arriving in the city the dervish inquired the way to the house of 'Abdallāh the Doorkeeper, and met him, saying, "I was in the desert, and I saw an old man who told me, 'Go to 'Abdallāh the Doorkeeper, give him my Salām, and ask him to recite the Fātiḥa for the preservation of my faith.' " At this, 'Abdallāh recited the Fātiḥa, and said to the dervish, "Go back." The dervish however said, "Sir, may the identity of that Shaykh be known to me?" 'Abdallāh replied, "Pass by, and do not ask that question." But the dervish was insistent that absolutely it should be made known to him who the shaykh was, and after a long struggle 'Abdallāh finally said, "It was Khiḍr." The dervish said, "I have so often met shaykhs in the desert! How do you know that this one was lord Khiḍr?" He replied, "I know." At this, the dervish said, "Master! This is the station of the saints! Whence has this grace come to you, in such guise?" The doorkeeper said, "What the Ṣūfī shaykhs do in a corner of the khānqāh, I do in the street, the bazār, my house, and the palace. When a third of the night has passed, I rise and perform the ablutions and occupy myself with reading the Qur'ān and mentioning God's name until dawn. Then I perform new ablutions, seat myself on my prayer-carpet, and busy myself with litanies until sunrise. Then I pray the ishrāq prayers and go to the palace, and on the whole way my tongue repeats the praises of God. When I arrive at the palace, I say "O my God, I see none but Thee, as if I stood before Thee." Then I go to serve the chamberlain. I have a covenant with God that I shall help everyone who has business with milord by every means that God has put in my power, be it by my words or my acts or my possessions. After, at the time of the supererogatory chasht prayers I come home, renew my ablutions, offer the prayer, and occupy myself until late morning when I have a short nap and then rise, repeat the ablution and perform the supererogatory part of the noon–prayer at home and the obligatory part at the mosque. Then I go back to the palace and give myself over to remembrance of God. I go home at the time of the afternoon prayer and perform it and the evening prayer at the mosque, so that they will be communal prayers. Then I go home and perform the supererogatory *bayn al 'ishā'ayn* prayer. Immediately after, I offer the night prayer and repeat *dhikrs* until midnight. What other shaykhs perform in prayers, devotion, fasting and good works I perform, fasting every day. What some do in the khānqāh, I do in the palace, on the road, and at home." The point here is, that although he was engaged in a worldly occupation, he could still attain the station of the shaykhs in it. Because he had a good relation with God, his work in the world did no harm, so that even Khwāja Khiḍr asked for his prayers.

After this, the Master remarked that, seeing how Khwāja Khiḍr had asked for the Fātiḥa of the doorkeeper, we can never know what the final result of an action may come to; whether good, or—we take refuge in God!—in evil. Matters are judged by their final result. Then he recited this ḥadīth: The Messenger of God, on whom be God's peace and benediction, said "A man cannot escape the reward of his actions—if they are good, his reward will be good; if they are bad, it will be bad." And the circumstances of this ḥadīth were this: a woman came to the Mother of the Believers 'A'isha, God be well pleased with her, and said, "Last night I had a dream. The resurrection had come, and I was going along a road. Then there were two ways before me, and I took the right way. I saw my father standing at a tank, and he was giving people to drink. When I came to him, I said, 'Father, where is Mother?' He replied, 'Your mother has not come to me.' Then I left my father and took the left way. I saw my mother standing at a tank, crying 'Oh, my thirst, my thirst!' I went up, and said, 'Mother, the tank is in front of you. Why do you cry, and do not drink water? She said, 'Because my hand cannot reach the water.' I went and took some water, and poured it in her mouth, and I heard a voice say, 'Withered is the hand that gives her water!' Then I awoke, and lo! my hand had withered.' " When 'A'isha told this story to the Messenger—God bless him, and give him peace!—he said, "Go, 'A'isha, and ask this woman what sort of man was her father, and what sort of woman was her mother?" She said, "My father was a righteous man, and did many good things, but my mother was just the other way." 'A'isha then told the Messenger this, and he said, "A man shall not escape the reward of his actions."

Then the Master told this story. "A certain 'alim was a qāḍī, and a poor man came to him and said, 'The king has taken a piece of land belonging to me and built a castle upon it.' The qāḍī called a bailiff and gave him the decree which had appointed him to the qāḍīship, and ordered him, 'Go to the king, and say three things. First say "I come to tell you of the Law." Then see what he will do, and whether he respects the Law or no. If he does not show respect, kiss the appointment and lay it before him, and say "The qāḍī says 'give the appointment of qāḍī to another.' " If he shows respect and listens, say that he has taken the land of a man wrongfully and raised a castle upon it. Come and answer to the plaintiff, or summon the plaintiff and give him satisfaction. If he does neither, then kiss the deed of appointment, lay it at his feet, and say 'The qāḍī says, "Give this work to another." '

"The bailiff put the appointment in his sleeve and went to the king's palace and said, 'Tell the king "I come to tell you of the Law." They informed the king, and he summoned the bailiff. When he came before the throne the king rose, and stood and said, 'What is it you would say?' The bailiff said, 'A poor man has brought a case saying that you have taken a piece of land belonging to him and built a castle on it. The qāḍī says come and answer him, or send for the man and satisfy him. If you do not choose to do either, here is the deed of appointment. Take it, and give this work to another.' The king said, 'Take the deed of appointment and give it to the qāḍī and say, "The qāḍīship is yours, and if you like I will come to you, or send the man to me and I shall give him satisfaction." Then they brought the poor man, and the king said 'Good man, why did you go to the qāḍī? If you had come to me, I would not have wronged you.' Thereupon he commanded, 'Go where the man says and wherever he shows you, destroy the castle and give him back his land.' Then they went where the man led, and the king gave orders to pull down the castle. But the man said 'O King, I give up my claim. Do not order them to destroy your castle!' The king replied 'Oh no! Come, tear it down.' Then the man said, 'My lord, I wish to die! My king, do not say that word! Before God, I withdraw!' Then the king said 'What was the measure of your land?' The poor man said 'So many feet.' Then he ordered, 'Measure this land, and for every square foot give him a gold *tanka*.' Then they measured the land and he gave him that many pieces of gold, and a robe, and a deed of security. Then the king said, 'Now I have settled your claim. Are you content?' The man replied, 'Indeed I am content.' After that the king mounted and went to visit the qāḍī. At that moment the qāḍī was affixing his seal to a legal opinion, and paid no attention. When he had sealed it, he showed his respect for his king, and gave him half of his prayer carpet to sit upon, saying 'Please be seated.' Then they sat side by side on the prayer rug, and the qāḍī ordered a bowl of sherbet to be brought, and they brought it. Then the qāḍī drank, and handed the bowl to the king, and he drank. Thus all the qāḍī's orders were carried out. Respect was shown for the Law, the plaintiff was satisfied, and the king paid a visit to the qāḍī."

When he finished, I cried, "How good a reign! How good a qāḍī! And how good a king!" Then the Shaykh said, "Yes, such things do not happen just anywhere. Only a qāḍī who is ready to give up being a qāḍī can act like that." When the Master had finished this story we sat savoring it for awhile. Just then a man came in, and asked him what he did. He said, "I am a jeweller." Someone remarked here that some people do not believe in dervishes. [i.e. in poverty.—Ed.]. The Master then spoke these blessed words:

"There was once a shaykh who had great sanctity, and at the same time there was a qāḍī, who was a master of self-discipline. He saw many miracles of the saint, but he did not become his disciple. One day the qāḍī came to visit the shaykh, and a jeweller came in and gave a pearl of great price to the shaykh as an offering. The shaykh took the pearl in his hand, and said, 'O Qāḍī, what is this?' The qāḍī said, 'It is a pearl.' Then he poured it into the qāḍī's palm and said 'What is it, O Qāḍī?' and the pearl turned to water. The qāḍī said, 'It is water.' Then the shaykh poured the water on the ground. The qāḍī was astonished to see such a miracle, but still he did not become a disciple.

"After that, he said to the shaykh, 'I shall only become your disciple when you perform a forty days' retreat with me.' Now the qāḍī was very severe in austerities. The shaykh replied, 'Shall it be the forty days' retreat of men, or the forty days of women?' The qāḍī wondered, for he had never found such expressions in any book. He asked, 'What might the forty days of men and the forty days of women be?' The shaykh said, 'The forty days of women is that on the first day one performs the little and the great ablution, and goes into retreat, and eats nothing for forty days. Then he comes out still pure from the ablution of the first day. The forty days of men is that at the end of each day's fast, one eats two roast sheep and two *manns* (about 120 pounds) of bread, and on the fortieth day comes out still pure from the first ablution.' The qāḍī's wonder increased, and he said, 'It is possible for a man to live without eating for forty days, or even fifty, but it is not possible to eat two sheep and two manns of bread every day, and not have to perform ablutions (necessary after using the latrine or dirtying one's hands) by the fortieth!' Nevertheless, he said 'Let it be the forty days of men!' Now at the shaykh's there was a courtyard with two cells on two sides of it, so the qāḍī said, 'You take that cell, and I shall take the one opposite.'

"When the first day had passed, the time of breaking fast arrived. They brought two sheep and two manns of bread to each of them, and put a lamp in front of each cell. The shaykh rose and came forward, the qāḍī did likewise, and they began to eat. The shaykh soon dispatched his two sheep and two manns of bread. The qāḍī, however, was a master of self-discipline, who had never eaten his fill, even of bread. He ate a few loaves, and then could eat no more. The shaykh looked up and saw the qāḍī's discomfort, so he came to the qāḍī and said, 'One must give rest to a friend.' Then he sat down and likewise polished off the qāḍī's food, and retired to his cell, and performed the night prayer without the need of any ablution. The qāḍī's stomach however began to rumble, and he could scarcely perform his prostrations. Then the shaykh came to the qāḍī, and said, 'Qāḍī, such prayer is not recommended. Rise, and break off your forty days.' The qāḍī came out of his cell, and broke off his devotions, and fell at the feet of the shaykh. But the shaykh said, 'The thing we began must now be finished.' Each day they brought four sheep and four manns of bread to the shaykh, and the shaykh ate them, until the twentieth day. Then he said 'In a sense, my forty days are completed.' Then without having needed any ablution but that of the first day, he came out and offered up his prayers. The qāḍī then came forward and became his disciple."

When this strange tale was finished, the Master of blessed memory ordered sherbet and sweets to be brought in. When he handed the sherbet to me, I drank it. Now it was summer, and extremely hot, so I recited this verse:

> "With this sherbet you have given life to my heart;
> May the Lord let you drink in the sight of His face!"

Really, it was a most excellent evening.[34]

Later Indian walīs came to settle at the capitals of the local sultanates that rose in the provinces after the Tughluqs of Dehli.

The following notices of holy men of Gujarat, the western province, were compiled by 'Ali Muḥammad Khān, the son of an official of the last of the strong Mughal emperors, Awrangzīb (d. 1707), whose great-grandfather Akbar had conquered the province for the Mughal Empire. 'Ali Muḥammad lived to see Gujarat overrun by the Hindu

Marathas (from 1725 to 1758) and attempted to salvage the local Muslim history of his province.

A characteristic teaching of the Ṣūfī saints was that learning as well as asceticism are good and useful means to the end of friendship with God, but that those who are truly committed to Him worship Him in love, with joyful hearts. Also, one should submit oneself to the teaching of friends of God.

Shaykh 'Alī of Gujarat
from The Aḥmadī Reflection *(Supplement)*
by 'Alī Muḥammad Khān (ca. A.H. *1163/*A.D. *1750)*

Shaykh 'Alī, better known as Khaṭīb Shaykh 'Alī the Ascetic: At the age of twelve he devoted himself to the service of God, and abstaining from food obtained by men's labour, lived on fruits and wild herbs. For twelve years he fasted continuously until at last he heard the hallelujas of the Seraphim. It so happened that every day when he went to the river Sābar for (ablutions) he was accosted by a mystic, who was wont to sit by the way and call out to him, " 'Alī, be a Muslim!" The Shaykh, understanding not the meaning of the mystic utterance, increased his bodily mortifications and rigid asceticism.

One day that mystic had cooked food and was giving it to the (poor), when the Shaykh happened to pass. The mystic attacked the Shaykh, and throwing him down sat on his chest and struck him, and with each blow thrust a morsel of food into his mouth. Then he left him and said, "Go, 'Alī, be a Muslim." The Shaykh, panting and covered with dust, returned home and fell down in a swoon. But, when he recovered, the meaning of that mystic utterance flashed upon him, and he determined to become the disciple of some great saint. There were two such saints at that time: Ḥazrat–i Quṭb al–'Alam, and Ḥazrat–i Ganj Bakhsh. As the former tolerated music, he would not go to him. So, he drove to Sarkhaj to wait on Ḥazrat–i Ganj Bakhsh. But the oxen stood still on the way, and a mysterious hand pulled the Shaykh by the collar. "Let the beasts have their will!" exclaimed the Shaykh, and the cart was drawn towards the convent of Ḥazrat–i Quṭb (d. 1480 A.D.).

The Saint was sitting at meal with his disciples when the Shaykh came, and he was given a portion of food. His eyes were now opened, and he saw the hollowness of his self–imposed mortifications. Love was kindled in his heart, and his hard nature was softened, and he wept. Then, filled with ecstacy, he rose up and poured forth his heart as a Dervish does, till even the musical instruments responded. The Saint then ordered his *qawwāls* (singers of mystical poetry) to sing, and the whole assembly was entertained. Afterwards the Shaykh was admited as a disciple of the Saint and given the privilege of making disciples himself and teaching publicly. He is buried at Qadampūr, which along with Quṭbpūr belongs to his descendants.[35]

A Child Saint
from The Aḥmadī Reflection *(Supplement)*
by ʻAlī Muḥammad Khān (ca. A.H. *1163*/A.D. *1750)*

Shāh Bhikan: he died at the age of nine or ten. The story of his death is recorded by the author of the *Mir'at–i Sikandarī* on the authority of Malik Fakhr al–Dīn (Sulṭān Aḥmad's son–in–law), who heard it from his father Malik Sayf al–Dīn. Says the Malik, "I was born as an outcome of the saint's blessings. Once, in my childhood, I swooned, and men took me to be dead. Mad with sorrow my father ran to Saint Quṭb al–ʻAlam, his preceptor, taking with him his cap and Ṣūfī (silsila), determined to give them back and abjure his fealty if the Saint failed to revive his child. The Saint referred him to his son (Saint) Shāh ʻAlam, who consoled my father, bidding him to accept the Divine decree. 'Wilt thou reply in the same way in the intercession of the next world?' answered my father, provoking him. The Saint ignored this reply and went home. Then my father went to the young Shāh Bhikan, and persuaded him to speak to his father, Saint Shāh ʻAlam. 'Art thou prepared,' said the Saint to his son, 'to offer thyself for a sacrifice?' 'Yes, my father,' replied the boy, even as Abraham's son, and he went into a room, and he died. The Saint came out and spoke to my father thus: 'Go home, and see thy son, who is perchance in a swoon and not dead.' Afterwards my father heard of the death of the Saint's son, and was grieved thereat."

Shāh Bhikan is buried with his mother Bībī Murkī in the tomb of Jām Juva on the west of the city (of Aḥmadabād) by the riverside. The 14th of Rajab is the date of his anniversary celebration.[36]

The great Mughal Akbar (d. 1605 A.D.) was so much influenced by the teachings of Ṣūfī friends of God that his legalist detractors even accused him of trying to found a new religion (it was in fact more on the order of a ṭarīqa).

His son Salīm, the later Jahāngīr, writes in his memoirs of the role a Chishtī walī played at his own birth.

Shaykh Salīm Foretells the Birth of Akbar's Heir.
from the Memoirs *of Jahāngīr*
by the Emperor Jahāngīr (d. A.H. *1037/*A.D. *1627)*

Until the twenty-eighth year of his age, my father had no son born to him. With a view to having an (heir), he used constantly to have recourses to those dervishes and recluses who are possessed of an affinity to the Divine Court. Since the great saint Khwāja Mu'īn al-Dīn Chishtī was the fountainhead, as it were, of the saints of Hind, he conceived the idea of repairing on foot to his sacred threshhold at Ajmer in order to obtain this his desire. In the year A.H. 977/A.D. 1569, on Wednesday the 17th of the month of Rabī' al-Awwal, when seven hours of the day had passed, under the auspices of the 24th degree of Libra, the Most High God brought me into existence from behind the veil of nonbeing.

At the time that my illustrious father was desiring a son, a certain Shaykh Salīm Chishtī, a dervish of ecstatic habits, who had traversed already the stages of (the mystic) life, came and took up his abode in a mountain near to the village of Sīkrī, which is one of the villages of Agra, and the people of that neighbourhood placed the most perfect confidence in him. Since my father was in the habit of treating with dervishes, he was also introduced to Shaykh Salīm. One day he asked him, "Shall I have sons?" The Shaykh replied, "He who gives without grudging will grant you three sons." My father said, "I make this vow: I shall have my first son brought up by you, and make you his guardian and protector. If the Shaykh consents and gives his blessing, I will name my son after him."

Accordingly when the time for my mother's (the Rajput princess of Amber) delivery drew near, my father sent her to the Shaykh's house, so that I was born at that place. After my birth he gave me the name of Sulṭān Salīm. But I never heard from his blessed lips, either in drunkenness or sobriety, this title; he always used to call me, "Shaykhu Bābā" (Father Shaykh).

My illustrious father always used to consider the village of Sīkrī, which was my birthplace, as a place especially lucky for him, and so made it the imperial residence. In the course of fourteen or fifteen years that mountain and jungle, which had been full of wild beasts and deer, became a city containing all sorts of gardens and buildings, and pleasant and lofty palaces, and delightful seductive places. After the conquest of Gujarat, Sīkrī was known as Fatḥpūr.

When I became Emperor, it struck me that I ought to change my name, since it was liable to be confounded with the names of the Sulṭans of Turkey. The Inspirer of Secrets put it into my mind that the business of kings is "Dominion," so I called myself Jahāngīr, and took the title of Nūr al-Dīn, because my accession took place at the time of the rising of the "Greater Light" and the illuminating of the world. Moreover while I was the heir apparent I had heard some of the learned men of Hindustān say that after the reign of Jalāl al-Dīn Akbar Padishāh, one Nūr al-Dīn would become manager of the affairs of the empire. This also was in my mind, and for these reasons I fixed on Nūr al-Dīn Jahāngīr as my name and title.[37]

A MODERN FRIEND OF GOD

Although we have not had space to mention them, Ṣūfī saints have been important in Africa, where they played a role in the Islamizing movements of the sub-Sahara, and have also been active in North Africa.

We may close with a recollection by an agnostic French doctor of Shaykh Aḥmad al-'Alawī, a mystic of Algeria, whose influence converted several Europeans to Islam, and touched hundreds of North Africans as well in this century.

Recollections of Shaykh Aḥmad al-'Alawī
by Dr. Marcel Carret
from A Moslem Saint of the Twentieth Century, *by Martin Lings, (1961)*

When I first met the Shaykh, the present *zāwiya* (khānqāh) had not yet been built. A group of faqīrs (dervishes) had bought the ground and made a present of it to the Shaykh, and the foundations had already been laid. . . . The way in which this zāwiya was built is both eloquent and typical: there was neither architect—at least, not in the ordinary sense—nor master-builder, and all the workmen were volunteers. The architect was the Shaykh himself—not that he ever drew up a plan or manipulated a set-square. He simply said what he wanted, and his conception was understood by the builders. They were by no means all from that part of the country. Many had come from Morocco, especially from the Riff, and some from Tunis. . . . The news had gone round that work on the zāwiya could be started and that was all that was needed. . . . Among the Shaykh's North African disciples there began an exodus: masons some, carpenters others, stone–cutters, workers on the roads, or even ordinary labourers, they knotted a few meager provisions in a handkerchief and set out. . . . They received no wages. They were fed, that was all; and they camped out in tents. But every evening, an hour before the prayer, the Shaykh brought them together and gave them spiritual instruction. This was their reward. . . .

They worked in this way for two months, sometimes three. . . . Others took their place and after a certain time went off in their turn. . . . This went on for two years, by the end of which the building was finished. . . . Here, in the mid–twentieth century, was the same fervour that had built the cathedrals of the Middle Ages.

As soon as the zāwiya was finished, the fuqarā' said that they would like to have a big festival to celebrate its inauguration, and the Shaykh gave his consent. . . . At my expression of surprise he gave an imperceptible shrug of the shoulders, and said more or less —I do not remember the exact words—"You are right. Such things are superfluous. . . . (But) not all can find complete satisfaction in pure intelligence and contemplation. They have a need now and then to gather together and to feel that their own ideas are shared by a great many others. That is all they are asking for now. Besides, there is no question of the sort of festivity that you must have seen at some of the Muslim places of pilgrimage, with pistol–shots, displays of riding, various games and far too much food. For my disciples a festival means spiritual rejoicing. It is simply a reunion for the exchange of ideas and for communal prayer."

According to what the Shaykh had told me, I had expected no more than a sort of congress where the academically–minded hope to shine. . . . As far as I could gather it was in fact something of the sort, especially among the younger disciples. It was not there, however, that the interest lay, but with the older disciples who did not talk and who were rapt in deep meditation. I was especially struck by the most humble of them all, the Riff mountaineers. . . . I watched them, drinking in the atmosphere as if plunged in a kind of beatitude through the very fact of being there, penetrated by the holiness of the place, in the Presence of God. . . .

At other times, after remaining motionless and silent for hours at a time, the disciples would softly start up a lingering chant. Then they would divide up into circular groups, and holding hands would begin to sway forwards and then backwards, slowly and rhythmically, pronouncing clearly, in time to each movement, the Name "Allāh!" Little by little the speed of the rhythm increased. The slow swaying to and fro gave place to an up and down movement with knees bent and then suddenly straightened. . . . They began to gasp, and the voices became hoarse, the up and down movement became more and more violent, jerky and almost convulsive. The Name of God was now no more than a breath, and so it went on, always quicker and quicker, until the breathing itself was no longer heard. Some of them would fall to the ground in a state of exhaustion.

This exercise, analogous to those of the whirling dervishes, is evidently intended to produce a particular state of soul.[38]

What the doctor had witnessed was the Ṣūfī dhikr, or "mentioning;" sometimes made with music and even dance, but all intended to produce a state of ecstacy in which the devotee forgets himself, and remembers the Divine Friend.

The tradition of the friends of God is not in eclipse in Islamic Society today. In refined forms, it seems to offer a particular certainty to many highly educated Muslims in a modern world.

NOTES

1. Bukhārī, Book 59. Chapter 6, no. 3. Leiden edition. (Editor's translation.)

2. Al-Sarrāj, *Kitāb al-Luma'*. London, 1914. pp. 383–84. Translated by A. J. Arberry in *Reason and Revelation in Islam,* (London, 1957) pp. 95–96.

3. Ibn Sa'd, *al-Tabāqāt al-Kubra.* Leiden, 1908. Vol. IV, II, p. 26. (Editor's translation and abridgement.)

4. Al-Sulamī, *Tabāqāt al-Ṣūfiya.* Cairo, 1953. pp. 30–31. (Editor's translation.)

5. Al-'Aṭṭar, *Tadhkirāt al-Awliyā'*. Translated by A. J. Arberry in *Muslim Saints and Mystics,* (London, 1966) p. 78.

6. Ibid. pp. 68–70. (Editor's abridgement.)

7. Quoted by A. J. Arberry in *Sufism,* London, 1950, p. 37.

8. Al-Niffārī. *Mawāqif and Mukhāṭabāt.* Translated by A. J. Arberry, (London 1935) pp. 70–72.

9. Translated by A. J. Arberry, in *Revelation and Reason in Islam,* (London, 1957) pp. 95–98.

10. *Kitāb al-Tawahhum.* Cairo, 1937. pp. 39–41. (Editor's translation.)

11. Ibid. Translated by A. J. Arberry, in *Revelation and Reason in Islam,* (London, 1957) pp. 46–47.

12. Al-Tirmidhī, *Khatm al-Awliyā'*. Beirut,, 1965. pp. 336–47. (Editor's translation and abridgement.)

13. Ibid. pp. 371–72.

14. *Kashf al-Mahjūb.* Translated by R. A. Nicholson, London, 1911, pp. 210–15. (Editor's abridgement.)

15. Ibid. pp. 225–27.
16. Ibid. p. 228.
17. Ibid. pp. 239–40.
18. Translated by A. J. Arberry as *The Doctrine of the Ṣūfīs,* (Cambridge, 1935) pp. 57–66.
19. *Nishwār al-Muḥādara.* translated by D. S. Margoliouth as *Table-Talk of a Mesopotamian Judge,* (London, 1922) pp. 289–92. (Here abridged.)
20. Al-Hujwīrī. *op. cit.* pp. 75–79.
21. Al-Rāzī. *Kitāb al-Naqs.* Teheran, 1951. p. 197. (Translated by Professor Mahdī Muḥaqqiq.)
22. Sayyid Hoseyn Nasr. *Ideals and Realities of Islam,* London, 1966. pp. 161–63.
23. Al-Dhahabī, in *Journal of the Royal Asiatic Society,* 1907, p. 286ff. (Editor's translation and abridgement.)
24. Ibn Yazdānyār. *Rawḍat al-Murīdīn.* mss. Cairo, Princeton, Istanbul, Paris, Berlin. (Edited and translated by editor.)
25. Translated by A. J. Arberry in *Aspects of Islamic Civilization,* (London, 1964) pp. 329–34. (Here abridged.)
26. Evliya Chelebi. *Siyahat-Name.* Translated by J. von Hammer, (London, 1834–46–50) Vol. II, pp. 19–21.
27. Ibid. p. 70–72.
28. Ibid. p. 106.
29. Ibn al-'Arabī. *Fuṣūṣ al-Ḥikam.* Afifi edition. Cairo, 1946. pp. 58–68. (Editor's translation and abridgement.)
30. Ibid. p. 135ff.
31. Ibid. p. 214ff.
32. Barānī. *Tarikh-i Fīrūz Shāhī.* Translated by K. A. Nizami in *The Life and Times of Shaikh Farīd-u'd-Dīn Ganj-i Shakar,* (Aligarh, 1955) p. 75ff.
33. Appendix to K. A. Nizami's *Religion and Politics in India* (New Delhi, 1961) p. 351ff. (Editor's translation.)
34. *Khayr al-Majālis.* Aligarh, 1959. p. 12–20. (Editor's translation.)
35. *Supplement to the Mir'āt-i-Ahmed.* Translated by Syed Nawab Ali and C. N. Seddon. Baroda, 1924. p. 34–35.
36. Ibid. p. 41.
37. *Tuzak-i Jahāngīrī.* Translated by W. H. Lowe. Calcutta, 1889. p. 1–3.
38. Martin Lings. *A Moslem Saint of the Twentieth Century.* London, 1961. pp. 18–21.

Bibliography

In addition to the bibliography contained in the footnotes, the following list of titles is appended for those who may wish to read further.

The Qur'ān:

The author has made his own translations of the passages cited here, but the best literary translation available is certainly A.J. Arberry's *The Koran Interpreted,* (Oxford, University Press, 1964).

Introductions to Islam as Religion:

The classical introduction is H.A.R. Gibb's *Mohammadanism* (in many editions). A somewhat different approach, using translations from original Islamic sources put together so as to let Islam "speak for itself" will be found in my *Islam* (New York, 1961; Washington Square Paperbacks, 1964). Most recently, an admirable presentation by a modern Muslim is to be found in Fazlur–Rahman's *Islam* (New York, 1966; Anchor Paperbacks, 1968).

The Life of Muḥammad:

The *Sīra,* or biography of the Prophet gathered by Ibn Isḥāq in the ninth century and edited later by Ibn Hishām of Baṣra, has been translated by A. Guillaume as *The Life of Muḥammad,* (Oxford University Press, 1955). A Shī'ī treatment may be found in James L. Merrick's old translation of Majlisī's *Hayāt al–Qulūb,* published as *The Life and Religion of Mohammad* (Boston, 1850). A brief and excellent modern treatment is *Muḥammad Prophet and Statesman,* by Montgomery Watt (Oxford University Press, 1964). This in turn is a summation of Professor Watt's two detailed critical studies: *Muḥammad at Mecca,* (Clarendon Press, Oxford, 1953), and *Muḥammad at Medina* (Clarendon Press, Oxford, 1960).

Ḥadīth:

One of the great medieval collections from the Sunnī canonical works, Tibrīzī's *Mishkāt al–Maṣābīh,* has been translated by James Robson,

(Lahore, 1963–1965). The approach of Muslim scholarship is examined in Robson's *Introduction to the Science of Tradition* (London, 1953). The most authoritative collection of all, Bukhārī's *Ṣaḥiḥ*, has also been completely translated into French by O. Houdas and W. Marçais (Paris, 1903–1914), and into English, in selections, by C. C. Torrey (Leiden, 1948).

Islamic Law:

Greatly to be recommended is the late Professor Joseph Schacht's *Introduction to Islamic Law* (Oxford, Clarendon Press, 1964).

An old but good translation of one of the leading Ḥanafī legal works, the *Hedāya* of al-Marghinānī, exists in the translation of Charles Hamilton (London, 1870 and Lahore, 1957).

The Mālikī manual of Ibn Abī Zayd al-Qayrawānī has been translated into French by L. Bercher (Algiers, 1952).

For Shāfi'ī Law, there is the important *Minhāj al-Ṭalibīn* of al-Nawawī, edited and translated into French by L.W.C. Van Den Berg (Batavia, 1882). There is also a rather unsatisfactory English paraphrase of al-Shāfi'ī's *Risāla*, or treatise, by Majid Khadduri (Baltimore, 1961).

Ḥanbalī law is probably best studied in the French translation of Ibn Qudāma's legal work, translated to French by Henri Laoust as *Le Précis de Droit d'Ibn Qudāma* (Beirut, 1950). The important Ḥanbalī scholar Ibn Taymīya has been admirably studied also by Professor Laoust in his *Essai sur les doctrines sociales et politiques d'Ibn Taymīya* (Damascus, 1939).

Twelver Shī'ī Law is accessible in A. Querry's *Receuil de lois concernant les musulmanes shy'ites* (Paris, 1871–72), which is mainly a translation of Muḥaqqiq al-Ḥillī's *Sharā'i' al-Islam.*

A manual of Ḥisba regulations, the *Ma'ālim al-Qurba* of the Mamlūk scholar Ibn al-Ukhūwa, has been edited in Arabic with an English abstract, by R. Levy in the E.J.W. Gibb Memorial Series (London, 1938). There is also "A Zaydī Manual of Ḥisba of the Third Century," edited with an English abstract by R. Serjeant in *Rivista degli studi orientali* (1953), vol. 28.

Institutions and Political Theory:

The best introduction to political theory is probably E. I. J. Rosenthal's *Political Thought in Medieval Islam* (Cambridge University Press, 1958). The great *al-Aḥkām al-Sulṭānīya* of al-Māwardī is still not available in English, but may be found in a French translation by E. Fagnan (Algiers, 1927) as *Les statuts gouvernementaux*. However there are excellent translations of Niẓām al-Mulk's *Siyāsat-Nāma*, Kay Ka'ūs ibn Iskandar's *Qābūs-Nāma*, and al-Ghazālī's *Nasīḥat al-Mulūk*, all of which I have drawn upon for this book. Particulars will be found in the footnotes. Ibn Ṭiqṭiqā's agreeable history of the Caliphate and advice to a Mongol Prince, *al–Fakhrī h*as been rendered in an English version which leaves much to be desired, by C. Whitting (London, 1947).

For the institution of the caliphate, the excellent book by Sir Thomas Arnold, *The Caliphate,* can still stand (Oxford, Clarendon Press, 1924). One should however also consult Sir Hamilton Gibb's essay on the caliphate in *Studies in the Civilization of Islam,* edited by S. J. Shaw and W. R. Polk (Boston, 1962).

Religious and Sectarian Development:

The best introductory book in English is still D.B. MacDonald's *Development of Muslim Theology, Jurisprudence, and Constitutional Theory* (reprinted; Beirut, 1964). Also to be cited is his *The Religious Attitude and Life in Islam* (Chicago University Press, 1909).

Valuable introductions to particular questions are found in W.M. Watt's *Free Will and Predestination in Early Islam (*London, 1948) and A. J. Arberry's *Revelation and Reason in Islam (*London, 1957).

Twelver Shī'ism has been studied by D. M. Donaldson in *The Shi'ite Religion* (London, 1933), and two important Twelver creedal statements have been translated into English: that of Ibn Babūya (d. A.H. 991), by A.A.A. Fyzee, as *A Shi'ite Creed* (London, 1942) and that of 'Allāma al–Ḥillī (d. 1326 A.D.), with its commentary by Miqdād–ī Fāḍil, by W. McE. Miller (London, 1958).

Much information on the Ismā'īlīs is to be found in the works of W. Iwanow; here we may cite his *Brief Survey of the Evolution of Ismailism* (Leiden, 1952), *Studies in Early Persian Ismailism* (Bombay, 1955), and *A Creed of the Fatimids,* a paraphrase of the *Tāj al–'Aqā'id* (Bombay, 1936). The medieval Nizārī sect of Ismā'īlīs are studied in a splendidly lucid historical treatment by Bernard Lewis: *The Assassins: a Radical Sect in Islam* (London, 1967), and a detailed study by M.G.S. Hodgson: *The Order of the Assassins* (The Hague, 1955).

The Shī'a of India, by John Hollister (London, 1953), contains very interesting material on the history of the various sects of the Shī'a in India.

The Mu'tazila may be studied in A. Nader's *Le système philosophique des Mu'tazila* (Beirut, 1956) and the Khawārij in E. Salem's *The Political Theory and Institutions of the Khawārij* (Baltimore, 1956).

Ṣūfism:

The subject of Islamic mysticism has received especially sustained and careful consideration by orientalist scholars. Among these, the most prolific was the late Professor A.J. Arberry, whose small historical work, *Sufism* (London, 1950) should perhaps be read first. Arberry's predecessor, R. A. Nicholson, wrote the invaluable *The Mystics of*

Islam (Cambridge University Press, 1921), as well as *Studies in Islamic Mysticism* (Cambridge University Press, 1921), which consists of very good translations of original works with comments, and also translated Jalāl al-Dīn Rūmī's great *Mathnavī* (London, 1925–40). Rūmī's *Fīhi mā Fīhī* has been translated by Arberry, as *Discourses of Rumi* (London, 1961). Also recommended is Margaret Smith's *Readings from the Mystics of Islam* (London, 1950).

The Bektāshī dervishes have been studied by John K. Birge: *The Bektashi Order of Dervishes* (London, 1937). Excellent studies of activities of the Ṣūfī shaykhs in medieval India are to be found in K.A. Nizami's *Life and Times of Shaikh Farīd ud-Dīn Ganj-i Shakar* (Aligarh, 1955) and *Religion and Politics in India in the 13th Century* (Delhi, 1961).

Ibn al-'Arabī's *Fuṣūṣ al-Ḥikam* is not available in an English translation, regrettably. Here one must turn to T. Burckhardt's French paraphrase, *La sagesse des prophètes* (Paris, 1965). There is however a study of Ibn al-'Arabī's ideas in A.E. 'Affīfī's *The Mystical Philosophy of Muḥyīd Dīn Ibn ul 'Arabī,* (Cambridge, 1939).

Islamic Culture and Literature:

A collection of English adaptations of translations in European languages, which therefore lacks accuracy, but is done with superb literary taste and sensitivity, is Eric Schroeder's *Muhammad's People* (Portland, 1955). Another valuable collection is A. J. Arberry's *Aspects of Islamic Civilization* (London, 1964; and Ann Arbor Paperbacks, 1967).

A classic study of Islamic culture in the middle ages is G.E. Von Grunebaum's erudite and eminently readable *Medieval Islam* (University of Chicago, 1953).

Monographs on individual cities of the Islamic world are found in the University of Oklahoma "Centers of Civilization" series. Here we may particularly cite A.J. Arberry, *Shiraz, Persian City of Saints and Poets* (Norman, 1960); B. Lewis, *Istanbul and the Civilization of the Ottoman Empire* (Norman, 1963); and R. Le Tourneau, *Fez Under the Merinids* (Norman, 1961). Also, but not of the same quality, there is G. Wiet's *Cairo* (Norman, 1964). A handsome text with many photographs on Isfahan is by Wilfrid Blunt: *Isfahan, Pearl of Persia* (London and Toronto, 1966). Ibn Ḥazm's treatise on courtly love, which is also a most valuable source for the life of Cordoba under the Spanish Umawīs, has been translated by A.J. Arberry as *The Ring of the Dove, A Treatise on the Art and Practise of Arab Love* (London, 1953). Here we may also cite Arberry's collection of the Arabic poetry of medieval Andalusia, *Moorish Poetry* (London, 1953).

For the history of Islamic literature there is the brief but excellent *Arabic Literature: An Introduction* by Sir Hamilton Gibb (revised ed.,

London, 1963), and the fuller and more documented *Literary History of the Arabs* by R. A. Nicholson (Cambridge, 1930). The four volume *Literary History of Persia* of E. G. Browne (Cambridge, 1928–30) has never been surpassed, but A.J. Arberry's *Classical Persian Literature* (London, 1958) is very good. E. J. W. Gibb's *History of Ottoman Poetry* in six volumes (London, 1900–1909) is not nearly so readable, but is most informative.

Because it should be cited somewhere, Reuben Levy's *The Social Structure of Islam* (revised ed. Cambridge, 1957), may come next before we turn to general histories. Here the best thing one can do is refer the reader to another bibliography by Jean Sauvaget and Claude Cahen: *Introduction to the History of the Muslim East* (University of California, 1965).

The great medieval *penseur* and scholar Ibn Khaldūn, whom I have quoted more than once in this book, can best be approached through Muhsin Mahdi: *Ibn Khaldūn's Philosophy of History* (London, 1957). Ibn Khaldūn's *Muqaddimah* is available in an English version by F. Rosenthal (London and New York, 1958).

Islam Today:

Two excellent books still contain the essential insights on the situation of Muslims today. These are: (Sir) H.A.R. Gibb's *Modern Trends in Islam* (University of Chicago, 1947); and *Islam in Modern History* by Wilfred Cantwell Smith (Princeton, 1957, and Mentor Paperbacks).

A Reader's Guide to the Great Religions, ed. by Charles J. Adams (New York and London, 1965) has a very fine bibliographical article on Islam past and present, written also by Professor Adams.

Index

Italicized references are to commentary by the editor.
References in roman type refer to works quoted.